# JUNK FICTION

## Borgo Press Books by S. T. JOSHI

*H. P. Lovecraft: The Decline of the West*
*Junk Fiction: America's Obsession with Bestsellers*
*A Subtler Magic: The Writings and Philosophy of H. P. Lovecraft*
*The Weird Tale*

# JUNK FICTION

## AMERICA'S OBSESSION WITH BESTSELLERS

by

# S. T. Joshi

## THE BORGO PRESS

*An Imprint of Wildside Press LLC*

**MMIX**

*I.O. Evans Studies in the Philosophy and Criticism of Literature*
ISSN 0271-9061

**Number Forty-Six**

www.wildsidepress.com

FIRST EDITION

# CONTENTS

# For Leslie

*without whom . . .*

# INTRODUCTION

In 1973, Gore Vidal wrote a two-part essay in the *New York Review of Books* entitled "The Ashes of Hollywood"; as reprinted in his essay collection *Matters of Fact and of Fiction* (1977), it was retitled "The Top Ten Best Sellers According to the Sunday *New York Times* as of January 7, 1973." Its opening line—"Shit has its own integrity" (purportedly a quotation from the "Wise Hack at the Writers' Table at the MGM commissary")—pretty much conveys Vidal's take on the ten books he forced himself to consume.[1] Although by no means uniformly condemnatory—Vidal found some merit in Mary Renault's historical novel *The Persian Boy* and a few other titles—the article found little good to say about the most popular fictional works read by the American public in early 1973. (Vidal's point that most of these books were heavily influenced by film, and indeed were in effect film wannabes, is an issue I shall take up later.) As I am incapable of matching Vidal's wit and pungency, I can at least study this issue more exhaustively than Vidal could trouble himself to do. Accordingly, this book studies, from a purely aesthetic perspective, individual titles—all of them bestsellers—by some of the most popular writers among the Anglo-American reading public, in an effort to ascertain whether they are indeed as much beneath contempt as the majority of highbrow critics—aside from those academic critics who enjoy slumming in popular writing to prove that, in spite of their Ph.D.s, they are one with the people—seem, by their very avoidance of any detailed discussion of these works or authors, to believe. I am not principally, or indeed at all, interested in the sociological significance of popular writing or popular reading, and will have little to say of it except in portions of this introduction and in my conclusion.

There has been remarkably little study of the bestseller as a (quasi-)literary, or even a sociological, phenomenon. Alice Payne Hackett's *Fifty Years of Best Sellers*—first published in 1946 and subsequently revised in 1956, 1967, and 1977—is a mere year-by-year catalogue of best sellers, with minimal commentary on any given title. Q. D. Leavis's pioneering study, *Fiction and the Reading Public* (1932), is a brilliant work that anticipates some of my conclusions, but it of course cannot take account of recent developments in the mass media. Frank Luther Mott's *Golden Multitudes* (1947) and James D. Hart's *The Popular Book* (1950) are insightful historical treatises but have little relevance to contemporary writing. Keith L. Justice's *Best Seller Index* (1998) is a highly useful reference work but contains no analysis at all. The astute British critic John Sutherland has recently issued *Bestsellers: A Very Short Introduction* (2007), but the brevity of his book and the extensive scope of its historical coverage render it disappointingly insubstantial. It is symptomatic of the nearly universal neglect of the bestseller that, of the twenty titles published after 1990 studied in this book, only five were reviewed, even in capsule reviews, in the *New York Times Book Review;*[2] four others were reviewed in the daily *New York Times.*[3] For all practical purposes, in the judgment of our "nation's paper of record" these authors and titles do not, for all practical purposes, exist. To be sure, the *Times* dutifully lists them on its hardcover or paperback bestseller lists, but those lists are always relegated to the back of the issue and, in recent years, they have been augmented with an "Editor's Choice" section in which works of genuine literary merit (in the editors' judgment) are listed in a probably futile attempt to steer readers away from schlock.

The attitude that I have here outlined is generally referred to—and derided as—elitism. I will admit openly that I am myself an elitist, but of a very specific sort. There is, in short, good elitism and bad elitism. Good elitism embodies an unremitting quest for excellence and an intolerance for mediocrity; bad elitism, while seeming to seek excellence, declares *a priori* that certain realms cannot possibly produce excellence and therefore maintains that these realms are aesthetically off-limits before even examining them in any detail. I trust that I am not the latter sort of elitist. I have spent a significant proportion of my career vaunting the excellence of certain literary products in a domain (supernatural literature) that has had its share of blanket condemnations from bad elitists, among others. It will not take much effort to ascertain that I in fact do find some of the bestsellers I have read to have some literary merit, even though it is unlikely that any of them will enter the canon of American literature anytime soon, or have a very lofty place in it even if they do.

There are multiple theoretical issues confronting us as we examine the literary merit—or lack of it—of the bestseller. What are the criteria to be used in gauging literary merit or its converse? What is the validity of these criteria? What does it say about the Anglo-American public that it seems to care little whether bestsellers have the literary deficiencies I have outlined? In the space of this introduction I cannot hope to provide comprehensive answers to these questions, but some hints of an answer may emerge from my discussion of individual titles.

For now, I can assert the brute fact that the great majority of bestsellers have not in fact entered the American canon. Let us consider the number one best sellers of the years 1901 to 1975, as recorded in Alice Payne Hackett and James Henry Burke's *80 Years of Best Sellers: 1895–1975:*[4]

| Year | Title |
|------|-------|
| 1901 | *The Crisis* by Winston Churchill |
| 1902 | *The Virginian* by Owen Wister |
| 1903 | *Lady Rose's Daughter* by Mrs. Humphry Ward |
| 1904 | *The Crossing* by Winston Churchill |
| 1905 | *The Marriage of William Ashe* by Mrs. Humphry Ward |
| 1906 | *Coniston* by Winston Churchill |
| 1907 | *The Lady of the Decoration* by Frances Little |
| 1908 | *Mr. Crewe's Career* by Winston Churchill |
| 1909 | *The Inner Shrine* by Anonymous (Basil King) |
| 1910 | *The Rosary* by Florence Barclay |
| 1911 | *The Broad Highway* by Jeffrey Farnol |
| 1912 | *The Harvester* by Gene Stratton Porter |
| 1913 | *The Inside of the Cup* by Winston Churchill |
| 1914 | *The Eyes of the World* by Harold Bell Wright |
| 1915 | *The Turmoil* by Booth Tarkington |
| 1916 | *Seventeen* by Booth Tarkington |
| 1917 | *Mr. Britling Sees It Through* by H. G. Wells |
| 1918 | *The U. P. Trail* by Zane Grey |
| 1919 | *The Four Horsemen of the Apocalypse* by V. Blasco Ibáñez |
| 1920 | *The Man of the Forest* by Zane Grey |
| 1921 | *Main Street* by Sinclair Lewis |
| 1922 | *If Winter Comes* by A. S. M. Hutchinson |
| 1923 | *Black Oxen* by Gertrude Atherton |
| 1924 | *So Big* by Edna Ferber |
| 1925 | *Soundings* by A. Hamilton Gibbs |
| 1926 | *The Private Life of Helen of Troy* by John Erskine |
| 1927 | *Elmer Gantry* by Sinclair Lewis |
| 1928 | *The Bridge of San Luis Rey* by Thornton Wilder |
| 1929 | *All Quiet on the Western Front* by Erich Maria Remarque |

1930   *Cimarron* by Edna Ferber
1931   *The Good Earth* by Pearl S. Buck
1932   *The Good Earth* by Pearl S. Buck
1933   *Anthony Adverse* by Hervey Allen
1934   *Anthony Adverse* by Hervey Allen
1935   *Green Light* by Lloyd C. Douglas
1936   *Gone with the Wind* by Margaret Mitchell
1937   *Gone with the Wind* by Margaret Mitchell
1938   *The Yearling* by Marjorie Kinnan Rawlings
1939   *The Grapes of Wrath* by John Steinbeck
1940   *How Green Was My Valley* by Richard Llewellyn
1941   *The Keys of the Kingdom* by A. J. Cronin
1942   *The Song of Bernadette* by Franz Werfel
1943   *The Robe* by Lloyd C. Douglas
1944   *Strange Fruit* by Lillian Smith
1945   *Forever Amber* by Kathleen Winsor
1946   *The King's General* by Daphne du Maurier
1947   *The Miracle of the Bells* by Russell Janney
1948   *The Big Fisherman* by Lloyd C. Douglas
1949   *The Egyptian* by Mika Waltari
1950   *The Cardinal* by Henry Morton Robinson
1951   *From Here to Eternity* by James Jones
1952   *The Silver Chalice* by Thomas B. Costain
1953   *The Robe* by Lloyd C. Douglas
1954   *Not as a Stranger* by Morton Thompson
1955   *Marjorie Morningstar* by Herman Wouk
1956   *Don't Go Near the Water* by William Brinkley
1957   *By Love Possessed* by James Gould Cozzens
1958   *Doctor Zhivago* by Boris Pasternak
1959   *Exodus* by Leon Uris
1960   *Advise and Consent* by Allen Drury
1961   *The Agony and the Ecstasy* by Irving Stone
1962   *Ship of Fools* by Katherine Anne Porter
1963   *The Shoes of the Fisherman* by Morris L. West
1964   *The Spy Who Came In from the Cold* by John le Carré
1965   *The Source* by James Michener
1966   *Valley of the Dolls* by Jacqueline Susann
1967   *The Arrangement* by Elia Kazan
1968   *Airport* by Arthur Hailey
1969   *Portnoy's Complaint* by Philip Roth
1970   *Love Story* by Erich Segal
1971   *Wheels* by Arthur Hailey
1972   *Jonathan Livingston Seagull* by Richard Bach

1973   *Jonathan Livingston Seagull* by Richard Bach
1974   *Centennial* by James A. Michener
1975   *Ragtime* by E. L. Doctorow

Of these seventy-five titles, no more than six have genuinely entered the American canon (I exclude works by British or European authors): Sinclair Lewis's *Main Street* (1921 [actually published in 1920]) and *Elmer Gantry* (1927), John Steinbeck's *The Grapes of Wrath* (1939), James Jones's *From Here to Eternity* (1951), Philip Roth's *Portnoy's Complaint* (1969), and E. L. Doctorow's *Ragtime* (1975)—and even some of these are a bit on the edge. In some other cases (e.g., H. G. Wells's *Mr. Britling Sees It Through* and Katherine Anne Porter's *Ship of Fools*) the authors are notable but the bestselling works are less so. Thornton Wilder's *The Bridge of San Luis Rey* won a Pulitzer Prize, but its merits were probably exaggerated in its day. Pearl S. Buck's *The Good Earth* also won a Pulitzer and enjoyed critical esteem for some years, but I believe it is now commonly regarded as a pretty lightweight title, fit for high school students (as is much of Steinbeck) but not worthy of rank as serious literature.

As for the other authors, they are a motley farrago of the once-popular, even the once-esteemed, but now almost universally forgotten, even by diligent graduate students seeking something fresh to write about. It is particularly revealing that those super-bestsellers that dominated the lists for two years running—Buck's *The Good Earth,* Hervey Allen's *Anthony Adverse* (an historical novel), Margaret Mitchell's *Gone with the Wind,* and Richard Bach's *Jonathan Livingston Seagull*—have all been consigned to the Gehenna of popular hackdom. (Lloyd C. Douglas's *The Robe* was on the bestseller list ten years apart, in the latter instance as a result of the appearance of the film adaptation.)

It should be noted that this list of number one bestsellers does not fully convey the thoroughly trashy nature of the bestseller lists. Hackett and Burke list fifteen fiction titles that have sold more than seven million copies in hardcover and paperback; they are as follows (listed in order of sales):

Mario Puzo, *The Godfather* (1969)
William Peter Blatty, *The Exorcist* (1971)
Harper Lee, *To Kill a Mockingbird* (1960)
Grace Metalious, *Peyton Place* (1956)
Erich Segal, *Love Story* (1970)
Jacqueline Susann, *Valley of the Dolls* (1966)

Peter Benchley, *Jaws* (1974)
Richard Bach, *Jonathan Livingston Seagull* (1970)
Margaret Mitchell, *Gone with the Wind* (1936)
Erskine Caldwell, *God's Little Acre* (1933)
George Orwell, *Nineteen Eighty-four* (1949)
Charles Monroe Sheldon, *In His Steps* (1897)
Harold Robbins, *The Carpetbaggers* (1961)
Xaviera Hollander, *The Happy Hooker* (1972)
George Orwell, *Animal Farm* (1946)

Here the lack of canonical status becomes painfully evident. Aside from *To Kill a Mockingbird* and the two Orwell novels (conveniently sold in paperback to generations of high school and college students), not a single work is anything but a potboiler. Blatty's *The Exorcist* is a far from contemptible work of horror fiction, but it cannot be said to rank with the loftiest examples of this literary mode. The number of the above titles that were made into blockbuster films is also noteworthy; indeed, many works only attained super-bestseller status upon the emergence of the film version.

Is the relegation of these authors and works to literary oblivion the result of some evil conspiracy on the part of highbrow critics and university professors—those self-appointed guardians of literary canonicity—to foil the implied consensus of the mass reading public? I suppose there may be some—even some literary critics, sociologists, and other advocates of the common people—who think so; but I suspect the majority of reputable critics would conclude that these bestsellers have disappeared—and, more significantly, disappeared even from popular interest, superseded by more contemporary fare that in its turn is also probably destined to vanish—because they do not have the staying power that could lead to canonicity. They are, in effect, inferior works embodying certain recognised flaws that doom them to insignificance, and their popularity during their heyday was based largely upon their hitting a popular nerve and—one might as well come out and say it—their appeal to a broad mass of ill-educated and uncultivated readers.

We are getting to the heart of the matter. What makes a good book? What makes a bad one? On what basis can we make such judgments? Can such judgments ever be valid, and do they reveal anything other than the opinions—or, worse, the prejudices—of the person making them? We return to the elitism issue. In our democratic society the very quest for excellence—a quest that may be beyond the reach (as it is certainly beyond the interest) of the common person—is inherently suspicious. The only type of excellence that the average person can endure is celebrity, which is the excellence of numbers, and hence acceptable to democracy. When democracy is conjoined with capitalism, numbers rule inexorably. A "good" book must be the one that sells the greatest number of copies. The old Latin dictum *pulchrum est paucorum hominum* ("Beauty is for the few") is both paradoxical and subtly evil to the democrat.

And yet, even the democrat will be forced to pause when certain awkward facts are brought to his attention. Why is it that A. S. M. Hutchinson's *If Winter Comes* (1922) has faded from both popular and critical esteem, while another work of 1922, James Joyce's *Ulysses*, has not? Is it possible that *Ulysses* offers certain intellectual and aesthetic nourishment that *If Winter Comes* does not? If so, what kind of nourishment might that be?

If there are two elements that would seem to have universal validity as markers of genuine as opposed to bogus literature, they are *realism* and *sincerity*. Both elements must be treated carefully. *Realism* does not necessarily refer to realism of incident; for in that case, the entire literature of fantasy and the supernatural would be relegated to non-literary status. The realism that good literature strives for is realism as pertains to human emotions, and to the human being's relation to society and to the universe. The works studied in this book contain all manner of scenarios where characters act in ways that no human being in that situation would ever act, and to that degree they are false and meretricious. In the great majority of popular writing of whatever genre, both incidents and characters are stylised—the product of the author's adherence to certain standardised conventions that become over time increasingly separated from reality. In other words, they become stereotypes. These stereotypes become comforting markers for readers to fall back on, thereby situating the work in a given genre or mode and offering very largely the same kind of unadventurous regularity found in television sitcoms, sporting events, or even fast food.

*Sincerity* has come under much suspicion among literary critics because it appears to raise the spectre of "authorial intention," something that many critics believe should be banished from criticism because, in their judgment, it is impossible to ascertain what an author had in mind when writing a given literary work. But literary criticism is not an exact science, and in the great majority of cases an approximate sense of an author's sincerity in the portrayal of characters and events can be deduced by the application of *critical judgment*—the one element that distinguishes literary criticism from all other kinds of intellectual activity. A work whose characters are hackneyed and stereotyped, whose incidents are derived not from life but from other books or films, whose overall scenario is designed not to probe serious issues relating to human life but to provide transient amusement—this work (regardless of what the author had in mind) can be deemed *insincere* and therefore false and meretricious.

Various other failings of popular writing can be identified. The question of *prose style* is perhaps a bit tricky. Under the influence of Modernism, many critics for a substantial portion of the twentieth century maintained that only the spare, barebones prose of a Hemingway or a James T. Farrell constituted a legitimate vehicle for serious prose expression, and that anything approaching flamboyance in prose writing was in itself a sign of a lack of seriousness and maturity. This view persisted in the face of numerous counterexamples—most notably the dense and rich prose of Faulkner, whose superiority to Hemingway and Farrell was widely acknowledged. In recent decades, with the return of Asianic prose in the work of writers as diverse as Thomas Pynchon and Gore Vidal, a broader view of the parameters of acceptable prose style has emerged, and has helped to resurrect the reputations of a number of older writers, from Poe to H. P. Lovecraft, whose utilization of florid prose was central to their aesthetic practice.

The prose of most popular writers tends to be flat, bland, and elementary—a kind of dumbed-down Hemingway, entirely lacking the careful word-choice and keen attention to telling symbol and metaphor found in the work of even the most spare of prose minimalists. It is death to a popular writer to be perceived as anything other than "easy reading": since one of the prime goals of the popular writer is the ability to keep the reader turning the pages, any style that smacks of complexity or difficulty is anathema.

In a broader sense, popular writers as a whole also tend to avoid genuine emotional engagement, especially any plot whose dénouement could be termed sad, depressing, or tragic. In spite of the fact that a substantial majority of the world's great literature is tragic, the evocation of tragedy—even if it were within the capacities of popular writers—would be strenuously avoided, because no popular writer wishes to be perceived as a "downer." Tragedy must be clearly distinguished from the *melodrama* utilised, generally in a pretty calculating manner, by romance and sentimental writers who wish to offer their (largely female) readers a "good cry." Even these writers generally insist on some kind of happy ending to counteract the superficial elements of sadness and disappointment that have peppered their novels prior to that point.

As it is, most popular writers rely upon *plot*—and in particular the construction of an involved and cleverly executed plot, with numerous complications and surprises along the way—to carry the reader along. But this facility in plot-weaving is a relatively low-order literary skill; it is, in effect, the work of literary mechanics. Readers of popular writing tend to castigate serious literature as "slow moving," or as work where "nothing happens." On this point Gerard Manley Hopkins wrote a criticism of Robert Louis Stevenson (then and now regarded as, at best, occupying the second rank of literary greatness) that remains pertinent today:

> His doctrine, if I apprehend him, is something like this. The essence of Romance is incident and that only, the type of pure Romance the *Arabian Nights:* those stories have no moral, no character-drawing, they run altogether on interesting incident. The incidents must of course have a connection, but it need be nothing more than that they happen to the same person, are aggravations and so on. As history consists essentially of events likely or unlikely, consequences of causes chronicled before or what may be called chance, just retributions or nothing of the sort, so Romance, which is fictitious history, consists of event, of incident. His own stories are written on this principle; they are very good and he has all the gifts a writer of fiction should have, and at first you notice no more than an ordinary well told story, but on looking back in the light of this doctrine you see that the persons illustrate the incident or strains of incident, the plot, *the story,* not the story and incidents the persons.[5]

This is, indeed, a very charitable opinion even of Stevenson, let alone any other popular writer; but the fundamental thrust of Hopkins's criticism—that "incident" in a popular work deflects the reader's attention from the plain fact that the characters in the work are stereotyped and uninteresting, or at any rate that there is no meaningful probing of the characters' thoughts and feelings and therefore no attempt to hold these figures up as representative or symbolic of any segment of human society—remains valid. The inveterate tendency of popular writers to tie up all loose plot threads neatly at the end is a telltale sign that they wish to provide their readers an artificial resolution that has no relation to real life, where few issues are tied up neatly.

Popular writers owe their appeal heavily to the inveterate human curiosity to *find out what happens*. No matter how poorly written a book is (and books by, say, Danielle Steel or James Patterson are very poorly written indeed, by any conceivable aesthetic yardstick), no matter how hackneyed or unrealistic the characters are, readers of a certain mentality (who in general have little perception of the niceties of prose expression and who are willing to swallow the most outrageous departures from reality in character portrayal and in incident) will keep turning the pages because they want to know how the plot resolves. This is especially true in the case of the mystery/suspense genre, whose entire *raison d'être* is the concluding revelation of the murderer or criminal; but it applies nearly as strongly to other genres as well.

The response of most popular writers to criticisms like the above is that they are not intending to write weighty works that "probe serious issues relating to human life," but are instead merely striving to "entertain." But this seemingly straightforward statement is itself highly problematical and complex. In what sense does a lightweight literary work "entertain"? Whom does it entertain? And how? I daresay that pornography entertains those who choose to partake of it, but I don't imagine that most people would think this confers any value to it. If a popular work only "entertains" a popular audience in the manner of a crossword puzzle or a football game, what aesthetic status does it occupy? Presumably these works do *not* entertain readers of a higher aesthetic level. Certainly, I derived little "entertainment" from the great majority of works I discuss in this book, and I would not have finished—or even begun—them had I not decided to undertake a study of them. My greatest source of pleasure in each of these books was coming to the last page.

\* \* \* \* \* \* \*

Some further light may be shed by a necessarily brief examination of the history of popular reading, especially in the United States. It has become fashionable for some critics to maintain that the popular author of today becomes the canonical author of tomorrow; Shakespeare and Dickens are usually hauled out to prove the truth of this assertion. These commentators conveniently forget that, even if popular authors who later entered the canon can be found, the immense number of once-popular authors (most of them unknown except to specialists in literary history) have been universally and deservedly forgotten. Does one really wish to make a case that, say, Marie Corelli or Charlotte Mary Yonge are, or ever will be, canonical? This whole matter is immensely complex, having to do with the spread of literacy, developments in the technology of publishing, the power of advertising and marketing, and numerous other factors, but some broad features of the issue can be outlined here.

For nearly the whole of human civilised history, reading—especially the reading of literary works—was restricted to a tiny segment of the adult population who had the social status and the economic means to educate themselves. This education was, on the whole, intense enough to render this narrow elite capable of appreciating the highest fruits of literary expression, so that authors—who were rarely of that elite themselves—necessarily directed their writings toward it. There was, for all practical purposes, no such thing as "popular writing" or, more broadly, popular culture prior to the later nineteenth century, because there was (at least as far as writing is concerned) no market for it.[6] The plays of Shakespeare attracted a wide and diverse audience because they were, first and foremost, visual spectacles that could be appreciated on many different levels by viewers of highly differentiated educational levels.

It has been maintained that the novel was, at its inception, a "popular" form, but the term appears to be a misnomer if actual levels of literacy in early eighteenth-century England—the birthplace of the novel—are taken into consideration. In 1714 the base literacy rate in England was 45% for men and 25% for women, and this rate actually declined in some areas of England as the century proceeded.[7] Moreover, this rate measured only those who could sign their names; the literacy level required to read a novel by Fielding, Smollett, or Richardson was considerably higher than this. The best that can be said of the novel at this stage was that it appealed to a slightly broader but still relatively small minority of the English adult population.

It should also be noted that the cost of books was prohibitively high at this time, and for a considerable period thereafter. As late as 1821, the price of Sir Walter Scott's novel *Kenilworth* was 31s. 6d—equivalent to a week's wages for a manual labourer.[8] Circulating libraries were beginning to flourish at this juncture, but even they required a membership fee that was often beyond the means of the working class.

Charles Dickens did indeed make a conscious effort to appeal to a lower stratum of society—or, rather, to include that stratum in his readership along with higher strata—by the technological innovation of publishing his novels serially (usually on a monthly basis) in "parts." This was a clever move, in that his readers—assuming they liked the work in question—assured him of regular sales for as many as twenty or thirty months. And yet, the number of readers Dickens reached was still a minuscule portion of the overall English population. In 1849–50, he issued *David Copperfield* in twenty monthly parts; the first part had a print run of 30,000 copies, the others somewhat less. Given that the adult British population was at this time just under seven million, one could hardly say that Dickens was reaching a mass audience. Book sales of *David Copperfield* in 1851–53 averaged only 1,500 a year.[9] To say that Dickens was a "bestseller" is a serious misconstrual of the term.

It was only with the Education Act of 1870 (the very year of Dickens's death), requiring school boards to ensure that all children in their districts met minimum standards of school attendance, that literacy began to approach universality in England. In 1840, 41% of the populace was literate; in 1870, the number had risen to 70%; and by 1900 it was 85%.[10] Keep in mind, however, that these percentages denote only basic literacy; the level required to read books—to say nothing of the interest in doing so—remained beyond the reach of a substantial proportion of the population. As we shall see presently, it is telling that "popular" literature during the nineteenth and well into the twentieth century took the form of newspapers, magazines, and other non-book material—because it was only this material, which could be picked up and put down without serious loss of continuity, that appealed to a popular audience of limited patience, limited means, and limited leisure time for reading.

In the United States the expansion of education to the working classes roughly followed that of England, so that by the turn of the twentieth century nearly universal basic literacy had been achieved. But another key element that was central to the birth and proliferation of popular writing was economic advance. Individuals could obviously not absorb popular writing if they could not read; but they could also not absorb it if they did not have the economic means to obtain it or the leisure time to appreciate it. It required such modifications of laissez-faire capitalism as the eight-hour law, unionization, and collective bargaining to allow the working classes sufficient disposable income and sufficient leisure to make them consumers of popular culture. As a result of these radical developments, the average work week for American labourers declined from 70 hours in 1850 to 60 hours in 1890 to 50 hours in 1920 to 40 hours in 1950.[11] Wages underwent a startling rise in approximately this same period: from 1890 to 1926, union wages rose 205%, while non-union wages rose (surprisingly) 237%; this figure was not matched until the period 1914–47, when union wages rose 401% and non-union wages rose 406%. It was, therefore, only in the later nineteenth and twentieth centuries that a mass audience with the money to purchase entertainment products and the leisure to enjoy them emerged.[12]

It is, therefore, no accident that popular literature did not take hold much earlier than the latter decades of the nineteenth century. The first form it took was the dime novel, perhaps a successor to the "penny dreadfuls" that had been distributed in England beginning in the 1830s.[13] The first dime novel was published in 1860, when the firm later known as Beadle & Adams reprinted, in a 128-page paper-covered volume, Ann Sophia Winterbotham Stephens's *Malaeska: The Indian Wife of the White Hunter*. The fact that it was a reprint was critical, for it allowed the firm to claim that here was "a dollar book for a dime."[14] Beadle & Adams was the leading publisher of dime novels until it folded in 1898, having been driven out of business by the bold and innovative publishing practices of Street & Smith, which entered the dime novel market in 1889.

It should not be assumed that dime novels were merely action thrillers, although many of them were; there were westerns (Deadwood Dick from Beadle & Adams; Diamond Dick from Street & Smith), detective or espionage stories (Nick Carter from Street & Smith; Old King Brady from Frank Tousey), tales of high school and college life (Frank Merriwell from Street & Smith), and even pious tales of moral uprightness (Horatio Alger, Jr., wrote prolifically for Street & Smith in the 1890s). Their principal features were their price, their format (paper covers, 128 pages or less), and, in general, their linguistically simple, action-packed narrative style. The leading dime novel series were, of course, priced at 10¢, although there was a wide array of smaller books, called "nickel libraries," at 5¢ aimed at younger readers.

The inexpensiveness of these books was critical, for at this time—and, indeed, throughout the twentieth century—there was a fairly direct correlation between the number of books purchased by a given household and that household's personal income. In 1918–19, only 5.4% of those in the lowest income level (those making under $900 a year) purchased books; in the highest income level (those making more than $2,500 a year), the percentage was 29.2. In 1972, the percentage in the lowest income level (under $3,000 a year) was 31.2; in the highest (more than $25,000), it was 83.3.[15] So the price of a given literary product was a highly relevant factor in its purchase by the working classes. Michael Denning has shown conclusively that the chief audience for dime novels was the working class.[16]

The bestseller, as a literary or commercial phenomenon, only dates to the later nineteenth century. Lew Wallace's *Ben-Hur* (1880) sold two million copies, far exceeding the sales of Dickens and other purportedly "popular" authors. The New York magazine *Bookman* was the first to run bestseller lists, in 1895; *Publishers' Weekly,* although it had been founded in 1872, did not begin its list until 1912.

The dime novels ultimately gave way to the pulp magazines. The history of pulp magazines—usually costing anywhere from a dime to a quarter, and therefore accessible to the pocketbooks of the working class—is highly involved, but its roots can be traced to 1882, when Frank A. Munsey launched the *Golden Argosy* (later the *Argosy*) as the first all-fiction pulp magazine. He later established numerous other fiction magazines, and his chief claim to fame resides in his discovery of Edgar Rice Burroughs, whose first Mars novel (*Under the Moons of Mars*) and first Tarzan novel (*Tarzan of the Apes*) both appeared in 1912. By that time, Street & Smith had gotten into the act with the *Popular Magazine,* and other publishers contributed their own ventures.[17]

It was in the pulps that the genres as we know them—the western, the horror story, the detective story, the love story, the science fiction tale—all became viable forms of popular writing. Each of these genres has a history—and often a distinguished history in "high" literature (such as Henry James's ghost story *The Turn of the Screw* [1898], the "scientific romances" of H. G. Wells, and so on)—that extends well before the pulps of the early twentieth century, but it was the pulps that lent them widespread popularity among the masses. Indeed, it was exactly at this time that mainstream or "slick" magazines tended to banish genre fiction (particularly the horror, detective, and science fiction tale) from its pages, except when written by especially eminent authors. The end result was the ghettoization of these genres for decades; even today certain snobbish critics disdain this work on principle.[18] To be sure, much of the writing in the pulps was subliterary and deserves permanent inhumation, but given the difficulty of selling work to other venues, such now canonical writers as H. P. Lovecraft, Dashiell Hammett, Raymond Chandler, Arthur C. Clarke, and Ray Bradbury had little option but to appear in its pages.

This period—roughly the first half of the twentieth century—constituted the first occasion in which, in both the United States and Europe, a mass audience for entertainment products existed; and it was, somewhat fortuitously, the same time that other modes of mass entertainment aside from printed matter emerged—the radio, the movie, music (including the musical drama), and later television. The result, as far as the economics of the entertainment industry (of which books, even bestsellers, constituted a relatively small portion) was concerned, was inevitable: media outlets began a wholesale shift in their output to cater to the (relatively crude and ill-formed) tastes of the mass public. What else could they do? That was where the money was. In sheer numbers, the mass audience dwarfed the now tiny elite of the educated to such a degree that the latter were rendered insignificant as consumers. H. P. Lovecraft, who was a reluctant contributor to the pulp magazine *Weird Tales* but who strove valiantly to preserve his aesthetic integrity, saw this at first hand, as he wrote to a colleague in early 1937:

> Bourgois capitalism gave artistic excellence & sincerity a death-blow by enthroning cheap *amusement-value* at the expense of that *intrinsic excellence* which only cultivated, non-acquisitive persons of assured position can enjoy. The determinant market for written, pictorial, musical, dramatic, decorative, architectural, & other heretofore aesthetic material ceased to be a small circle of truly educated persons, but became a substantially larger (even with a vast proportion of society starved & crushed into a sodden, inarticulate helplessness through commercial & commercial-satellitic greed & callousness) circle of mixed origin numerically dominated by crude, half-educated clods whose systematically perverted ideals (worship of low cunning, material acquisition, cheap comfort & smoothness, worldly success, ostentation, speed, intrinsic magnitude, surface glitter, &c.) prevented them from ever achieving the tastes and perspectives of the gentlefolk whose dress & speech & external manners they so assiduously mimicked. This herd of acquisitive boors brought up from the shop & the counting-house a complete set of artificial attitudes, oversimplifications, & mawkish sentimentalities which no sincere art or literature could gratify— & they so outnumbered the remaining educated gentlefolk that most of the purveying agencies became at once reoriented to them. Literature & art lost most of their market; & writing, painting, drama, &c. became

engulfed more & more in the domain of *amusement enterprises.*[19]

This assessment may be a trifle harsh, but in essentials it seems largely valid. The plain fact is that even those who have received college educations are rarely taught to make the fundamental critical distinctions that would allow them to sort the wheat from the chaff when it comes to art—the original from the hackneyed, the distinctive from the trite, the sincere from the calculated, and so on. As early as 1956, Gore Vidal was lamenting that the serious literary novel was dead—not because of a dearth of good writers, but rather because of a lack of educated readers:

> The fault, if it be a fault, is not the novelist's (I doubt if there ever have been so many interesting and excellent writers as there are now working) but of the audience, an unpleasant accusation to make in a democracy where, ultimately, the taste of the majority is the measure of all things. Nevertheless, appalling education combined with clever new toys has distracted that large public which found pleasure in prose fictions.

When Vidal presented a counter-argument that paperbacks (which became the successors to the pulp magazines when the latter faded in the 1940s) were being purchased in great numbers, he replied to it as follows: ". . .it may be argued that the large sales of paperback books, both good and bad, are proof that there are millions out there in the dark, hungering for literature. But though it is true that all those books must go *somewhere,* I suggest that their public is not a serious one, that it is simply pursuing secret vices from one bright cover picture to another—consuming, not reading."[20]

The proliferation of the mass media (in which publishers, especially paperback publishers, must now be included) only exacerbated the situation. It was impossible for any of the mass media to survive economically by appealing to a coterie audience: even today, cable television channels of seemingly specialised subject matter still have subscription lists in the millions, or even tens of millions. Media such as television, film, and even radio require such enormous expenditures of capital that they can only make a profit by addressing the interests of the widest possible audience. In book publishing, the profit margin has always been quite small; for paperbacks it is even smaller, so that only the most popular books ever achieve a profit when published in "mass-market" paperback editions.[21] It is, however, a curious, and quite counter-intuitive, fact that the ratio between expenditures for books and for other media has not shifted radically for the better part of a century. In 1929, out of a total personal expenditure of $471.4 billion dollars (converted to 1982 dollars), the spending on all forms of mass media amounted to $14.2 billion, of which books constituted $1.8 billion, or about 12%. In 1986, spending on mass media amounted to $77.7 billion, of which books constituted $6.7 billion, or about 9%.[22] So spending on books has indeed declined in relation to spending on other forms of mass media, but not as precipitously as many have feared; and the recent popularity of books like Dan Brown's *The Da Vinci Code,* which sold 40 million copies worldwide to the end of 2005,[23] or (among juveniles and young adults) J. K. Rowling's books about Harry Potter speak strongly for the continued power of certain popular books or genres to maintain their allegiance among readers.

But the media have had, on the whole, a deleterious effect on book production, especially of the popular sort. There is so much money involved in the media adaptation of literary products (an author can often earn far more on such an adaptation than on the total sales of the book itself) that popular authors now strive to secure film or television rights as part of the initial package of sales of their product; and the best way to do this is to write, as it were, novelised screenplays that can be readily adapted (sometimes by themselves) for the screen. Accordingly, we are today bombarded with books whose very short chapters, rapid change of scene, exaggerated emotional conflicts, and frequent plot twists are meant to mimic the special-effects-laden blockbuster films at the local Cineplex. This may have contributed to the very plain, ordinary, unadventurous prose of contemporary bestsellers: anything resembling a complex or idiosyncratic prose style will hamper the quick *visual* absorption of the scenario and therefore render less likely the prospects of a media adaptation. The brutal truth, however, is that there is no way that any book, no matter how visually adept, can match the adrenalin rush of a contemporary film's action sequence or torrid love scene; but that doesn't prevent our valiant bestsellers from trying.

The dominance of the media has had deleterious effects on "serious" fiction as well. Just as popular bestselling authors become, in effect, brand names once they achieve the bestseller lists, so too do certain authors of a higher grade land (briefly) on the bestseller lists chiefly for their notoriety rather than for the intrinsic merit of their writing. Gore Vidal is an illuminating case. Although he reached the bestseller lists as early as 1948 with *The City and the Pillar,* one of the first openly homosexual novels to receive wide distribution, he subsequently faced hostility from publishers and readers for breaking a taboo, and so in 1954 he abandoned the novel. But he stayed in the limelight by writing or co-writing a number of major screenplays (including uncredited work on *Ben-Hur*) as well as by appearing on television talk shows and on game shows such as "What's My Line?" Accordingly, when he returned to novel writing in 1964 with the historical novel *Julian*, he reached the bestseller lists again— largely on the basis of his personal celebrity and not on the superlative merits of his book. After still more media work (including a celebrated verbal duel with William F. Buckley, Jr., on ABC at the Democratic National Convention of 1968), he became a kind of brand name with *Myra Breckinridge* (1968), which achieved spectacular sales in paperback—no doubt among many who sought out its "naughty bits" and couldn't care less for its pungent and wide-ranging satire. Norman Mailer is another author who not only became a celebrity for actions quite unrelated to his writing, but who also sought to capture a popular audience with works carefully aimed for a lowbrow readership, such as his biography of Marilyn Monroe.

It has been remarked that bestsellers today are dominated by what is generally termed genre fiction. Luc Sante, with a considerable degree of exaggeration, has recently noted: "Older readers may remember a time when there existed something called 'mainstream' fiction.... [But] the Top 10 charts these days are stuffed with thrillers, very nearly to the exclusion of everything else."[24] If we look at our list of bestsellers from 1901 to 1975, we find that a work of genre fiction (by which one means a work of detective/crime fiction, horror fiction, science fiction, western, action/adventure, or romance) achieved the top of the bestseller lists only in 1964, with John le Carré's espionage novel *The Spy Who Came In from the Cold.* (There are any number of historical novels on the list prior to this date, but the historical novel was not then, and perhaps is not now, considered a "genre" in the sense that the others mentioned are.) Even after this date, genre fiction does not dominate the lists down to 1975; but it does when we come to look at the fifteen leading bestsellers of this period. Of the top seven, five can be considered genre fiction: Mario Puzo's *The Godfather* (crime); William Peter Blatty's *The Exorcist* (horror); Grace Metalious's *Peyton Place* and Erich Segal's *Love Story* (romance); and Peter Benchley's *Jaws* (action/adventure). In the thirty subsequent years, with such writers as Stephen King and Dean Koontz (horror), Danielle Steel and Barbara Taylor Bradford (romance), and James Patterson and

Robert Ludlum (crime/suspense) repeatedly appearing on the best seller lists, we can say that genre fiction definitively monopolises the realm of popular writing.

What genre fiction, even more than popular fiction of a more "mainstream" sort, appears to do is to enhance the reader's wish-fulfillment fantasies. The romance novel allows women readers the wish-fulfillment of finding the perfect lover; the crime/suspense novel places the reader in the position of the brave detective or crime-fighter battling evil criminals; the sex/glamour novel allows the reader the wish-fulfillment of becoming a voyeur to the intimacies of the beautiful and the celebrated; even the horror novel delivers a shiver to those readers who seek the wish-fulfillment fantasy of vicariously experiencing a terrifying scenario, knowing full well that they are really not in danger. Individual titles within these genres may perhaps break the stereotype or even utilise the stylised conventions in an aesthetically effective way, but these are exceptions to the rule that rarely achieve bestseller status. The sociological significance of this indulgence in wish-fulfillment is, as I have suggested, beyond the scope of this study and largely beyond the scope of my interest; but I think that those frenzied defenders of popular culture would be better off if they ceased to deny that this effect is widely prevalent in popular writing of all sorts.

\* \* \* \* \* \* \*

This book might—if I wished to be particularly pompous and self-important—be considered a kind of personal odyssey through bestseller land. Aside from Stephen King and Irving Wallace (the latter of whom I devoured avidly as a teenager, when he was a big seller), I had not previously read any of the authors I discuss, and I knew their work only by what little I had heard from the mainstream media.[25] In spite of appearances, I did not enter into my reading campaign with an unwavering prejudice against these authors or their books, nor have I gone out of my way to point out their failings and to ignore or minimise their virtues. But it strikes me that only a careful dissection of individual bestselling novels can truly reveal either their failings or their virtues, and I have sought to do that with a minimum of unwarranted sarcasm. If I have not entirely succeeded in this latter attempt, it is only a testament to the truth of Juvenal's old dictum, *Difficile est saturam non scribere* (It is difficult not to write satire). The literary criteria I have used to evaluate these works are fairly orthodox ones that have been considered valid for centuries, and I don't imagine that they reveal any notable biases or prejudices one way or the other.

I believe I have covered most of the standard genres or modes of bestseller writing—the romance novel, the novel of pseudo-profundity, the detective novel (and its offshoots, the suspense or action/adventure novel and the spy novel), the horror novel, the sex/glamour novel, and the novel that deliberately exploits controversial subjects. I have not discussed the western (because it has, in the past thirty years, largely faded from the scene as a form of popular entertainment) nor the science fiction or fantasy tale (which, in spite of the renewed popularity of Tolkien's *The Lord of the Rings* as a result of the recent films, has not produced blockbuster best sellers of late), but no doubt a similar analysis of these genres, among others, could be made.

My conclusion—that the great majority of these books are subliterary—is, I daresay, not surprising, but I think we need to have a clearer idea of exactly *how* these books are subliterary in order to deal with the broader issue of why these books are read in such numbers and what, if anything, can be done to steer readers to better fare. I shall address these issues in my conclusion.

# I.

# QUEENS OF ROMANCE

## DANIELLE STEEL, BARBARA TAYLOR BRADFORD, AND NORA ROBERTS

It would, I suppose, be possible to trace the origin of romance writing to the dawn of literary history. *Oedipus Rex* is a love story, if one wishes to look at it that way. But in the realms of English and American literature, romance—the love of a man and a woman (lesbian or gay love being, of course, *verboten*) as a central feature of a narrative—emerges at the very commencement of the novel as a distinct literary mode. There is plenty of lovemaking in the eighteenth-century novels of Henry Fielding, Tobias Smollett, and especially Samuel Richardson, whose sentimentality was pilloried by critics of his day and of ours. Richardson's *Pamela; or, Virtue Rewarded* (1740–41), in which a young woman valiantly defends her virtue against the onslaughts of a cruel aristocrat, Mr. B., before finally yielding to him and marrying him (by which time he has apparently reformed his horrible, lustful ways to become a model husband), was pungently satirised by Fielding in *Shamela* (1741). Richardson's immense novel *Clarissa* (1748–49), more than a million words in length, is somewhat along the same pattern, with the heroine continually dodging rape and brutalization. It was the direct inspiration for the novel *Charlotte Temple* (1794), an immense bestseller by a British transplant to America, Susanna Rowson, and hence perhaps the first American romance novel.

But if romance reached a level of high literature in the work of Jane Austen and the Brontë sisters, it descended close to the level of the subliterary in the work of such writers as the Americans Catherine Maria Sedgwick (1789–1867) and E. D. E. N. Southworth (1819–1899). Toward the end of the nineteenth century, the reading public was gobbling up the work of such women writers as Margaret Oliphant (1828–1897), Ouida (1839–1908), and Charlotte Mary Yonge (1823–1901), the last of whom may have been, in terms of actual wordage, the most prolific writer of the nineteenth century. These and other writers wrote romances set in their own day, historical romances (following the lead of Sir Walter Scott), or what came to be called Gothic romances, deriving from the work of Ann Radcliffe (1764–1823) and placing beauteous heroines in peril in scenarios that suggested the supernatural.

It is no accident that most of the writers of what we would now call romance novels were women. By the turn of the twentieth century, H. L. Mencken was already complaining about the "feminization" of literature—the fact that literature, whether actually written by men or women, was being directed at female readers rather than male readers. The stereotype emerged of the "tired business man," the wage slave who worked so hard at his job that he had no time or energy to enjoy a good book (or a book of any kind) when he came home. Meanwhile, his stay-at-home wife, with the advent of various labour-saving devices that made housework easier and less time-consuming, could indulge in the literature that suited her.

Accordingly, we find such writers as the American Robert W. Chambers (1865–1933)—who, curiously enough, began his career as a skilful writer of supernatural tales—becoming a perennial best-seller with a long succession of romance novels, either contemporary or historical, that specifically catered to young women. These novels, generally set in an urban milieu (Chambers was born in Brooklyn, spent time as an art student in Paris, and lived for most of his life in the New York City area), featured vivacious heroines pursuing, or being pursued by, their male counterparts in the worlds of business or finance, and after a suitable number of complications settling down to married bliss. In England, Georgette Heyer (1902–1974) began her long series of romance novels in 1921; twenty years later appeared the first novel of Victoria Holt (1906–1993), a pseudonym of Eleanor Hibbert who also published under her own name and under the names Philippa Carr, Jean Plaidy, and other pseudonyms. She produced 188 novels in the fifty years of her career, alternating between historical and Gothic romance. The only American to come close to her achievement was Phyllis Whitney (b. 1903), whose first novel dates to 1943.

British writer Barbara Cartland (1901–2000) began her career so early as 1925, but did not hit her stride until the 1970s—perhaps because it was at this time that she began dictating her novels to a stenographer. She boasted that she could complete a novel in seven working days. By the end of her life, 600 million copies of her novels were in print. Many of her earlier novels were published by the British publishing company Mills & Boon, which in 1949 opened a Canadian branch called Harlequin. Since that time, Harlequin Enterprises has dominated the romance book industry, with nearly 4,000 titles published (they currently publish 780 a year).

Perhaps more than any other genre of writing studied in this book, romance writing caters quite deliberately to the wish-fulfillment fantasies of its (almost exclusively female) readers. It does so by fostering scenarios that a substantial number of women yearn for in their lives but in general find lacking—most notably, the existence of a loving, caring husband who, aside from his good looks (and, more recently, his prowess in bed, always with the understanding that he is as interested in pleasing his partner as he is in pleasing himself), is sensitive to a woman's needs and desires, emotional as well as sexual, and is sufficiently well-to-do to provide for his wife in the manner in which she wishes to become accustomed.

One of the purest wish-fulfillment fantasies of recent years is Robert James Waller's *The Bridges of Madison County* (1992), which establishes the extraordinarily unlikely scenario of a photographer (Robert Kincaid) who encounters a lonely farm wife, Francesca Johnson (her husband and children are conveniently away), and engages in a four-day affair with her. Waller is careful to maintain a sufficiently romantic and elegiac air so as to guard against the suggestion that mere sex is at the heart of the enterprise; and, upon Kincaid's inevitable departure, Francesca can now look back with tender longing on a fling that in no way harms her otherwise sound marriage.

What we have, in effect, are three different levels of romance writing: writing (by such figures as Edith Wharton, Anne Tyler, and Terry McMillan) that is (or at least purports to be) a serious treatment of domestic issues, in which love and romance are central features; romance novels of a lower grade, generally published in hardcover but being somewhat more predictable and stereotypical in their scenarios and outcomes; and the frankly subliterary Harlequin type, which are expressly written to a formula supplied by the publisher, whose guidelines specify that certain incidents (the first kiss, the first sexual situation, and so forth) must take place at precise stages of the narrative. It is the novels of the second group that I propose to treat here, and their chief proponents—as far as the bestseller lists are concerned—appear to be Danielle Steel, Barbara Taylor Bradford, and Nora Roberts.

Danielle Steel (b. 1947) was born in New York City and gradu-ated from New York University. She has been married at least three times, which no doubt gives her some kind of first-hand expertise in affairs of the heart. After working in public relations and advertising (useful professions for a budding bestseller), she turned to writing with the novel *Going Home* (1973). Since that time she has written sixty-seven additional novels down to the end of 2006—a rate of more than two a year. This figure does not include fifteen children's books published between 1985 and 1992, a volume of *Love Poems* (1981), a nonfiction treatise, *Having a Baby* (1984), and a biography (1998) of Nick Traina, her troubled son—a rock singer who was a manic-depressive and died at the age of nineteen. Twenty-one of her books have been adapted for film or television, although the major-ity of these appear to have been in the form of TV miniseries rather than blockbuster movies. At least 450 million copies of her books are in print, putting her a somewhat distant second to Barbara Cart-land but certainly no slouch in the tree-destroying profession.

Steel is apparently known for dealing with "tough" issues in the course of her romance novels—perhaps as a result of her experience with her son, Nick—but there is also every indication that she pre-fers to give her readers just what they want: a nice, sentimental ro-mance, not without complications and with no great emphasis on sex, but ultimately leading to a satisfactory union. I have no idea whether the novel of hers that I read, *Bittersweet* (1999),[1] is repre-sentative of her work, but I have no reason to believe that it isn't. At any rate, it provides a good introduction both to Steel's work and to the romance novel in its contemporary incarnation.

In *Bittersweet,* we are introduced to India Taylor. The exotic first name and the run-of-the-mill second name (her husband's, no doubt) is meant to convey a significant duality to readers: she is ex-traordinary, but not so extraordinary as to be beyond the power of (women) readers to envision themselves in her place. Naturally, she is gorgeous, even in the relatively advanced age in which we find her as the novel opens:

> There were wisps of wheat-colored hair framing her face, and she never thought much about what she looked like. She was lucky, she didn't have to. She had clean, healthy, classic looks, and the braid she wore suited her. Her skin was good, and she looked about thirty-five instead of forty-three, with a long, slim figure that looked well in shirts and turtlenecks

and jeans, which was the uniform she wore daily. (20–21)

But India's virtues go well beyond mere appearance. We learn that she is "bright and beautiful and talented" (36). She lives in Westport, Connecticut (hence has no mundane worries about where the next meal is coming from), and she is the daughter of a *New York Times* photographer—not just any photographer, but one who went "on dangerous assignments in war zones" (2) and ended up winning a Pulitzer Prize for his troubles (4). India initially followed in his footsteps, winning prizes "for her coverage, her insight, and her courage" (3). But India does not wish to repeat some of her father's mistakes; in particular, she certainly does not wish to die on an assignment, as he had done, and she also recognises that his work adversely affected his marriage.

India marries Doug Taylor at the age of twenty-six, and for two years she continues to work. But Doug is anxious to have children, and he gives her an ultimatum: "He had told her that if she wanted a future with him, she had better 'get her ass back to New York' and stop risking her life in Pakistan and Kenya" (4). Moreover, "Doug had made it very clear to her when they got married that once they had children, she had to give up her career" (4). After some soul-searching, India does so, and gives birth to four children in five years.

At this point, we might think that India is meant to represent Steel's answer to feminism, and a rejection of the notion that you can't have it all. India reflects that "giving it [her career] up was the price she had had to pay for having children. There was just no other way to do it" (6). Evidently India has not heard of equal parenting; at this point it seems beyond her powers to conceive that Doug could somehow curtail *his* career to lend a hand with childrearing. And even though India tries to convince herself that "Doug appreciated all that she'd given up for him" (13)—a phrase repeated almost verbatim a few pages later: "she knew that Doug appreciated what she was doing" (19)—it is quite plain that Doug is not in fact very appreciative. Not only does he scorn India's father's career ("He was lucky, and you know it. . . . He got paid for what he liked to do. Hanging out and watching people. That's kind of a fortuitous accident, wouldn't you say?" [23]), but her own ("I think you had a hell of a good time doing what you did for a while. It was a good excuse to stay out and play, probably a little longer than you should have" [24]).

But the real problem with India is not that life has become "virtually the same" (7) for the past fourteen years, with the usual responsibilities of raising children ("Driving, diapers, teething, nursing, fevers, play groups, and one pregnancy after another" [5]), but that Doug really doesn't love her anymore. His "adventuring days were over" (10), and, in spite of his own dashing appearance ("He was tall and lean and lanky, with athletic good looks, and a boyish face. At forty-five, he was still very handsome, and looked like a college football hero" [22]), his passion has cooled considerably. During a particularly tense argument, Doug admits that at the age of forty-five it is unreasonable to expect people to be "in love" anymore. In answer to India's pungent query, asked in a "strangled voice": "What *can* you expect?" (46), he replies blandly: "Companionship, decency, respect, someone to take care of the kids. Someone you can rely on. That's about all anyone should expect from marriage" (46). Indeed, "Being married to someone just isn't romantic" (47).

By now Steel's agenda is becoming clearer. Here is a beautiful, desirable woman—technically middle-aged, but still a knockout—who, like the great majority of her readers, "was wasting her life cleaning out the barbecue and driving car pools" (36). All she had become was "a maid, a short-order cook, and a chauffeur" (41)! If this can happen to someone as transcendent as India, it could happen to anyone—and, indeed, *has* happened to a majority of married women in the West, in spite of the advances of feminism. And on top of it all, she has to take care of an ungrateful husband who doesn't even love her—at least, not in the way India wants to be loved. She wants romance, exactly as her readers do.

In this scenario, India's friend Gail Jones plays a critical role. Gail, a former lawyer who had similarly given up her career to raise children in Westport, admits to India that she has had several affairs over the twenty-two years she has been married to her husband, Jeff. Gail symbolises the bad choice that Steel wants to make sure her readers don't follow. For although Gail herself maintains that these affairs "had actually improved their marriage," India thinks to herself: "It was a form of 'improvement' India had never been drawn to, nor approved of" (11). And later: "India couldn't even imagine sleeping with anyone else" (19). The figure of Gail, who pops up every so often throughout the novel, usually with a different married man in tow, allows Steel to titillate her readers with sexual suggestion (although nothing even remotely explicit is supplied) without sullying her sainted protagonist.

Things go from bad to worse with India and Doug. Her agent, Raoul Lopez, who has always wanted her to return to professional photography, offers India an assignment in South Korea, where an adoption agency is killing unwanted children. It is just the kind of heart-rending, do-gooder assignment India yearns for, but she knows that Doug would disapprove, and so she regretfully turns it down. We are, of course, meant to think poorly, not of her, but of Doug for so clipping her wings. It is just at this point that she and Doug have the bitter argument in which he confess he is no longer "in love" with her.

The Taylors have established the pattern of spending the summers in a cottage on Cape Cod, and they head out there as usual—but Doug has to work nights at his advertising office, so he can't come very often. (For a moment the reader is led to wonder whether *he* is having an affair, but no such luck. He is too devoted to his work for that.) Things take a dramatic turn when a friend informs India that the celebrated writer Serena Smith and her husband will be arriving soon. Serena "was on the bestseller list constantly with her steamy novels," and India "had always had the impression that she was an interesting woman" (61). Aren't all bestselling writers interesting? Serena's husband is one Paul Ward, a banker who has received the remarkable—perhaps unprecedented—honour of being on the cover of *Time* magazine *twice*—"in the past few years" (62)!

Clearly, Paul is no ordinary banker. As Steel lovingly describes him, he becomes the ideal man—at least, for India and all those who yearn for romance with a man who combines financial success, moral values, sensitivity, and passion. He is no hard-headed money man, but has been involved in "airlifts to some very out-of-the-way places," including "a number of missions into Bosnia, to help the children [naturally] while things were rough there. And of course Rwanda" (77). Of course. But there is more:

> He was fascinating to talk to. He had an extensive knowledge of the world and the arts, a passion for politics, and a lot of strong opinions and interesting views. And at the same time, he had a gentleness, a kindness, and a wisdom that endeared him to her. And more than once, he had her laughing at stories he told on himself. He had a sense of mischief as well, and a wicked sense of humor. (78)

What more could one ask for? Did I mention good looks? "He had intense blue eyes, and a handsome chiseled face, and he was wearing white shorts and a bright red T-shirt, over powerful shoulders and a long, lean, athletic-looking body" (72). And in contrast to Doug, he immediately takes India's son Sam under his wing, letting Sam spend a wonderful afternoon on his sailboat. In a pregnant utterance, Paul notes whimsically, "I think I'm falling desperately in love with your son" (78)—especially since his own grown-up son doesn't like boats at all!

By now the scenario should be clear to any reader: India and Paul are meant for each other. But how to dispose of the other spouses in the picture? Doug may not be so much of a problem, but Serena is Paul's second wife, and he loves her devotedly. In spite of the fact that he is attracted to India ("There was something quiet and magnetic about her that drew her to him" [80]), especially given that Serena herself is somewhat hard and forceful, unlike the gentle India, and in spite of the fact that, in true romance fashion, "she felt their eyes lock for a moment" (84) as they are parting, India knows well that neither she nor Paul wish to have an affair.

But India takes the first faltering steps, even if they are only mental. She envisions what life would be like without Doug, and does not find the prospect so terrifying. ". . .what if Doug left her? If he died? Would her life be so different? Would she feel more alone than she did now, knowing that she was just a tool to him, a convenience? What would happen to her if she lost him?" (91). And again:

> What did their marriage mean to her now? Now that she knew what Doug was thinking. It changed everything, like the subtle turn of a dial that changed the music from sweet melody to endless static that hurt one's eardrums. And she could no longer pretend to herself that what she heard was music. It wasn't. Hadn't been for weeks. Maybe longer than that. Maybe it never had been. That was the worst thought. (92)

Then she imagines being on Paul's boat and taking a long journey with him. It is, of course, a luxurious boat, as India discovers when she comes to her stateroom after agreeing to a short trip with Paul (with Sam discreetly in tow to make sure no funny business occurs): "The room was more beautiful than any hotel room. The walls were paneled in mahogany, there were shiny brass fittings on all the drawers and closets. The room was large and airy, with several portholes, and a huge closet, and there was a fabulous white marble bathroom, with a bathtub and a shower" (94). Women must have their nice bathrooms!

But in spite of Paul's attraction, and his sensitivity to India's plight with Doug ("It's a very dangerous thing clipping a woman's wings" [100], he intones sagely), Paul admits to being entirely happy with Serena, even though they do not in fact seem a particularly good match: "'I'm happy now,' he said to India. 'Serena is an extraordinary woman. She doesn't take a lot of guff from me, and I respect her for it'" (102). Matters are made worse when India gets to know Serena herself: she admires Serena for refusing to kowtow to a man and give up her career. What is more, Serena asks India to take some new author photographs for her next book, and during the course of the photo session India admits to herself that she likes Serena. It is becoming clear that she will never do anything deliberately to take Paul away from her.

Meanwhile, India's and Doug's marriage is degenerating fast. She confronts him about her life and career, telling him she feels unsatisfied and unfulfilled. He flings back in her face a classic guilt-inducing taunt: "You're being a spoiled brat, and you're letting me and the kids down" (132). In fairness to Steel, some of these arguments between India and Doug ring fairly true and have a certain emotive power, although it is derived more from realism than from any literary artistry in which they are expressed. And Steel can still manage to descend to bathos with such clumsy metaphors as: "The angry seeds that had been sown in June had grown into a tree whose branches had begun to choke them" (144). I am not sure how a branch can choke anyone. In any case, the upshot of this latest marital bout is that India folds under the pressure and gives in, stating that she would remove her name from the roster of photographers and "won't take any assignments if they call" (149). It is a tough decision for her to make, and she is more than irked when Doug "didn't thank her, didn't praise her, didn't tell her she'd done a great thing for mankind, or for him, and that he was grateful for it" (149). Instead, he actually makes an effort to have sex with her, in his clumsy and unfeeling way ("he reached a hand around her in silence and touched her breast, and she could feel her whole body turn to granite" [149]). But failing to get a response from her, he gives up and goes to sleep.

Well, this is a pretty pickle. Things look bleak for India, and we're less than halfway through the novel. It's time for a little *deus ex machina,* and Steel doesn't disappoint. She kills Serena in a plane crash.

If there is any authorial trickery more underhanded than getting rid of inconvenient characters by killing them off, I can't imagine what it is. The crash takes out some other notables—"a congress-woman from Iowa, a British M.P., a well-known ABC newscaster returning from a special he had done the week before in Jerusalem" (161), but Serena is the most notable victim. Needless to say, India is horrified and genuinely saddened. Her thoughts go out to both Serena and her husband: "She was thinking about Paul, and about his wife, and their ruptured life, that had exploded in a million tiny shards over the Atlantic" (165). She attends Serena's funeral but does not make any effort to meet or talk to Paul: he must be left to grieve without interference from her. But the very day after the funeral, Paul calls her. Their talk is cordial and sympathetic, but no more. And he concludes by saying: "Call me sometime. I'd love to hear from you" (179). It is not Paul, but Steel, who is teasing here: Steel knows that every one of her readers wants Paul to get together with India, but she is not going to make it easy. We are now exactly halfway through the book, and the ultimate union, however inevitable, must be drawn out to its maximum limit of wrenching emotion.

There are, in effect, two issues requiring resolution here: How is India to resurrect her career (as she manifestly wants to do), and how is she to unite with Paul? The answer to the first comes quickly, as Raoul Lopez offers her a double assignment: a royal wedding in London and, at the same time, "some kind of underground prostitution ring, somewhere in the West End, involving ten- to fourteen-year-olds" (190). It is an assignment that would combine glamour and moral uprightness, and—in spite of the promise she had made to Doug only a short time earlier—she accepts it. She boldly confronts Doug on the matter, who is of course outraged. India responds hotly: "I'm not going to let you bully me anymore, or blackmail me. This is who I am, who you married. You can lay down all the rules you want, but you can't threaten me" (195). So India is a budding feminist after all!

She goes to London, where she meets an Irish photographer who delivers a sob story about the plane crash that killed Serena: "Damn shame. I hate stories like that. I always think about the children. Kill an army. Bomb a missile plant. But don't, for God's sake, kill the children. The bastards always do, though. Every damn country that gets pissed off, they kill the children" (206). Yes, my friends, that is a direct quote. Steel is not likely to rise to eminence in political philosophy on the basis of things like this. In any event, India telephones Paul frequently from London, and on one occasion admits to herself that she needed him: "He was like a drug she had become addicted to, without realizing how it had happened. But it had. They needed each other. More than either of them were willing to admit, or knew. But little by little, over time, and from a great distance, they were moving slowly toward each other" (217–18). That "little by little" is the key. The central issue now is the fact that Paul's emotions are still tied up with Serena. He tells India: "I don't think I could ever love another woman" (223). The finality of that utterance seems daunting, but neither India, nor Steel, nor her readers are going to take no for an answer. India realises that she must move carefully and gently, but she is determined to move.

The situation is relieved in one sense when India comes home. She had not in fact told Doug about the double nature of the assignment, mentioning only the royal wedding as a relatively harmless task that could not possibly endanger her life or Doug's stability. But he finds out about the prostitution story when he sees a magazine with India's photographs in it, and is enraged—both because India had lied to him and because he thought the story itself "total smut. The worst garbage I've ever seen" (239). He doesn't grasp that India's photographs were meant to provoke outrage at the appalling degradation of children. He storms out of the house, vowing to stay in a hotel. India's first thought is not for him but for Paul: "the hope [of getting together with Paul], slim as it was, was becoming increasingly appealing" (246). But Paul seems to throw cold water on that idea: "'I wish I could tell you I'd be there for you, India. I wish I could be. But I know I won't be. I'm not going to be the light at the end of the tunnel for you. I can't even be there for myself anymore, let alone for someone else'" (250).

Then Doug finds out about the many calls that India made to Paul while in London; he is furious and demands a divorce: "I've had it. I'm finished. You're not the woman I married, or the one I want. I don't want to be married to you anymore. It's as simple as that. . . . I'm calling my lawyer on Monday" (254). Well, that takes care of him. Now that Doug is essentially out of the picture, India can focus on Paul. But although they telephone each other frequently, there doesn't seem to be much advance in their relationship. After several months, Paul—who has been sailing around the world in his yacht to work out his grief for Serena—suddenly decides to come to New York. Evidently his business partners are getting annoyed at his protracted absence and require his keen banking instincts to maintain their edge over their competitors. Paul is friendly with India, but no more than that. However, after one particularly nice dinner, the two of them go back to Paul's room at the Carlyle, at which point Steel finally rewards her long-suffering readers with what they have been waiting for: "He said nothing more to her then, but leaned over very quietly, took her in his arms, and kissed her. And as she felt his lips on hers, she had the answers to all her questions. It was a long time before they spoke again, and when they did, his voice was soft and hoarse with passion. 'I think I've fallen in love with you, India,' he whispered" (290). Hot dawg! Ring the bell, throw the confetti! And it gets better, for they actually retreat to the bed: "He peeled the black suit away, and everything he found beneath it, and they clung to each other with a hunger neither of them had realised they had for each other" (291). Steel valiantly attempts to wax poetic in describing the act:

> They met and held and danced in the skies, as together they found what they had been looking for, in the arms of someone whom they not only loved, but who loved them. It was everything neither of them had had before, and only discovered now, with each other. It was like being born again, for both of them, as they clung to life and hope and the dreams they each had forgotten, and long since ceased to believe in. And as she moaned softly in his arms, he brought her to places she had never known, and had only dimly realized she had longed for. And when it was over, it was not an end, but a beginning. (291)

With each passing sentence one wants to beg Steel to shut up while she is ahead; but she just digs herself deeper and deeper into grotesque bathos. Of course, she is not the sort of girl—er, writer—to describe the sexual act in any kind of salacious detail; there is no unseemly mention of, or even allusion to, private parts or bodily fluids. Instead, Steel wishes to lend it a high and poetic meaning full of deep emotion. But she is just not up to the task; for later she writes preposterously, "Their relationship had leapt full blown from birth to manhood" (298)!

But note that we are still about seventy pages from the end of the book. Clearly we haven't reached the "happily ever after" stage yet. For it transpires that Paul is now wracked with guilt over what he regards as his betrayal of the memory of Serena, and he takes the dramatic step of breaking off all relations with India; he tells her exactly what she doesn't want to hear: "Go home, India. . . . Go back to your kids. They need you" (305). He says he is going back on his boat for a long trip and asks India not to call him. Can this be the appalling end of what is, so far, nothing but a brief fling? But everyone—Steel, India, and her readers—knows that this is not in fact the end of the matter.

Raoul Lopez calls up and offers India an assignment in Rwanda about the orphans in a hospital there. India accepts, asking Doug to take care of the children for three weeks while she is away. He agrees, especially given that he already has a girlfriend, a substantially younger woman named Tanya, whom (of course) the kids hate. India goes to Rwanda—where she meets Paul! Remember Paul's airlift missions in the interest of world peace? Well, he is back at it, attempting to assuage his guilt over both Serena and India. It is most awkward, and Steel attempts to justify the otherwise meaningless title of her book with the remark: "It was bittersweet irony that they had both come to the same place" (329). India proposes that they attempt to be friends. Paul doesn't know if he can do that, but he will make the effort. Nothing particularly dramatic happens in Rwanda, aside from the fact that India hears that her son Sam has been injured—but it turns out to be merely a broken wrist playing baseball. India and Paul seem reconciled to being "just friends," and when she returns home she is not surprised to learn that Doug and Tanya are going to marry.

As usual, India takes her children to Cape Cod during the summer. There is a threat of bad weather, but no one realises exactly how bad until the Taylors find themselves in the midst of a full-blown hurricane. But as the hurricane is arriving . . . so does Paul on his trusty yacht! It fulfils a hope that India had made a little while before in regard to her ideal mate:

> "I want him to be crazy about me. I want him to think I'm the best thing in his life, that he is so god-damn lucky to have me, he can hardly see straight. I've always been the one who's done the loving and the giving, and made all the concessions. Maybe it's time to turn the tables, and get some of what I've been giving. . . . I want a man who would cross heaven and earth because he cared for me . . . come through a hurricane for me, if he had to." (349)

And Steel make sure this time not to disappoint her readers in this wish-fulfillment fantasy, for we have now reached the end of the book and Paul and India (and, of course, the children) are reunited forever.

What makes *Bittersweet* such a venture into hackdom is that, once the book is finished (or, for that matter, even while it is being read), it becomes plain that the various plot elements are all transparently contrived to lead to the expected conclusion. The convenient death of Serena is only the most obvious of these; but even the summer vacationing of the Taylors in Cape Cod is manifestly fashioned for the purpose of introducing the hurricane that will allow Paul Ward to become the knight in shining armor coming to rescue the maiden (although this one is hardly a maiden, with her four bairns around her) from harm. Doug's almost caricaturish insensitivity to India's quest for fulfillment in a career is meant to deflect sympathy from him and therefore make his departure from India's life a relief rather than a tragedy. Doug doesn't even care much for his own children, in contrast to the dashing Paul, whom the children like almost at first meeting.

The most noticeable thing about Steel is the utter mundanity of her prose. This is, in fact, a novel so entirely absent of distinguishing characteristics—in prose, in character development, in plot—that it could have been written by anyone, or by a computer. The opening chapters are massively repetitious in delineating the crumbling of India's and Doug's marriage, and at times Steel's narrative voice can descend close to the plebeian: "It sounded like he had already had a bad morning, and listening to him, India was hoping he wasn't going to ask her to do something totally insane. Sometimes, despite the limitations she had set on him for years, he still did that. He was also upset because he had lost one of his star clients, a hell of a nice guy and a good friend . . ." (30). But in light of Steel's disastrous attempts at poetic prose (as in the sex scene), one perhaps should be grateful that most of her writing consists of harmless banalities like this.

Lest it be thought that *Bittersweet* has some kind of sociological value as a document in feminism, it should be borne in mind that, by the time of the novel's publication, several decades had passed since women had entered the workface in numbers, and the great majority of husbands had become largely reconciled to their wives' devotion to their careers. In this sense, Doug's furious hostility to India's attempts to work at a job she is manifestly good at are ludicrously anachronistic. His attitude might have been plausible in 1969, but not in 1999.

But the greatest flaw of *Bittersweet* is that every reader knows, from the moment Paul Ward enters the stage, that he and India will be united at the end. No amount of teasing and delaying by Steel, no amount of plot twists that thrust Paul and India apart, can convince any reader that the ultimate resolution of the plot will not be to everyone's satisfaction.

My mother, who has read the complete works of Danielle Steel, has informed me that one of her novels, *The Ring* (1980),[2] stands out above the rest as a "serious" work of art and not just a literary lollipop for lonely widows. So I felt it incumbent upon me to read and digest this work.

The focus of the first "book" of *The Ring* is Kassandra von Gotthard, an aristocratic German in Berlin. She is romantically involved with a thirty-three-year-old writer, Dolff Sterne, author of the recent novel *Der Kiss* (*The Kiss*). Needless to say, he is supremely talented—

> In his outspoken fashion, he had shocked all of Germany for a time, but the book had nonetheless won him still more acclaim than his first. The story had been deeply sensitive and erotic and his seat at the pinnacle of Germany's contemporary literary movement seemed assured. He was controversial, he was modern, he was at times outrageous, and he was also very, very talented. (4)

—and she is supremely beautiful:

> Her beauty had left him breathless the night they met. He had heard of her; everyone in Berlin knew who she was. She seemed untouchable, unreachable, and she looked frighteningly fragile. Dolff felt something akin to a shaft of pain when he first saw her, wearing a silky, clinging dress of woven gold, her shimmering hair barely covered in a tiny golden cap, a sable coat draped over one arm. But it wasn't the gold or the sable that had stunned him, it was her presence, her separateness and silence in the clamor of the room, and finally her eyes. When she turned and smiled at him, for an instant he felt as though he might die. (4)

But lest we think this is merely another conventional love story, Steel has several tricks up her sleeve. Aside from the fact that Kassandra and Dolff first kiss, then have sex, in the very first chapter ("Taking her hand gently, he led her to his bed and peeled away the fine gray silk of her dress and creamy beige satin of her slip, until he reached the exquisite lace that lay beneath, and the velvet of her flesh" [11]), we quickly learn that Kassandra is actually *married*—to the fifty-eight-year-old Walmar von Gotthard. She also has two children. But unlike the casual affairs in which the later Gail Jones engages in *Bittersweet,* Kassandra's passion for Dolff is the real thing—high romance in the grand manner. This is emphasised by the very sequence in which we are introduced to the protagonists—first Kassandra and Dolff, and only then Kassandra's husband and children, who are in fact raised by a nurse and are virtual "strangers" (21) to her. Moreover, Steel reveals only on page 25 that it is the year 1934, suddenly transforming this seemingly routine tale of a love triangle into an historical novel with, potentially, significant sociopolitical implications.

Walmar, as it turns out, knows about the affair, and he now confronts her about it—not in anger or even much hostility, but out of sincere solicitude for her own standing and ever her safety. For Dolff is a Jew, and Walmar knows this could lead to all kinds of trouble: ". . . it makes me sick to tell you that, because I think that what is starting to happen in this country is disgusting, but the fact is that it *is happening* and you are my wife and the mother of my children and I won't have you murdered or put in jail!" (34). Walmar himself, a respected banker, is hostile to the Nazis but dares not oppose them openly. All this sounds promising as a serious treatment of conditions in pre-war Nazi Germany, but Steel cannot resist lavishing her attention on Kassandra's appearance and attire, as in this glimpse of her at the Spring Ball: "She wore her full-length ermine over a starkly simple white velvet gown. The top was cut halter fashion, and the skirt fell in total perfection from her waist to her white satin-clad feet. Her hair was an upswept mass of delicate tendrils, and she looked lovelier than ever and as though she had not a care in the world" (41).

But things turn ugly very quickly. Just after Kassandra and Dolff have concluded a lovemaking session in his apartment, four policemen burst into the room, beat him up, and take him away. They even threaten to rape Kassandra herself, thinking her a Jew ("You've lost your boyfriend, little Jewess, but now you will find out what it is to be had by a better race. I am going to teach you a little lesson, dear one" [45]). But she announces her identity, and out of prudence the policemen leave her alone, although the leader does proceed to strike her across the breasts with his belt. Later she reads in a newspaper that Dolff has been killed. In grief, Kassandra kills herself by slitting her wrists in the bathtub.

This is pretty strong stuff for the first six chapters of a Danielle Steel novel, and it seems to suggest at least the potential of a work that may approach literature. The next "book" concerns Ariana, Kassandra's daughter and elder child. It is now 1942, and she has turned sixteen. Naturally, she is also beautiful:

> She looked young and fresh and lovely, but more than that, there was a lure to Ariana, a quiet power that pulled at anyone who looked into those deep blue eyes. It was as though she had the answers to a secret. . . . It was a quality that hypnotized most men. It was the quiet face, the gentle eyes, and then the sudden smile, like summer sunshine on a lake. There was a quality to Ariana that drew one, a magic and a spirit of which one wanted to know more, despite her youth. (63)

Let it not be said that Steel cannot write prose-poetry! In any case, Walmar is attempting to assist a friend, Max Thomas, to escape from Germany. Max, a German, had been married to a Jew, and his wife and children have already been killed. Shattered as he is by this tragedy, he nonetheless can't resist thinking romantically of the lovely Ariana; but in fact nothing much is made of this—yet. It is only now that Walmar tells Ariana the true story of her mother, Kassandra, and her love affair with Dolff. Ariana is deeply impressed, feeling sorrow for all concerned. Walmar manages to help Max get to Lucerne, Switzerland, and hears from him no more.

By the fall of 1944, Ariana's brother, Gerhard, has turned sixteen and has been drafted. At this point Walmar decides that the entire family must leave Germany. After considerable effort and trickery, Walmar and Gerhard reach Zürich (or Zurich, as Steel has it). But the von Gottards' servants, who are pro-Nazi, have long had their suspicions about the family's doings, and they make a report to the government. A Nazi lieutenant comes to their lavish house and takes Ariana away for questioning. It is at this point that the novel takes a remarkable turn, for the chapters involving Ariana's imprisonment in a dank, fetid cell are quite grim in their realism, and Steel pulls no punches:

> She was then shoved into the cell and the lieutenant stood by as the woman locked the doors. In cells around them women were calling and crying, and once she thought she heard the wails of a child. But she couldn't see any faces, the doors were solid slabs of metal with barred windows only a few inches

square. It was the most terrifying place Ariana could imagine, and once inside the dark cell, she had to fight every moment so as not to scream and totally lose control. In the tiny shaft of light that came through the minute window, she could see what she thought was a toilet, and discovered moments later was only a large white metal bowl. (110)

How different from the white marble bathroom on Paul Ward's boat! In all seriousness, a passage like this would come close to literature if it were not written in such bland prose and with the aesthetic cheap shot of the "wails of a child."

But Steel isn't finished yet. Walmar, having found a relatively secure place for Gerhard, now attempts to come back to Berlin to fetch Ariana. Although he is in disguise, he is stopped at one point by Nazi soldiers, who find a large wad of bills in his wallet—and shoot him dead. I will be honest and say that this event took me aback, for I had been expecting Steel to give in to the convention of the happy ending and have Walmar successfully pluck Ariana from Berlin to safety. In a sense, however, Walmar's death (about which Ariana is in ignorance for many months) is necessary to liberate her emotionally for the next part of her adventure.

For now, however, all is misery. She has spent weeks in prison, and at one point comes close to being whipped and raped by a thuggish guard, Hildebrand; but, just like her mother, she escapes this fate, this time by the intervention of Hildebrand's superior, Manfred von Tripp, who, though a Nazi, turns out to be a singularly soft-hearted fellow. Von Tripp allows her to go back to her house (by this time appropriated by a Nazi general), collect a few things, and go to a workhouse. Ariana confronts her old servants, gives them a well-deserved tongue-lashing for their betrayal of the family, and takes some possessions—including a fake book that has concealed within it a signet ring belonging to her mother (which, in turn, belonged to Kassandra's own mother).

Meanwhile, Manfred is developing a sincere regard for Ariana and sympathises with her fall from wealth and prominence. He learns that another officer, General Ritter (who, as a young man, had attempted to dance with Ariana at the Spring Ball but had been rebuffed by her) wishes to seize her as his concubine; eager to spare her this fate worse than death, he takes her away himself to protect her. To be sure, Manfred is attracted by Ariana's beauty (still present, even though "faintly obscured by the drab clothes and her distress" [139]) and her sweetness of temperament, but his overriding intentions are more honourable. Ariana, for her part, cannot believe that she has been taken into the house of a Nazi officer who doesn't wish to have sex with her—or, at any rate, who won't force her to have sex with him. Manfred later tells Ariana that his own family—wife, children, parents, sister—were killed in the Allied bombing of Dresden; at which point we are evidently to conclude that the horrors of war affect everyone indiscriminately.

Even though Ariana vows not to open up to Manfred ("She didn't want to see his pity, his compassion, his own sorrow—it was all she could do to cope with her own" [150]), their continual proximity, and the decency with which he continues to treat her, lead to the inevitable: they fall in love. What is more, they have sex: "'I love you, Manfred.' She hadn't even known until then that she meant that, but as he held her next to his wildly pounding heart, she knew that she did. And moments later they lay together, and he took her with the tenderness of a man very much in love. He loved her expertly and gently and again and again" (155). Good man! Those euphemistic code-words for the sexual act ("took" and "loved"), so beloved of romance writers too squeamish to write about sex honestly and straightforwardly, destroy what is otherwise a reasonably elegant and convincing passage in which Ariana's initial repugnance at being the virtual prisoner of a Nazi softens first into tolerance, then affection, then actual love. Steel also gives in to the inveterate habit of the hack historical writer by introducing celebrated individuals for no meaningful purpose—in this case, by having Ariana touched by Hitler ("just a quick touch on the arm" [165]).

In any event, Manfred and Ariana decide to marry. The war is winding down, and the Germans know that they will probably lose. As the happy couple is leaving the church after the ceremony has been completed, the church blows up. This leads to some tolerably gripping pages describing the fall of Berlin, during which Manfred, in spite of his general hostility to the Nazi agenda, feels obligated to perform his duty: he dies while defending the Reichstag. Ariana later finds his body: "She lay there beside him for almost an hour, until suddenly, terrified, she understood what it meant now, and with a last kiss on the sleeping eyes, she touched his face and ran away" (183).

There now begins a period of trauma equaling in horror her weeks of imprisonment. She flees Germany, thinking to find safety with an old schoolmate of her husband's, Jean-Pierre Marne, who lives in Paris. She first drives her car and, after it breaks down, begins an incredible trek on foot. Along the way she is nearly raped by a surly farmer:

He grabbed her roughly, letting himself down hard on top of her, at the same time pushing up her skirt and pulling at her pants, while in astonishment she pushed at him, fighting wildly and flailing at his face with both her hands. But she was indifferent to her lack of interest in his seduction; he pushed hard at her with his hands and body, and then with something hard and warm she felt pulsing between her legs, and then just before he could enter her there was a stirring, a shout, and a shot fired in the air. (189)

She is saved in the nick of time by an American soldier. These repeated close shaves, so reminiscent of the hapless Joan of Arc in Voltaire's mock epic *La Pucelle d'Orléans* (1755), become comical after a time: a Steel protagonist can suffer every possible indignity, but rape is beyond the pale. It is worth noting that the above passage is far more explicit (in spite of the mealy-mouthed "something hard and warm" for the male member) than any passages describing consensual sex: the latter can only be described in the dreamy, pseudo-poetic imagery that masks carnality by the wish-fulfillment of romance.

Ariana manages to make it to Jean-Pierre's apartment in Paris. She immediately asks him to make inquiries regarding the fate of her brother, Gerhard, who now appears to be missing. Jean-Pierre tenderly advises her to brace herself for the very real possibility that Gerhard may be dead. The moment this possibility is uttered, every reader knows—or ought to know—that Gerhard will somehow be pulled out of a hat in some fashion or other. Steel does not disappoint, but extends the plot in nearly unbelievable ways in order to delay the final resolution for another 150 pages.

Jean-Pierre persuades Ariana to go on a refugee ship to the United States, where there appear to be more opportunities for work and for leading some semblance of a normal life. She does so, although she is violently ill on the ship. She is placed in a hospital in New York, where a social worker, Ruth Liebman (there is no secret as to her ethnic origin), feels so sorry for her that she wishes to take her into her own home, thinking that Ariana is Jewish. Ruth's husband, Sam, is not very keen on the idea—after all, there are countless refugees coming in from Europe, and one can't take them all in—but after visiting Ariana in the hospital, he is touched with her charm and her frailty, almost thinking of her as another daughter.

The Liebmans already have two almost-grown daughters, Julia and Deborah, and they both take to Ariana immediately. There is, in addition, a brother, Paul, who is about to return from military service. Ariana wonders what he could be like, and naturally the reader wonders about the possibility of a romance ("the high school pictures that lined the room showed a tall, smiling, athletic-looking boy with broad shoulders and a mischievous light in his eyes" [240]). Steel doesn't disappoint: upon his return, Paul and Ariana spend plenty of time together, and Paul quickly admits his affection ("I'm saying that I care for you very, very much. I've been drawn to you, I think, since that first day" [252]). It should be noted that Paul also thinks that Ariana is Jewish; Ariana, in fact, is well aware that the family believes her to be a Jew, but she has been so overwhelmed with gratitude to them—and has also taken a certain time in recovering her health—that the opportunity to disabuse them has never arisen.

Things take a dramatic turn when a doctor finds that Ariana is pregnant. This cannot be from Paul, for they have not had sexual relations. Ariana is pleased, realizing that she has found a tangible way to preserve her memory of Manfred. (It is about seven weeks since his death.) But the doctor advises her to marry Paul for the baby's sake—this is, after all, 1945, and an unwed mother is a social liability. Ariana does not feel she can tell the Liebmans about her past life, especially her marriage to a Nazi, albeit a decent and honourable one. While the family is spending the summer in the Hamptons (where else?), Paul confesses his love for Ariana and presents her with an engagement ring. Although she doesn't love Paul, she cares deeply for him—enough to have sex with him that night (273).

Paul quickly takes her to Maryland to marry. It is never explained why they need to go to Maryland (Ariana pointedly asks "Maryland? Why?" [275], but never receives an answer); perhaps the marriage laws are a bit more liberalised there, allowing for quick elopements. In any case, they go, get married by a justice of the peace, and return to the family. Everything looks peachy . . . until one day Paul finds Ariana gazing at a photograph of Manfred. What reason would there be for her to look at a picture of a Nazi officer? Ariana confesses the entire story, in spite of Paul's increasing rage and disbelief. She admits that the baby is Manfred's. Paul immediately sues for divorce, and the Liebman family feels betrayed: "How dared she have pretended to be a Jew. It was, as Ariana had always suspected it would be, the ultimate betrayal, not to mention the fact that she was pregnant with 'some Nazi's' child" (285). Amidst the turmoil, Ariana's baby is born early—on Christmas day.

It is at this point (we are now well into the third "book") that Steel shatters an otherwise moderately respectable novel with a series of grotesque coincidences, uncorked merely for the sake of resolving the plot in a suitably satisfactory way. Ariana goes to the German consulate to apply for reparations for goods and property stolen by the Nazis. There she meets . . . Max Thomas! How convenient. They immediately talk over old times, and it is clear that their old friendship has revived. It has with a vengeance: by the very next chapter, the first of "book" four, twenty-five years have passed, and Max "had been [Ariana's] constant companion" (297) for all that time. It is not entirely clear whether they have had sexual congress; he is nineteen years older than her, meaning that he is now sixty-four; in any case, they still occupy separate living quarters. Ariana's son, Noel, has just spent seven years at Harvard (where else?), graduating with a law degree. Noel doesn't want to plunge into work just yet; instead, he wants to spend part of the summer in a trip to Europe. Max and Ariana have never returned to Europe, thinking that the memories might be too painful; but they allow Max to go. He goes to Berlin, looking up the house that had belonged to Walmar von Gotthard, his grandfather; he is actually allowed to take a tour inside the house.

Noel, it transpires, is going steady with a girl named Tammy. He brings her to New York to meet his mother and "Uncle Max" (who has finally persuaded Ariana to marry him). It turns out that Tammy is Tamara Liebman, the granddaughter of . . . you guessed it . . . Ruth and Sam Liebman, and the daughter of Paul and Marjorie (whoever she may be) Liebman! This coincidence to beat all coincidences is devised simply for the purpose of reconciling Paul and Ariana—and also to advance the plot in another significant way. Noel wants to marry Tamara, but Ariana tells of her past history with Tamara's father and thinks it highly unlikely that Paul would give his consent. Noel confronts Paul in his office, saying that he will marry Tamara in spite of his objections. Ariana then intervenes, meeting Paul again for the first time in decades and persuades Paul to drop his objections to the marriage. He finally does so.

But Steel has one final coincidence up her sleeve. Noel and Tamara go to Paris and meet a friend her hers, Brigitte Goddard, the daughter of Gérard Goddard, who now runs an art gallery. The moment this name is mentioned, any astute reader should be able to guess the outcome, especially after we learn that Gérard is "haunted by ghosts" (337). When Noel meets Gérard, "It was almost as though he knew him" (340). Conveniently, Ariana had given Tamara her mother's signet ring, which she had managed to keep all this time. When Gérard sees it, the truth comes out. He tells the story of his life to the young couple, and the novel ends with his flying to New York to meet his long-lost sister.

*The Ring* is, to be sure, superior to *Bittersweet,* and perhaps to most of Steel's other novels, if only for the realism of some of the grimmer scenes in Nazi Germany, and for the fact that not *everyone* escapes unscathed—poor Walmar did succumb in an unfortunate way, not to mention Manfred, who emerges as virtually a co-star next to Ariana. But Steel's furious attempt to tie up all loose ends and conclude the novel with a cheerfully happy ending has betrayed her into pulling her punches at key moments and in fashioning the plot in a highly implausible manner. By using the title *The Ring* one would suppose that she intends some deep symbolism with the signet ring—but in fact it is merely a makeshift contrivance devised to effect the ultimate reunion of Ariana and her brother. Accordingly, the very setting of the early parts of the novel in Nazi Germany really signify very little and cannot qualify as a serious historical treatment. There is some minimal virtue in Steel's demonstration that not all Nazis were complete scoundrels, but overall she dodges the broad social and political implications of the scenario she has devised. But I suppose it is at least creditable that a popular writer, especially a romance writer, has faced such a serious issue at all, however superficially and tentatively.

\* \* \* \* \* \* \*

Barbara Taylor Bradford (b. 1933), our next victim, is an Englishwoman, but she emigrated to the United States in 1963 and retains dual UK/US citizenship. In England she was educated in private schools (no college, apparently) and became a newspaperwoman at the tender age of sixteen, working diligently on a number of different papers until her move to the United States. Here she worked on several decorating and design magazines. Before writing her first romance novel, *A Woman of Substance* (1979), she produced five children's books and ten works of nonfiction—including, revealingly, a three-volume series called *How to Be the Perfect Wife* (1969–70). In extenuation of Bradford, these were written just prior to the latest wave of feminism beginning in the early 1970s. In any event, *A Woman of Substance* became a spectacular bestseller, selling more than nineteen million copies worldwide. She has written twenty-one novels down to the end of 2006, a relatively modest figure as far as best-selling writers are concerned. Ten of her novels have been adapted for film or television. For no compelling reason, the work of hers I have chosen to analyse is *A Sudden Change of Heart* (1999).[3]

The novel opens in the year 1972. We are introduced to seven-year-old Laura Valiant, whose father, Richard, is a composer and conductor, and her mother, Maggie, is a painter. Evidently there are no unaccomplished or undistinguished persons in a Bradford novel, for we learn that Laura's grandmother, Megan, is a former Broadway star. But it gets better: much later we are told that Megan "was *the* great musical stage star of the 1930s, 1940s, 1950s, and even well into the 1960s" (139)! Greater than Ethel Merman or Liza Minnelli? A pretty tall order! Laura's parents appear to be so consumed with their careers that Laura and her four-year-old brother, Dylan, are largely raised by grandparents. This vaguely antifeminist streak runs through the novel, popping up at odd moments.

The Valiant family lives in New York City but is vacationing in rural Connecticut. Nearby is twelve-year-old Claire Benson, who is Laura's best friend. On one occasion Laura saves Claire from drowning, thereby cementing their bond still further. But this incident is merely an excuse to reveal (when the two girls are being toweled off) that Claire has odd bruises on her back (14). Even the most obtuse reader, one supposes, should be able to pick up on the obvious implication here, especially when we learn that Claire's parents are considered "a bit odd" (15). And yet, Bradford, as we shall see, wishes to hold this "surprise" revelation until the very end of the novel.

This is merely the prologue to the book. The novel proper begins in the winter of 1996. By now Laura is a successful businesswoman, running a company called Art Acquisitions. She had studied art history in Paris when she was eighteen, and had translated her learning into a two-woman firm that advises wealthy clients on the purchase of expensive paintings. A nice job if you can get it. . . . Currently she is in Paris on an assignment, and we find her (or, rather, Bradford) gushing over a Renoir in a museum:

> She stood for a long time in front of *Nude in Sunlight*. Renoir had painted it in 1875, and yet it looked so fresh, as if he had created it only yesterday. How beautiful it was; she never tired of looking at it. The pearly tints and pink-bluish tones of the model's skin were incomparable, set off by the pale, faintly blue shadows on her shoulders that seemed to emanate from the foliage surrounding her. (22)

This is not likely to put her in the company of Bernard Berenson or Roger Fry, but regrettably descriptions like this—and worse—pepper the novel from beginning to end.

In the museum, Laura encounters one Philippe Lavillard and his mother. There is some peculiar and unexplained tension between the parties, but it is presently elucidated. Just as Laura has turned her thoughts to her old friend, Claire, there she is, standing in front of her! It happens that Claire has long lived in Paris, and gradually we learn that she was once married to Philippe—unhappily, it appears, although a daughter, Natasha, resulted from it. So traumatised is Claire from this marriage that she has vowed never to love again, leading Laura to reflect (again a bit antifeministically): "There was something oddly sterile about a woman's life if she did not have love in it, if she didn't have a man to cherish" (32). Evidently lesbian love doesn't cut the mustard with Bradford. But Claire is adamant on the matter: "Marriage is a battlefield, and I have the scars to prove it. I won the war by getting off the battlefield, and I've no intention of putting myself in the line of fire ever again" (46).

Laura, for her part, is married to one Douglas Casson, a lawyer, and their relations seem idyllic: "They were a perfect fit, compatible, attuned to each other in the best of ways" (31). And yet Laura ponders worriedly: "But lately he worked too hard. She smiled inwardly at this thought. Didn't he say the same thing about her?" (31). Doug now arrives in Paris as a surprise, and it doesn't take long for things to heat up. Consider this: "he began to caress one of her breasts *sensually* [my emphasis], drawing small sighs from her" (72). I am not sure how it is possible to caress breasts in any other fashion, unless one happens to be a gynecologist. But Bradford doesn't stop there; throwing to the winds any Steel-like delicacy in describing the sexual act, she plunges into the breach:

> Doug's excitement was mounting. He returned her fervent kisses and with suddenness, almost abruptness, he rolled them over so that he was on top of her. Their mouths stayed locked together. Her tongue grazed his and they shared a moment of intense intimacy [??] before Doug pushed his hands under Laura's buttocks [!] and fitted her long, lean body into the curve of his. And at last he was hard enough [!!] to slip inside her, easily and expertly, and within moments they had a rhythm, were rising and falling together, their movements swifter, almost frenzied. Her legs went high around his back [!!!] and

he shafted deeper into her, sinking deeply into the warmth. (72-73)

But lest she be accused of being merely pornographic, Bradford now follows Steel's example by engaging in a bout of poetic prose:

> Soon Doug felt as though he were falling through dark blue water, falling down, falling farther and farther down into a bottomless dark blue sea. The waves washed over him, beat against him. He squeezed his eyes tighter shut. Images danced behind his lids. Oh, yes, he thought, oh, yes, and as he began the long slide down into total ecstasy [!!!!], he saw that face, trapped as it was in his mind. . . . (73)

I won't explain that last phrase yet; but, in spite of Laura's pleas ("Now. Please. Oh, please, don't stop, darling" [73]), Doug does exactly that. Something is very wrong. Is it merely that he is tired from the long trip? preoccupied with thoughts of work? something still worse? We are left hanging—just as Laura is.

At a dinner party at Claire's apartment, an old friend of Laura's, Hercule Junot, a celebrated (naturally) interior designer, arrives— with the loathed Philippe in tow. Hercule, incidentally, has been introduced to us with the classic broken English beloved of hack writers putting foreigners on stage, as in this bit of dialogue with Laura:

> The Frenchman chuckled. "Ah, Claire, so many questions you fire, rat-a-tat, and you make the jest, *n'est-ce pas?*"
> "No, I'm being serious."
> "The room is superb. *Formidable, oui.* You have the wonderful taste." (34)

I cannot bear to quote any more: Agatha Christie's Hercule Poirot could not have done better (or worse). Do all people named Hercule speak like this? But let it pass. Hercule has brought Philippe (who, in fact, turns out to be not a bad sort at all) because the latter wishes to see his daughter, Natasha. Claire grudgingly agrees, and Laura and Hercule wonder why Claire has developed such a sense of hatred for Philippe. For his part, Philippe tells his daughter: "I have a feeling your mother has an enormous and deep-rooted distrust of men for some reason" (92). Readers, note well! Bradford is giving you a hint . . .

But our attention is now brought back to Laura and Doug. In a dramatic one-sentence paragraph, Doug ponders: "His marriage was in trouble." He elaborates to himself:

> The problems had nothing to do with their inability to produce a child together. This did not even worry him much anymore. Rather, it had to do with *them*, with their relationship, and their future together. Of late they had spent a lot of time apart, traveling because of their careers. And were they not growing apart? Emotionally and physically. *He* believed they were, but he was quite certain Laura had no conception of this. None at all. Not because she wasn't smart, she was one of the savviest people he knew. But because he was different now; he had changed. (108)

Again, there is something ominous about Doug that we are not yet privy to. But he tries to get back in the saddle, making love to Laura again—but again failing to ring the bell. In embarrassment, he blames it on the wine he had at lunch and slinks away.

By this time Laura is concerned over Doug and the state of their marriage, and she talks about it with her confidante, Grandma Megan. Megan has also noticed things: during Christmas she spied Doug at one point, "and he looked quite miserable to me" (154), but neither can figure out why. Doug is now spending increasing amounts of time at the office, and in fact has hastily arranged to go to the West Coast on business, at which point Laura reflects morosely: "Somehow he's drawing further and further away from me and I don't know the reason why" (163).

When Doug returns from his business trip, Laura comes to a sudden conclusion: "Laura knew instinctively, and deep within herself, that their marriage was over" (182). Quite frankly, in spite of Doug's bouts of sexual impotence and a few other troubles, this conclusion seems hasty and ill-informed: Bradford has not sufficiently prepared the psychological framework to make this decision of Laura's seem even remotely plausible. But Laura's mind is made up: in spite of the fact that Doug takes her to a nice restaurant, she still thinks to herself that "she had lost Doug, at least a large part of him" (184). Upon returning to their apartment, they discuss their situation further. Doug announces that he has been offered a position with a Los Angeles law firm, and he is inclined to accept it. Laura wonders what will happen to their marriage; she asks him: "Did you wish you were in another place? With another person perhaps? With another woman?" (191). Doug, who now admits to himself that this was the "end of their marriage" (192), nevertheless only wants a trial separation.

But shortly thereafter, Doug makes a shocking revelation: he is really leaving Laura for a person named Robin—a *man!* Doug has realised that he is bisexual. This conclusion is also almost entirely unprepared for, aside from a curious mention of Robin during the second failed sexual episode. At least Bradford is contemporary enough not to condemn Doug as some kind of pervert; Laura herself takes the matter philosophically: "Her marriage had started off so well, and then it had gone away, and he had fallen in love with someone else. Man or woman, it really didn't matter, because the outcome was the same. He had chosen someone else over her" (197). Laura doesn't want merely a trial separation, but an actual divorce—and, cheerfully enough, it proves to be amicable ("we're friends, and we'll stay friends for the rest of our lives, I feel sure of that" [199]). Whether this is meant to contrast with Claire's bitter divorce is not entirely clear. At all events, Grandma Megan offers Laura some pearls of wisdom at this point, replying to Laura's complaint about life ("it's a bit hard at times" [201]) with this sage advice:

> "Of *course* it's hard, but then, life *is* hard, and it always has been. And don't let anyone tell you otherwise. It's never been easy, not for anyone. The important thing is how you handle life and all of its hardships and pain. I've always believed you've got to deal with life's trouble [*sic*] standing up, fists raised, fighting hard. It's vital to battle through and come out triumphant. You're a winner, darling, of that I'm absolutely sure." (201)

We now turn our attention back to Claire. Laura's divorce has made her even more cynical about men ("Nothing that happened between a man and a woman should surprise her, of all people" [207]). But now Claire makes a startling revelation: she has breast cancer. Laura is appalled and saddened by the news, of course. Claire announces that she will not tell Philippe about her condition, and that she wants Laura to take care of Natasha if she were to die. But Laura persuades Claire to let Philippe know, and she does so. Philippe now learns of Laura's divorce, and his reaction is of interest: "As he continued to regard Laura across her desk, Philippe was struck again by the vividness of her eyes. She was a beautiful woman" (237–38). Can he possibly be attracted to her? Well, why not? She is only thirty-one, and in the prime of life . . .

Megan plays a key role in this whole business by surreptitiously inviting Philippe and his mother to her New York apartment for dinner with Laura. (It is remarkable how all the protagonists flit back and forth from Paris and New York with the greatest of ease—and the Concorde isn't even flying anymore!) We are given a long and inconsequential chapter about Rosa's hard life during World War II, but otherwise this meeting is quite obviously meant as a set-up for the eventual union of Laura and Philippe, the sealing bond being the girl Natasha. Claire herself has now moved back to New York for cancer treatment, and she visits Megan and Laura in their Connecticut vacation retreat. At Natasha's urging, Claire agrees to let Philippe visit her, uttering a sentence that is presumably meant to justify the title of the novel: "I've had a sudden change of heart" (304), even though a change of heart over the small point of allowing her ex-husband to visit his daughter seems pretty innocuous. It is, at any rate, at this point that Claire, slowly weakening and clearly dying, unleashes the revelation that no reader can have failed to guess from the opening chapter: her father abused her. She announces: "My father made me hate men, distrust them" (299). What is more, Claire now blames her father for her cancer—and Laura agrees! Laura opines: "You believe that your repression of all of this for so many years left you vulnerable to cancer" (300). Well, I suppose this is no more absurd than Phyllis Schlafly's contention that cervical cancer is caused by promiscuity.[4]

Claire dies, and we are rapidly approaching the obvious and telegraphed conclusion. A year passes, and Natasha realises that Philippe and Laura are in love with each other. Their union is delayed irksomely by a long and tedious account of the discovery of a painting from Rosa Lavillard's art gallery that had been stolen by the Nazis, but on the very last page of the book Laura and Philippe admit their love:

> ". . . But how *do* you feel?" she asked, her eyes riveted on his face.
>
> "I'm crazily, madly, in love with you," he answered.
>
> "Then we feel the same way," she said, and moved back into his arms. "And that's the way I'm going to feel for the rest of my life."

"The rest of *our* lives," he murmured against her hair. (350)

I suppose we are not to consider the high probability that Laura and Doug made these precise confessions to each other at the beginning of their six-year marriage.

I trust I have quoted enough of *A Sudden Change of Heart* to demonstrate that, on the level of prose, Barbara Taylor Bradford is, if such a thing is possible, an even worse writer than Danielle Steel—endowed with a prose style of singular flatness and banality. But there is more to it than that: on a distressing number of intervals she descends to actual illiteracy, as in such usages as "moreso" (38) and "humongous" (239). Elsewhere Bradford writes clumsily that Laura was "waiting for the sick feeling to *go away* [my emphasis]" (182)—when a word like *subside* or *dissipate* is wanted. On page 202 she misspells "augur" as "auger"—and this is no typo, for she repeats the mistake on page 307. But my favorite occurs on page 83: "Claire stared at her old friend without uttering a word, blinking rapidly, as if suddenly afflicted with a nervous *tick* [my emphasis]"! That must have been one annoying insect! One would have supposed that Bradford, an Englishwoman, had received a superior education than her American counterparts, but apparently not. One would also have assumed that her copyeditors, whether British or American, would have tactfully corrected these transparent errors—but perhaps she has reached that lofty elevation of bestsellerdom that prohibits lowly copyeditors from sullying her deathless prose.

But the problems with *A Sudden Change of Heart* are far deeper than merely verbal imbecilities. There are large stretches of the book that have no appreciable bearing on the plot, especially one long subplot (which I have deliberately avoided discussing until now) about a Gauguin painting, *Tahitian Dreams,* that was stolen by the Nazis from a Jewish family, the Westheims. Laura is representing Sir Maxim West, a descendant of the family, who wishes to reclaim the painting. It is currently in the hands of another collector, Norman Grant, and Laura finally manages to pressure Grant (by threatening to publicise his ownership of the stolen painting, and also the fact that he himself is Jewish, thereby bringing opprobrium upon him for being a kind of posthumous collaborator with the Nazis) into giving up the painting. This entire digression is in no way germane to the book, just as the fate of Rosa Lavillard and *her* paintings stolen by the Nazis is not germane to the book; these sections merely add bulk to a novel that might otherwise be disappointingly thin to its readers, who expect more substance (or, at any rate, more pages) for their money.

As in the work of Danielle Steel and other hacks, every plot twist in *A Sudden Change of Heart* is obviously and clumsily designed for the purpose of bringing together the leading sympathetic characters of the book. Just as in Steel's *Bittersweet,* certain characters who are impediments to the final resolution must somehow be dispensed with: Doug is cast aside by virtue of his bisexuality, and Claire is conveniently wiped out of the picture by her cancer. Neither of these individuals can be allowed to prevail, since Doug's sexual irregularities (however much Bradford refuses to condemn them openly) make him a problematical figure, while Claire's bitterness and rage end up deflecting the reader's sympathy from her. This leaves only Laura and Philippe standing, with the young Natasha as the glue holding them together; and their happy union becomes inevitable long before the final page is reached.

Bradford also has a knack for producing the most unnatural and stilted dialogue imaginable, as in this exchange between Doug and Laura as the latter is contemplating taking over care of Natasha in the event of Claire's death:

> "A lot of things change lives, Doug darling. That's the way life is." Laura gave him a pointed look. "Like divorce. That changes lives. It's certainly changed mine."
>
> He took he hand in his. "I'm sorry, Laura, so sorry we didn't make it."
>
> "I know you are. So am I."
>
> "I worry about you and about this situation, should it develop."
>
> "Don't, Doug. I'll be okay, really I will. Even if I have to bring up Natasha, I'll be okay. I'll make it, Doug."
>
> "Yes, you will." He gave her an appraising look and continued. "You're very strong and courageous, I've always admired your strength. There aren't many like you, you know."
>
> She smiled at him. "Thanks for those kind words, but I think there are a lot of strong women in this world, women who are brave and dependable, loyal and indomitable. Take Grandma Megan, she's indomitable, not to mention unbeatable."

"That she is. But you're still something of an original. I spotted that about you right away. In the very beginning." (233-34)

This passage is phony from beginning to end; people don't talk this way in real life—only in books. Bad ones, that is.

* * * * * * *

American writer Nora Roberts (b. 1950) attended public schools in Silver Spring, Maryland; like Barbara Taylor Bradford, she passed up the opportunity to go to college. She has been married twice and is currently married—rather charmingly—to a carpenter. Her first novel was *Blithe Images* (1982), and this opened the flood-gates to an extraordinary deluge of work, many of which are in series of recurring characters. The total (down to the end of 2006) appears to be as follows:

Works without a series character: 87 novels
The "Macgregor" series: 14 novels
The "Irish" series: 3 novels
The "Cordina" series: 3 novels
The "O'Hurley" series: 4 novels
The "Those Wild Unknown" series: 6 novels
The "Night" series: 5 novels
The "Calhoun" series: 5 novels
The "Hornblower" series: 2 novels
The "Born in . . ." series: 4 novels
The "MacKade" series: 4 novels
The "Star" series: 3 novels
The "Donovan Legacy" series: 5 novels
The "Quinn Brothers" trilogy: 3 novels
The "Dream" trilogy: 3 novels
The "Three Sisters Island" trilogy: 3 novels
The "Ireland" trilogy: 3 novels
The "Once upon a . . ." series (with others): 5 novels
The "Key" series: 3 novels
Novels written (or cowritten) as by J. D. Robb: 24 novels

This gives a total of 189 novels, or nearly eight novels a year. Her website boasts that in 2001, 34 of her novels were sold every minute. The assumption, evidently, is that there is some kind of virtue in this statistic.

Although only three years younger than Danielle Steel, Roberts appears to be of a different, and younger, generation than Steel and Bradford. She is much more open about sexuality (although apparently it is almost exclusively heterosexual), and at times her language and episodes can become quite coarse. She seems to be fond of mingling romance with other genres, especially mystery, fantasy, horror, and even science fiction (the J. D. Robb novels are straight mystery stories). Incredibly, no films of her work have been made, although several novels have been optioned. I am confident that the novel (not part of a series) that I read, *Midnight Bayou* (2001),[5] is fairly representative of her work.

*Midnight Bayou* opens with a flashback on December 30, 1899. The young Abigail Manet, wife of Lucian Manet, is tending to her three-month-old daughter, Marie Rose, at Manet Hall, in Louisiana. We learn that she is Cajun and is a maid in the house; but evidently her beauty has impelled the aristocratic Lucian to fall in love with her. We are treated to Abigail's memory of her first sight of Lucian, at a ball: "They had danced, to that lovely, sad song in the moonlit garden with the house a regal white and gold shadow behind them. Her in her simple cotton dress, and Lucian in his handsome evening clothes. And as such things were possible in fairy tales, they fell in love during that lovely, sad song" (9). But the fairy tale ends a bit abruptly. Lucian's brother, Julian, bursts into the nursery, insults her ("Bitch! Whore!" [13]) by throwing her low birth in her face, and then rapes and kills her. Pretty strong stuff! The matriarch of the family, Josephine, cannot let this crime destroy the family, so she promptly takes the situation in hand and disposes of the body in the bayou; she plans to tell Lucian—who is conveniently away somewhere—that Abigail has run off with a man she was seeing. After all, what can one expect of Cajuns? Roberts is deliberately vague on the fate of the little baby Marie Rose.

Much of the rest of the novel is a series of leaps back and forth in time, from the late nineteenth century to the early twenty-first, but for the sake of simplicity I shall recount the events of the past here. When Lucian returns and is told the story of Abigail's disappearance, he refuses to believe it. He spends considerable time looking for Abigail, but of course to no avail. Later, we find Julian at a whorehouse; evidently he is a regular customer there:

> Julian was drunk, as he preferred to be. He had a
> half-naked whore in his lap, and her heavy breast
> cupped in his hand. The old black man played a

jumpy tune on the piano, and the sound mixed nicely in his head with wild female laughter. . . .

He's selected the prostitute because she was blond and lush of build, vacant of brain. He could tell himself later, when he rode her, he wouldn't see Abigail's face staring back at him. (249)

All of a sudden, Lucian bursts into this pretty picture. Julian taunts Lucian about Abigail ("I'm not embarrassed to pay for a whore. . . . Now if I married one, it would be a different matter" [250]); they come to blows. A bouncer throws them out on to the street, but they continue their fisticuffs there. Julian pulls out a knife and stabs Lucian, but he is in turn stabbed by him. Roberts had earlier stated, in one of the scenes set in the present day, that both brothers had died young, so we can assume that both injuries here are fatal.

The bulk of the novel is set in the year 2002. In January of that year, young Declan Fitzgerald has acquired Manet Hall; as the scion of a wealthy Boston lawyer, he evidently has ready cash at his disposal, and in any case Manet Hall has apparently been vacant since the Manets had left and has fallen to rack and ruin. So Declan sets his mind to restoring it. Right from the beginning, he appears to have visions of the past, seeing the house as it was in its heyday, and also feels a sense of fear when approaching the locked door of the nursery, as Roberts explains in classic hack-novel fashion:

In an instant he knew a fear so huge, so great, he wanted to run screaming. Instead he stumbled back, braced himself against the wall while terror and dread choked him like murderous hands.

*Don't go in there. Don't go in.*

Wherever the voice in his head came from, he was inclined to listen to it. He knew the house was rumored to be haunted. He did mind such things.

Or thought he didn't mind them. (33)

Those one-sentence paragraphs, and especially the italicised interior monologue, are dead giveaways. And Roberts compounds the corniness by having Declan hear a baby crying in the house at night (39).

Presently Declan meets the youthful owner of a local bar, Angelina (Lena) Simone. He is immediately bowled over by her:

> She wasn't beautiful, not in any classic sense.
> What she was, was spectacular.
> Her hair was midnight black, a gypsy mane that
> spilled wild curls over her shoulders. Her face was
> fox-sharp—the narrow, somewhat aristocratic nose,
> the high, planed cheeks, the tapered chin. Her eyes
> were long and heavy-lidded, her mouth wide, full and
> painted blood-lust red. . . .
> She was small, almost delicately built, and wore
> a tight scooped-neck shirt the color of poppies that
> showed off the lean muscles of her arms, the firm
> curve of her breasts. Tucked into the valley of those
> breasts was a silver chain with a tiny silver key.
> Her skin was dusky, her eyes, when they flicked
> to his, the deep, rich brown of bitter chocolate. (51)

And so on and so forth. In spite of the rather incongruous mention of her "aristocratic" nose, it is plain that Lena is being set up as a kind of reincarnation of the Cajun Abigail: it is she who has to work hard at operating a bar, whereas it is Declan who is as close to the leisure class as our contemporary society allows. From the moment he meets her, the reader is lured into the expectation that they shall eventually be united—but Roberts has 300 more pages to fill, so she doesn't plan to allow the union to occur anytime soon, or without the inevitable complications.

As they begin going out, Lena is determined to maintain her own independence, and also to maintain the relationship at the tempo she has set. Here is their first kiss:

> She rose on her toes, swayed in. Her hand
> slipped around to the back of his neck as she brought
> his mouth down to hers.
> He felt himself sink. As if he'd been walking on
> solid ground that had suddenly turned to water. It was
> a long, steep drop that had a thousand impressions
> rushing by his senses.
> The silky slide of her lips and tongue, the warm
> brush of her skin, the drugging scent of her perfume.
> By the time he'd begun to separate them, she
> eased back.
> "You're good at that," she murmured, and laid a
> fingertip on his lips. "I had a feeling. 'Night, *cher*."
> (73–74)

But that is all—for now. Note that it is Lena who has initiated the kiss, and Lena who terminates it before it leads to anything further. No shrinking violet she, melting at the first touch of a man's rough caress!

Declan has a friend, Remy Payne, a local lawyer—the two had gone to law school together. It was Remy who had told Declan that Manet Hall was for sale, leading to Declan's acquisition of it. Remy now surprises Declan by telling him that he had had a fling with Lena when he was seventeen and she fifteen. Although it did not work out, they have remained friends. Just at that moment, Effie, Remy's fiancée, sees a ghostly presence—a dead woman lying on the bed in an upstairs bedroom. We have already learned that Effie is a sceptic in regard to supernatural phenomena ("Remy grinned. 'Effie doesn't believe in ghosts'" [69]), so this vision is presumably meant to be taken as veridical. Throughout the novel, indeed, various characters witness ghostly visions, and since Roberts has already outlined the century-old crime that triggered them, we are expected to interpret them as "real" and not mere hallucinations.

Meanwhile, things between Declan and Lena are heating up. They're getting close to the ultimate act, but not yet:

> She didn't try to pull away, but lifted her face so his lips could meet hers. She liked the easy glide from warmth to heat, the fluid ride offered by a man who took his time.
>
> She understood desire. A man's. Her own. And she knew some of those desires could be sated only in quick, hot couplings in the dark.
>
> From time to time, she'd sated hers in just that fashion.
>
> There was more here, and it came like a yearning. Yearnings, even met, could cause a pain desire never could.
>
> Still, she couldn't resist laying hands on his face, letting the kiss spin out. (103)

Note the profusion of one-sentence paragraphs, not to mention sentence fragments ("A man's. Her own"). Are they meant to duplicate the pantings of pre-sexual passion? But Lena isn't ready to make Declan's day just yet—he has to court her, in proper fashion, and she insists on his taking her out on a formal date, explicitly including a "fancy dinner" (104). Even then, she doesn't plan to be dessert: "Take me dancing after, then walk me back to my door and kiss me good-night" (104). Perhaps, after several more of these dates, during which Declan spends considerable sums of his unearned money, something might eventuate. . . .

Declan, meanwhile, has learned from Lena more about the fate of Abigail, and begins to suspect that, far from running away, she was murdered. He vows to find out what happened. For her part, Lena is pondering over her relationship with Declan, which is clearly something more than the teenage back-seat-of-the-car fling she had with Remy (and goodness knows how many others). The big issue is sex:

> The problem was, Declan had the talent for putting her in the mood for sex all the damn time. She was *not* in the habit of being guided by her hormones.
> The wisest, safest thing for a woman to do about sex was to be in control of it. To decide the when, the where, the who and how. Men, well, they were just randy by nature. She couldn't blame them for it.
> And women who claimed not to try to stir men up were either cold-blooded or liars. (128)

We definitely see a more modern sensibility here than in the *oeuvre* of Danielle Steel or Barbara Taylor Bradford: it assumes the feminist stance that a woman will be strong, both in physique and in spirit, and similarly assumes that a woman will use her sexual wiles to her own advantage. Even if it also falls into the Victorian stereotype (one that, however, is also prevalent in many facets of feminism) of a universal sex-obsession in the human male, it nonetheless sees sexual activity as a normal and welcome feature of a healthy relationship. The only problem with Roberts's formulation is that it is expressed so banally.

What is more, in her attempt to endow the Lena-Declan relationship with a complexity (beyond their obvious distinctions in upbringing and social class) that one might find in a real novel, Roberts exaggerates the overall scenario beyond credibility. Lena thinks to herself that Declan wants more out of the relationship than just sex: "there was more to him than that. Too many layers to him, she thought, and she couldn't seem to get through them all and figure him out" (129). But nothing in the novel up to this point—nor, for that matter, in what follows—justifies this verdict: there are no more "layers" to Declan than what one might find in the average personable, rich young man just out of law school.

True to his word, Declan follows through on the orders he has received from Lena, and Roberts allows her readers the wish-fulfillment fantasy of a date from heaven. He picks her up in a limousine, with champagne waiting for her pleasure; he takes her to a fine French restaurant, where *he* does all the ordering; he takes her dancing (he's a great dancer, naturally). And what is the culmination? Is he just going to kiss her goodnight at her door and walk away? *Non, non, mon ami!* She ends up being dessert after all. The sex scene Roberts unleashes goes on for pages, and like the best sex, the great majority of it is foreplay—teasing, kissing, undressing, and so forth. But Roberts does not fail to deliver the payoff:

> Flesh glided over flesh, silky friction. Music, the tragic sob of it from her living room, a sudden celebratory burst of it from the street below, merged together in his head with her quickening breaths.
> She tensed beneath him, her head going back to bare the line of her throat for his lips. She tightened around him, shuddered, shuddered. Once again he buried his face in her hair, and this time, let himself fly with her. (142–43)

I like that "silky friction"—perhaps this paradox is meant to suggest the complexity of their relationship! And yet, Roberts turns out to be surprisingly delicate, even a bit squeamish, in her mention of body parts. Earlier we had had a fleeting reference to "the hot wet velvet of her" (142), and she can't help mentioning that he was "hard as stone" (142), but otherwise she ends up being only a tad less chaste than Danielle Steel. What is manifest is Roberts's hankering to paint the perfect sexual experience from a woman's point of view. At one point Lena interrupts their antics by asking: "Did you take lessons on what to say to have women falling for you?" (137)—something that countless millions of women would wish they could say to their loutish husbands or boyfriends. Meanwhile, Declan falls into the pattern by remarking: "I'd like to take my time with this, if it's all the same to you" (138)—a wish-fulfillment fantasy (for women) if ever there was one. But Roberts makes the matter explicit by noting in her own narrative voice: "She was every man's fantasy. Dusky skin, tumbled hair, full, high breasts barely restrained in that fancy of lace. The slim torso, the gently rounded hips with more midnight lace riding low. Shapely legs in sheer black stockings and man-killer heels" (140). This is not meant for Roberts's (nonexistent) male readers—they can find their fantasies fulfilled in any porn magazine or video; rather, Roberts's bountiful female audience can swoon by imagining themselves with both the impossible physique of slim torsos and high, full breasts and the seductive get-up that their male partners want to peel off at the first opportunity.

It would seem that this episode, coming well before the novel is half over, might lead to an anticlimax. But of course Roberts is relying on the reader's interest in the resolution of the old Abigail matter to keep them turning the pages; and of course one sexual bout, however heavenly, doesn't make a relationship. Declan actually wants to marry Lena, but Remy warns him to be careful, thinking that he is only infatuated. Lena, in turn, wants to appear strong and even untouchable, presenting herself as the voice of reason ("We had ourselves a real good time, too, didn't we? But you don't want to be making more out of it than it was" [166])—but she melts when he kisses her roughly: "She couldn't resist it. Not when the punch of emotions slammed into her system, liberating needs she'd hoped to lock down. On a muffled oath, she wrapped her arms around his neck and met the ferocity of the kiss" (166). Maybe men would like reading Roberts after all: here is certainly a classic instance of a man assuming that "no" means "yes"! Still later, Declan, for no apparent reason, comes to Lena's apartment and has what can euphemistically be called rough sex with her—and what would in other contexts be called rape. She protests at first, but then gives in, yielding by the elegant French expression *"J'ai besoin"* (271)—which the ever-helpful Roberts translates ("I need") for those of her readership who might be ignorant of French. But in reality, Roberts's female readers know that Lena has yielded only because Declan is the man of her dreams—emotionally as well as physically.

But Lena's worries about going too fast are genuine. As she talks matters over with her sage grandmother, Odette, she ponders: "That house over there [Manet Hall] . . . it's a symbol of what happens when two people don't belong in the same place" (169). Manifestly, she is thinking of the pairing of Lucian and Abigail—seemingly a love-match, but one destroyed by racial and class distinctions too vast to overcome—and wonders whether her own involvement with Declan might be afflicted with analogous obstacles.

Mardi Gras comes to New Orleans, and there is plenty of sex all about, by both men and women. (Incredibly, however, there is not a hint of gay sex: is everyone in New Orleans heterosexual?) Lena puts in long hours at her bar, and Declan is right there to help her. Afterwards, her gives her . . . a foot rub! He must certainly be the ideal man ("Mmmm. Declan, you do have a good pair of hands"

[181]). This is followed by a full body massage—but still no sex. Lena falls asleep after his ministrations. Later she asks him about it—doesn't she appeal to him anymore? Declan actually gets angry, saying he was only thinking of her ("I rubbed your feet because I figured you'd been on them about twelve hours straight. Then I let you sleep because you needed to sleep. Hasn't anyone ever done you a favor?" [185]). If this is supposed to be an example of Declan's "layers," then so be it. In any event, both of them now hear a baby crying, not to mention doors slamming, in Manet Hall. Declan has a vision of Abigail and Julian arguing (this is a scene that occurred some months before the murder). Lena now suggests that perhaps reincarnation is at work ("Maybe you're Lucian, come back after all these years for his Abigail" [205]). Declan scoffs at the suggestion, and nothing more is made of it for now.

Declan goes to a jewelry store and buys Lena a ring (not quite an engagement ring, but close enough) and some earrings. While there he finds a watch that *Abigail* had given to *Lucian*—although how on earth a maid could have secured the funds for such a purchase is unexplained. In another classic wish-fulfillment fantasy, Lena swoons when hearing that Declan wants to spend the day obtaining various items for the house: "I've never seen a man so crazy to shop" (236). A wrinkle now enters the picture: Lena's dissolute mother, Lilibeth, shows up. This good-for-nothing woman had deserted Lena a week after giving birth to her at the age of sixteen, and of course she has no money and no prospects. Lena, unable to endure her presence, sends her packing. A little later Lilibeth comes to visit Declan at Manet Hall—and tries to seduce him! Needless to say, he is repulsed and speaks sharply to her, whereupon she hurls insults at her own daughter:

> "All those fine doctors and lawyers and Indian chiefs up there in Boston, how are they gonna like the idea of their golden boy hooking up with some bastard child from the bayou? No money, no pedigree. Runs a second-rate bar and has a grandmama who sews for other people to earn extra pennies. Gonna cut you right out of the will, sugar. Leave you high and dry with this big white elephant of a house on your hands. Especially when I tell them you slept with her mama, too." (260–61)

Certainly a nasty piece of work. But Declan handles her with aplomb, throwing her out of the house and slamming the door in her face. Lilibeth, however, is nothing if not persistent: she later returns to Manet Hall, sneaking in to steal whatever money she can find in the place. She goes to the third floor, where the nursery was—and sees Julian raping and killing Abigail! She flees in terror, never to be heard from again.

But there are more pressing issues at hand. In a convenient *deus ex machina* development, an old plantation house where Remy and Effie were to have their wedding has suffered fire damage, prompting Declan to offer Manet Hall for the event. At once, all parties engage in detailed preparations for the ceremony, and it is transparently obvious that all this pother is meant to plant in the reader's mind the thought of a similar ceremony with Declan and Lena as the principals. But the matter of Abigail must be resolved. Lena now has the brilliant idea that reincarnation is indeed involved, but not in the way she had initially assumed; it is not that Declan is the reincarnation of Lucian, but that he is the reincarnation of *Abigail!* She reasons from the fact that he is the one who had repeatedly heard a baby crying: "Mothers do, before anyone else" (294). We are evidently to take this idea seriously, but there are immediate problems with it: much earlier, Declan had had a touching vision of Lucian, Abigail, and the baby (127), something he could not possibly have had—at least, not in that manner—if he himself were the reincarnation of Abigail. But this half-baked "explanation" of the supernatural phenomena really doesn't amount to much, in spite of Odette's owlish utterance, "Sometimes, old souls search for new life" (299). It is only when Lena finally agrees to marry Declan that, in Roberts's reconstruction, the supernatural manifestations will end.

We have seen that the mingling of romance and supernaturalism is a hallmark of Roberts's work; but her handling of it is clumsy in the extreme, and the novel would have been better (or less poor) without it. As it is, Roberts destroys a potentially serious and dramatic concluding scene—where Declan mentally experiences Abigail's rape and murder at the hands of Julian (339f.)—with jejune humor, as Declan remarks at the end: "I'm trying to figure out if I need an exorcist, a psychiatrist, or if I should cash in and see about starring in a remake of *The Three Faces of Eve*" (343). In the end, it seems that the whole subplot of Lucian and Abigail was designed merely to highlight how, with the progress of a century, a pair of interracial lovers can now find true love instead of horror and death. But Roberts really has no particular interest in a searching examination of class, race, money, and power: she just wants to present a pleasing love story, and the supernatural paraphernalia is meant as a kind of *lagniappe*—and, perhaps, to extend the book to suitable length. But neither the old nor the new love story is handled in anything like an effective manner: if the involvement of Lucian and Abigail is marred by stereotypes (the tender-hearted aristocrat, his cruel and jealous brother, the saintly but impoverished maid lifted up to a level beyond her station, the domineering mother intent on preserving the family's good name), the relationship of Declan and Lena is scarcely less riddled with conventionality and predictability: good sex but a teasing prolongation of the final decision to marry until the very end, the sage old Cajun grandmother full of wise old saws drawn from long experience, the scoundrelly mother who receives her deserved comeuppance, and so on and so forth. There is nothing in *Midnight Bayou* that has not been found in hundreds of works of the same ilk, and Roberts's ham-fisted prose, full of clichés and those tell-tale one-sentence paragraphs, makes virtually every plot twist either contrived or predictable.

* * * * * * *

The romance novel has lately received a certain modicum of critical and even scholarly scrutiny, chiefly by academicians who seek to determine whether the novels in question do or do not conform to currently fashionable tenets of feminism.[6] I am perfectly willing to believe, as these scholars have maintained, that some of these novels are not quite as socially reactionary as they are customarily thought to be; but I am struck by the fact that very few critics and scholars treat these novels from a purely aesthetic perspective. Perhaps this is not so surprising, for—gauged by the novels of Danielle Steel, Barbara Taylor Bradford, and Nora Roberts examined here—any kind of aesthetic value is pretty hard to come by.

# II.

# AN AESTHETIC PRETENDER

## JOHN GRISHAM

The tradition of the Aesthetic Pretender is a venerable one in literature—the author who professes to great profundity and the serious treatment of weighty issues, but who in fact avoids truly and sincerely coming to grips with the issues at hand by a series of literary dodges and sleights-of-hand. At times such an author can even bamboozle contemporary critics into accepting his pretensions, but a telltale sign of his or her aesthetic vacuity emerges when the work promptly falls by the wayside after—or, in some mortifying cases, even before—the author's death.

If one had asked a well-educated person in 1850 who the four leading American poets of the day were, more than one would have rattled off the names of Ralph Waldo Emerson, Henry Wadsworth Longfellow, Edgar Allan Poe (who had died the preceding year), and . . . Fitz-Greene Halleck. Fitz-Greene who? Halleck (1790–1867), generally a comic poet, issued his *Poetical Works* in 1847, and it went through many editions; but he is now scarcely a blip in the annals of nineteenth-century literature and provides meager fodder even for academicians desperate for a fresh topic to escape the inevitable Melville-Emerson-Whitman rut.

H. L. Mencken, who displayed a remarkable ability to sort the wheat from the chaff, performed perhaps his most notable—at all events, his most heroic—efforts in slapping down Aesthetic Pretenders at every turn. One of his frequent victims was Winston Churchill—the once-popular but now almost universally forgotten American novelist, not the British prime minister—who, as we have seen, was the best-selling novelist of 1901, 1904, 1906, 1908, and 1913. Mencken's dissection of Churchill's novel *A Far Country*

(1915), dealing with the conflict of business and labour, gets to the heart of the ways and means of the Aesthetic Pretender:

> It is, in fact, much less a work of the imagination than a piece of pamphleteering, and if it fails as the latter it fails even more certainly as the former. The story that Mr. Churchill tells is not only incoherent and unconvincing; it is also quite uninteresting. It is heavy with small details, but they are details that burden the reader without either enlightening him or diverting him. Page follows page and chapter follows chapter; finely printed, laborious and meticulous, but at the end one sees Hugh Paget only dimly. What are his vices? What is his notion of beauty? What is his view of women, the sex war? Who are his heroes at forty-five? Reading the book from end to end, I get no satisfactory answers to these questions. Paget passes through it like a shadow, one never sees clearly into his soul, one never comes to actual grips with him.[1]

Consider now the virtually forgotten phenomenon of Richard Bach's *Jonathan Livingston Seagull*. This book came out with relatively little fanfare in 1970, but an aggressive advertising campaign thrust it into the bestseller lists in 1972, and it became the top-selling book of that year and of the year following. In addition to that, certain naïve newspaper and magazine critics convinced themselves that there was deep meaning in the book. *Time* magazine—not noted for its critical acuity—devoted a cover story to it on November 13, 1972, writing at the outset of a long article: "People are beginning to compare *Jonathan* to Saint-Exupery's *The Little Prince* and Kahlil Gibran's *The Prophet* (favorably or not, according to taste) as a book likely to stay around forever."[2] This comparison to two books almost as lightweight is not encouraging, even if the author (wisely hiding behind anonymity) attributes this judgment to unnamed "people." But the learned critic goes on to probe *Jonathan's* religious and philosophical depths:

> In his own ingenious way, Richard Bach has explained the message of *Jonathan.* "Find out what you love to do, and do your darndest to make it happen." That urging is what most of the thousands of people who have written to Bach seem to take to heart. . . .

Says Science Fiction Writer Ray Bradbury, a great friend and fan of Bach's: "*Jonathan* is a great Rorschach test. You read your own mystical principles into it." Rorschach test or not, *Jonathan* owes something to science fiction (thought movement, for example). It is also a mélange of contradictory religious messages. One is Hinduism (the goal of life is absolute perfection). Yet *Jonathan* emphasizes the self over all else, and that runs counter to Eastern religions. Insistence on the power of the self also undercuts the book's Christian overtones. For Jonathan is no fallen flyer needing God's help but an idea of perfection that can fulfill itself.[3]

I trust we are now in agreement that *Jonathan Livingston Seagull* is an utterly vapid and empty work that perfectly encapsulates the equally vapid and empty era in which it was written; its chances of entering the American literary canon are about as good as the Montreal Expos' chances of winning the World Series. (For the enlightenment of baseball ignoramuses, the Montreal Expos no longer exist as a professional franchise.) I don't believe the book is even in print anymore. Bach, of course, has gone on to write several more books, and (because he became a brand name by means of *Jonathan*) several of them became bestsellers; but they too have been swallowed up by the maw of oblivion, and Bach is about to join them, if he hasn't done so already.

There are a number of telltale signs of the Aesthetic Pretender. One is the cold-bloodedly calculating way in which an author will deal with a currently fashionable political, social, or cultural issue, not to probe the issue itself but to exploit its popularity (Michael Crichton has mastered this technique in such books as *Disclosure* [1994], about sexual harassment, and, still more notoriously, *State of Fear* [2004], about global warming). These books frequently indulge in such patented devices of the hack novel as the happy ending, the artificially neat resolution of all plot details, and the absence of a genuine catharsis by an evasion or mitigation of a tragic dénouement. For after all, Aesthetic Pretenders have no real desire to come to grips with the issues they are purportedly treating; they wish to "entertain," and they know that their generally untutored readers will not tolerate anything too sad or depressing. That's not "entertainment" for them.

A prime recent instance of the Aesthetic Pretender is John Grisham (b. 1955). It is not sufficient to say that Grisham has capitalised on the sensational legal novel as popularised by Scott Turow and others; as a practicing lawyer born and raised in Mississippi, he has repeatedly dealt with the lingering racism of his native region. He has written eighteen novels and one work of nonfiction, beginning with *A Time to Kill* (1989). His first bestseller was his second novel, *The Firm* (1991), which achieved popularity largely on the basis of the blockbuster film. Seven other of his books have been adapted into film. Grisham, at least implicitly, claims a superior status to the Danielle Steels and James Pattersons of the world by virtue of his subject-matter, so it is worth examining at least two of his novels to see exactly how he addresses—or evades—the serious issues he purports to treat.

*The Chamber* (1994)[4] opens in Greenville, Mississippi, in 1967. Three white men—Jeremiah (Jerry) Dogan, Sam Cayhall, and Rollie Wedge, all members of the Ku Klux Klan—plan to blow up the office of a "radical Jew lawyer" (1), Marvin Kramer. They do so, and in the ensuing explosion Kramer's twin five-year-old sons die, while Marvin has both his legs amputated. His sons were not supposed to be in the office at the time, but all three had arrived there early in the morning, before the boys were to be taken to nursery school. Sam Cayhall was near the office at the time of the blast and was slightly injured. He drove off in a car but, almost by accident, he was stopped by police and arrested. The car he was driving was traced to Jerry Dogan. The first trial, with an all-white jury, ends in a mistrial. The second trial ends in a hung jury. The entire incident continues to have unfortunate ramifications on the Kramer family: Marvin and his wife separate in 1970, and Marvin commits suicide the next year.

In 1979, Dogan is indicted for tax evasion. He makes a plea agreement with the FBI to testify against Cayhall in a murder trial. In this third trial, Cayhall is convicted and given the death sentence. Ten years pass.

A young lawyer, Adam Hall, at an immense Chicago law firm, Kravitz & Bane, wishes to work on the Cayhall case in conjunction with an ageing and somewhat embittered pro bono lawyer, E. Gardner Goodman. We learn quickly that Adam is Sam Cayhall's grandson, the son of Sam's son, Eddie, who had gone to California and changed his name. Goodman, although reluctant to let Adam work on a case that has such deep personal resonances with him, grudgingly agrees. He is convinced that there was another accomplice in the bombing; if he could somehow get Sam to name this person, Sam might get off death row. The matter takes on urgency because David McAllister, the district attorney who had convicted Cayhall, has now become governor of Mississippi and wants to speed up the execution.

Adam now learns more about his grandfather from his aunt Lee in Memphis. In spite of the fact that Sam had, many years before, killed a black man in an altercation, never serving time for the act, Adam wonders whether Sam really intended to kill Marvin Kramer and his two small children. Could he have been just trying to scare the lawyer, setting off a bomb at a time when he thought the office would be empty?

Adam now goes to the Mississippi State Prison and talks with the prison attorney, Lucas Mann, who tells Adam that Sam is to be executed four weeks from that day, or August 8. Adam meets Sam himself, who declares that he is a "political prisoner": "I didn't do what the jury said I did" (82). It doesn't take long for Sam to recognise Adam, who sounds like his father. Sam grudgingly lets Adam represent him in what is likely to be his last legal imbroglio—but lays down the dictum that Adam must not speak with Governor McAllister, whom Sam despises. This presumably means that Adam cannot appeal to McAllister for clemency, something that the latter is pretty unlikely to grant in any event.

Adam presses Sam to tell him of the other accomplice, but Sam refuses, claiming there was no such person. He does let out the fact that Jerry Dogan and his wife died in a house fire that occurred exactly a year after Dogan had testified against Sam in the third trial: the obvious implication is that Rollie Wedge was responsible, and that he was sending Sam a message not to be similarly loquacious regarding Rollie's role in the old killing.

The title of the novel alludes to the gas chamber where Sam is presumably to die, and we are now regaled with a succession of hideous stories of executions gone awry. Here is one, as Sam himself (now an expert on the matter) relates:

> "A 1984 case from North Carolina. The man's name was Jimmy Old, and evidently Jimmy did not want to die. They had to drag him into the chamber, kicking and screaming, and it took a while to strap him in. They slammed the door and dropped the gas, and his chin crashed onto his chest. Then his head rolled back and began twitching. He turned to the witnesses who could see nothing but the whites of his eyeballs, and he began salivating. His head rocked and swung around forever while his body shook and his mouth foamed. It went on and on, and one of the

witnesses, a journalist, vomited. The warden got fed up with it and closed the black curtains so the witnesses couldn't see anymore. They estimate it took fourteen minutes for Jimmy Old to die." (179)

Therefore, one of the strategies Adam now devises is to declare the gas chamber unconstitutional, although he acknowledges that this is just a means of buying time while pursuing more substantial methods of overturning the death sentence.

We are now introduced to a person named Roland Forchin, who, it becomes quickly evident, is Rollie Wedge. Roland runs a secret compound full of weapons, communications equipment, and the like. He has graduated from the Klan to the Aryan Nation and other, less savory groups; as Grisham states with heavy-handed irony, "he was a proud fascist" (185). He reads press reports of Adam's work on Sam's case—and feels a certain monitoring of the situation is in order. So we learn that he is making his way to Memphis. . . .

Adam now interviews an ex-FBI agent who had handled Sam's case, Wyn Lettner; he tries to get Lettner to admit that Sam had an accomplice. Wyn does so with alacrity: "Of course he [Sam] had some help" (194). Wyn had learned from an employee of Jerry Dogan's that Dogan had hired a man from another state to do the bombing, since neither Sam nor Jerry had much experience with the particular kind of time-bomb used in the Kramer killing. But beyond this, Wyn has no information to offer.

At a meeting with a federal judge, Adam meets Governor McAllister, who tells him in private that he is not sure Sam should die: he thinks Sam may have had an accomplice, and that Dogan was a notorious liar. They have an interesting conversation, part of which goes like this:

> [McAllister:] "There are a lot of people in this state who secretly do not wish to see Sam executed." McAllister was now watching Adam closely.
> "Are you one of them?"
> "I don't know. But what if Sam didn't plan to kill either Marvin Kramer or his sons? Sure Sam was there, right in the thick of it. But what if someone else possessed the intent to murder?"
> "Then Sam isn't as guilty as we think."
> "Right. He's certainly not innocent, but not guilty enough to be executed either." (230–31)

E. Gardner Goodman now comes to Memphis to meet with Adam. It appears that Daniel Rosen, a leading figure in the firm, is trying to get Adam dismissed for deceiving the firm about his relationship with Sam. But Goodman and others are rallying members of the Termination Subcommittee, as it is called, to preserve Adam's job. Sure enough, they prevail, although it is a close call. But a much closer call is at hand, one that Adam knows nothing about: Rollie Wedge has come to Memphis and knows that Adam is staying with his aunt.

Lee now tells Adam the painful story of Adam's murder of the black man, Joe Lincoln, in 1950. It is all rather sordid, involving Sam's son Eddie accusing one of Joe's sons, Quince, of stealing, Sam chastising and beating Quince, Quince running to get his father's help, and Sam blowing Joe Lincoln away with a shotgun. It is far and away the most gripping passage in the entire novel and comes close to justifying Grisham's pose as a novelist of literary substance. But it takes up only four or five pages in the book.

Adam now talks with Elliot Kramer, Marvin's father. Understandably, Elliot is very embittered over the death of his son and grandchildren, and the two engage in a heated discussion over life and death:

> [Adam:] "I assure you he's not being coddled. Death row is a horrible place. I just left it."
>
> "Yeah, but he's alive. He's living and breathing and watching television and reading books. He's talking to you. He's filing lawsuits. And when and if death gets near, he'll have plenty of time to make plans for it. He can say his good-byes. Say his prayers. My grandsons didn't have time to say good-bye, Mr. Hall. They didn't get to hug their parents and give them farewell kisses. They were simply blown to bits while they were playing."
>
> "I understand that, Mr. Kramer. But killing Sam will not bring them back."
>
> "No, it won't. But it'll make us feel a helluva lot better. It'll ease a lot of pain. I've prayed a million times that I'll live long enough to see him dead. I had a heart attack five years ago. They had me strapped to machines for two weeks, and the one thing that kept me alive was my desire to outlive Sam Cayhall. I'll be there, Mr. Hall, if my doctors allow it. I'll be there

to watch him die, then I'll come home and count my days." (286–87)

Wyn Lettner now visits Sam in prison. He tells Sam that he never thought Dogan's death was an accident, for around the same time Dogan's son went AWOL from the army and was also probably killed. Moreover, Sam's former lawyer, Clovis Brazelton, died in a plane crash. All this, I must say, reveals pretty clever and relentless work on the part of Rollie Wedge, especially given that he was never caught or charged in any of these crimes. Wyn thinks Sam may also be in danger. His fears are quickly realised: Rollie Wedge boldly comes Sam's prison and visits him, pretending to be Sam's brother. He threatens to kill Sam if he reveals anything about Wedge's involvement in the case.

Lee now spills the beans further about Sam: she tells Adam that Sam, when he was fifteen in 1936, was involved in a lynching. She tells of a photograph in a book published in 1947 that seems to show Sam: "Smiling from ear to ear. They're standing under the tree and the black guy's feet are dangling just above their heads. Everybody's having a ball. Just another nigger lynching" (303). Adam, for his part, is increasingly concerned about Lee, who has already admitted that she is an alcoholic and who is apparently descending back into alcoholism. Matters are not helped by a newspaper article that reveals Lee's relation to Sam.

Adam has filed a plea on the cruelty of the gas chamber before the Fifth Court of Appeals, but Sam how tells him that he is tired of fighting for a stay of execution. Can this be the influence of Rollie Wedge? Goodman goes to see Governor McAllister to ask for a clemency hearing. McAllister will grant it only if Sam names his accomplice. Goodman now resorts to a clever scheme, hiring several local law students to telephone the governor's office repeatedly and express their opposition to the execution. The ruse appears to be working, for the governor's staff now wonders whether executing Sam would prove to be highly unpopular and endanger his reelection prospects.

Meanwhile, Sam himself is undergoing some changes of heart. Although portrayed throughout the novel as an unrepentant racist, he now writes a letter of apology to Joe Lincoln's son, Quince, instructing Adam: "Tell him that I died with a lot of guilt" (377). Sam also admits that he killed two white men who had killed his father: "me and my brothers waited patiently. We killed both of them, but I never felt bad about it, to be honest. They were scum, and they'd killed my father" (404). The best that Adam can say is: "Killing is always wrong, Sam" (404). Adam, meanwhile, has found the 1947 book with the photograph of the lynching scene in which Sam was present: "He was just a boy, born and reared in a household where hatred of blacks and others was simply a way of life. How much of it could be blamed on him?" (400).

In spite of the repeated setbacks that Adam has suffered in his various pleas and motions, there now seems to be a hint of a last-minute reprieve. Judge Slattery calls a hearing to gauge whether Sam is mentally competent to be executed. A psychiatrist hired by Kravitz & Bane, a Dr. Swinn, says that Sam is unaware of his imminent execution, but the state calls prison officials who testify to the reverse. The judge denies the plea of mental incompetency. As the execution seems to be nearing, protesters of various sorts gather outside the prison. One of the groups is the Klan, and Sam has Adam read a statement he has prepared:

> Adam glanced at the stern faces of the Klansmen, all hot and dripping with perspiration. "The last paragraph reads as follows, and I quote: 'I am no longer a member of the Ku Klux Klan. I repudiate that organization and all that it stands for. I would be a free man today had I never heard of the Ku Klux Klan.' It's signed Sam Cayhall." Adam flipped it over and thrust it toward the Kluckers, all of whom were speechless and stunned. (449)

But Sam's last hopes seem to be dashed when Governor McAllister denies clemency. In a statement he notes bombastically: "It is my fervent hope that the execution of Sam Cayhall will help erase a painful chapter in our state's tortured history. I call upon all Mississippians to come together from this sad night forward, and work for equality. May God have mercy on his soul" (464). Sam finally makes a telling admission:

> "And I didn't kill those Kramer boys," Sam said, his voice shaking. "I had no business being there, and I was wrong to be involved in that mess. I've regretted it for many years, all of it. It was wrong to be in the Klan, hating everybody and planting bombs. But I didn't kill those boys. There was no intent to harm anyone. That bomb was supposed to go off in the middle of the night when no one would be anywhere near it. That's what I truly believed. But it was wired

by someone else, not me. I was just a lookout, a driver, a flunky. This other person rigged the bomb to go off much later than I thought. I've never known for sure if he intended to kill anyone, but I suspect he did." (468)

But will Sam actually name this accomplice? No; he wishes to protect Adam, since Wedge could easily come after him.

Sam is executed. Adam makes the fateful decision to practice death penalty litigation in Mississippi.

I gather that *The Chamber* is a somewhat more bleak and cheerless novel than many that Grisham has written, and also lacks the fast pacing that renders many of them turn-the-page legal thrillers. Adam's repeated disappointments as he tries one legal move after another to prevent the execution of his grandfather have a certain lugubrious element of suspense to them, but that is about all. And yet, one cannot help feeling that this novel falls between two stools: it is not quite serious enough to be a genuinely literary novel, and it is not crude enough to be a mindless legal adventure story.

Throughout, we are repeatedly struck by Grisham's refusal to deal compellingly and profoundly with the racial, moral, and legal ramifications of the incidents he relates. Perhaps he feels that they speak for themselves, but they do not. Grisham is to be praised for having as the focus of his novel a genuinely unsympathetic character in Sam Cayhall, who—until his rather unconvincing conversion toward the end—remains racist, embittered, and, to put it mildly, unlikable. And there is a certain cleverness in the trap Grisham has laid for his more liberal readers, who are presumably opposed in principle to the death penalty but who also do not wish in any way to sanction the racial crimes of which Sam is guilty.

As Grisham gradually relates Sam's life story, we come to learn some of the reasons why Sam has evolved into the person he is. But in only one passage does Adam forthrightly confront Sam in regard to his hatred and racism:

> "Why do you hate, Sam? Why does it come to easy? Why were you taught to hate blacks and Jews and Catholics and anyone slightly different from you? Have you ever asked yourself why?"
> "No. Don't plan to."
> "So, it's just you, right. It's your character, your composition, same as your height and blue eyes. It's something you were born with and can't change. It

was passed down in the genes from your father and grandfather, faithful Kluckers all, and it's something you'll proudly take to the grave, right?"

"It was a way of life. It was all I knew." (206–7)

This is not very helpful, and the debate soon peters out as Adam ironically accuses Sam of failing to inculcate his son, Eddie, Adam's own father, into the pattern of hate that had claimed his family for generations.

And then there is the matter of Rollie Wedge. Clearly Grisham has inserted this baleful figure to lend a certain sense of danger and tension to a novel whose only other element of suspense is whether an unrepentant Klansman will face the gas chamber or not. But Rollie's cartoonish portrayal as a racist and fascist, his remarkable ability to silence his opponents, and his final confrontation with Sam only days before the latter's execution actually diminish the novel's seriousness by rendering him a James-Pattersonish super-villain. And to top it off, Grisham appears to forget all about him at the end and fails to provide an account of his ultimate fate after Sam's execution. Does he simply go back to his secret compound, or does he continue on his campaign of murder? Is he ever brought to justice, or does he continue to lurk in the shadows? We never learn the answer.

And Grisham does not, it seems to me, genuinely confront the many and complex issues surrounding the death penalty, which presumably is the focus of his novel. Goodman tells Adam early in the story:

> ". . . the death penalty may be very popular in our country, but the people who are forced to impose it are not supporters. You're about to meet these people: the guards who get close to the inmates; the administrators who must plan for an efficient killing; the prison employees who rehearse for a month beforehand. It's a strange little corner of the world, and a very depressing one." (42)

But Adam rarely, in fact, has any meaningful discussions with these individuals, and, aside from the passage where Sam recounts those cases of grotesque mishandling of executions, we are never given much of an account of what it actually means, legally and morally, for the state to kill one of its own citizens. We are told (twice) that death row inmates tend to sleep as much as sixteen hours a day (110, 119), and Sam undergoes a certain transformation—not entirely convincing, as I have mentioned—as the day of doom approaches. And while Grisham is to be praised for not uncorking some sort of jack-in-the-box surprise whereby Sam is providentially saved at the end, one develops the impression that Grisham does not wish to depress his readers too much with excessive focusing on the death penalty, or to offend his millions of readers—who are bound to have very diverse views on the legality and morality of capital punishment—with too strident an argument on one side or the other. The end result is a tiptoeing around what is putatively the central issue of the novel.

* * * * * * *

Thinking that *The Chamber* was not entirely representative of Grisham's work, I decided to sample another and more recent work—to wit, *The King of Torts* (2003).[5]

The novel opens dramatically with the killing in Washington, D.C., of a young man nicknamed Pumpkin, whose real name is Ramón Pumphrey, by a "boy" (1)—the twenty-year-old Tequila Watson. Watson is, of course, black. A young lawyer in the Office of the Public Defender, Clay Carter II, is asked by the judge to handle Watson's defense, much to Clay's discomfort. After five years in the public defender's office, Clay is already burned out: it was not the life he had envisioned for himself, being the son of a well-known Washington lawyer. Clay talks with Tequila in jail, trying to ascertain his motives in killing Pumphrey. All Tequila can say is: "I had a gun, and I wanted to shoot somebody. Anybody, it didn't matter" (23). In spite of the brutal world of the Washington slums, this seems unusually callous and irrational, so Clay decides to dig further.

He talks with a person known only as Talmadge X, a counselor at the Deliverance Camp, a rehab facility in downtown Washington where Tequila had been staying. Talmadge makes the odd claim that Tequila was actually "afraid of violence" (32), so the mystery of his sudden descent into killing becomes more inexplicable. Clay later learns a bit more about his client:

> . . . Tequila began his slide at the age of eight when he and his brother stole a case of beer off a delivery truck. They drank half and sold half, and with the proceeds bought a gallon of cheap wine. He'd been kicked out of various schools and somewhere around

the age of twelve, about the time he discovered crack, he'd dropped out altogether. Stealing became a way of survival. (48)

This sounds all too familiar, but there is still something inexplicable about it: "As depressing as the history was, there was a remarkable absence of violence in it. Tequila had been arrested and convicted five times for burglary, once for shoplifting, and twice for misdemeanor possession. Tequila had never used a weapon to commit a crime, at least not one for that he had been nabbed for" (49).

Meanwhile, Clay's personal life is not going well either. He is in love with a woman named Rebecca Van Horn, the daughter of Bennett and Barbara Van Horn. Bennett is a big real estate tycoon in northern Virginia who has earned the nickname Bennett the Bulldozer. Why? We learn quickly:

> Bennett the Bulldozer struck gold in the late eighties when he invaded the rolling hills of the Virginia countryside. Deals fell into place. Partners were found. He didn't invent the slash-and-burn style of suburban development, but he certainly perfected it. On pristine hills he built malls. Near a hallowed battleground, he built a subdivision. He leveled an entire village for one of his planned developments— apartments, condos, big houses, small houses, a park in the center with a shallow muddy pond and two tennis courts, a quaint little shopping district that looked nice in the architect's office but never got built. Ironically, though irony was lost on Bennett, he named his cookie-cutter projects after the landscape he was destroying—Rolling Meadows, Whispering Oaks, Forest Hills, etcetera. (35)

At dinner with the Van Horns at the McClean Country Club, where Bennett's money has bought him a membership, Bennett makes a startling proposal to Clay: He says he can get Clay a job with the Speaker of the House in the Virginia legislature. It would, of course, entail a move to Richmond. The Van Horns (and, for that matter, Rebecca herself) make no secret of the fact that they want a somewhat more prosperous husband for their daughter, who (although she herself has a busy job in a congressman's office) has been brought up with the idea that her husband should support her while she stays home and has babies.

Clay doesn't cotton to the idea of moving to Richmond and working for some sleazy politician who is likely in Bennett's pocket; more significantly, he does not wish to be forever indebted to Bennett for his career. So he declines the offer, greatly offending Bennett and actually causing a breakup with Rebecca. He seems genuinely in love with her (although the fact that they have sex five times a week must be something of a factor) and does his best to put the whole incident behind him.

Matters take a much more fateful turn when someone named Max Pace tells Clay that a big pharmaceutical company had manufactured an anti-addiction drug known as Tarvan, testing it (illegally) on human patients overseas and also among African Americans in Washington, D.C. The drug seems to be remarkably effective, but in a very small number of cases it causes them to turn to random killing. Tequila Watson is one of these. Pace now wants Clay to represent the families of five or six murder victims and negotiate a quick and quiet settlement with the drug company, which is never named. Clay would get $10 million dollars for his work, while the families would each get $4 million. Clay goes to the Bahamas to consult with his father, Jarrett Carter, who has had to retire there because of a succession of misfortunes at his once-powerful law firm, including suspicions that he had cooked the books. But Jarrett is no help, his interests now extending solely to women and alcohol. Clay comes back to Washington, meets again with Pace, and demands $15 million for himself and $5 million for the families. Pace agrees with alacrity. Clay quickly gets a cool $5 million upon the signing of the contract and immediately resigns from the public defender's office.

Clay calls upon his former colleague, Rodney Albritton, to help him sign up the families (now numbering seven) who would be involved in the settlement. As an African American, Rodney would presumably have greater credibility with the black families in question. Rodney does his work well, and all the families sign up, although some a bit reluctantly. The settlement is quickly put through, and Clay gets the remainder of the money owed to him.

He is now wealthy beyond his wildest dreams and has already bought a home in Georgetown worth $1.3 million. But now Pace wants him to take on an even bigger case: a drug called Dyloft, made by Ackerman Labs, a leading competitor of the company that had manufactured Tarvan, has a powerful anti-inflammatory drug taken by arthritis sufferers. The Tarvan company has had a similar drug on the market for years, which is one of their biggest sellers; but now they have confidential information that the competitor's drug has serious side effects: "it's been linked to the creation of small tumors in the bladder" (120). (It later turns out that many of these tumors are benign, but nevertheless the matter is of considerable consequence.) Pace wants Clay to set up an immense class-action lawsuit, involving tens of thousands of patients, against the maker of Dyloft. His cut would be perhaps in excess of $30 million, depending on how many clients he signed up.

Clay, now besotted with the idea of making this kind of un-dreamed-of money, goes down to New Orleans, where a private conference (the entry fee is $5,000) among all the leading mass tort lawyers in the nation is being held. Pace wants Clay to get some background on how such a large class-action suit is to be managed. The star of the show is one Patton French, who delivers a lecture on the virtues of his trade:

> He spoke again at one, after a buffet lunch fea-turing Cajun food and Dixie beer. His cheeks were red, his tongue loose and colorful. Without notes he launched into a brief history of the American tort sys-tem and how crucial it was in protecting the masses from the greed and corruption of big corporations that make dangerous products. And, while he was at it, he didn't like insurance companies and banks and multinationals and Republicans, either. Unbridled capitalism created the need for people like those hardy souls in the Circle of Barristers, those down in the trenches who were unafraid to attack big business on behalf of the working people, the little people. (131)

But, of course, there is something to be said for all the money to be made:

> French's war stories poured forth effortlessly. A $400 million class-action settlement for a bad choles-terol drug. A billion for a diabetes drug that killed at least a hundred patients. For faulty electrical wiring put into two hundred thousand homes that caused fif-teen hundred fires killing seventeen people and burn-ing another forty, $150 million. The lawyers hung on every word. Sprinkled throughout were indications of where his money had gone. "That cost 'em a new Gulfstream," he cracked at one point and the crowd

actually applauded. Clay knew, after hanging around the Royal Sonesta for less than twenty-four hours, that a Gulfstream was the finest of all personal jets and a new one sold for about $5 million. (131)

Clay has not yet descended to this level of avariciousness. He doesn't actually learn very much about how to handle mass tort cases, but upon his return to Washington he realises that his office will have to be considerably expanded to deal with such a large affair as the Dyloft case. He hires a number of lawyers and paralegals to hunt up Dyloft patients and sign them up for the class-action suit. An advertising blitz on television costs $2 million. Patton French now approaches Clay, taking him on his private plane and suggesting that they team up on Dyloft. Patton habitually files his cases in Mississippi, where he is well known and well liked. He thinks that this action will force Ackerman to make a quick settlement. Patton offers to cover the $2 million that will be needed for the medical testing of all the afflicted patients. Clay wants to check with Max Pace to make sure that this collaborative enterprise suits his (and his company's) interests. Pace is enthusiastic, and several other leading tort lawyers also now get into the act, although the number of their clients pales in comparison with Clay's.

Matters are moving fast. Clay's staff is harried by the number of cases they have unearthed and claim that more lawyers and other employees, including a doctor, need to be hired. Clay now hears that Philo Products has offered "to buy the outstanding common stock of Ackerman Labs for $50 a share, a merger with a price tag of $14 billion" (191). Clay is suspicious: is Philo the maker of Tarvan, and was this class-action suit simply a means of allowing Philo to swallow up its competitor? More significantly, Clay wonders whether he is now becoming corrupted by the vast amounts of money he stands to gain. He has already contemplated buying a Gulfstream jet for himself, even though it is still a bit out of his range; he decides only to lease it. He has also purchased some Ackerman stock and makes a quick $6 million when Philo buys it at $53 a share.

A group of tort lawyers, including Clay, calling themselves the Dyloft Plaintiffs' Steering Committee now meets with a team of Ackerman lawyers. They have agreed to settle the "Group One" plaintiffs' case (those with only benign tumors, making up the largest number of plaintiffs) for $62,000 each; accordingly, Clay's estimated gross fees for these settlements comes to a whopping $106 million. Clay becomes a celebrity overnight. He is featured in the *Wall Street Journal,* where he is called "The King of Torts." With his new-found wealth, Clay buys a $3 million boat for his father. He also meets a Russian model named Ridley (her real name is Ridal Petashnakol), largely to have a pretty face to accompany him to important social functions. One of these functions proves to be the wedding of Rebecca Van Horn and a suitable husband dug up for her by her parents. Clay calls up Rebecca, jocularly trying to dissuade her from marrying the fellow; he fails, but at least he can try to upstage her by bringing the Russian bombshell to her wedding reception. Clay is, however, also generous: he gives $10 million of his fee to his old friend Rodney, and also to two other of the original partners of his law firm.

Matters, however, start taking a turn for the worse pretty quickly. A number of the Dyloft patients are unhappy with the relatively meager settlement they received—which comes down to $43,000 after Clay's legal fees are subtracted. But Clay can put this unpleasantness behind him for the time being. While lounging with Ridley on a Caribbean island, he is visited again by the redoubtable Max Pace, who now proposes yet another mass tort case. There is another bad drug out there—a female hormone drug called Maxatil—made by a venerable and powerful American company, Goffman ("the bluest of all blue-chips" [229]). In a small number of women, "the drug greatly increases the risk of breast cancer, heart attacks, and strokes" (229). This sounds pretty bad, and Max now insists that he receive 25% of the gross attorney's fees. There is some little mystery about how Max is getting all this information, but Clay doesn't seem overly concerned, and so he plunges into this newest case.

Clay is, however, astounded to find that Patton French and others are reluctant to join in the litigation, even though it could be far more lucrative than their previous endeavors. French had himself considered taking on the Maxatil case, but had passed on it: "Causation could be a real problem" (244). That is, it might be difficult to prove that actual cases of breast cancer and the like contracted by Maxatil patients was caused directly by the drug. The media response to this newest class-action case is quite hostile: since Goffman is such a well-respected firm, there is widespread suspicion that Clay is engaging in a frivolous lawsuit just for the money.

Clay, a bit shaken by these developments, meets with Dale Mooneyham, a lawyer in Tucson who is suing Goffman in a single-party suit over Maxatil. Mooneyham is a very careful, tough lawyer who has not lost a case in twenty years. He utters what appears to be the overall moral of the book:

"Class actions are a fraud, at least the way you and your pals handle them. Mass torts are a scam, a consumer rip-off, a lottery driven by greed that will one day harm all of us. Unbridled greed will swing the pendulum to the other side. Reforms will take place, and they'll be severe. You boys will be out of business but you won't care because you'll have the money. The people who'll get harmed are all the future plaintiffs out there, all the little people who won't be able to sue for bad products because you boys have screwed up the law." (250–51)

Nevertheless, Clay puts much of his hope on Mooneyham's case, for if he prevails, then Goffman will very likely settle Clay's class-action suit. Meanwhile, Clay's firm is spending immense amounts of money on all kinds of overhead. Clay, for his part, is informally shacking up with Ridley and has purchased a $3 million property in the Caribbean—which he labels a "bargain" (276).

But trouble is brewing. FBI agents come to Clay's office and ask about Max Pace. It appears that Pace is part of an SEC investigation: "Pace has a history of securities fraud, insider trading" (282). Clay honestly tells the agents that he hasn't heard from Pace in weeks. Clay's law firm now takes another hit: the manufacturer of a diet pill colloquially known as Skinny Ben, in which Clay's firm had invested considerable money in the expectation of reaping millions, declares bankruptcy, in effect robbing the firm of an expected $15 million in revenue. Clay's insurance company calls up, cancelling the firm's $10 million malpractice insurance. This amount, in any case, would be chicken feed if the Maxatil case goes bad and Clay is countersued by Goffman.

Still worse news is on the horizon. Some of the Group One Dyloft patients are now developing malignant tumors. Helen Warshaw, a tort lawyer who has made a specialty of going after other tort lawyers, sues Clay, Patton French, and others over these cases. The FBI agents pay Clay another visit, all but accusing him of securities fraud for his involvement in dealing with the Ackerman stocks. Clay feels it is time to consult a lawyer himself, and he sees Zack Battle, an old friend of his father's. Zack tells him that Clay is in fact guilty of insider trading—which would mean "Five years in the slammer" (305)—but his complicity could only be revealed if Max Pace testified against him. But, fortunately, Pace is nowhere to be found.

The only piece of good news for Clay is that he hears, both from word of mouth and from Rebecca herself, that her marriage is not going well. She admits to him that she is "very lonely" (288), since her husband seems immersed in his work. Later she visits him in his office, communicating her marriage troubles to him but refusing his whimsical offer to engage in adultery.

Clay realises that the fate of his Maxatil case depends on the outcome of Mooneyham's trial in Flagstaff. But Clay is other concerns also. He had engaged in a smallish class-action case against Hanna Portland Cement Co., of Reedsburg, Pennsylvania, which had unwittingly used bad mortar for a number of houses in Baltimore. Clay, demanding too much money from the company, had forced it into bankruptcy. The company was forced to lay off a thousand workers, something it had never had to do before. Clay actually visits Reedsburg (without revealing his identity, of course), and is pained at the toll that the company's troubles have had on the close-knit community.

The dénouement is rapidly approaching. Clay receives a peculiar phone call from someone who wants to talk about the Hanna Portland case. He is asked to come to a Washington hotel for the purpose. As he is on his way there, on foot, he is attacked by two white men, who pummel him and injure him seriously. Later a Hanna Portland cement bag is found under his Porsche.

As he is recovering in the hospital, Clay finally gets some good news. The SEC is suspending its investigation into his stock trades, because the doctor whom Clay had hired in the Dyloft matter—Max Snelling, who could have created trouble for Clay if he had admitted that he had shown a report of Dyloft's dangers to Clay in advance of his selling the stock—is not talking, so no action can be taken against Clay. Mooneyham's case, reports of which Clay hears from his hospital bed, is going splendidly, so Clay's firm may be soon out of its serious financial troubles. He hears that Goffman is leaning toward settling the class-action case (Mooneyham, on principle, refuses to settle). But when the verdict comes in, both Clay and Mooneyham are stunned to find that the jury has sided with Goffman.

Meanwhile, Helen Warshaw is still on the warpath. Clay feels he has no option but to declare bankruptcy. His bankruptcy lawyer supplies a quick summary of Clay's assets and expenditures:

> In the seventeen months since he'd left OPD, Clay had earned $121 million in fees—$30 million had been paid to Rodney, Paulette, and Jonah as bonuses; $20 million had gone for office expenses and the Gulfstream; $16 million down the drain for ad-

vertising and testing for Dyloft, Maxatil, and Skinny Bens; $34 million for taxes, either paid or accrued; $4 million for the villa; $3 million for the sailboat. A million here and there—the town house, the "loan" to Max Pace, and the usual and expected extravagances of the newly rich. (365)

But there is good news: Clay and Rebecca have definitively gotten back together, and they decide to spend six months in London while the bankruptcy proceedings take effect. What is more, Rodney and Paulette promise to give Clay some of the $10 million he had given them—so his landing is, if not exactly a golden parachute, relatively soft.

And that is *The King of Torts.*

It can be seen immediately that Grisham has pulled a number of punches and dodged a number of bullets on behalf of his protagonist. While seeming to present a classic tragic parabola of a figure who starts in humble circumstances, attains fabulous wealth and celebrity, and then loses it all through overreaching and hubris, in reality Clay ends up quite a bit better than he was at the start, in spite of the loss of all the pretty toys he had treated himself to during his year and a half of imitating Midas. And the fact that his pals are willing to lend a hand financially at the end means that he and his lady love can count on getting by at least comfortably, if not luxuriously, upon their return from London. His mugging by the disgruntled Pennsylvanians also goes for naught, since he recovers fully from his injuries.

And while Clay is never portrayed as purely a money-grubbing villain and repeatedly expresses a certain element of guilt and remorse over the bad things he has done, his concluding reflections on his life as a tort lawyer are banal in the extreme. All he can conclude is: "He was ashamed of his greed and embarrassed by his stupidity" (366). In the hospital he also notes that he feels "tortured" (367)—an obvious allusion to "tort," which (as the back cover helpfully states) is derived from the Latin *torquere,* to twist, and *tortus,* twisted, wrested aside. The suggestion is clearly that it is the tort lawyers themselves who are "twisted" (i.e., morally perverted). And while Grisham, as a former lawyer, is clearly not writing from the perspective of the "right-wing, trial lawyer–hating, tort-bashing, corporate mouthpiece" (325) of a reporter who on one occasion confronts Clay, the moral of the story—neatly outlined for us by Dale Mooneyham, as quoted above—is itself not exactly profound or earth-shaking.

Then there is the matter of Max Pace. We are never given any account of how he emerged from the shadows to plague Clay, or what happened to him after he had thrown the Maxatil case into Clay's lap. He simply disappears from the latter part of the novel, and at the end his whereabouts, not to mention his origin, are left entirely unaccounted for. All we hear about is this:

> Clay couldn't help but think of Max Pace, his old pal who'd gotten him into the Maxatil business. Pace, one of at least five aliases, had been indicted for securities fraud, but had not been found. His indictment claimed that he used insider information to sell almost a million shares of Goffman before Clay filed suit. Later, he covered his sale and slipped out of the country with around $15 million. Run, Max, run. If he was caught and hauled back for a trial he might spill all their dirty secrets. (364)

But of course Max does not come back to spill any secrets. But how did he get those confidential medical reports that revealed the failings of the drugs he encouraged Clay to go after? We never learn.

And if Grisham thinks that he is to be ranked as some kind of satirist on the basis of his portrayals of various seedy characters in the novel, he had better think again. His characterization of the real estate tycoon Bennet Van Horn is straight out of central casting, without subtlety or nuance. His various passages on the wealthy but still greedy tort lawyers are moderately engaging, especially the convention in New Orleans, but they too pall after a time. There is no depth or shading in any of the characters in the book, not even Clay or Rebecca. In part this is a result of the rapid pacing of the book, whereby Grisham shows himself desperate to grip his readers' attention with turn-the-page twists and turns; he succeeds so well at his task that he leaves little room for rumination on or by the characters, who seem like so many marionettes going through motions dictated from an outside source.

* * * * * * *

There is every reason to believe that the aesthetic and emotional dodges in which Grisham has engaged in these two novels are representative of his work overall. His very first novel, *A Time to Kill*, chickens out at the end in very much the same way as *The King of Torts:* here we have a sympathetic black man (a Vietnam war veteran) who, right in front of the courthouse, guns down two white men accused of raping and beating a young black woman, and who is ultimately found not guilty (even though he is clearly guilty) by a sympathetic jury upon whom the man's (white) lawyer has worked his gifted eloquence. Nothing in this dénouement, or in the novel as a whole, indicates that Grisham has come to grips with the complex interplay of race, violence, and justice that he has so artificially staged. Some naïve and ill-informed reviewers continue to make preposterous comparisons of Grisham to William Faulkner, but it is far more plausible to believe that Grisham is the Fitz-Greene Halleck or Richard Bach of our time.

# III.

# MISTRESSES OF MYSTERY

## MARY HIGGINS CLARK, SUE GRAFTON, AND PATRICIA CORNWELL

This is not the place for anything approaching an exhaustive history of the mystery or detective story. The job, in any event, has been done capably by other hands.[1] Edgar Allan Poe's three or four stories of the 1840s, featuring C. Auguste Dupin, have a claim to literature by virtue of their initiation of the genre (although antecedents have been traced back through Voltaire's *Zadig* all the way to Herodotus), their piquant style, and their elevation of the principle of "ratiocination"—the power of reason to penetrate the fog of circumstance to the hidden core of truth. But this last feature has become so commonplace and conventionalised that it can no longer constitute a rationale for considering the detective story, as such, a contribution to literature in the absence of other virtues—virtues that the overwhelming majority of detective writers do not possess.

The mystery or detective story took its time establishing itself after Poe. Wilkie Collins's *The Moonstone* (1868) is rightly regarded as a landmark, but it is so only as one of the earliest novel-length detective stories; aside from cleverness in the execution of the plot, its literary values are not high. The same must, regrettably, be said for Sir Arthur Conan Doyle's tales and novels of Sherlock Holmes (1887f.), which have not only evoked countless imitators but a legion of devotees who seek to elevate their idol far beyond his merits as an author. The Sherlock Holmes tales constitute, at best, literature of the third or fourth rank: their generally literate prose elevates them above the crassest forms of popular or pulp writing, and their evocation—more by accident than design—of the "gaslight" era of the late nineteenth century endows them with a certain sociological significance that can translate into a sort of faux nostalgia; but the tales have no broader message to convey and rarely probe the psychology or morality of crime, two factors that might conceivably have lent them an augmented literary value. G. K. Chesterton attempted to do so in his Father Brown stories (1911f.), but the heavy-handed religious morality he injects in these tales becomes quickly off-putting in its laboured didacticism.

The modern detective story is, very largely, the offspring of Agatha Christie (1890–1976). Her first novel, *The Mysterious Affair at Styles* (1920), not only introduced her celebrated detective, Hercule Poirot, but was the first of a seemingly unending array of novels and short stories that Christie produced like clockwork over the next half-century. She came to dominate the detective field to such an extent that other authors either became frank imitators of her or strove consciously to avoid her influence. But Christie's work is, quite frankly, on a lower level than even Conan Doyle's: afflicted with a prose style of almost intolerable blandness, an inability to portray character except by artificial idiosyncrasies, and a marked disinclination to engage in any kind of meaningful commentary on a world that underwent extraordinary change through her long writing career, Christie carried her readers—who, like readers of popular fiction everywhere, care little for style or characterization or engagement with the real world—solely on the strength of her undeniable cleverness. But she also created what became the ultimately stultifying prototype of the "cozy" British detective story: a story laid usually in a British village, sometimes even a nobleman's castle, where a suitable number of suspects could be conveniently gathered so that, both before and after the murder, the author could deftly shift suspicion from one individual to the other before finally revealing the culprit by slight-of-hand.

In the first few decades after 1920, however, Christie did have some competition for supremacy in detection. The Americans John Dickson Carr and Rex Stout and the Englishwomen Dorothy L. Sayers and Margery Allingham produced substantial series of mystery novels, although none of them attained Christie's spectacular popularity. I have, for my sins, read every one of John Dickson Carr's novels and tales and have even produced a "critical study" of them; but while enjoying them richly as a frankly guilty pleasure, I am not deceived as to their lack of literary substance:

> . . . if one does not have anything to say, it makes no difference how cleverly or entertainingly one says it. Carr, fundamentally, had nothing to say. This brutal

truth—that Carr had no significant or profound view of the world or of human relations to convey through his work—is what will rank him even lower than such figures in detective fiction as Margery Allingham or Rex Stout, who cannot approach Carr's pure narrative skill. . . . No one's view of life will be changed by reading Carr.[2]

The same could be said for almost every mystery writer who has ever written.

The "cozy" British detective story produced a strong reaction in certain literary figures, chiefly American, who came to be called hard-boiled writers. The earliest, and still the best, of these—all of them Californians, oddly enough—were Dashiell Hammett, James M. Cain, Raymond Chandler, and Erle Stanley Gardner. The first three of these deserve enshrinement as genuine contributors to literature if only because they lifted the murder tale from what it became all too frequently in the work of Christie and her successors—a kind of literary crossword puzzle, where the actual murder is regarded merely as a conundrum to be solved, with no particular emphasis placed on the moral, emotional, or psychological effects that sudden death produces in real people. To be sure, some of the work of the hard-boiled writers was itself somewhat stylised, and it does not always come much closer to the gritty realism they claimed for themselves than the British mysteries they despised; but, whatever their failings, their novels and tales did place a far greater emphasis on the seriousness of the crimes being committed in them and the tough, often sordid, methods that detectives (private or official) sometimes utilised to solve them. And the prose of Cain and Chandler, at any rate, merits high regard for its own sake.

Gardner, sadly enough, began promisingly but then deteriorated into a formula writer when he discovered how easily he could contrive short but complex plots focusing on his central figure, Perry Mason, who would later become a popular icon in television and film. As the years passed Gardner took to recording his novels into a Dictaphone, anticipating Barbara Cartland in that regard by a few decades. The result is that these novels are thin in every sense of the word: skimpy on scene description, skeletonic in character portrayal, and largely carried forward by dialogue, they amount to little but fleshed-out plays or screenplays.

The hard-boiled school led to the development of what can generally be called crime writing, where the emphasis is on the crime rather than on some presumably charismatic detective chosen to solve it. Perhaps the best writer of this sort is Patricia Highsmith, whose work of the 1950s and 1960s is so chilling in its ruthless analysis of the psychology of crime that it achieves genuine literary status. But Highsmith's dour, even misanthropic, worldview is not likely to win her a popular audience. Another very clever writer is Margaret Millar, who at roughly the same period produced a succession of psychological crime novels endowed with powerful and subtle character portrayal and a prose style of marked fluidity and grace. *A Stranger in My Grave* (1960) is, to my mind, an unrecognised classic of the form, and a number of her other novels are not far behind. The work of John D. MacDonald and Ross Macdonald (the husband of Margaret Millar), falling somewhere between the hard-boiled novel and the crime novel, has some merits beyond mere cleverness of execution, especially the latter.

It need hardly be remarked that the detective or crime story has flourished in the media of television and film. The great majority of persons—at least of a certain generation—who, when attempting to picture Sherlock Holmes, will undoubtedly conjure up the image of Basil Rathbone. Raymond Burr *is,* for all practical purposes, Perry Mason. Dorothy L. Sayers's Lord Peter Wimsey has been featured in two different series on British television. And, of course, the *film noir* of the 1940s and 1950s is a direct evolution of the hard-boiled crime novel. The pure detective story is not as frequently adapted for film or television today as in the past, perhaps as a result of the proliferation of television shows focusing on crime or detection, ranging from "Murder, She Wrote" to "Law and Order" to "CSI." A mystery novel today has to be spectacularly popular to make it to the big screen, and even some of our most popular bestsellers have to settle for the rare television miniseries.

It is curious how many women writers have excelled—if that is the term—at the detective story. The list seems well nigh endless: one can go all the way back to Anna Katherine Green and Mary Roberts Rinehart, and on through Christie, Sayers, and Allingham to Josephine Tey, Ellis Peters, Ngaio Marsh, Gladys Mitchell, and on to the present with P. D. James (much of whose later work is genuine literature, although in a few cases rather self-consciously so) and Ruth Rendell. Three of the most popular mystery writers of today— Mary Higgins Clark, Sue Grafton, and Patricia Cornwell—represent three distinct phases of the contemporary detective story, and each has established herself as a perennial bestseller.

\* \* \* \* \* \* \*

Mary Higgins Clark (b. 1929) took to writing relatively late in life. After receiving a B.A. from New York University, she was, for a time, a flight attendant before becoming a radio scriptwriter and producer for Robert G. Jennings Co.; she later became vice president of radio programming for Aerial Communications. Her first novel, *Where Are the Children?* (1975), appeared when she was forty-six, and a widow with five children. She has, in all, written twenty-eight novels, six short story collections, and two novels co-written with her daughter, Carol Higgins Clark. Six or seven of her novels have been adapted for film or television. A bestseller almost from the beginning, she has sold at least fifty million copies worldwide.

Clark is a fair representative of the orthodox whodunit stretching back to Agatha Christie and Dorothy L. Sayers. Although, as an American, she sets her novels chiefly on this side of the water, their atmosphere is surprisingly similar to that of the "cozy" mysteries of two or three generations ago. I have little reason to believe that the novel of hers that I sampled, *Moonlight Becomes You* (1996),[3] is in any way unrepresentative of her work.

The novel opens dramatically with a two-page chapter, entirely in italics and dated October 8, depicting someone named Maggie who appears to have been buried alive. Well, that sounds promising! Very quickly we learn, as the book proper begins (on the date of September 20), that this is one Maggie Holloway, who is attending a family reunion of her old boyfriend, Liam Moore Payne, in New York City. There she meets her ex-stepmother Nuala Moore, who lives in Newport. She and Maggie had become very close in the years when Nuala was married to Maggie's father.

We now move to September 27—less than two weeks away from Maggie's live interment—and find Maggie in Newport, awaiting a dinner party that Nuala is holding in her honour. In another brief chapter we find that an unidentified man comes early and pays Nuala a visit—surely to no good end. In another chapter we learn that Malcolm Norton, Nuala's lawyer, is eyeing her property covetously because he hopes he can make an immense profit on it if he could buy it from Nuala, as she had tentatively agreed, and then re-sell it. Manifestly, this is nothing less than a Motive for Murder. Other characters who will play a role in the case are also introduced, although in a less sinister fashion. Sure enough, when Maggie comes to Nuala's house, she finds Nuala inside—dead. Clearly she has been murdered. But the house has also been ransacked, as if the murderer had been looking for something—what could it be? We quickly learn that, only the day before, Nuala had changed her will, cancelling the sale of the house to Norton and leaving all her effects to Maggie. This is one of the most venerable tools in the detective writer's arsenal—the new will that changes everything. How often this actually happens in real life, let alone how often it leads to murder, does not trouble our valiant and prolific authors of whodunits. But the one thing we know is that Maggie herself cannot possibly be a suspect in the crime, if only because of that opening chapter where we saw her interred alive. In any event, several chapters have related her activities in the hours before the scheduled dinner party, so there is no possibility of her having committed the murder.

Norton, meanwhile, is in deep trouble because he has already taken out a second mortgage on his own house in the expectation of buying Nuala's; now he will have to try to persuade Maggie to sell the property. Another person whose hopes are dashed is Barbara Hoffman, Norton's secretary. They have been having an affair, and she was setting store on the prospect of Norton's divorcing his shrewish wife, Janice, and marrying her; but now she doubts whether that will happen, and she is contemplating leaving his office and departing for parts unknown. Another chapter reveals that Janice knows all about her husband's philandering, and in fact holds him in deep contempt for his repeated failures to make something of his life.

Maggie concludes that Nuala was not killed by a random thief; there was no violent break-in, and she would only have opened the door to someone she knew. Could it have been one of the prospective dinner-guests? This scenario also replays one of the hoariest devices of mystery writing: the convenient gathering of a suitable number (at least five or six) of suspects, around whom suspicion can revolve from one to the other as evidence of motive, opportunity, and temperament is gradually revealed. Chet Brower, the chief of police, also thinks the murderer was known to Nuala. Brower, incidentally, plays relatively little role in the whole business, and the chief exercise of deduction is conducted by Maggie herself, who fulfills the dual role of (nominal) suspect and investigator.

Maggie is disinclined to sell the house to Norton, in spite of his repeated importunings. Maybe she will live there, in spite of the dreadfulness of knowing that her ex-stepmother was killed on its premises. A new wrinkle is introduced when Greta Shipley, an elderly friend of Nuala's who is residing at an expensive retirement home called Latham Manor, dies. To be sure, she was old—but is this death entirely natural? Did Dr. William Lane, who operates the home, want her removed so that Eleanor Robinson Chandler, a spectacularly wealthy heiress, could occupy Greta's room? What is more, could the room that Greta occupied have been the same one that had previously been occupied by Constance Rhinelander, who has also died recently? At this point Clark reports a thought going through Lane's mind: "*Be careful,* Lane warned himself. In future you've got to be much more careful" (145). This would seem to be a dead giveaway, but as we are less than halfway through the book, it cannot possibly be a revelation of the identity of the murderer. So we read on.

Maggie finds herself in a nearby cemetery. (It is now October 4.) She finds something very curious: several of the graves have bells on them. Do they reflect some local superstition? Then she hears of a legend told to the residents of Latham Manor by Earl Bateman, a young professor of anthropology at Hutchinson College (fictitious) in Providence, that these bells are connected by a string to the interred body so that the latter can summon aid in the event of premature burial. Very shortly there after she finds A Clue: dirt in the pocket of one of Nuala's raincoats. Where could it have come from?

More sinister things are afoot. Janice Norton and her nephew, Douglas Hansen, are involved in a scheme whereby old ladies at Latham Manor are bilked of their savings through bad investments. Meanwhile, Maggie observes that the women whose graves have the bells on them had all died—presumably in their sleep—at Latham Manor. Things do not look good for the hapless Dr. Lane. Some time thereafter, Maggie finds a bell in one of Nuala's shoes: it must be the bell Nuala had removed from Constance Rhinelander's grave, as the bell was missing there. Is that what the murderer was looking for when he ransacked Nuala's house? If so, why?

Maggie had earlier been taken through a funeral museum that Earl Bateman—a rather morbid individual—had established in his home. One evening she goes back there: she wants to make sure that there are only six bells, or twelve as Bateman had originally stated were made for him. In a chapter in which Clark attempts to stoke up the suspense by depicting the hideous museum in the dark—

> Likewise, she tried not to *think* about the exhibits on the second floor, as she switched on the flashlight at the top of the first staircase. Keeping the beam pointed down, she continued up the next flight. Still, the memory of what she had seen there earlier haunted her—those two large end rooms, one depicting an ancient Roman aristocrat's funeral, the other, the coffin room. Both were grisly, but she found the

sight of all those coffins in one room to be the most disturbing. (266)

—Maggie learns that there are only six bells. It is not entirely clear what significance this business of the bells has: can Bateman be the killer, having put the bells on the graves as some sort of morbid joke? Clearly Maggie sees the matter as fraught with baleful significance: "Suddenly she was almost desperate to be safely away from this place, outside with her proof that Earl Bateman was certainly a liar, possibly even a murderer" (269). But it is too late: she is hit on the head, and we are now to understand that she has been interred in the grave, as indicated at the outset.

Things aren't exactly chipper for other characters. Malcolm Norton finds out about the activities of his wife and her nephew. Thinking that his life has come to nothing—he will not make any money from Nuala's home, his squeeze of a secretary has left him, he seems all around to be a failure at everything he has attempted—he kills himself, after preparing material on Janice and Doug Hansen to be turned over to the police. But what of poor Maggie? The opening chapter has revealed to us that there is indeed a bell on the grave in which she is interred, with a string leading down into the coffin—but the clapper has been removed from the bell, so that her increasingly frantic efforts to ring it will presumably have no effect. Who could have been responsible? The slimy Earl Bateman? One passage late in the book suggests another suspect, as Dr. Lane's wife, Odile, questions him: "You were supposed to be rushing home to see Mrs. Bainbridge last night. Not that you'd have been allowed anywhere near her, but I hear you didn't show up at the residence till nearly eleven. What were you *doing* until then?" (280).

Earl Bateman now comes to the fore. He reports to Chief Brower that one of his caskets has been stolen during the night. Does this clear him of complicity in Maggie's interment? Surely he would not proffer this information on his own, as he does, if he were involved. But the matter comes to a head very quickly. The murderer stands over Maggie's grave, taunting her. It becomes immediately evident that it is not Dr. Lane, as the murderer notes, "When they exhume those women, they'll blame Dr. Lane for their deaths" (297). Is it Bateman after all? No: the murderer is the person who (secretly) owns Latham Manor. This person is revealed, a bit later, to be . . . Liam Moore Payne. This revelation occurs, almost in passing, a full six chapters prior to the end, and seems oddly telegraphed and lacking in fanfare. All that remains, therefore, is to see how Liam is finally caught—and, of course, the small point of how

Maggie is to be rescued from her interment. As for the former: we are treated to lugubrious reflections on the part of the murderer:

> It was all unraveling, he thought glumly. They knew he owned the residence. Earl had already started to suspect that he had been the one in the museum last night. The bodies were going to be exhumed, and they'd find that the women had been given improper medications. If he was lucky, Dr. Lane would be blamed, but Odile was ready to crack. They would get a confession out of her in no time. And Hansen? He would do *anything* to save his own skin.
>
> So that leaves *me,* Liam thought. All that work for nothing! The dream of being the second Squire Moore, powerful and rich, was gone. After all the risks he had taken—borrowing from his clients' securities; buying the residence on a shoestring and pouring money into it; figuring out Squire-like ways to get other people's money—he was, after all that, just another failed Moore. Everything was slipping through his fingers. (323)

The only mystery in this the role of Odile, Dr. Lane's wife. We later learn that it was Odile who, on Liam's orders, switched medications on some of Lane's patients, so that they would die. (This would be convenient for them, because residents at Latham Manor paid an immense sum up front for their care, so that it was to the advantage of the owners that their stay be as short as possible.) Lane, for his part, is not guilty of murder, but merely of medical incompetence. Maggie, for her part, is rescued by Chief Brower along with Neil Stephens, a friend who has rather coyly been holding a torch for her.

My initial reaction to Mary Higgins Clark as I was reading *Moonlight Becomes You* is that, even among bestselling writers, her prose is unusually flat, stale, and lifeless. Even when dealing with presumably strong emotions, she can never raise the temperature of her prose beyond the lukewarm, as in this passage where Greta Shipley and Maggie are discussing the recent death of Constance Rhinelander:

"Was she a close friend?" Maggie asked.

"Not nearly as close as Nuala, but she lived in Latham Manor, and I had gotten to know her very well." She paused. "It's sudden, it's all so sudden," she said, then turned to Maggie and smiled. "I'd better get back. I'm afraid I'm a bit tired. It's so hard to lose so many people you care about."

"I know." Maggie put her arm around the older woman and realized just how frail she seemed. (75–76)

It is difficult to get more banal than this. It stupefies me how Mary Higgins Clark could have attracted the audience she has. For all that the detective story, as conventionally practiced, is a highly artificial genre with virtually no relationship to the real world and how the real world (and real human emotions) operates, one can at least say that the most distinguished—or, at any rate, popular—mystery writers have had something distinctive about them: the unique air of gaslight London in the Sherlock Holmes tales; the highbrow air of aristocracy of Dorothy L. Sayers; the fiendishly convoluted plots of John Dickson Carr, frequently spiced by a suggestion of the supernatural; the quietly clever scenarios of Agatha Christie; and so forth. There is nothing even remotely distinctive about Mary Higgins Clark. Her prose is soporific; her attempts to shift suspicion from one character to the other are predictable and mechanical (and further marred by artificial attempts to create suspense: "He could not shake the ominous feeling that something was wrong" [173]); her characters are all cardboard, and their supposed flaws of temperament—in this case, Norton's thirst for money, Odile Lane's desire to be well respected in the community, Earl Bateman's morbid obsession with death—are all transparently contrived merely for the sake of throwing suspicion upon them. It would be hard to contend that *Moonlight Becomes You* (a title that has virtually no bearing on the scenario) is a poor specimen of her work, for it is her sixteenth book overall and her thirteenth novel. The dust jacket of the book proclaims that all her previous books have been bestsellers, so presumably this is no better or worse than any of the others.

Clark is also guilty of an unusual number of simple gaffes that one would not expect a practiced writer to commit. Aside from the nearly universal error of writing "disinterestedly" when she means "uninterestedly" (286), she misspells the adjective "tony" as "toney" (178). In a book of 332 pages of very large type and generous leading, she has 93 chapters, not counting the opening italicised two-pager about Maggie's interment. Some of these chapters (e.g., 44 [164–66]) are less than two pages long.

But the worst thing about *Moonlight Becomes You,* as with this kind of puzzle-mystery in general, is the author's (and, presumably, her many readers') staggering lack of concern over the actual death by violence of a human being. Readers of mystery fiction have been so conditioned to accept this dreadful act as merely the trigger for a presumably entertaining conundrum and hunt for the perpetrator that all the emotive force behind the notion of murder is drained at the outset. It simply doesn't *matter* whether someone has been killed; all that matters is that, with the crime, a pleasurable chase can begin. And the fact that, even with the purportedly strong motives of monetary gain or sexual jealousy or any of the other motives put forth as potential incitements to crime, the great majority of human beings would be hardly likely to commit an act of murder is blithely ignored: there must be a body, after all, and even these motives are rarely treated with the seriousness they deserve, being instead merely pinned on to the various characters so that the reader can be tickled at the prospect of a substantial group of individuals each of whom is theoretically capable of committing the ultimate crime. Death, in a murder mystery of this sort, is about as real as in a video game.

* * * * * * *

Sue Grafton (b. 1940) is quite a bit younger than Mary Higgins Clark, but her literary career began more than a decade before Clark's. Her first novel, *Keziah Dane,* dates to 1967; it was followed by *The Lolly-Madonna War* (1969). Her "alphabet" series began with *"A" Is for Alibi* (1982). In all, she has written twenty-one novels and one short story collection. Only one of her novels, her first, has been adapted for film; in fact, she co-wrote the screenplay herself, along with one Rodney Carr-Smith. She has done several other screenplays and teleplays, including the adaptation of two novels by Agatha Christie.

Surprisingly, Sue Grafton writes hard-boiled detective novels. I say surprisingly because, up to recent years, this subgenre has been the exclusive bailiwick of male writers—from Hammett and Chandler in the 1920s and 1930s to James Ellroy and Elmore Leonard in the present day. But Grafton, along with Sara Paretsky, has invaded his domain successfully. A rather more regrettable tendency to which she is addicted is the corny use of sequential or related titles, as exemplified in her "alphabet" series. It is difficult to know when this tendency began—at least in detective fiction—but one may trace its origins at least to the novels of John D. Macdonald, nearly all of whose titles have colours of one sort or another in them (e.g., *The Deep Blue Good-by* [1964]). In the 1960s and 1970s Harry Kemelman wrote a dozen novels about a rabbi detective, many of them citing a day of the week or (after he had run out of them) merely the word "day." We are also faced today with writers such as Lilian Jackson Braun with her "cat" mysteries and Janet Evanovich's Stephanie Plum series, each of which features a number in the title. It is not entirely clear what purpose is served by this kind of quasi-uniformity of title: does it really promote sales by compelling readers to buy each novel in the series as it appears? If readers like a novelist, they will buy his or her work in any case; if they don't, they are not likely to be influenced by the suggestion (largely false, as it happens) that the newest book is part of an ongoing and intimately connected series that must be read—and purchased—sequentially.

But no matter. This is a minor flaw in a writer who proves to be surprisingly creditable. Let us turn to her actual work.

*"O" Is for Outlaw* (1999)[4] is a kind of historical detective novel, set in the remote period 1986—a time when, as the author informs us in a prefatory letter "to the reader," her plucky detective, Kinsey Millhone, is "without access to cell phones, the Internet, or other high-tech equipment used by modern-day private investigators." Millhone is thirty-six years old at this time and living in Santa Teresa, California. She is startled when a scavenger, Ted Rich, who makes a kind of living by buying up property abandoned in self-storage units and put on auction, tells her that he has some personal items belonging to her (school reports, a yearbook, and the like). They had belonged to an ex-cop, John Russell. But Millhone, in her first-person narration, quickly tells us that "'John Russell' was the alias for a former Santa Teresa vice detective named Mickey Magruder, my first ex-husband. What the hell was going on?" (16). What the hell, indeed. I find it rather remarkable that the existence of this ex-husband was not revealed, or even alluded to, in Grafton's fourteen previous novels, all of which deal with Millhone and presumably inform us in scrupulous detail of her past history. But there it is. (Shortly thereafter we learn that Millhone's parents had died when she was five years old [30]—another fact that, evidently, had not been revealed in previous novels.)

Millhone initially scorns Rich's offer to buy back the material. Instead, she takes more decisive action. She manages to find out where Rich lives, breaks into his house, and finds the name of the storage company where the material had been stored. In the process, she is almost caught by Rich and his dog, but narrowly manages to escape. Millhone ponders why Mickey let the rent on his storage unit lapse—does he need money, or is he in worse trouble? Mickey had left the force after a confrontation with one Benny Quintero:

> This was March 17, St. Patrick's Day, and Mickey was off duty, drinking at the Honky-Tonk with a bunch of buddies, who supported his account. He claimed the man was drunk and abusive and exhibited threatening behavior. Mickey removed him bodily to the parking lot, where the two engaged in a brief shoving match. To hear Mickey tell it, he'd pushed the guy around some, but only in response to the drunk's attack. Witnesses swore he hadn't landed any blows. Benny Quintero had left the scene, and that was the last anyone reported seeing him until his body was discovered the next day, beaten and bloody, dumped by the side of Highway 154. (43–44)

Mickey resigned to avoid questioning from Internal Affairs as well as from the district attorney's office. No charges were ultimately filed, in spite of the fact that Mickey's whereabouts for four hours of that night were unaccounted for: could he have met Quintero later and beaten him to death? It was at this time that Millhone divorced him, apparently because Mickey had asked her to cover for him for those four missing hours.

In the package of material obtained by Rich, however, is a letter from Millhone that she had never opened and read. It is from Dixie Hightower, a bartender at the Honky-Tonk, who admits that Mickey was sleeping with her that night. In her illiterate way she writes poignantly: "He's completly innocent and desperetly needs your help. What difference does it make where he was as long as he didn't do it? If you love him, you should take his part insted of being such a bitch" (39). Well, that's not the kind of letter to soften up the tough Millhone, but nevertheless she feels enormous guilt that she never opened the letter and took appropriate action that might have saved Mickey's career—for, as the letter states, "Being a cop is his whole life, please don't take that away from him" (39).

Dixie is now married to a crippled and embittered Vietnam War veteran, Eric Hightower. This sounds hackneyed enough, but Grafton effects a clever twist: they have implausibly become fabulously wealthy by manufacturing designer wheelchairs. As an old friend of Mickey's, Peter Shackelford, explains: "Custom jobs with all the bells and whistles, depending on the disability. Now he's added sports chairs and prostheses. He has a plant in Taiwan, too, making parts for other companies. Donates a ton of stuff to children's hospitals across the country" (55). Millhone visits the Hightowers' palatial estate. Grafton is good on portraying the social gulf that separates the two women, as Millhone is unused to gallivanting around high society:

> Like her, I wore jeans, though mine were cut without style, the kind worn to wash cars or clean hair clots from the bathroom standpipe. In the years since I'd seen her, she'd risen in social stature, acquiring an almost indescribable air of elegance. No need to wear diamonds when plastic would do. Her jacket was wrinkled in the manner of expensive fabrics . . . linens and silks . . . you know how it is with that shit. (60)

Dixie, however, does not know where Mickey is and dismisses Millhone's quiet outrage at her philandering with her husband ("He and I were an item long before the two of you met. He broke it off for a while and then he came back. Why attach anything to it?" [64]). Millhone, however, manages to get Mickey's address from Mark Bethel, Mickey's former lawyer. Just as she is about to take further action, she is startled to learn from two policemen who come to interview her that Mickey has been shot twice and is in critical condition. The policemen are there because Millhone's gun, which Mickey had given her (touchingly) as a wedding present, was found at the scene. The policemen further inform her that Mickey had placed a thirty-minute phone call to Millhone's number. She is, of course, astounded, as she never spoke to Mickey then.

So Millhone again cuts through a lot of red tape . . . and breaks into Mickey's bungalow. Searching the place thoroughly, as only a private detective can, she finds all kinds of interesting items: fake identification cards for any number of Mickey's aliases, a large roll of twenty-dollar bills inserted into a metal curtain rod, and a "handful of gold coins" in a pipe in the bathroom. On the way out, Millhone talks to Mickey's elderly landladies, who tell her that had had a recurrent visitor of late—"one of those motorcycle types" (116). She is considering renting the place herself, in order to examine it more carefully. She is there one night when a man comes calling gruffly for Mickey, then actually breaks a window with the evident intention of entering the place. But eventually the man slinks off. A neighbor who caught a glimpse of the intruder says that this person had a habit of showing up every few weeks. Is there some kind of collusion—or, worse, blackmail—going on?

Millhone discovers that Mickey had lent Tim Littenberg, the son of a deceased policeman, $10,000. What could this possibly have been for? She later finds that Tim is now the owner of the Honky-Tonk bar—very suspicious! A further curious fact emerges: a week before he was shot, Mickey had gone to Louisville, evidently to track down a boy at the Louisville Male High School, one Duncan Oaks, who had become a reporter and had died on assignment in Vietnam in 1965. Meanwhile, back in Santa Teresa, Millhone sees a man on a motorcycle going into the Honky-Tonk and talking with Tim Littenberg. Does this have any significance?

Millhone, invited to a cocktail party by the Hightowers, is startled to find Dixie wearing a necklace that was in Mickey's room the first time that Millhone was there, but that subsequently went missing. The mysterious man on the motorcycle is now identified as one Carlin Duffy—who proves to be none other than the brother of the late Benny Quintero. At the Honky-Tonk she meets an individual named Delbert Amburgey—but this was one of the names on the batch of fake identification cards in Mickey's bungalow. Could Mickey have been involved in a phony identification business being run out of the Honky-Tonk? She quickly informs the Secret Service. Meanwhile, she manages to talk with Carlin Duffy, who claims he has actually become friends with Mickey—he (Carlin) accepts Mickey's account of the confrontation with Benny and holds no hard feelings.

Millhone now goes to Louisville, for she feels the business of Duncan Oaks may be the key to the whole case. She talks with a retired newspaper editor, Porter Yount, who had hired Duncan. Although supposedly killed in Vietnam, his body was never recovered. Is Duncan actually alive? She then goes to the Louisville Male School and looks at an old high school yearbook. The prom king is Duncan; the prom queen is one Darlene LaDestro—but Millhone recognises her as Laddie Bethel, the wife of Mickey's former lawyer, Mark Bethel, who had also been in Vietnam. Had Duncan fooled around with Darlene, and had Mark found out and killed him in Vietnam? And did Benny Quintero, who had also been in Vietnam, learn about it? Did Mark—who has aspirations for political office and can't risk having skeletons from his past come out at an inopportune time—kill Benny, then shoot Mickey, who had also pieced together the whole sordid business with Duncan Oaks? It would seem so, as Millhone, confronting Bethel, gets him to confess to the crimes. But he also discovers that Millhone is wearing a hidden tape recorder, and so he pursues her in his wife's BMW. She heads for Duffy's ramshackle house, and as she is confronted by Mark, the latter is dispatched by Duffy by running him over with a tractor:

> The metal lip banged into Mark's chest with an impact that nearly lifted him off his feet, driving him back against the side of the wall of the shed. For a moment, he hung there, pinned between the bucket and the wall. He struggled, his weight pulling him down until the lip of the bucket rested squarely against his throat. Duffy looked over at me, and I could see his expression soften. He propelled the tractor forward, and Mark's nearly severed head thumped in the bucket like a cantaloupe. (314-15)

In an epilogue we learn that Tim Littenberg and others are busted for their fake identification scheme. Mickey ends up dying from his gunshot wounds.

Somewhat surprisingly, of all the writers studied in this book Sue Grafton probably has the most substantial claims to literary respectability. There are, to be sure, some gaffes in her prose: the now universal "disinterested" for "uninterested" (86), the nearly universal "disassociated" for "dissociated" (26), and so forth. There is also the overriding problem, in this novel, as to who the titular "outlaw" is: has this word been chosen to any meaningful purpose? Is the outlaw Mickey Magruder; the biker, Carlin Duffy; the late lamented Benny Quintero? One gains the suspicion that *"O" Is for Outlaw* was chosen as the title only because it sounds good, not because it has any vital significance to the scenario.

A more serious flaw is Grafton's penchant for describing Millhone's actions in painful detail, even when these have little relevance to the advancing action. Consider this passage:

> I woke to the smell of coffee. I was still wearing Mickey's jacket, but someone had placed a heavy afghan across my legs. I put a hand above my head, feeling across the pillow, but Dorothy [a cat] was gone. The door was open a crack. Sunlight made the curtains glow. I looked at my watch and saw that it

was close to eight. I put my feet over the side of the bed and ran a hand through my hair, yawning. I was getting too old to horse around at all hours of the night. I went to the bathroom and brushed my teeth, then showered and dressed again. In the end, I looked much as I had when I'd arrived. (135–36)

It will be observed that seven of these nine sentences begin with "I"—that dangerous pitfall of first-person narration for inexperienced writers, but one that an author of Grafton's advanced years should by no means have committed.

On the whole, however, Grafton's prose, while certainly not rivaling the rich, metaphor-laden lyricism of Raymond Chandler, achieves its purpose in its hard-edged, tight-lipped grimness, laced with flashes of dry humor. Her plot is executed with cleverness and subtlety, and it is complex enough to require a fairly lengthy novel (by hard-boiled detective standards) to execute. It may be argued that the whole business of the fake identification scheme at the Honky-Tonk has no intimate bearing on the rest of the case, which involves the tracking down of an old crime committed in Vietnam; but it is a nice way to link all the central figures together, and it adds richness and interest to the core plot.

There are also some moving passages, coming close to profundity, whereby Millhone reflects upon her past life and her relations with her ex-husband. On the whole, the hard-boiled detective school—in accordance with its model, the school of Hemingway—is determined to let actions speak for themselves, and to let these actions reveal fine shades of character and mood; but sometimes a passage like this needs utterance:

> Soon after the wedding, I began to realize he was out of control . . . at least from the perspective of someone with my basically fearful nature. I wasn't comfortable with what I perceived as his dissipation and his self-indulgence. My Aunt Gin had taught me to be moderate—in my personal habits if not in my choice of cusswords. At first, Mickey's hedonism had been appealing. I remembered experiencing a nearly giddy relief at his gluttony, his love of intoxication, his insatiable appetite for sex. What he offered was a tacit permission to explore my lustiness, unawakened until then. I related to his disdain for authority and I was fascinated by his disregard for the system, even

while he was employed in a job dedicated to upholding law and order. I, too, had tended to operate outside accepted social boundaries. In grade school and, later, junior and senior high schools, I was often tardy or truant, dawn to the lowlife students, in part because they represented my own defiance and belligerence. Unfortunately, by the age of twenty, when I met Mickey, I was already on my way back from the outer fringes of bad behavior. While Mickey was beginning to embrace his inner demons, I was already in the process of retreating from mine. (147)

There is a quiet honesty in this passage that manages to etch an entire life in a single paragraph—and does so without sentimentality or self-pity. As a result of passages like this—and, really, as a result of the entire course of Millhone's first-person narration—we gain a sense of her as a full-blooded, real-life figure and not merely a character in a book. Her flaws and limitations—her readiness to bend or break the law to suit her purposes; her lack of social skills or experience with her social betters, as exemplified in her owning only a single black dress to wear on formal occasions; her perhaps excessive control of her emotions, as embodied in her clipped, laconic prose—are exhibited for all to see, but not gloried in. Sue Grafton is the one writer, among those I have read for this book, whose other work I would be happy to read.

* * * * * * *

Patricia Cornwell (b. 1956) was a police reporter in Charlotte, N.C., for two years after she graduated from Davidson College; she then served for six years (1985–91) in the office of the chief medical examiner of Virginia in Richmond, where she manifestly gained the technical knowledge that serves her to this day in her detective novels, which feature Kay Scarpetta, who is in fact the chief medical examiner of the state of Virginia. Her first novel was *Postmortem* (1990), and in all she has written nineteen novels and five works of nonfiction, including the somewhat bombastically titled (or subtitled) *Portrait of a Killer: Jack the Ripper—Case Closed* (2002), in which Cornwell claims to have definitively solved the Jack the Ripper case. Others, including most authorities on Jack the Ripper, have thought otherwise. None of Cornwell's books have been adapted for film or television, although there appear to be ongoing negotiations for film rights to two or three novels.

Cornwell fits approximately into the "police procedural" sub-genre of the detective story, in which nearly the entire focus is not on potential suspects (as in the whodunit) or the criminal (as in the crime/suspense novel), but on the police who are investigating the crime. The police procedural probably grew out of the hard-boiled detective story, with its intense focus on the private detective's pursuit of crime and criminals; but the emphasis upon the police investigation frequently involves questions of legal maneuverings (including the deliberate bending of criminal statutes to follow a lead or capture a criminal) and the day-to-day operations of a police force, from the lowly policeman on the beat to the police chief and his or her assistants. Ed McBain's compact novels of the 87th Precinct are good examples of the form, and Cornwell has attracted a following with her presumably charismatic female medical examiner.

*Black Notice* (1999)[5] opens with a letter written by one Benton Wesley on December 6, 1996. In this letter, written to Kay Scarpetta, he announces a bit melodramatically: "You are reading this because I am dead." The letter really does not amount to much, merely encouraging Kay to reconcile with her niece, Lucy, and a person named Marino. Very quickly we learn that Lucy is Lucy Farinelli, who is now with the Bureau of Alcohol, Tobacco, and Firearms (ATF) in Miami, while Marino is Pete Marino, a police captain in Richmond. Benton was Scarpetta's lover and appears to have died in some hideous fashion that is never clarified in this book: he himself was, it appears, an agent with the FBI and perished after being tortured, or something of the sort. Perhaps Cornwell's previous book expounded on the matter, but, if so, it seems a trifle presumptuous for the author to pass over this point so cavalierly in the expectation that her devoted readers will have read book after book of her *oeuvre* and would therefore be clued in on the matter.

At any rate, the book proper begins with the discovery of a decomposing body found in a cargo container of the ship *Sirius*. The container was carrying German camera equipment and was sealed. The ship had sailed from Antwerp via Chester, Pennsylvania. There are no signs of injury on the body, so that it is not entirely clear whether he was even murdered or just happened to die in the container. On one box in the container is found the phrase: "Bon voyage, le loup-garou" (32). Incredibly, neither Scarpetta nor Marino, who are investigating the case, have any idea what "loup-garou" means, and Scarpetta has to call up the chef at a French restaurant to learn that it means "werewolf."

At this point the novel takes a curious turn. For large stretches we are asked to forget all about the decomposing body and turn our attention to Scarpetta's personal problems. She is, of course, traumatised by Benton's death and is not shy about admitting (in this first-person narrative) the deep emotions she feels over the matter, in spite of her otherwise grimly clipped prose. Lucy and her partner (professionally and emotionally), Jo Sanders, pay Scarpetta a surprise visit, having learned of the existence of Benton's letter from Senator Frank Lord. Lucy is herself even tougher, in exterior, than Scarpetta herself, and sparks fly as the two engage in banter on various subjects; Scarpetta wants Lucy to get out of the undercover cop business, but Lucy likes it, especially as she and Jo (who works with the Drug Enforcement Agency [DEA]) are involved in a case centering on nasty drug traffickers from South America.

Meanwhile, Scarpetta and, especially, Marino are having all kinds of difficulties with a new deputy chief of police, Diane Bray, who is making life miserable for them for reasons that are never entirely clarified. She has just demoted Marino so that he has to fit his rather corpulent frame into a police uniform, and she is also attempting to have the medical examiner's office subsumed under the control of the police department. Is it merely that she is grabbing power, or that she resents another strong female whom she envisions as a rival? Cornwell never answers—indeed, rarely even addresses—these questions; and what is worse, she takes an excruciatingly long time explaining to her hapless readers why they should even be concerned about these matters and how they relate to what the police call the Container Man. In the end all these matters do link up, but for much of the novel we appear to be dealing not with a single case but with a kind of "Day [more properly a Week or more] in the Life of a Medical Examiner."

Scarpetta finally gets around to conducting an autopsy on Container Man, at which point Cornwell, in the tried-and-true fashion of popular novelists, unleashes an impressive arsenal of technical knowledge that is presumably meant to reassure the reader that she knows whereof she speaks:

> More to the point, odors are important. They have their own story to tell. A sweet smell might point at ethchlorvynol, while chloral hydrate smells like pears. Both might make me wonder about an overdose of hypnotics, while a hint of garlic might point at arsenic. Phenols and nitrobenzene bring to mind ether and shoe polish respectively, and ethylene

glycol smells exactly like antifreeze because that's exactly what it is. Isolating potentially significant spells from the awful stench of dirty bodies and rotting flesh is rather much like archaeology. You focus on what you are there to find and not on the miserable conditions around it. (80)

I trust I am not the only reader to stumble over that curious expression "rather much." It is no typo, I assure you, for it appears several more times in the novel, so clearly it is a locution much favored by Cornwell. But, so far as I can tell, it is not English.

Scarpetta ascertains that the man in the container had actually drowned. Clearly he was killed somewhere else and then placed in the container, which was then sealed. It is at this point that we are given the rationale for the novel's title. In the language of Interpol, "An unidentified body is a black notice. . . . Usually suspected fugitives with international ties" (98). Well, that's straightforward enough.

But we now once again turn, apparently, to Scarpetta's difficulties on the job. Her assistant, Chuck Ruffin, confronts her and says that she has been acting strangely ever since Benton died: "Fact is, everyone thinks you're on your way out" (106). Angered by this revelation, she demands more information, but Ruffin is reluctant to provide it. He does say, however, that she has been failing to accept calls from grieving family members regarding the bodies she deals with, and she has also apparently been leaving curious messages on a chat room on the Internet. She is even more astounded, and is convinced that someone is impersonating her on the Internet, not to mention sending e-mails in her name (which would require that the person has obtained her theoretically secret password). Scarpetta's suspicions fall on Ruffin himself: perhaps he is seeking to replace her. She conveys her suspicions to Sinclair Wagner, secretary of health and human services. He first disbelieves her, thinking that she has become paranoid from grief; but he is quickly forced to accept her story when he discovers that she never received several e-mail messages he had sent saying that her office may be transferred to the department of public safety, a move designed to place her under the thumb of the police department. This move is being engineered by a state representative, and Scarpetta suspects Diane Bray's hand—or, more precisely, other parts of her anatomy—in the matter. (It is needless to remark, of course, that Bray is lovely—but in a tough, hard way that is presumably off-putting to those men who like something a bit softer to cuddle up with: "Diane Bray was a haughty beauty with black hair and perfect features. Her figure was stunning" [39]).

Scarpetta isn't going to take any of this lying down. She and Marino confront Bray outside of a fashionable Richmond restaurant, but they get little out of her. In any case, Scarpetta now has other concerns: Lucy calls, saying that in the course of a sting operation that went wrong she has been forced to shoot and kill two drug dealers, and that her partner Jo has been shot and is in rather a bad way. The drug cartel immediately planted bombs under her and Jo's cars, but the police defused them without injury. The police, however, feel that Lucy had best lay low, and so she hides out in Washington, D.C. Scarpetta then takes on Chuck Ruffin, who all but admits his guilt in impersonating his boss on the Internet. He also admits that Diane Bray persuaded him to act behind Scarpetta's back, and he (a basically weak man) fears that Bray is going to ask him deliberately to mess up the investigation of the Container Man case in order to make Scarpetta look bad.

This finally gets us back to Container Man. Scarpetta discovers that he had a tattoo on his back. Could this be of any significance? Scarpetta takes the unusual option of visiting Richmond's most experienced tattoo artist, a fellow named John Pit. Pit informs Scarpetta—as he looks unflappably at a section of Container Man's back that Scarpetta had brought for the occasion—that there are in fact two tattoos there, one placed directly over the other. The tattoo on top may be the figure of a bird, perhaps an owl, with two yellow dots for eyes. Scarpetta files this information away, not knowing quite what to make of it.

There are now further confrontations with Bray and her various underlings, including one Rene [no accent] Anderson, a new female police detective who appears to be Bray's dog's body. Bray, for her part, has suspended Marino without pay for insubordination—but this does not stop him from horning in on a homicide at a convenience store in Richmond, where an Asian store clerk, Kim Luong, has been hideously murdered:

> It was as if a wild animal had dragged her dying body off to its lair and mauled it. Her sweater and bra had been ripped open, her shoes and socks removed and tossed nearby. She was a fleshy woman with matronly hips and breasts, and the only way I had a clue about what she had looked like was the driver's license I was shown. Kim Luong had been pertty with a shy smile and shiny long black hair. (211)

Scarpetta is outraged that some crime-scene technicians are already at the scene and examining the body, usurping her role; it doesn't help that they are making serious blunders in the process. When Bray appears, Scarpetta is harsh with her: "I don't ever want to walk in on a scene like this again . . ." (216). This certainly doesn't ingratiate Scarpetta with Bray, but it is Marino who explodes with pent-up rage, claiming that her underlings' bumbling may render it impossible to secure a guilty verdict for the murder: "'This lady's beat-up face ain't about politics and sound bites, you goddamn-motherfucking-bitch! How'd you like it if it was your sister? Oh hell! What am I saying?' Marino threw his talc-dusted hands up in the air. 'You wouldn't know the first fucking thing about caring about anybody!'" (218).

As the body of Kim Luong is examined more carefully, it is ascertained that bite marks are found on various parts of it. What is more, there are curious long blond hairs on the body—clearly identical to hairs found in the clothing of Container Man. Scarpetta momentarily thinks the hairs may be from a baby, but dismisses the conjecture as preposterous.

More personal troubles develop. Scarpetta's secretary, Rose (last name evidently never provided), feels that she is being followed by someone in a car. She also tells her boss that she thinks Ruffin is stealing prescription drugs from crime victims. Many of these victims have died with hundreds of pills in their possession, and Ruffin—who theoretically is supposed to count them meticulously and then destroy them—might find it tempting to practice a lucrative business selling these medications on the sly. Meanwhile, the situation with Lucy is not improving. Lucy's mother, Scarpetta's sister Dorothy, comes to Richmond and gives Scarpetta an earful about turning her own daughter against her. Lucy also shows up: she admits that it was one of her bullets that hit Jo in the leg, and she is consumed with guilt about the whole incident. Matters are made worse by the fact that Jo's conservative parents won't let Lucy enter Jo's room in the hospital. (Jo has been transferred to a hospital in Richmond, conveniently enough.)

The Container Man case takes an even more bizarre twist when one Jay Talley, an ATF liaison at Interpol, calls Scarpetta and asks her and Marino to come to Lyon, France, immediately. Scarpetta is suspicious, but Senator Lord confirms Talley's identity and convinces her that the matter is highly urgent. Scarpetta and Marino make their way to France on the Concorde and meet with the secretary-general of Interpol, George Mirot. He informs them that there is a serial killer in Paris who calls himself Loup-Garou. Can Container Man be Loup-Garou? No: Loup-Garou has no tattoo—but his brother did. What is more, members of the One-Sixty-Five drug cartel—the very cartel that Lucy had become involved in—all have a distinctive tattoo consisting of two yellow dots. (The cartel's name derives from the high-caliber ammunition they are fond of using.) It appears that Container Man is one Thomas Chadonne, the son of the apparent boss of the One-Sixty-Fivers. He was apparently killed for betraying the family and the cartel. Did Loup-Garou murder his own brother and then switch clothes with him? Is this why the blond hairs are found on the *inside* of the dead man's clothing? And could Loup-Garou, having come aboard the *Sirius,* have embarked at Richmond and then killed Kim Luong? At last—three-fourths of the way through the book—most (but not all) of the variegated facets of the novel are connecting up.

Talley wants Scarpetta to see the chief medical examiner of France, Ruth Stvan, and discuss the other murders with her. She has been reluctant to talk about them, but Talley thinks that Scarpetta, as a woman and a colleague, can induce her to reveal what she knows. Scarpetta initially thinks that Talley is asking her actually to steal evidence, but Talley assures her this is not the case. Reluctantly, Scarpetta talks with Stvan, who reveals that Loup-Garou had actually tried to kill her, but had failed in the task. Stvan shows Scarpetta some of the evidence she has collected—including the long blond hairs found on several bodies. Scarpetta now thinks that Loup-Garou is afflicted with a rare condition known as hypertrichosis:

> In most hypertrichotic people, hairiness progressively increases until the only areas spared are mucous membranes and palms and soles, and in some extreme cases, unless the person frequently shaves, the hair on the face and brow can become so long it has to be curled so the person can see. Other symptoms can be anomalies of the teeth, stunted genitalia, more than the normal number of fingers and toes and nipples, and an asymmetrical face. (334)

In other words, the person would look like the conventional image of a werewolf.

It is at this point that Cornwell commits the mild gaffe of having Scarpetta and Talley have a quick sexual encounter, in spite of the fact that she is more than ten years his senior and is still grieving for the lamented Benton:

"God, you're so beautiful," he said into my mouth. "Christ, you've been driving me insane . . .!" He tore off a button and bent hooks. "Sitting there in front of the fucking secretary-general and I'm trying not to stare at your breasts."

He gathered them into his hands. I wanted it raw and without limits. I wanted the violence in me to make love to his violence, because I didn't want to be reminded of Benton, who had known how to slowly smooth me like a stone and skip me through erotic waters. (342)

But this descent into Danielle Steel-land—for it appears that Talley is actually in love with Scarpetta, or thinks he is—doesn't last long, and pretty soon Scarpetta and Marino (who has found out about his partner's dalliance and is furious—perhaps with jealousy) are on their way back to Richmond.

But if this gaffe is of small proportions, Scarpetta now another of much greater consequence—nothing more than the murder of the pestiferous Diane Bray. It is no help that the murderer is, without doubt, the notorious Loup-Garou, who apparently has a penchant for killing off any member of the police or related parties who are investigating his crimes, especially if they happen to be women; the elimination of this thorn in Scarpetta's side in such a manner has all the earmarks of a convenient *deus ex machina.* Things like this don't happen in real life, and Cornwell's whole tone throughout this book (and, presumably, her others) is an almost fanatical devotion to the grim realities of real life. Bray's sidekick, Rene Anderson, is momentarily implicated, and she does admit to having a pizza with Bray shortly before she was killed; but clearly she is not the murderer. Scarpetta and Marino do ascertain, however, that it was Anderson who had been following both Rose and Scarpetta in her car, and that she (and perhaps Bray herself) was involved in Chuck Ruffin's scheme to steal prescription drugs and resell them covertly.

Scarpetta, examining the murder site, finds some curious marks in blood on Bray's bed. She goes to a hardware store, where she determines that the marks were made by a chipping hammer—a tool used relatively rarely, and usually in construction. Marino then points out that a vacant house nearby has been under construction, as workers have been putting on a new roof. Could Loup-Garou be staying there? It appears so; but, as Marino discovers, he is not there now. Scarpetta, at her home, is startled to hear the house alarm go off. When the police come, they see that someone has tried to pry her garage door open. Shortly thereafter, someone announcing himself as the police (without a foreign accent) comes to her door. It is, of course, Loup-Garou. Evidently the simple expedient of having a small window, or even a peep-hole, in her door could have prevented her being victimised by this loathsome person. At any rate, he pursues her through the house, and she resorts to throwing a bottle of formalin (a liquid preservative used in autopsies) in his face. She then rushes outside, but falls down and breaks her elbow in the snow and ice. She is therefore unable to use her gun on the marauder. Loup-Garou follows her outside, but is still writhing in pain and nearly incapacitated. Lucy comes suddenly on the scene and wants to blow him away, just as she blew away those drug dealers in Miami; but Scarpetta, sensing that Lucy has become trigger-happy as a result of her various experiences, pleads with her not to shoot. Naturally, Lucy restrains herself. Then, in a final and even more implausible *deus ex machina,* Scarpetta's long-lost lover Jay Talley suddenly emerges on the scene and comes to take her away to a hospital.

This absurdly contrived ending leaves a bad taste in the mouth, for otherwise *Black Notice* is by no means a discreditable performance. I have mentioned that it takes a very long time for all the disparate elements of the book to come together into a unity, but in fact they do so, and in a reasonably satisfying manner. It can be seen, however, that there are really two plots in the book: the case of Loup-Garou and the troubles in Scarpetta's office involving Diane Bray, Chuck Ruffin, and others; these two threads are only fortuitously united by Loup-Garou's killing of Bray. He could have killed anyone else and the crime could have been solved just as satisfactorily.

It is a bit surprising that Cornwell has become so popular, for—at least on the basis of this book—the general atmosphere that she strives to evoke is grim to the point of lugubriousness, and I have noted that depressing writers are, on the whole, shunned by the mob. Her prose does have a few imperfections: she writes of "the *unpleasantries* of the job" (80) when she means "unpleasantnesses," and—most amusingly for a crime writer—she writes "jury-rigged" (169) when she means "jerry-rigged." Otherwise, her prose is cold, clinical, and clipped, but nevertheless capable of inducing strong emotion in the reader. One gains a clear sense of Kay Scarpetta as a woman who does not suffer fools gladly, who does her own work with ruthless competence, and who resents any encroachment upon her professional—and perhaps personal—terrain. The portrayal of

Pete Marino is perhaps rather less successful: he is nothing more than the stereotypical heavy-set, loud-mouthed cop who has the guts to say what others are thinking but are afraid to articulate. After a time, though, he simply becomes a blow-hard, and one desperately wishes that he might be the Loup-Garou's next victim.

Overall, though, *Black Notice,* like so many other detective novels, has no broader message to convey. It is simply a puzzle story, and the reader is expected to be interested in, and satisfied by, the outcome. Perhaps Cornwell made something more of the feminist implications of Scarpetta's lofty position in earlier novels; certainly, her portrayal of the odious Diane Bray, who (as Cornwell hints on a number of occasions) may well have slept her way to her place of eminence in the hierarchy of crime fighting, does not suggest that all women in positions of authority deserve to be there. In the end she even turns out to be a petty criminal, and then is cast aside by her author as merely another murder victim.

What other messages are we to draw from *Black Notice?* That a rare disease like hypertrichosis is likely to lead to psychological trauma and then to violence? That government workers who function largely unsupervised are likely to be corrupt? That lesbians are quick to the trigger? These points are either banally obvious or preposterously false, but there is nothing else in *Black Notice* that could raise it to a level of actual literature. Cornwell's prose is capable and suitable for her subject, no more; her manner of executing her plots is clever but troubled by convenient contrivances to get her to where she wants to get; and her overall purpose seems simply to present her heroine, Kay Scarpetta, going about her duties with a dogged determination that ultimately leads to a solution, as every reader could have known from the opening page. With books like this—and there is no reason to think that any of Cornwell's, or that of any other leading mystery writer's today, are any different—the suspicion that detective fiction is little more than a literary crossword puzzle is likely to linger.

# IV.

# PULSE-POUNDING SUSPENSE

## JAMES PATTERSON AND NELSON DEMILLE

The suspense novel can be considered a spin-off of the mystery or detective tale, for its chief distinction is that the identity of the killer or criminal is deliberately revealed, so that the central interest resides in the manner in which the criminal is caught—if, indeed, he is caught. By removing the "whodunit" element from the plot, suspense novels can frequently do without a know-it-all detective, one of the main aesthetic drawbacks of the standard mystery story; but a number of suspense novels do in fact involve the police or other law enforcement figures or agencies intent on tracking down the criminal. (The use of the CIA, the Secret Service, or "spies" in general, involving as it does geopolitical considerations and other elements generally absent from mystery or suspense novels, is treated in a separate chapter.)

The history of suspense fiction is, accordingly, virtually coeval with that of mystery fiction itself. Two stellar examples that come close to genuine literature are Francis Iles's novels *Malice Aforethought* (1931) and *Before the Fact* (1932). Iles is the pseudonym of British writer Anthony Berkeley Cox, who as Anthony Berkeley wrote orthodox whodunits featuring the detective Roger Sheringham; but most of these have been forgotten, while the two Francis Iles novels remain as near-classics in their field. *Malice Aforethought* is a tour-de-force in being one of the first novels in which the criminal—a doctor who murders his wife and apparently escapes detection—is known from the beginning. It is symptomatic of the influence of popular prejudice upon art that when Alfred Hitchcock filmed *Before the Fact* as *Suspicion* (1941), he was forced to change the ending (in which a man poisons his wife, with her deliberate contrivance) so that viewers would not be outraged at the portrayal of Cary Grant as a murderer.

A fair number of hard-boiled detective novels—by James M. Cain, Cornell Woolrich, Jim Thompson, and others—prove to be suspense novels of this sort, oftentimes featuring the criminal as a kind of anti-hero whose increasingly harried attempts to escape from justice become the focus of the reader's interest. Patricia Highsmith wrote *Strangers on a Train* (1951) and many other suspense novels of this sort, but her work has a grimness, literary artistry, and even an element of misanthropy that lift it far above popular writing. With the decay of the standard whodunit from a surfeit of mediocrity and an increasing sense of its complete dissociation from anything approaching reality, the suspense novel in recent decades has gained prominence in the ranks of bestsellers. Whereas only a very small number of conventional mystery writers achieve bestseller status, the suspense or adventure novel—the prototypical instigator of the "what-happens-next" syndrome designed to keep readers turning the pages—has gained immense popularity. Two of its more prominent recent practitioners are James Patterson and Nelson De-Mille.

\* \* \* \* \* \* \*

James Patterson (b. 1947) proves, surprisingly, to be better educated than most popular writers—he has a B.A. from Manhattan College and an M.A. from Vanderbilt. I am surprised because, in fact, his work is much poorer in every regard than that of nearly any of the authors considered here. Patterson began as a copywriter for the advertising firm of J. Walter Thompson Co., moving doggedly up the ladder until he actually attained the position of chief executive officer in 1988. His first novel was *The Thomas Berryman Number* (1976), and he has so far written a total of forty-one novels, some co-written with others. He is also the editor of an anthology, *Thriller: Stories to Keep You Up All Night* (2006), which pretty much sums up his own lofty aims as a writer. Four of his novels have been adapted for film or television, notably *Along Came a Spider* and *Kiss the Girls.* The first of these (1993) was his first bestseller; its predecessors had evidently sold well enough but not spectacularly, which is no doubt why he didn't give up his day job. *Along Came a Spider* also introduced his recurring hero, Alex Cross, one of whose distinctions, presumably, is that he is an African American. Amusingly, Patterson has also written two romance novels.

My own reading of Patterson has been rather more diligent than that of many of the other bestsellers discussed in this book, for reasons that will become apparent. I have kept to the focus of this book by reading only the novels of his that are actually bestsellers, although I rather doubt that these are much better or poorer than his earlier work. I began, quite at random, with a work called *The Lake House* (2003).[1]

This novel is largely the story of Frannie O'Neill, a veterinarian, and her lover, the FBI agent Thomas Brennan. In a flashback, we learn that Frannie, driving along a highway in Colorado, is startled to see a young girl—with wings! This girl, named Max, proves to be one of six children who have been genetically engineered to have wings—a practice that, as our scientifically gifted author informs us, is going on right now "in out law labs across the United States and in other countries as well" (12). Frannie and Kit rescue these six children from a dreadful place called the School, where they were being trained for some nefarious purpose. The children were turned over to their biological parents, but in the interim had bonded with Frannie and Kit, and now the latter are waging a court battle to regain custody of them. Of course, the children are distinguished by other than their bodily apparatus: "each of the six had a genius IQ" (23). It would not do to have non-genius children endowed with wings. For their part, Kit and Frannie seem made for each other. In an unwitting commentary on the violence of American life, we are soberly informed that Kit's family had died in a plane crash, while Frannie's husband was killed in a holdup.

During a break in the trial, the children choose the occasion to fly through the air, purely for relief: they become fidgety and ill-at-ease if they do not use their novel endowments from time to time. At one point a sniper named Marco Vincenti (is he with the Mafia?) is taking aim at the children—but then a mysterious voice speaking through his earphones tells him not to harm them. Well, we know now, as if we didn't earlier, that these children have bull's-eyes on their backs. But, in fact, we have already learned that possibly a worse fate is in store for them.

*The Lake House* opens with a chapter about one Dr. Ethan Kane—whose name, a homonym of Cain, immediately brands him as a villain. Even if it did not, the fact that he is a misogynist ("He considered the nurse inferior in every way, including the fact that she was female" [3]) is, as Patterson knows all too well, enough to deem him a scoundrel. But it gets worse: Kane "hated pets and, even more, those who kept them" (37), thereby condemning himself in the eyes of tens of millions of us guardians of our beloved furry or feathery friends; and there is at least one more thing: "Plus, he was paranoid" (37). I love that "plus": what would we do without the American vulgate?

It is, however, manifest that Kane is involved in some kind of diabolical medical experimentation. The prologue in which we are introduced to him is titled "Resurrection," and he is working at a place simply called "the Hospital." Is he interested in the resurrection of the dead? Would that he were involved in something so tame! It is no doubt he who countermanded Vincenti's orders to blow the winged children away. To be sure, Kane himself is scarcely one to eschew violence: earlier, he had raided Frannie's office and looked through her files, and when an assistant came to investigate, he "pulled a handgun from his jacket pocket and shot the large woman twice" (38). I guess she needed two bullets, being so large.

What is worst of all, in terms of our judgment of Kane, is the fact that he is married to some kind of android or Stepford wife. As he comes home from a hard day's work playing the mad scientist and randomly killing those who stand in his way, he is greeted by Juliette, his wife. He then pushes some buttons on a "compact black case from his pocket" (124), and a bit later the two of them head to the bedroom: "'Let's go up to bed, darling,' he whispered against her ear as she lightly stroked the front of his trousers. He put one hand on a pert, nicely rounded breast, the other between her legs. What waited there for him was the perfect *fit*. Kane knew that for certain. He'd measured" (124). All the most beautiful breasts, somehow, turn out to be "pert."

But back to the trial. The judge, after listening to testimony from all sides, issues his ruling:

> "Here is my decision. . . . The petitioners, Dr. O'Neill and Mr. Brennan, have taken on the task of demonstrating that the custody of these minors by their parents would be detrimental to their well-being. They state that the children will not be happy, or *safe*, with their biological parents. The children seem to believe this as well. That's important to this court. It carries weight with me. But Dr. O'Neill and Mr. Brennan have not sufficiently proved their case. Not today anyway. Accordingly, I must rule that the children stay with their parents." (60–61)

Naturally, Frannie and Kit are crushed; but that "Not today anyway" is the giveaway: every reader knows that the children will ultimately end up with their rescuers, so this is merely a temporary setback that allows Patterson to get on with the plot.

Max, aged thirteen, appears to be the leader of the band of children. At one point a reporter, Linda Schein, tries to query her about something called the Resurrection Project at the Hospital. Now of course the reader knows that *something* of the sort is going on there, but doesn't know exactly what. Max herself is frightened and refuses to answer the reporter's questions; in fact, she warns her: "Don't dig into this subject, Ms. Schein. Please believe me. If you talk about it, you could die. I'm not exaggerating. *You talk, you die*" (102). But the heedless reporter pays no attention, and presently she is Kane's next victim.

Kane is intent on capturing at least Max and the next-oldest child, Matthew, alive. But Max is on to his plans, and she arranges for all six to flee their respective homes and come to the waterfront cabin owned by Frannie, which they call the Lake House. This is the place where Frannie and Kit first tended to them after they had escaped from the School. But Kane is no slouch, and he knows that that is where they are headed. (It is only at this point that we discover that Frannie's husband was killed because he had learned at least something about the School, as Frannie reflects with originality: "He had found out too much about the School, and the bastards had killed him" [165].) Kane and his cohorts have surrounded the Lake House and seem on the verge of capturing their victims, but Frannie burns down the cabin to create a diversion and then flees in her SUV (I'm glad to know these gas-guzzlers are good for something). Kit later joins them. But they are scarcely out of the woods. A new batch of gunmen track them down in their motel, but the children—with Kit lending a hand—by some miracle manage to subdue them.

At this point, the FBI intervenes. Taking charge of all the children, as well as Kit and Frannie, the agency takes them back to Washington, D.C. The FBI believes that the Hospital is somewhere in Maryland—perhaps the Liberty General Hospital, within which is the Hauer Institute (note the sinister, German-sounding name), run by one . . . Dr. Ethan Kane! Kane is, on the surface, involved in some cutting-edge research; in fact, he has won the "American Society of Transplant Surgeons' Pioneer Award" for "breakthrough research with stem-cell therapies" (260). But there is more to it than this: Kane admits that he is experimenting with the transplantation, not of single organs, but of entire organ systems, which appears to work better and involve less rejection of the transplanted material by the host body. All this sounds noble and valuable, but of course we the readers know that something much more evil is going on.

A bit later, Kane and his gang confront Max and the other children at a motel (Frannie and Kit have conveniently gone shopping). The redoubtable Marco Vincenti has now returned to the scene. He is focusing his gun on a child named Ozymandias (evidently Patterson thinks we ought to be impressed that he has read at least one sonnet by Shelley), nicknamed Oz, who is flying right toward him. Marco shoots—does he hit him? Marco doesn't have time to enjoy the achievement, for another winged child, Peter, now comes at him with a rock in his hand and kills the sniper. Max, in the interim, has been caught in a net and taken away by Kane.

Oz has in fact been killed, and it becomes quickly evident that Patterson expects us to pat him on the back for this expression of grim realism and the eschewing of a conventionally happy ending where all the good guys are saved from the bad guys. Max reflects:

> Pictures floated before her eyes; she heard his laughter. She imagined flying with him, soaring above the clouds, caressing him.
> *But that is all such fake bullshit. Ozymandias is dead. This is no fairy tale with happy endings.*
> *This is the world—as humans see it, as they wish it to be. So sad, such a waste of potential, such a shame.* (299)

But the expression of such pompous and inane sentiments robs this incident of any genuine poignancy. In any event, it is quickly forgotten amidst the book's further adventures.

It is only at this point that we actually learn what Kane and his cohorts are up to. He has selected thirty important men (they are all men, including a former president of the United States) to come to his hospital and have their internal organs replaced by young donors. Kane himself proves to be one Dr. Harold Hauer, who was thought to have died in a car accident eleven years before; in fact, he has resurrected himself and is in the pink of health, although he is ninety-four years old. We still, however, do not know the role of the winged children in this entire nefarious scheme. Frannie, who herself has now been captured, along with Kit, ponders the matter: "Were we [Frannie and Kit] to be used as bargaining leverage? Was that it? It had to be. Kit and I were alive because we might be needed to influence the children in the next few hours. What part were they supposed to play in what was going on? What Max called

Resurrection. *Why were they so important?* The question was driving me crazy" (308). No doubt Patterson is hoping that the question is driving his readers crazy also—at least to the point where they want to keep on turning those pages to learn the answer. But he has a lot more pulse-pounding action in store.

Max, by some means or other, manages to escape her bonds and frees the other children. Then, in a spectacular encounter, she flies at Kane again and again, apparently killing him. But this is too simple a solution: it is only a clone of Kane's—one of three that exist—who has bitten the dust. (We had been introduced to these individuals earlier [265], so the reader is somewhat prepared for this eventuality.) And yet, somehow the killing of this clone results in the collapse of the entire Resurrection enterprise, in a manner that Patterson inexplicably refuses to elucidate. But the end result is that the immense climax that Patterson clearly has in mind falls completely flat.

We are, of course, not quite at the end. Although Frannie is distressed that nothing about the Resurrection Project is mentioned in the press, she has other fish to fry. A new custody hearing is held, and—in spite of the fact that the winged children have been in all kinds of near-death experiences while under the nominal care of Kit and Frannie—the kindly judge this time awards them the custody of the children. What is more, Max has given birth—to two large eggs, the product of an earlier love affair with the departed Ozymandias. So he lives, after a fashion! But the evil Dr. Kane hasn't finished his machinations. He now comes to take the eggs. This is, of course, the real Kane (or Hauer), and he finally explains why he wanted the winged children: "'Do you know why I'm here, Max? Do you know why I kept you alive all this time? Want to know the big secret? You're even bigger than Resurrection. Really and truly you are. These eggs were more important than anything I've done. I've seen the future, Max, and it flies!'" (373). The thinking is that Max has passed her winged form down to her offspring, and that this will be the new shape the human race will take—and Hauer wants to control it. But of course he first has to get rid of Max first. Uttering villainies ("I'll show you something. I'll show you pain. Then *death*" [374]), he tries to push her out the window. (How exactly this will kill her, given her ability to fly, is not entirely apparent.) But she tricks him: she grabs on to him, taking him out the window with her, then releases him: "She saw him hit a tree, then carom to the ground with a sickening thud, then he lay very still. Crumpled, twisted, *still*. As she had hoped, as she'd solemnly promised Ozymandias, she'd broken the bastard's neck" (375). And that, mercifully, is the end.

It is difficult to describe, short of profanity, the utter imbecility of *The Lake House*. Its fatuities begin remarkably early—namely, with an author's note at the beginning. Here Patterson talks about the scientific foundations for the book: "When I researched it I interviewed dozens of scientists. All of them said that things *like* what happens in *The Lake House* will happen *in our lifetime*. In fact, a scientist in New England claims that he can put wings on humans right now. I'll bet he can." And I'll bet there's a bridge somewhere in Brooklyn that I can sell to Mr. Patterson. I have no idea what quacks Patterson interviewed, but the idea that people can be genetically engineered to have wings—and, in complete defiance of Darwin, to pass on this trait to their immediate offspring—is so preposterous that it can be laughed out of court at the start. As a premise for an adventure novel, I suppose it is no worse than many others, but let us not kid ourselves into believing that it could actually happen.

The elementary aesthetic principle behind this book, and behind much of Patterson's writing, is the facile trick of letting readers know just a bit more than some of the characters, but not everything; in this way, readers can experience the requisite amount of suspense wondering when the protagonists are actually going to figure out what the whole business is about, while they themselves keep turning the pages in search of the full solution. By letting us know something, but not too much, of what Kane-Hauer is up to—all we know is that it is something unsavory and potentially evil—we are supposed to be vicariously apprehensive for Frannie and Kit as they deal with the shadowy threat he symbolises.

But the worst thing about the book, and about the work of Patterson overall, is its prose. It is *simply dreadful*. Patterson is far and away the worst stylist of any of the authors covered here—worse than the bland Danielle Steel, worse than Barbara Taylor Bradford with her "nervous ticks," worse even than the stolid Clive Cussler or the gushing Jackie Collins. He is in particular addicted to the one-sentence paragraph, thinking with touching naïveté that he can generate tension and suspense thereby:

> Max was up very late that night, getting absolutely nothing accomplished, futzing about her room.
> Anxious.
> Uncomfortable.
> Angry without reason.
> Couldn't sit still.
> Could not.

Sit.
Still. (128)

To which all I can say is:
Please.
Shut.
Up.

But it goes beyond mere sentences. Patterson, preeminently, is the writer for the ADHD crowd. *The Lake House,* consisting of 376 pages of very large print, has 107 chapters, or an average of just over three pages a chapter. Some chapters are exactly two pages. I have not found any chapter of one page (as we will find in *The Da Vinci Code*), but no doubt Patterson will get to that in the course of time, if he hasn't already done so in his other books. What is more, Patterson's constant shuffling between first-person narration (Frannie) and omniscient third-person narration is confusing and irritating—and is undertaken for the sole purpose of moving the plot forward at points where Frannie could not possibly know what is going on.

*The Lake House* exemplifies in a particularly egregious manner the ludicrous improbabilities that readers are expected to swallow in order to get to the big payoff at the end. No matter how implausible the premise, the overall scenario, or the course of action, readers are expected to take it in stride in order to come away satisfied with a slam-bang ending. But even here Patterson fails us, for his double climax—the collapse of the Resurrection Project and the death of Kane-Hauer—are both narrated in such a way as to rob them of the spectacular thrills the reader is pining for. Even on its own terms the novel fails as a work of suspense.

If there is any "message" embedded in *The Lake House* amidst its flurry of action, it is the problematical role of science in human affairs. But this is handled with typical superficiality and ineptitude. The novel consistently betrays an anti-science bias by portraying scientific advance as amoral and potentially evil, as a technician in Kane's hospital ruminates after an eighteen-year-old boy has been killed for medical research: "*This is science,* she told herself. It was important, necessary, and it was happening all around the world, but especially in China and Japan. It was essential that the United States keep up and, ultimately, surpass other countries, wasn't it?" (156). And of course, what would a novel like this be without its cardboard villain, without the faintest trace of redeeming characteristics (although evidently the American Society of Transplant Surgeons thought otherwise)? This kind of mad scientist has been a staple of pulp fiction for more than a century, and he has been stale and hack-neyed for just about that same period.

\* \* \* \* \* \* \*

Plagued by the belief that the pseudo-scientific premise of *The Lake House* (although it is in fact so preposterous as to be virtually supernatural) was not representative of Patterson's *oeuvre,* I felt the obligation to read another work of his that presumably did not fea-ture so eccentric a plot. I chose *Honeymoon* (2005),[2] co-written with one Howard Roughan. The dust jacket of this book boasts that it is the "2005 International Thriller of the Year," so presumably those in the know have passed judgment on it and found it meritorious.

At the outset of *Honeymoon,* we are introduced to Nora Sin-clair, who is distinguished (note carefully) by "small, pert breasts" (8). (I suppose it is difficult for large breasts to have a sufficiency of pertness; they are more likely to be "voluptuous.") She and her man (husband? boyfriend? sex partner?) Connor Brown live in an im-mense house in Westchester County, New York:

> It was also impeccably furnished—every room a superb blending of form and function, style and com-fort. The very best New York City antiques shops meet the best of Connecticut—Eleish–Van Breems, New Canaan Antiques, the Silk Purse, the Cellar. Signature works by Monet, Hudson River School star Thomas Cole, Magritte. A George III secretary in the library that had once been owned by J. P. Morgan. A humidor originally presented to Castro by Richard Nixon, with provenance documentation. A walk-in wine cellar that held four thousand bottles and was nearly full. (10)

Ah, what a pleasure it is to be rich! This paragraph probably cost the Floridian Patterson a certain amount of tedious research on the Internet. I especially like the bit about the "star" Thomas Cole, mak-ing him sound like the painter's equivalent of Derek Jeter or Madonna.

But it gets better. Nora is an interior decorator—hence the "im-peccably furnished" house—while Connor is a hedge-fund manager. Rather charmingly, they sit down to a meal and have double cheese-burgers . . . with caviar (11)! They met only six weeks ago, and Connor now takes it upon himself to propose to her; she gushingly accepts. "She quickly dressed, and moments later, as the limousine started to drive away, Nora called to Connor out the open back window. *'I'm the luckiest girl in the world!'"* (12).

But lest the reader think this is one of Patterson's romance novels, things take a sinister turn very quickly. Nora goes to Boston, ostensibly on business. There she meets Jeffrey Sage Walker, with whom she seems to be on terms of surprising familiarity: "Jeffrey Walker hurried down to the foyer. Then he swept Nora up in his arms. He twirled her around as they kissed for a full minute. Then they kissed again" (15). Not to be outdone in distinction by Nora or Connor, Jeffrey turns out to be an "international bestselling author of historical fiction" (16). It turns out that Jeffrey is her husband.

At once the question of plausibility rears its ugly head. How is it possible that an international bestseller's family life is not known? Only much later (see 120) do we learn that in some manner or other Jeffrey has kept his marriage secret from his adoring fans and from the press—an explanation that only compounds the difficulty. In any event, we are now informed that Nora's first husband, Dr. Tom Hollis, has died—or, rather, that he was murdered (28). It is becoming pretty clear that Nora is the culprit, especially when an interior monologue lets us in on some of Nora's thoughts:

> The fact was, Nora loved being with Connor and Jeffrey equally. Which made her decision that much harder.
> *Which one was she going to kill?*
> *First?* (30)

Passages like this make one wish that italics—and paragraphs—had never been invented.

Connor is the first to bite the dust. He is killed by something Nora slips into his drink. Let us experience his last moments:

> The glass fell from his hands and shattered. His body violently convulsed, and he was writhing in pain. His hands reached for his neck, desperate for air.
> He tried to scream. Couldn't. Nothing came out of his mouth.
> He tried to reach for Nora. She took a step back.
> She didn't want to watch and yet she couldn't turn away. All she could do was wait for the shaking and convulsing to stop again, which it finally did.

Permanently.

Conner was lying on the floor of one of the bathrooms in his 11,000-square-foot Colonial.

Dead. (49)

Well, I should say so. I don't imagine that Patterson's beginning two consecutive paragraphs with "He tried to" is his attempt to be alliterative—I doubt that he knows the meaning of the word. In any case, upon killing him Nora transfers $4.2 million from Connor's Swiss bank account into her own account in the Cayman Islands. Once again the reader ought to do a reality check: Surely Connor's lawyer or accountant ought to be able to learn fairly quickly of this missing money and suspect something underhanded? But since this would put a crimp in the novel's development, nothing of the sort happens.

We suddenly shift gears and locations. The Pine Woods Psychiatric Facility is a state-run center some distance north of Westchester. Nora's mother, Olivia Sinclair, is an occupant there: she had shot and killed her husband ("So a jury said," a nurse ambiguously notes [75]). Olivia is so far gone in dementia that she doesn't even recognise her own daughter. Evidently we are to conclude that this is a "like mother, like daughter" situation—and only much later do we learn that Olivia had killed her husband while Nora watched (154).

Things quickly become uncomfortable for Nora. A person named Craig Reynolds shows up on her doorstep, stating that Connor Brown had had a $1.9 million insurance policy and that Nora is the sole beneficiary. But since Connor died under suspicious circumstances, the claim will have to be investigated. Something smells in this whole situation, and Nora is by no means unaware of it. On one occasion, after Craig has been to her house, she follows him. What she doesn't know is that Craig is aware of her tailing him, and he leads her to what seems an innocuous and genuine insurance office. Nora's suspicions are somewhat relieved, at least for the moment. Craig, in turn, follows Nora as she flies to Boston to meet Jeffrey. There she is alarmed to discover that he has given an interview to a reporter for *New York* magazine during which he revealed his marriage to Nora.

But the situation with Craig Reynolds is not going well either. He informs Nora that the insurance investigator, one John O'Hara, has contacted the FBI about the insurance policy, and that Connor's body is going to be exhumed. It is only at this point that we learn that Craig himself is O'Hara, and that he is a federal agent. It is also around this time that we learn that O'Hara is the figure that appeared in previous chapters as the Tourist—who on one occasion shot a man in broad daylight and took a duffel bag that had a flash disk with numbers of offshore bank accounts on it. Now O'Hara kills an intruder (disguised as a pizza delivery man) who tries to take the duffel bag back. So there appears to be something more going on here than merely a crazed husband-killer.

In any event, Connor's body is exhumed—at 2 A.M. one night. Nora is there observing the event surreptitiously. But when an autopsy is conducted on the body, nothing is found. How is that possible? We don't learn the answer to this conundrum yet. O'Hara, still believing that Nora is the person he is after, now tries to get her to let her guard down, and ends up sleeping with her. But this does little to allay Nora's own suspicions. At breakfast the next morning, she feeds him an omelet: he throws it up, but otherwise manages to survive.

And yet, it appears that Nora may be genuinely falling for O'Hara, who of course she thinks is Craig Reynolds. She is still a bit suspicious, however. One day she follows him back to his house, where a mailbox reads O'HARA. So she has been duped after all! Well, this is a fine pickle. Not long thereafter she goes to Boston to be with Jeffrey and ends up poisoning him just as she had Connor. O'Hara, for his part, manages to put the squeeze on Stephen Keppler, the lawyer who had set up Nora's Cayman Islands account. Patterson leaves it unclear exactly what information O'Hara pressured out of Keppler, but readers don't have to exercise their craniums too hard over that point.

Nora, not letting on that she has penetrated O'Hara's identity, invites him to spend some time with her at a remote cabin. (Why do so many murderers have remote cabins?) She tries once again to poison him, but the pestiferous agent again manages to survive. Now pulling out all the stops, she tries to shoot him, but only ends up wounding him in the shoulder. She then drives away. Later she calls O'Hara on his cell phone and threatens his family. But the end is on the horizon. Through Olivia, the FBI manages to track Nora to a Caribbean island, where she is about to practice her husband-killing wiles on a new victim, and capture her.

We are, however, still fourteen pages from the end of the book—far too long, in a work of this kind, to be taken up merely in a rumination over the case. It is, however, exactly at this point that the novel loses whatever credibility it has. O'Hara is stunned to discover that the FBI is dropping all charges against Nora: the fact is that the FBI has been monitoring all kinds of secret bank accounts, and it is less troubling to let one murderer go free than to have this spying revealed to the world. But Nora nevertheless gets her come-uppance in what Patterson desperately hopes is some kind of poetic justice: Connor's sister poisons Nora's water bottle and kills her.

But remember that flash disk? What exactly is on it? What is the significance of all those offshore accounts? O'Hara explains at the end:

> "What I think it is, somebody in the Bureau tracked money coming and going to several offshore accounts. People trying to hide cash, lots of it, close to a billion and a half dollars. And as best I can tell, Frank, *everyone* on the printout is a contributor or 'friend' of the political party not currently in power. How about them apples?
>
> "Now that *would* be embarrassing to the Bureau, and the administration, if it had come out during Nora Sinclair's murder trial. That would be considered very unlawful, highly unethical too. Even worse than screwing Nora Sinclair, which I'm incredibly ashamed of, by the way." (311)

Incredibly.

This is a fittingly grotesque ending to a novel that doesn't have a clue what it wants to be—a murder mystery, a tale of organised crime, or a political thriller. Patterson wants to present Nora as some kind of *femme fatale,* but her characterization is so flat that she seems to kill merely for the fun of it—or for the sake of acquiring more cash so she can decorate her various homes the more lavishly. The whole business with Nora's mother is also handled with incredible incompetence. At one point Olivia slips into Nora's purse a letter that "explained so many things she'd wanted to tell her daughter for so many years but knew she couldn't" (206), but this matter is apparently forgotten, as it plays no role in the outcome.

Patterson surpasses even *The Lake House* by uncorking 117 chapters in 311 pages, or well under three pages a chapter. His prose is just as plodding and banal as ever, and I am not a sufficient scholar on the work of Howard Roughan to have any idea of what he could possibly have contributed to this work. And once again Patterson jolts the reader with sudden shifts from omniscient third-person narration to first-person narration: on page 69 we suddenly see events through the eyes of John O'Hara, but only when it suits Patterson's plot outline to do so; whenever it is imperative to show

Nora doing something out of O'Hara's purview, the third-person narration returns.

* * * * * * *

Nevertheless, my devotion to fairness compelled me to assume that the shoddiness of *Honeymoon* may have rested at least in part on Patterson's collaborator, so I forged ahead and read a third novel that he wrote all by himself: *The Big Bad Wolf* (2003).[3] This one, in any case, is a novel involving Alex Cross, the African-American detective whom Morgan Freeman portrayed in the film versions of *Along Came a Spider* and *Kiss the Girls.*

In a purportedly dramatic opening chapter, Elizabeth (Lizzie) Connolly, an attractive mother of three in Atlanta, is brazenly kidnapped in the parking lot of a shopping mall. Very quickly we learn that this was done by the order of a Russian gangster known only as the Wolf. On page 16 (the beginning of chapter 3), we suddenly shift into the first person, as Cross introduces himself as he is getting ready to go to work. He is by no means the conventional policeman, as he himself observes:

> I'd already played the piano—Gershwin—for forty-five minutes. And eaten breakfast with Nana Mama. I had to be at Quantico by nine that morning for my orientation classes, but it left time for the walk to school at around seven-thirty. And that was what I'd been in search of lately, or so I believed. Time to be with my kids.
>
> Time to read a poet I'd discovered recently, Billy Collins. First I'd read his *Nine Horses,* and now it was *Sailing Alone Around the Room.* Billy Collins made the impossible seem so effortless, and so possible. (16–17)

A cop who plays the piano and reads poetry! But note the kind of music Cross plays: nothing so snooty and highbrow as Chopin or Charles Ives, but a nice, popular, American composer like Gershwin. And his poetry reading similarly eschews esoteric versifiers like Swinburne or even Wallace Stevens, sticking to nice, safe, American poets like Collins (the books cited are actual volumes, published in 2002 and 2001, respectively). And of course there is his concern for his children, a point that will come to play a significant role in this work.

The mention of Quantico is of interest, for it appears that Cross, who had spent fifteen years on the Washington, D.C., police force, has decided to join the FBI and is in training to be an agent. Cross had already "entered the Bureau with a reputation for catching pattern killers" (20), making his skills highly marketable. A certain portion of *Big Bad Wolf* is taken up with fatuous and predictable conflicts between Cross and some of his instructors or superiors, who in their dogmatism and intolerance for unconventional brilliance make Cross's life wearisome—and the reader's as well. Cross, having previously solved a hostage situation in Delaware (I am not sufficiently learned in Patterson's work to know whether this was dealt with in a previous novel), is sent down to Atlanta to investigate the Lizzie Connolly case. He soon discovers that there have been eight other kidnappings like this one all across the country—suburban white woman being abducted, no doubt for nefarious purposes. Are we dealing with some kind of white slave ring?

At this point we are introduced to the redoubtable Wolf, who happens to be throwing a party at a 20,000-square-foot waterfront house in Ft. Lauderdale, Florida:

> *The modern-day godfather.* A forty-seven-year-old Russian now living in America and known as the Wolf. Rumored to be fearless, hands-on, into everything from weapons sales, extortion, and drugs to legitimate businesses such as banking and venture capital. No one seemed to know his true identity, or his American name, or where he lived. *Clever. Invisible.* Safe from the FBI. And anybody else who might be looking for him. . . .
>
> At six-foot-two, this Wolf could carry 240 pounds and still move like a big and very powerful animal. He circulated among his guests, always smiling and joking, knowing that no one in the room understood why he smiled, not one of these so-called friends or business partners or social acquaintances had any idea who he was. (60–61)

Cardboard villain that he is, the Wolf must be made to seem impressively formidable in order to make a worthy opponent for Alex Cross, and to make his ultimate capture or defeat a particularly notable feather in Cross's cap.

It turns out that the Wolf's actual name is Pasha Sorokin, a former KGB agent who had "become one of the most ruthless cell leaders in Russian organized crime, the Red Mafiya" (60). He is keeping Lizzie Connolly right in his house in Ft. Lauderdale—safely concealed from his well-heeled guests, of course. Among his subordinates are a pair simply called the Couple, also Russians named Zoya and Slava. At a mall in King of Prussia, Pennsylvania, they kidnap a fashion designer named Audrey Meek (I have no idea whether Patterson intends an obvious pun with that last name). Strangely enough, her two children, who are with her at the time, are deliberately left behind: why would anyone wish to leave witnesses to their crime in this manner? However, the first chink in the Wolf's armor comes when some unspecified person leaks information to the *Washington Post* that the kidnappings of Connolly and Meek might be related. The Couple then kidnap a college student named Benjamin Coffey, a gay man attending a Rhode Island college, and sell him to a Mr. Potter. It is pretty obvious what Potter intends to do with the young man:

> The buyer's name was Mr. Potter.
> It was the code name he used when he wanted to make a purchase from Sterling, when he and the seller communicated for any reason. Potter was very happy with Benjamin and he'd told this to the Couple when they dropped the package at his farm in Webster, New Hampshire, population of a little more than fourteen hundred—a place where no one bothered you. Ever. The farmhouse he owned there was partially restored, with white antique wood shingling, two stories, a new roof. About a hundred yards behind it sat a red barn, the "guest house." This was where Benjamin would be kept, where the others before him had been stored as well. (110)

So this fellow is a repeat buyer! He proves to be Homer O. Taylor, an assistant professor of English at Dartmouth. But his purchase of Benjamin doesn't last long, and for reasons not entirely clear Taylor kills him soon after buying him. (Taylor could afford this purchase, no doubt very expensive, because he had conveniently "inherited a little over two million dollars" [158] five years earlier.) We are spared details of Benjamin's demise, but Patterson attempts with pitiable foolishness to probe Taylor's disturbed psyche: "*Benjamin, dear boy,* why couldn't you have been good? Why did you bring out the worst in me when there was so much to love?" (157).

An earlier death, however, is described in some specificity. This is when the Wolf himself comes to Long Island, where the Couple live, and dispatches them for their carelessness in leaving those children behind in Atlanta. Here is how the Wolf deals with Slava: "he twisted Slava's head as if he were opening a big jar of pickles. Slava's neck snapped, a sound that the Wolf had come to love over the years. His trademark in the Red Mafiya" (149). We do not learn precisely how he disposes of Zoya, but she bites the dust also, since the FBI later finds their bodies and determines that they are the ones who had kidnapped Audrey Meek. Meanwhile, the Wolf, not finished with killing, goes to a bar in New York City and meets his ex-wife, Yulya ("tall and slender, with large breasts he'd bought for her in Palm Beach, Florida" [150]). Evidently it was Yulya and her boyfriend, Mikhail Biryukov, who had paid off the Couple to leave those children behind as witnesses, in the belief that their evidence would eventually lead the FBI to the Wolf. The latter does not take kindly to this kind of betrayal: "With dazzling speed, the Wolf pulled an ice pick from his sleeve and stuck it into Biryukov's left eye. The gangster was blinded, and dead in an instant" (151). Yulya is similarly unfortunate: "The Wolf lifted Yulya even higher in the air. Her long legs kicked violently and one of her red mules went flying, scooting under a nearby table. . . . The Wolf took his left hand out of Yulya's hair and wrapped it around her throat. He twisted hard and Yulya's neck broke" (152). Understand that this is all going on in a crowded nightclub, with dozens of witnesses; but they are so terrified at the Wolf's reputation that no one reports the crimes—exactly as the Wolf predicted.

But there are further breaks for the FBI. The person who had bought Audrey Meek, known only as the Art Director, inexplicably decides to let her go in the Pennsylvania woods. Later the FBI comes upon the house where she had been kept. The Art Director himself is found inside, dead—apparently a suicide. He has left a note telling of a seven-year obsession with Audrey, an obsession he could not act upon until "I got the opportunity to take what I really wanted, what I needed" (179). The FBI focuses on this sentence, and it is becoming clear to the agency that some kind of kidnapping ring is involved, where white women (and men) are being taken to serve as very high-priced sex slaves (the note mentions that the Art Director had paid $250,000 for Audrey).

While all this is happening, we have been intermittently treated to Alex Cross's somewhat troubled but nonetheless wholesome and satisfying home life:

Nana was sitting over a cup of tea in the kitchen when I came in. She didn't even look up. I bypassed a lecture and headed upstairs in the hopes that Jannie might still be awake.

She was. My best little girl was sitting on her bed surrounded by several magazines, including *American Girl.* Her old favorite bear, Theo, was propped in her lap. Jannie had gone to sleep with Theo since she was less than a year old and her mother was still alive.

In one corner of the room Rosie the cat was curled up on a pile of Jannie's laundry. One of Nana's jobs for her and Damon was that they start doing their own laundry. (183)

This is not designed merely to humanise Cross, as we shall see presently.

But back to kidnapping. One Francis Deegan is abducted from Holy Cross College. He is a most fetching individual, as his friend (lover?) Vince ponders:

Francis could make either sex drool, and that was Vince's private joke when they were among coeds, *"Drool, fools!"* Francis was six-foot-one, without an ounce of fat. His white-blond hair was cut in the same style he had adopted as a sophomore at Christian Brothers Academy in New Jersey. He adored Vince with all his heart, and Vince worshipped him. (215)

How touching! But poor Francis is spirited away, no doubt destined for Taylor as a replacement for Benjamin Coffey. All of a sudden, however, the FBI seems to be on the brink of breaking the case, and from an entirely unexpected direction: a fourteen-year-old girl named Lili Olsen has hacked into a private website, called the Wolf's Den, run by the Wolf, and she reads the discussion of kidnapping that the members openly engage in. Presently the FBI discovers that the Wolf is Pasha Sorokin. As one agent states: "I can't quite believe Pasha Sorokin would be personally involved in this, but if he is, it's huge. We've been interested in Sorokin for six years! We're very interested in the Wolf" (232). Now that that point has been sufficiently emphasised, let's move on.

Lili tells the FBI that she can no longer hack into the website because they have installed an eye scan that permits only members to enter it. Nonetheless, the FBI manages to figure out that Mr. Potter is Homer O. Taylor, and they follow him back to his cabin in New Hampshire. They capture him, with his purchase, Francis Deegan, thankfully still alive: "He had no clothes on. Nothing. His chest and genitals were bloodied. *But Francis Deegan was alive!*" (256). Don't you just love those one-word sentences? So punchy, so dramatic. . . .

Cross is present when Taylor interrogated, and the latter jeers at him: "What are you . . .? The FBI's idea of affirmative action?" (259). After many hours of interrogation, they manage to compel Taylor into admitting that he had made his purchases from the Wolf. But Cross is still puzzled at the overall scenario:

> It took several more hours of talking, bargaining, and negotiating, but Potter finally told me some of what I wanted to know about the Wolf, this Russian mystery man who impressed him so. Late in the day, I wrote in my notes, *This makes no sense yet. None of it does, really. The Wolf's scheme seems insane. Is it?*
>
> Then I wrote my final thought, at least for the moment:
>
> *The brilliance of it may be that it makes no sense.*
>
> *To us.*
>
> *To me.* (262)

Cross must waste a lot of notepaper if he writes notes in short little paragraphs like that.

In any case, Cross uses Taylor's eye scan to log onto the Wolf's website. Pretending to be Taylor, he asks Wolf for another young man. Fellow agent Paul Gautier will act as bait. But the attempt to capture Gautier's kidnappers goes awry: one of the kidnappers is killed, and the other two flee and escape. What is worse, Gautier himself is hit. Of course we are quickly reassured that he is still alive (it would not do to have Cross bear the responsibility for the death of a fellow agent), but Cross lamentably concludes that "the whole operation had blown up in our faces" (296).

But all hope is not lost. The FBI has traced the transfer of money from Taylor's account to an account in Dallas. Could that be where the Wolf is? Apparently not: the account is held by one Lawrence Lipton, an American businessman. Cross interviews Lipton in his office, addressing him as "Sterling" (one of the other names on the private website). Although Lipton tries to bluff his way out, he is arrested. Switching conveniently to third-person narration, Patterson informs us that the Wolf (whose capabilities for travel seem boundless, not to mention his skill at being at the right place at the right time) sees Lipton being led away out of his office building. Wolf drives by the car into which Cross is about to put him and attempts to kill him—but Cross, somehow sensing trouble, throws Lipton to the ground and protects him. Evidently there is no attempt to pursue the Wolf, for we hear no more of this troubling incident.

Under intense interrogation, Lipton finally cracks. He says that the whole idea of the sex club was his idea; the Wolf wanted Lipton's computer expertise for other purposes, about which Lipton can only speculate: "Let me tell you where I think he was going with the club. He wanted to involve very rich, powerful men. We already had one, a senator from West Virginia. He had big plans" (329–30). (I hope he is not mistaking the dignified senator for a representative from Florida.)

Throughout all this time, we have been regaled by the Wolf's intermittent brutalization of poor Lizzie Connolly. On one occasion, when the poor woman is being raped by the big bad wolf, we are privy to her thoughts:

> *She couldn't be here in this horror house.*
> *She had to be somewhere else, anywhere else.*
> *Had to be!*
> *Had to be!*
> *Had to be!* (304)

Patterson sure knows how to squeeze the heart. But perhaps her liberation is in the offing. Lipton has figured out that the Wolf lives in Ft. Lauderdale. The FBI raids his house and finds Elizabeth. Cleverly, she had alerted them to her presence (she had been locked, bound and gagged, in a closet) by using a cigarette lighter to set her clothes on fire. During the ensuing confusion, however, the Wolf and his bodyguard manage to escape. A standard chase scene ensues, and the two fugitives are finally cornered in a Gap store. I have no idea what symbolism is meant by that. But at this point Sorokin makes a startling statement:

> "So you caught us," he called out. "Big deal! It doesn't matter, you know. I have a surprise for you, FBI. Ready? My name *is* Pasha Sorokin. But I'm not

the Wolf." He laughed. "I'm just some guy shopping in the Gap. My clothes got wet. I'm *not* the Wolf, Mr. FBI. Is that funny or what? Does it make your day? It makes mine. And it will make the Wolf's too." (348)

Exactly what we are to make of this is not immediately clear. In any event, Sorokin now identifies another name on the private website—the person who goes by the name of "Sphinx." He is none other than . . . Brendan Connolly, the husband of Elizabeth! Tracking him down, the FBI pursues him as he flees in his Porsche. Alex Cross personally hunts him down and then proceeds to beat him up:

> I threw a hard right-handed shot into the bridge of Connolly's nose. The perfect shot, or close to it. Probably broke it, from the crunch I heard. He went down on one knee—but he got up again. Former college jock. Former tough guy. Current asshole.
>
> His nose was hanging to one side. Good deal. I threw an uppercut into the pit of Connolly's stomach and liked the feeling so much I threw another. I crunched another right into his gut, which was softening to the touch. Then a quick, hard hook to his cheek. I was getting stronger.
>
> I jabbed his broken nose and Connolly moaned. I jabbed again. I looped a roundhouse at his chin, connected, bull's-eye. Brendan Connolly's blue eyes rolled back into his forehead. The lights went out and he dropped into the mud and stayed there, where he belonged. (356–57)

Well, how else is one to treat a fellow who sold his own wife, the mother of his children, to another man? And how else is a person who was explicitly described as resembling Muhammad Ali (18) to treat such a wretch?

Meanwhile, the Wolf's depredations are not over. He kills both Lipton (in spite of the fact that he is in a jail cell) and his entire family. Cross proceeds to trek to a "super-max prison in Florence, Colorado" (370), where a similar murder had taken place some time before, and talks with a murderer named Kyle Craig, "who had once been an FBI agent, and also a friend of mine" (370). Evidently Cross doesn't have a very rigorous screening process for his friends. Craig says he knows the true identity of the Wolf: he is one Andrei Prokopev, a prominent Russian businessman. They presently capture him, but a new twist emerges: the Russians say that this person is not actually the Wolf. As another agent observes: "They [the Russians] know what the Wolf looks like. He was KGB, after all. The real Wolf set us up to believe he was Prokopev. Andrei Prokopev was one of his rivals in the Red Mafiya" (380). So the chase continues.... In an epilogue, we see Pasha Sorokin being led to a courthouse in Miami. But the van he is riding in is assaulted by a team of thugs and assassins who shoot the accompanying police. The real (and I mean the really real) Wolf says blandly to Pasha, "I understand that you were going to turn me in" (390) and calmly dispatches him with a rocket launcher fired directly at his face.

Oh, yes, and one final note: Alex Cross's ex-wife, Christine, who has been contesting his custody of his youngest son, Alex Jr., wins custody of the boy because Alex is deemed "a lightning rod for danger" (385).

And that's the end.

Once again, the sheer absurdity and unbelievability of the events in *The Big Bad Wolf* are difficult to convey. The constant shuffling as to who exactly the Wolf is becomes tedious and confusing, and a serious case could be made that Patterson has illegitimately misled the reader by plainly stating the identity of the Wolf with Pasha Sorokin (in the rape scene it is explicitly stated: "The Wolf was inside her . . ." [304]). In any case, it is not entirely clear what the continued elusiveness of the Wolf is meant to accomplish: does it mean that he will simply be back for another bout with Cross? One might be inclined to think so, especially since the "big plans" mentioned by Lipton are never clarified: what, in fact, was the Wolf wanting to do with the computer expertise Lipton was to have provided? This matter is simply dropped in the frenetic chase scenes that conclude the novel.

As for Alex Cross, he comes across as little more than a cipher—just one more tough-guy policeman determined to get the bad guys. His supposed sensitivity as a piano player and poetry reader plays no role in the novel, and his devotion to his children is transparently contrived to earn him sympathy against his cruel ex-wife for taking his son and namesake away from him. And for all the fisticuffs and the high body count in the novel, it is noteworthy that Patterson cannot bring himself to kill off the two most prominent (I would hardly call them sympathetic, since there is scarcely any attempt to portray them as anything but victims) women kidnap victims, Elizabeth Connolly and Audrey Meek. Exactly how Elizabeth deals with the trauma of her own husband having sold her is never addressed, for Patterson is too concerned with chasing down the various Wolfs and pseudo-Wolfs to pay any attention to this matter. And I've mentioned before how Patterson cannot allow agent Paul Gautier to bite the dust, for his death would cause us to cast a baleful moral eye upon Cross himself; so Gautier is conveniently wounded but destined to recover.

Patterson's prose is, if possible, still worse in this novel than in the others I endured. Once again, his penchant for sequences precisely in imitation of action films is evident: 117 chapters, as well as a prologue and an epilogue, in 390 pages. Many chapters are less than two pages long. I have quoted only the most obviously corny means by which Patterson attempts to instill in the reader either a sense of pathos or of dramatic, fast-paced action; and, once again, the bewildering shifts from first- to third-person narration are contrived purely for the sake of moving the plot forward at a brisk clip.

* * * * * * *

Nelson DeMille (b. 1943), after serving in the U.S. Army in Vietnam (1966–69), received a B.A. from Hofstra University in 1970, whereupon he worked at a number of odd jobs, including carpentry, house painting, and the like, before becoming a full-time writer in 1973, when he published his first novel, *The Quest.* He has gone on to write fourteen other novels, seven "police novels," and two pseudonymous nonfiction books (including a biography of Barbara Walters). Twenty-four novels in thirty-three years is relatively restrained for a bestselling writer. Two of his novels have been made into films or television; others have been optioned.

In *Bag of Bones,* Stephen King referred to DeMille and Richard North Patterson as "probably the best of the current popular novelists."[4] That's pretty high praise from one bestseller to another, but whether DeMille deserves this kind of encomium is far from certain. King, in any case, has not exactly shown that he is endowed with the critical acumen of a Northrop Frye, as his error-sprinkled study of horror fiction, *Danse Macabre* (1981), attests. And on the basis of the one novel of DeMille's that I have read, *Plum Island* (1997),[5] it doesn't seem as if he stands out from the mass of bestsellerdom to any significant degree.

*Plum Island* focuses around John Corey, a New York City policeman who is recovering from gunshot wounds at his uncle's house on the North Fork—the northern peninsula at the very far eastern end of Long Island. The local police chief, Sylvester Maxwell (a stereotypically gruff and no-nonsense type of fellow), asks his help in the murder of Tom and Judy Gordon. Their boat had landed at 5:30 P.M. on a pier near their house; they were apparently each shot once in the head at around 5:45, according to a neighbor who heard the shots. However, if readers are under the impression that a straightforward murder mystery is on the agenda, they had better think again. It transpires that a nuclear facility, Brookhaven National Laboratory, as well as a "very top secret biological research site which is so scary it has to be housed on an island" (7)—Plum Island, to be exact—are nearby. The Gordons had been employed at this site, doing work whose exact nature is not well understood. The inside of the house has been ransacked, but no valuables are taken: clearly the presumed murderer was after other objects entirely.

A woman, Detective Elizabeth Penrose from the Suffolk County homicide division, is in charge of the investigation. From the moment he lays eyes on her, tough-guy John is uppity with her, refusing to explain his (unofficial) presence but continually telling her, "You'll have to speak to the chief" (16). It is no surprise that she is attractive:

> She was very good-looking, of course; if she'd been ugly, I'd have been much nicer. She was dressed . . . rather severely, but the body beneath the tailored clothes was a symphony of curves, a melody of flesh looking to break free. In fact, she looked like she was smuggling balloons. The second thing I noticed was that she wasn't wearing a wedding ring. Filling out the rest of the form: age, early thirties; hair, medium length, coppery color; eyes, blue-green; skin, fair, not much sun for this time of year, light makeup; pouty lips; no visible marks or scars; no earrings; no nail polish; pissed-off expression on her face. (17)

I suppose Corey, as a policeman, is paid to be observant. This pairing up of a man and a woman in police investigation has become very common in recent popular writing, no doubt in part to take account of societal changes reflecting women's enhanced job opportunities, but also to engender some obvious sexual sparks and undercurrents—something that DeMille can expect both his male and his female readers to appreciate. *Plum Island* is, however, written from so resolutely male a perspective—entirely through the eyes and words of John Corey—that one wonders whether many women are going to like this book. Corey openly admits to the reader that "I can

be annoying" (22), and later, when he goes to the biological facility
with others to investigate, he remarks that he lagged behind at one
point "because I wanted to check out [a secretary's] legs and butt. I
know I'm a pig—I could conceivably contract swine fever" (111).
This self-deprecating humor actually has the effect of reinforcing
and even validating Corey's red-blooded sexism, something a certain proportion of his male readers no doubt richly enjoy. Still later,
to much the same effect, Corey says of himself: "I'm an overbear-
ing, egocentric, and opinionated male chauvinist pig. That's my
comfort zone" (194). One detects more than a little trace of pride in
this purported self-derogation, and this is itself a signal that De-
Mille's male readers can similarly be proud to remain opinionated
male chauvinist pigs themselves.

But DeMille is not intent on presenting a straightforward romance between Corey and Penrose; in fact, she figures relatively
little in the overall narrative. As the investigation continues, it is
quickly learned that the Gordons had an aluminum chest on board
their boat; it is now missing. At once all kinds of conjectures as to
what could have been in the chest are made: could it have contained
dangerous viruses or other biohazards that the Gordons were somehow intent on unleashing upon the region, or the nation, or the
world? Our sleuths discover that the Gordons had left Plum Island at
around noon; as it is a relatively short boat ride from the island to
their home on the North Fork, what could they have been doing for
all that time? Were they drug-runners dropping off a shipment of
heroin or cocaine?

The investigative team is joined by George Foster of the FBI
and Ted Nash, ostensibly of the Department of Agriculture (which
runs the biological research site) but who Corey thinks is probably
CIA. Corey takes an immediate dislike to Nash, apparently seeing
him as a rival: "he was closer to my age, tanned, curly salt-and-
pepper hair, blue-gray eyes, impressive build, and all in all what the
ladies would call a hunk, which is one of the reasons I didn't like
him, I guess. I mean, how many hunks do you need in one room?"
(33). Nash conjectures that the facility might be involved in "defensive biological warfare" (41): although it is illegal for the United
States to engage in experimentation for actual biological warfare,
there may be good reason to conduct tests to defend against such
warfare at the hands of a host of nefarious enemies. Nash paints a
lurid picture of the dangers of the enterprise:

> "The problem is, of course, that these bacteria
> and virus cultures can be . . . I mean, if someone got

his hands on these micro-organisms, and has the knowledge to propagate more from the samples, then, well, you'd have a great deal of it reproducing, and if it got into the population somehow . . . then you may have a potential public health problem."

I asked, "You mean like an end-of-the-world plague with the dead piling up in the streets?"

"Yes, that kind of public health problem."

Silence. (42)

What would popular writers do without one-word paragraphs?

Corey himself thinks the Gordons may have been involved in drug-running: how else could they have afforded the very expensive boat they owned? Bank records seem to indicate that the Gordons were "overextended" (60). One curious expenditure is a check made out for $25,000 to one Margaret Wiley, a local resident. Incredibly, Corey telephones her—at two in the morning: he can't sleep, worrying that "a civilization-destroying plague could be spreading over the nation" (62). (He adds with a lame attempt at wry humor: "I hate when that happens" [62].) Margaret answers and tells him that she sold the Gordons a small piece of land. This land cannot by law be developed, but crops could conceivably be planted on it. Did Tom Gordon wish to start a winery as a hobby? The area has an abundance of wineries, but the piece of land Gordon bought is not good for growing grapes. So the mystery deepens.

John and others of the investigative team now take a trip to Plum Island. They are welcomed somewhat grudgingly by Paul Stevens, head of security of the research site, who leads them on an intolerably long and tedious tour throughout the entire facility. He explains that the Gordons were interested in archaeological sites on the island—remains from Indian settlements or from the Revolutionary War. The investigators finally meet Dr. Zollner, director of the facility, who think the Gordons might have been planning to sell a vaccine that they had secretly developed:

"The Gordons, who were wonderful people, but somewhat carefree and terrible with money, stole one of the new vaccines they were working on. I believe they were further advanced on the research of a vaccine than they led us to believe. Unfortunately, this sometimes happens in science. They may have made separate notes or even separate sequencing gels. . . . So, consider that the Gordons could have discovered a wonderful new vaccine for a terrible disease-causing virus—animal, human, or both—and kept this discovery secret, and over the months assembled all their notes, genetic gels, and the vaccine itself in some hidden area of the laboratory, or in a deserted building on the island. Their purpose, of course, would be to sell this to perhaps a foreign pharmaceutical firm. Perhaps they intended to resign from here, take a job with a private firm, and pretend to make the discovery there. Then, they would get a very handsome bonus amounting to millions of dollars. And the royalties could be tens of millions of dollars, depending on the vaccine." (130–31)

The Gordons had in fact been working on the simian Ebola virus, and in the preceding year they had gone to the Pirbright Laboratory in England. So it all sounds plausible, and much less dangerous than thinking that the Gordons were either planning to unleash a deadly virus into the world or that they were drug dealers. Several of the investigators are satisfied that this is the solution of the case, or at least of the motivation behind the murders; nevertheless, Corey flatly states to Zollner that he doesn't believe a word of it. Later, Corey and Penrose think this is a story that the government has come up with; as Penrose observes, "The cover-up was conceived, written, and directed late last night, early this morning. The lights burned all night in Washington and on Plum Island. This morning, we saw the play" (166).

So Corey and Penrose continue their investigations. They pay a visit to the small plot of land purchased by the Gordons from Margaret Wiley. It is at the very edge of the bluff looking out over the sea; under the bluff is a small man-made cave—empty. What possible reason could the Gordons have had for paying so high a sum for an apparently worthless piece of land? It is at this point that DeMille uncorks that tried-and-true method of generating suspense—or, rather, interest in the outcome: Corey already thinks he is on the brink of solving the case ("I needed a few more points of light, a half dozen little pings, and then I would have the answer to why Tom and Judy Gordon were murdered" [212]), in spite of the fact that we are less than halfway through the book. As it turns out, Corey could not possibly have come upon anything like a full-scale solution, or even the glimmer of the solution, to the case at this early stage; but the hackneyed indication that he is close to the answer will presumably keep the readers turning those pages.

Corey now begins a highly laborious and relatively uninteresting round of interviews with potential suspects or witnesses. A very long chapter is taken up with the interrogation of Frederic Tobin, a vintner who had been acquainted with the Gordons. At one point Corey discovers that Tobin had lied about what seems to be a relatively small point: he claimed that he never visited the Gordons in their home, but the neighbor who had heard the gunshots that had killed them informs Corey that Tobin had in fact come there in his white Porsche some months before.

Corey then interviews Emma Whitehouse, president of the Peconic Historical Society. Corey had been expecting a dried-up old prune of a woman, but the reality is very different:

> Okay, here's the deal: she was tall—only an inch or so shorter than I am—thin but shapely, shoulder-length brown hair that was washed but not ironed, light makeup, no nail polish, no jewelry, no earrings, no wedding or engagement ring. And she wasn't wearing much clothing either. She had on a knee-length, beige cotton summer dress with itty-bitty shoulder straps holding it up. Beneath this scanty number was little in the way of underwear. Certainly no bra, but I could see bikini panty lines. Also, she was barefoot. If I pictured Ms. Whitestone dressing this morning, she had slipped on the panties and the dress, put on a touch of lipstick, sort of combed her hair, and that was it. She could conceivably get out of that outfit in four seconds. Less with my help. (246–47)

That final little whimsy turns out to be no joke, for in an egregious realization of a male sex fantasy, Emma—after engaging in an extended interview with Corey about the Gordons—ends up sleeping with him! ("I knelt down at the side of my bed to say my prayers, and Emma got into the bed and wrapped her long, long legs around my neck" [270].) So Corey's slow-burning dalliance with Elizabeth Penrose takes a bit of a detour. . . .

Before jumping into the sack with him, Emma tells Corey that she herself had had an affair with Fredric Tobin, and that Tobin is (like the Gordons) living above his means. Can there be a connection to the murders? Fredric himself had approached Tom and befriended him (this is another point on which Tobin had lied to Corey), for reasons that remain unclear; Emma goes on to say that both Tobin and the Gordons took cocaine, but Corey (who had gotten to know the Gordons during his recuperation and liked them) doesn't believe this.

At any rate, perhaps sleeping with Emma has stimulated Corey's mind, for he again believes he is on the verge of cracking the case ("I yelled, 'That's it!' and exhaled so much air that I sank" [273]). Specifically, he has been fixated on figuring out what a sequence of numbers—44106818—found on the margin of the Gordons' navigation book—could mean. Emma says they are related to treasure supposedly buried in the general region by Captain Kidd: "Well, when Captain Kidd was held in a Boston jail charged with piracy, he smuggled a note to his wife, Sarah, and on the bottom of the note were those numbers" (273). But no one knows what they mean. Did the Gordons find the treasure on Plum Island (hence accounting for their purported interest in archaeological sites there), and, knowing that any treasure found on the site would belong to the government rather than to the finders, bury it on the acre of land they had bought from Margaret Wiley?

Corey now thinks that Tobin is more deeply involved: perhaps he learned of the treasure, took it from the Gordons, and killed them to keep them quiet. Corey talks with Tobin again, but on this occasion Tobin rebuffs him: he had already been offended at being grilled by Corey the first time, and says he has now spoken to his lawyer and refuses to cooperate with Corey.

Corey now confers with Elizabeth Penrose about the case. She is a bit put out that he is sleeping with Emma, but otherwise attempts to keep up a professional demeanor. The same cannot be said for Corey, who teases Penrose about his reconstruction of the case, daring her to guess it. Just as she is driving off, she suddenly comes upon the solution herself (yes, the solution I have just outlined is in fact the answer to the mystery). However, it is still unclear who learned of the Gordons' discovery of the treasure and, therefore, who killed them. So further unearthing must be done.

Corey begins the task by confronting Paul Stevens at his home in New London just before he is heading to work. Can he be the culprit? For reasons that are not entirely clear to me, Corey actually engages in fisticuffs with Stevens:

> I sprinted across the lawn, across the driveway,
> and caught up to him as he rounded the far end of the
> house and turned toward his backyard. He heard me,
> spun around, and reached into the pit for his gun, but
> much too late. I caught him on the chin with my fist,

and he made one of those *umph* sounds and did a little backspring with his arms and legs askew. It was
almost comical. (369)

Almost. But this John L. Sullivan routine turns out to be for naught,
for in spite of Corey's certainty that Stevens is concealing information ("he *knew* something. I was convinced of that" [372]), it does
not in fact appear that he is the murderer.

Corey's suspicions increasingly focus on Tobin. It is at this
point that DeMille, through his mouthpiece, belches forth another
time-tested contrivance of the suspense writer: the "had-I-but-
known" scenario: "But I forgot to consider Tobin as a thinking, cun-
ning animal because he struck me as such a fop, the same way I'd
struck him as a simpleton. We both knew better, but we'd both been
lulled a little bit by each other's act. In any event, I blame myself for
what happened" (389). These lugubrious reflections are stirred by
the fact that Emma Whitestone is now found murdered, as Penrose
breaks the news gently to him: "She was found in her bed . . . apparently killed by blows to the head with a fireplace poker that was
found on the floor . . . there was no sign of forced entry . . . the back
door was unlocked" (393). Since it is now virtually certain that
Tobin is the murderer of both the Gordons and of Emma (in revenge
for her telling Corey about him), we are evidently to be treated to
nearly 120 pages (for the book is 511 pages long) in which Tobin is
systematically hunted down. Why should it take so long to capture
and arrest this person? He is not exactly a Moriarty, or even James
Bond's nemesis, Blofeld. But DeMille evidently feels that at this
point his novel must metamorphose from a mystery-suspense story
into an adventure story, and he strives not to disappoint.

Corey recklessly goes to Tobin's winery and ransacks his office
(it is nighttime and the place is empty), looking for any kind of evidence with which to incriminate him. Evidently he is not concerned
that evidence obtained in this illegal fashion might be ruled inadmis-
sible; for her part, Penrose follows him reluctantly, attempting in
vain to restrain his headstrong indignation. Corey finds a treasure
map—but Penrose informs him that it is probably a forgery designed
by Tobin to indicate that Captain Kidd's treasure was buried on the
piece of land purchased by the Gordons. The two now head to
Tobin's house. A housekeeper informs them that he has gone out in
a boat—in spite of the fact that a near-hurricane is heading directly
for the area. She also tells them that Tobin had taken various articles
from the basement. They go down there and find an aluminum
chest—presumably the one that the Gordons had owned. Inside is a

human skull, along with pieces of rotten wood and four pieces of gold. Could this be part of Captain Kidd's treasure?

John now decides to pursue Tobin on his own. In her sensible, feminine way she tries to restrain him, but he is convinced that Tobin has gone to Plum Island and that most of the treasure is still there. At the last minute Penrose joins him. They head out in your usual storm at sea, encountering life-threatening danger at every moment:

> I pushed the throttles forward, and we cleared the boathouse into the driving rain. A second later, I saw a huge wave coming at us from the right, and it was going to hit us broadside. I cut the wheel right and got the bow into the wave. The boat road up, hung on to the crest as if it were in midair, then the wave broke behind me, leaving the boat literally in midair. The boat came down, bow first, digging into the swelling sea. Then the bow rose and the stern hit the water. The propellers caught, and we were off, but in the wrong direction. In the trough between waves, I swung the boat around 180 degrees and headed east. As we passed the boathouse, I heard a sharp crack and the entire structure leaned to the right, then col-lapsed onto the boiling sea. "Jeez!" (433)

Jeez, indeed. Amazing that the two survived at all—but of course we can't have our valiant protagonists perish at this critical juncture. All of a sudden they see Tobin's boat, the *Autumn Gold,* coming right at them. A chase ensues, and there is some gunfire on both sides—but no harm, no foul. Both boats, clearly, are headed for Plum Island. Corey admits to the reader that he is now filled with hatred against Tobin: "The truth was, I wanted to kill Fredric Tobin. When I thought he'd killed Tom and Judy, I would have been satis-fied seeing the great State of New York kill him. Now, after he mur-dered Emma, I had to kill him myself. Calling the Coast Guard or Plum Island security was not going to even the score" (449). It is unclear whether we are to regard these sentiments as admirable or otherwise; at any rate, we are evidently to believe that this motiva-tion is, if not commendable, at least an understandable sentiment on the part of one whose sex partner—er, lover—has been so cruelly rubbed out. Let it pass that Corey himself had earlier stated, "But a cop can't be a vigilante, and a vigilante can't be a cop" (396).

As Corey's boat is approaching Plum Island, it hits some obstruction and begins to sink—but a large wave providentially lifts it to shore. Tobin's boat has already arrived, and he has gone inland to get the treasure. Corey leaves Penrose at the shore as he pursues Tobin. As he approaches an old and abandoned fort, he hears gunshots; later he discovers that Tobin has killed two foremen and commandeered an ambulance, for ease in getting around the island. A siren now goes off: can it be a warning of some kind of biohazard? Corey thinks of heading back to shore, picking up Beth, and fleeing the island—but his thirst for vengeance against Tobin drives him on. If they both die, what of it? (Some readers are perhaps beginning to wonder the same thing.)

Corey enters some pitch-dark concrete room in a building on the fort. Of course, Tobin is there. Now for the showdown! A shotgun from Tobin goes off—it misses Corey. For his part, Corey fires the last remaining bullet in his revolver—and misses. (Of course he does: we still have 40 pages to go.) There is now a typical battle of words between good guy and bad guy, with Corey taunting Tobin in an effort to make him lose his cool and do something stupid. The taunts fly, in fact, in both directions, and Tobin actually admits that he doesn't know where the treasure is: the Gordons had moved it shortly before he killed them. Corey now pretends that he knows where the treasure is; he then dodges out of the range of the flashlight that Tobin had trained upon him, tackles him, gets his gun away from him, and begins pummeling Tobin with it, and with a knife that he has. This latter weapon is put to a most ingenious use, for Corey slices Tobin down the middle and hands him his own guts to eat. The chapter ends dramatically: "I stood, wiped my hands on my trousers, and walked away. Tobin's screams and cries echoed in the cold, cold room" (492).

But, alas, we still have nearly twenty pages to go. What could possibly occur in them? In spite of the fact that Corey, while engaged with Tobin, expressed a certain modicum of regret at his savagery in dealing with him ("I truly wanted to stand up and run out of there before I did something that was irretrievably evil, but the black heart that lurks in all of us had awoken in me" [492]), he very shortly thereafter jokes about it: "You'd think a guy would run out of screams after a while. I mean, once the initial horror has passed, then a guy should get a grip on and see about stuffing his guts back where they belong and shut up" (493). In any event, as Corey is making his way back to the shore to get off the island, he is met by Paul Stevens, rifle in hand. Stevens admits that *he* has the treasure, and also states that the siren that is still being heard is only a test.

Whew! no biohazard to deal with! As Corey is about to charge Stevens, the latter gets ready to shoot—but (naturally) Corey is saved in the nick of time . . . by Elizabeth Penrose, who shoots Stevens.

Even this is not the end. When Corey gets back to New York City, he finds a letter that the Gordons had mailed to him before their death; it opens ominously: "If you're reading this, it means we're dead" (502). It is by no means clear why this should be so: If the Gordons knew that Tobin was about to kill them, why didn't they just go to the police? If they didn't know, then why would they have written a melodramatic letter predicting their own demise? But people in suspense novels do not behave rationally at times. In any case, the letter spells out what we already know. Corey, for his part, has now retired from the NYPD and, as part of a plea bargain for all the various derelictions of which he is clearly guilty, is now teaching a class on homicide investigation at John Jay College. As class is beginning, who shows up but Beth Penrose. We now learn that the "eviscerated and scalped" (509) Fredric Tobin *actually survived* the near-gutting that Corey had inflicted upon him (Corey is not surprised: "I knew I hadn't delivered a necessarily mortal wound" [509], he observes blandly) and is about to be put on trial. Meanwhile, we are left to contemplate the budding romance of the ex-cop and the fetching female detective. . . .

*Plum Island* is such a deeply silly book that one scarcely needs to do anything but narrate its plot to reveal its multitude of absurdities and implausibilities. In the first place, it becomes clear at the end that the entire business of the research facility, and the possibility of leaking viruses or vaccines or such, is a gigantic and time-wasting red-herring with no bearing whatever upon the main plot. It is there simply to add space—to make a 500-page novel out of what, in substance, should have amounted only to a 300-page novel—and, perhaps, also to add a spurious layer of cataclysmic danger to what in the end proves to a pretty mundane tale of crime, murder, and vengeance. Perhaps, too, it is meant as a kind of cover for the hoary idea of "buried treasure," something that has not been used credibly even in popular fiction for a century or more. That DeMille can actually use such antique tricks of the adventure writer as treasure maps, pieces of eight, and the like is sufficient testimonial to his fundamental lack of originality even in the kind of hack fiction he has chosen to write.

The one distinguishing feature of the novel, at least in DeMille's impression, is the figure of the protagonist, John Corey. Evidently we are to regard Corey as an affectionate scamp in spite—or perhaps because—of his self-confessed sexism, boorishness, and hot temper. The use of first-person narration throughout the book fosters this impression. DeMille mercifully does not shift to third-person narration whenever he finds it convenient to do so, as so many other popular writers do; to that degree, one must give him a token commendation for managing the construction of his plot (ludicrous and contrived as it is) in such a way that Corey's narrative voice can tell it from beginning to end. The specific tone of that voice is clearly adopted for this novel, as other works by DeMille are written in a very different (and usually third-person) narrative tone. For my part, I found myself so disliking Corey that I yearned futilely for his demise in one of the number of near-death experiences he predictably came upon.

Overall, DeMille's style is free of obvious gaucheries, although we find such blunders as the misspelling (twice) of *cojones* as *cajones* (127, 392) and the curiously redundant phrase "circa about 1850s" (245). As a resident of Long Island, DeMille portrays his chosen local adequately enough, but with no great insight or distinction. The book predictably opens with a long list of "acknowledgments" to those individuals who provided DeMille with various bits of specialised information, ranging from the details of police investigation to the specifics of wine growing; an "Author's Note" relates that there is a "United States Department of Agriculture Animal Disease Center" on Plum Island, and that DeMille "took a small amount of literary license regarding the island and the work done there"—in the end a very small amount of license, for in fact it does not appear that, in the novel, anything potentially cataclysmic actually goes on there.

\* \* \* \* \* \* \*

I am aware that sober canons of realism do not seem relevant to the kind of action-packed suspense that writers like James Patterson and Nelson DeMille write, but after a time the intelligent and sensitive reader (assuming, for the sake of argument, that any such actually read these books) must pause in amazement at how so many incredible events—and, more pertinently, so many utterly unreal reactions to those events by the human characters—are choreographed for the reader's supposed delectation. *People simply do not behave in this manner.* It is not enough to say that the characters in these suspense novels are merely cardboard stick-figures: they, and the incidents swirling around them, are so ludicrous that the works, for all their superficial aura of tough-guy realism, become *works of fantasy,* where the author can in essence create his or her own universe in strict accordance to the kind of slam-bang action that these novels demand. There is in fact more genuine realism in genuine works of literary fantasy (as in the writings of Lord Dunsany or J. R. R. Tolkien) than in these popular suspense novels, for in the former a certain self-consistency, either in topography or in psychological motivation, must at least be maintained to render an imaginary world plausible, whereas in the latter virtually all notions of how human beings actually behave and what events can actually occur are thrown out the window merely to generate the adrenalin rush that readers are evidently seeking. Because these works *seem* to be set in the recognizable real world, readers seem willing to accept on faith that the events related in them could actually have occurred. But in reality, these readers—as the authors know full well—are simply not interested in realism of any profound or meaningful sort: they just want a patina of verisimilitude in setting and character so that the truly fantastic events being narrated can be swallowed for the sake of the thrills they generate. The alpha and omega of these novels is adrenalin production: they aspire to no loftier purpose.

# V.

# COPS, ROBBERS, AND SPIES

## ROBERT LUDLUM, TOM CLANCY, AND CLIVE CUSSLER

The spy story is, strictly speaking, a subset of the crime/suspense novel, but it has distinct features that justify segregating it into its own subclass. Chiefly, it differs from the majority of mystery/suspense tales by explicitly or implicitly playing upon geopolitical considerations that transcend the individuals involved in the adventure. It is, therefore, not surprising that the spy novel emerged and flourished during periods of particularly heightened tensions between nations or blocs of nations. The first spy novel that deserves the name is William Fenimore Cooper's mediocre novel *The Spy* (1821), set in the time of the American war of independence. But it took nearly a century before the spy novel became anything like a frequent contribution to popular—and, in a very few cases, genuine—literature. British novelist William Le Queux (1864–1927) could be said to have established the spy story as a popular form with dozens of novels published from 1890 to 1931, dealing with all manner of contemporary threats to world peace, from Russian anarchists to German infiltrators. Le Queux's work was acknowledged even by its own author as subliterary, and he is of interest today only to specialists of the form.

A bit higher on the literary scale, but not much, is John Buchan's *The Thirty-Nine Steps* (1915), in which the private adventurer Richard Hannay is involved in a series of extremely bizarre events in Scotland. It is no accident that the novel appeared shortly after the commencement of World War I, for Buchan was one of a succession of British writers, the most notable of whom was Rudyard Kipling, who felt the need to bolster their countrymen's patriotism by tales of

British heroics. Buchan also fed into the inveterate British prejudice that amateurs are superior in cleverness and resourcefulness than professionals, so that Hannay—who starred in several other novels over the next decade or so—consistently outwits both his (usually foreign) adversaries and the stodgy British secret service agents who are nominally entrusted with guarding the nation's security.

And yet, while works like Le Queux's and Buchan's were pouring from the press in the interwar years, a more serious and grimly realistic variety of spy story was being written by authors both humble and distinguished. Julian Symons refers to Erskine Childers's *The Riddle of the Sands* (1903) as "one of the best spy and adventure stories ever written."[1] It is a question whether Joseph Conrad's *The Secret Agent* (1907) and *Under Western Eyes* (1911) could or should be regarded as spy novels; what is not in doubt is the seriousness with which Conrad treats the political and psychological ramifications of his scenarios. W. Somerset Maugham's volume of connected short stories, *Ashenden* (1928), is a landmark in the realistic treatment of the trade of espionage, while Graham Greene's several novels—*The Confidential Agent* (1939), *The Power and the Glory* (1944), and others—are, in spite of their own author's dismissal of them as "entertainments," are so rich and complex in their moral and political overtones as to transcend popular fiction altogether. Rather less polished but still of considerable literary substance are the novels of British writer Eric Ambler, who with *A Coffin for Demetrios* (1939) and many others used the spy novel to convey leftist political sentiments—rather surprisingly, since the spy novel has on the whole been the purview of super-patriotic right-wingers. Following World War II, John le Carré in *The Spy Who Came In from the Cold* (1963) and its many successors have raised the spy novel to an art form that need fear no comparison with serious mainstream literature.

But the popular spy novel of today is very largely the creation of James Bond—not so much the novels of Ian Fleming as the films inspired by them. The films in particular have turned Bond into a parody of himself: aggressively patriotic, suave with the ladies, refined in his tastes in food and liquor, capable both of enduring excruciating punishment and of dishing it out, he is the perfect male wish-fulfillment fantasy. In the actual Ian Fleming novels he is not quite so stereotyped. The curious thing about the Bond novels, however, is that they are not as chauvinistically political as one might expect them to be. In *Thunderball* (1961), we learn of the creation of the crime syndicate SPECTRE, run by one Ernst Stavfo Blofeld. He and his colleagues are said to be "from six of the world's great criminal and subversive organizations,"[2] but to what end is this syndicate to be put? Evidently SPECTRE is merely a "private enterprise for private profit" (42)—which one might interpret as a veiled attack on capitalism if it were not so obvious that Fleming hasn't the faintest thought of any such intent.

In fact, the great majority of the James Bond novels involve individuals like Blofeld threatening the entire world, rather than just one particular nation; and while it is true that it is Bond, acting as an agent of the British secret service, who always foils these plots, he does so out of a kind of altruistic devotion to all humanity rather than specifically to the welfare of the British nation. The Bond novels are, of course, entirely preposterous in both the conception and the execution of the plot, and their prose style and characterization leave very much to be desired. It was to be expected that in *Thunderball* Bond should be said to have "dark, rather cruel good looks" (85), although in that novel's sequel, *On Her Majesty's Secret Service* (1963), we find Bond uttering such remarkable sentiments as: "I'm fed up with all these untidy, casual affairs that leave me with a bad conscience. I wouldn't mind having children."[3] Well, this will never do, and the poor woman to whom Bond has just proposed is conveniently dispatched at the end of the novel, leaving Bond free to continue his bedding a succession of lovelies for queen and country.

The Cold War was an enormous boon to American spy writers, for against its backdrop of ever-impending nuclear catastrophe it established a convenient dichotomy between valiant Americans and evil Soviets, with the well-meaning but oftentimes bumbling British somewhere in between. It was in this atmosphere of perennial geopolitical tension that such popular spy writers as Fletcher Knebel (*Fail-Safe,* 1962) and Frederick Forsythe (*The Odessa File,* 1974) were able to command the bestseller lists. Their successors—Robert Ludlum, Tom Clancy, and Clive Cussler—are, with the fall of the Soviet Union, now facing the awkwardness of finding new villains, and we shall see that they are having mixed success in the endeavor.

Robert Ludlum (1927–2001), like many spy writers, engaged in a stint of military service before graduating from Wesleyan. He worked as an actor and producer from 1952 to 1970 before writing his first novel, *The Scarlatti Inheritance* (1971). His array of twenty-nine novels, some written under pseudonyms and some collaborative, utilises one of the more irritating forms of uniform titles: "The" + proper name + noun. The resulting artificiality is at times painful to behold. Five of his novels have been adapted for film or television, several of them blockbusters. One of his latest novels, published just prior to his death, is *The Sigma Protocol* (2001),[4] which I take to be representative of his work as a whole.

The novel focuses around the figure of Ben Hartman, an international banker and the son of Max Hartman, a refugee from Nazi Germany who has established the powerful firm of Hartman Capital Management. Ben is in Zurich (a.k.a. Zürich) on business, but is pondering the fate of his twin brother, Peter, who had been killed four years earlier. Even though Ben has "just about zero interest in money" (3), he is nonetheless dutifully following in his father's footsteps. Unexpectedly, he encounters an old school friend, Jimmy Cavanaugh—but as Ben approaches Jimmy, the latter at first greets him cordially, then takes out a gun with a silencer and prepares to shoot him. Conveniently, Ben is carrying skis, so he manages to hit Jimmy over the head with one of them, and Jimmy's shot goes wide. Ben runs away. As Jimmy gives chase, various bystanders are incidentally killed. The two run into an underground shopping mall, where Ben manages to knock Jimmy out with a metal lantern. As Jimmy revives, Ben kills him with his own gun. At this point Ben makes the sage observation: "He was suffused with . . . the sense that nothing would ever be the same" (13).

This first chapter is representative of Ludlum's method: grab the reader by the throat, inflict a high body count, but leave the reader wondering what could possibly be the *motive* behind all the fisticuffs. Ben expresses such plangent mental reflections as *"Why was this happening?"* (13), dodging bullets all the while, and the reader is—for now—in a similar state. Ludlum continues the mystification in the opening of the next chapter, where we see what appears to be an entirely unrelated incident where a young man kills an old man in Nova Scotia, after which we are taken to a mysterious foundation in the Austrian Alps, where some evidently sinister kind of "fulfillment" (16) is about to take place. No doubt Ludlum will tie these threads into the main narrative in due course, and the reader is fully aware of the fact; but for now he is merely interested in establishing the worldwide scope of whatever conspiracy or "protocol" is involved, and therefore its presumable importance in geopolitical affairs.

But let's return to Ben and his puzzlement. As he is examining Jimmy's body, he finds no ID of any kind on him. He continues to make remarkable assertions to himself ("This was a crime scene *of sorts*" [17; my emphasis]—remember that several bystanders have already been killed by Jimmy's murderous onslaught). But when Ben leads some policemen back to the body, it is gone—there are not even any bloodstains. A bit later, Jimmy's gun is found in Ben's luggage in his hotel. Now it is becoming clear that Jimmy is just a pawn in some infinitely larger game—and perhaps Ben also.

The scene shifts again. Anna Navarro, in the Office of Special Investigations at the U.S. Justice Department, is asked to go on a case for the Internal Compliance Unit, whatever that may be. She is handed a list of eleven elderly men who have recently died—presumably of natural causes. All the men have died in a very short period of time. (The reader of course thinks of the poor geezer in Nova Scotia.) What connects these men is that they had all been given clearance by the CIA for some operation in the 1940s and 1950s called Sigma.

For a considerable period in the novel, the narrative of Anna Navarro and that of Ben Hartman are related alternately, although of course the reader is fully aware that they will eventually fuse into one. For now, we can pursue the Navarro narrative. She goes to Nova Scotia, to the home of the old man, Robert Mailhot, who had been killed. As she approaches the house, a car suddenly bears down on her, missing her narrowly (naturally) before driving away undetected. Anna learns that four months before his death, $1 million had been wired into Mailhot's account. For what purpose? Mailhot's widow provides a slight clue, stating that the couple had lately been supported by Charles Highsmith, a media baron who had died mysteriously three years earlier. Anna and others then conduct a detailed autopsy of Mailhot, at which point Ludlum presents the impressive medical erudition that appears to be *de rigueur* in works of this kind. Anna and a colleague, Arthur Hammond ("a scholar of poisons and poisonings back to the Dark Ages" [101]), are desperately attempting to ascertain the method of Mailhot's murder:

> [Hammond:] "It's either something in their drink or their food, or else an injection."
> "But we didn't find any puncture marks. And believe me, we went over that body carefully."
> "If they used a 25-gauge needle you won't see it, probably. And there's always sux."
> She knew he meant succinylcholine chloride, synthetic curare. "Think so."
> "Famous case back in '67 or '68—a doctor in Florida was convinced of murdering his wife with sux, which I'm sure you know is a skeletal muscle relaxant. You can't move, can't breathe. Looks like cardiac arrest. Famous trial, baffled forensic experts around the world." (102)

And so on. At long last they do find a puncture mark on Mailhot—after removing the entire skin from his body.

Let's get back to Ben, for his adventures—and what he learns from them—fill in some important segments of information. Ben calls a colleague to find out what he can about Jimmy Cavanaugh—but the colleague says that, for all practical purposes, Jimmy doesn't exist: all trace of him has been expunged from the public record. Ben quickly gets out of trouble with the Swiss police when it is conclusively demonstrated that he did not fire the gun. (Evidently Ben, in his tussle with Jimmy, had caused Jimmy's own finger to pull the trigger.) Ben is, of course, not out of the woods by any means: a cutaway to a scene in London lets the reader (but, obviously, not Ben) know that a person named Jean-Luc Passard has asked one Trevor Griffiths, formerly of a shadowy organization called "the Corporation" (56), to complete the job of killing Ben. Here again, the reader has been given at least one bit of information that the protagonist (Ben) lacks—specifically, the identity of the person determined to eliminate Ben—but not the full story (or indeed, at this point, any story) of *why* the rubout is to occur. Accordingly, a double suspense is generated: the reader is, as it were, looking over Ben's shoulder while some seemingly immense conspiracy is swirling all around him without his knowledge, but is left wondering as much as Ben himself as to the purpose or motives behind the action.

Ben, now driving to St. Moritz, senses that he is being followed by a blue Saab. After coming out of a tunnel, he sees the Saab barricading the road ahead, while a Renault is behind him. Ben, ever resourceful, simply barrels into the Saab and keeps going. The Renault does so also, and Ben is shot at. A police car comes, and the Renault gives up the chase and flees. Ben comes to a tavern, where he notices a green Audi that he thinks he saw before. A man in his fifties, with a ponytail, comes into the tavern. By a ruse Ben ends up stealing the Audi and takes off. Stopping at an inn, he is astounded by the presence of . . . his brother Peter.

Peter tells Ben that the pony-tailed man is a person named Dieter, his brother-in-law: he was actually protecting Ben. Peter says that the Corporation is after Ben, but doesn't know much about the organization ("Who the hell *knows* who they really are" [84]). Peter has stumbled upon evidence of a corporation of wealthy industrialists in Europe and the United States, established in early 1945, evidently for the purpose of preserving their profits after the war was over: "To them, the war was like a Harvard-Yale football game—a momentary distraction from more serious matters, like the pursuit of the almighty dollar" (88).

This is the first suggestion of some kind of broadly political undercurrent in the novel, but the manner in which it is here expressed suggests that Peter is merely indulging in some kind of leftist paranoia against business; and this is exactly the conclusion Ben comes to:

> Ben shook his head slowly. "Sorry, bro'. Just listen to yourself. It all sounds like the usual counterculture rap: property is theft, never trust anyone over thirty—all that overheated, dated conspiracy crap. Next you're going to tell me they were responsible for Love Canal." He set his cup of coffee down sharply, and it clanked loudly against the saucer. "Funny, there was a time when anything having to do with business bored you stiff. I guess you really *have* changed." (88)

But Peter shakes Ben out of his own complacent cynicism by noting that the treasurer of the Corporation was their own father, Max, who was "no Holocaust survivor, Ben. *Our father was a goddamned Nazi"* (89). Put that in your pipe and smoke it, Mr. International Banker!

After Peter, having learned about the Corporation (called Sigma AG), had confronted his father over this issue, there were several attempts on his life. And so Peter staged his own death to escape the heat. But he is not quite clever enough: as he is explaining all this to Ben, a gunshot bursts through the window and Peter is shot through the head. Ben (naturally) manages to escape in Peter's truck.

Ben himself now confronts his father, but after a heated argument he learns nothing. All he can do is conclude with a ponderous attempt at wit: *"The past isn't dead. It isn't even past"* (109). Ben now looks up Peter's girlfriend, Liesl; he wants her to give him the document revealing the origin of the Sigma Corporation. She advises him to consult with Matthias Deschner, Peter's lawyer. He and Matthias go to a bank where Peter had opened an account in Deschner's name, along with a safety deposit box. (While all this is happening, the reader knows, but Ben and Matthias do not, that they are being observed by a spy. Can it be Griffiths?) In the safety deposit box Ben finds only a photograph of his father with other important members of Sigma. The banker at this point intervenes: he has Ben arrested because Ben, in violation of his agreement with the

Zürich police over the incident with Jimmy Cavanaugh, has entered Switzerland illegally. Once again, the otherwise staid Ben shows surprising agility by taking the policeman's gun away from him and fleeing. (Note that Ludlum is careful not to have Ben commit any crimes against law enforcement or other "innocent" parties, thereby preserving his moral uprightness.)

At this point we need to backtrack and see what Anna Navarro is up to. When Anna comes home after her autopsy on Mailhot, she finds an intruder—a very young man, perhaps even an adolescent. She suspects he is no ordinary intruder. She tries to stun him with a Taser, but he escapes. Alan Bartlett, the director of the Internal Compliance Unit, who had hired Anna for the case, now tells her that Charles Highsmith was a member of Sigma. Anna is sent to Paraguay to investigate the death of Marcel Prosperi, who "essentially ran Marseilles during and after World War II, controlling the heroin, prostitution, and weapons dealings there" (130). He has recently been killed (as a brief scene a bit earlier had related) by a fake nurse who had infiltrated his home. Anna learns about this substitute nurse, but Prosperi's body has already been cremated, so obviously an autopsy cannot be conducted. Pressed by Anna, Alan Bartlett grudgingly shows her a complete list of the men in Sigma; three are still alive. One is Gaston Rossignol, apparently in Zürich. Anna plans to go there. Meanwhile, tests on Mailhot's ocular fluid establishes that he was poisoned by a synthetic molecule. Anna asks the U.S. Patent Office if any company had patented this molecule. We do not learn the answer to this critical question immediately.

It is here that the narratives of Ben and Anna finally link up. Liesl tells Ben the sordid tale of American and British businessmen's collaboration with their German counterparts during and after the war. It of course has to be kept very secret, in order not to offend world opinion; and the United States government was fully involved in the enterprise:

> "There was a young attorney in the Justice Department who dared make a speech about collaborations between American businessmen and the Nazis. He was immediately fired. After the war, German officials were called to task, some of them. And yet the citadel of Axis industrialists was never probed, never disturbed. Why prosecute German industrialists who had done business with Hitler—who had, really, made Hitler possible—given that they were just as happy now to do business with America? When

overzealous officials at Nuremberg had a few of them convicted, your John J. McCloy, the American High Commissioner, had their sentences pardoned. The 'excesses' of fascism were regrettable, but industrialists had to look after each other, right?" (178)

This is presented as hard fact, and I have no doubt that it is, in essentials, true. So maybe Ludlum is a leftist after all! Ben, for his part, has followed Liesl to a cabin in the woods where she had Peter had lived in secret, and he finds the all-important document there: the articles of incorporation, with all the names of the company's officers and directors clearly spelled out, including Max Hartman as treasurer.

Ben now learns that his father had abruptly left his house after receiving a telephone call from Professor John Barnes Goodwin, a famous historian at Princeton. Ben calls Goodwin, who says the call was merely routine, but directs Ben to one Carl Mercandetti, a professor at the University of Zürich. Ben shows Mercandetti the photograph, but the latter thinks it may be doctored: he can't believe that all these powerful industrialists were ever in one place at the same time. Mercandetti does say that Gaston Rossignol, who is on the list of Sigma members, lives in Zürich. Ben locates Rossignol's probable residence and finds a way in—but is appalled to discover that Rossignol has been recently killed, perhaps only minutes before. Ben flees, choosing to go to Vienna, where he suspects that the son of Gerhard Lenz, a Nazi and Sigma member, now lives.

Anna Navarro, soon thereafter, comes to Rossignol's residence and finds his dead body. The policeman who had arrested Ben at the beginning of the narrative now tells her that Ben's fingerprints are present in the house. So now Anna is on Ben's trail, thinking that at a minimum he is somehow involved, and at worst he could be the killer. Ben has other troubles to dodge. He has discovered that Gerhard Lenz's son, Jürgen, has become a noted anti-Nazi, so it would seem intrinsically unlikely that he could be involved in Sigma. Meanwhile, Trevor Griffiths is outside Jürgen's house, waiting to kill Ben. As Ben is leaving the house, Griffiths approaches him—but Anna recognises Griffiths and shoots him. Ben flees, but he is caught by the police. But the most remarkable part of these proceedings is that, although Anna appears to have fatally wounded Griffiths, he remains alive and manages to stagger back to his car and get away.

Ben and Anna now finally meet, in the course of an interrogation. It is highly confrontational, and he tells her nothing. The patent search that Anna had initiated now turns up the fact that the particular molecule used to kill Prosperi was patented by Vortex, a Philadelphia company. Ben, who just can't seem to stay out of trouble, encounters an intruder in his hotel room who almost kills him. At this point he does the sensible thing and offers to cooperate with Anna.

This is, no doubt, a consummation that every reader has devoutly wished for. However implausible, indeed preposterous, it is for a private individual to team up with a federal agent in the solution of this highly complex and dangerous case, it conforms to the contemporary tendency for a male/female partnership in crime solution—both as a way of enticing female readers, who might otherwise be repelled by the exclusively male realm of cops and robbers, but as a means of generating inevitable sexual tension as the two become enmeshed in increasingly hazardous investigations that may ultimately have a payoff in the bedroom during fleeting moments of downtime. The ploy therefore becomes a tactic to lure male readers also, since they can then envision themselves both as valiant defenders of the American way and as sexual powerhouses. Ludlum is feminist enough to portray Anna as a strong, competent figure who does not need defense from a mere man, but in our contemporary world this makes her even more sexy than otherwise.

Anna now meets a CIA agent named Phil Ostrow, who tries to persuade her to hand Ben over to the agency. Anna wonders about the exact purpose of this request, but her attention is distracted by an even more urgent call from Alan Bartlett, who chastises her and orders her back to Washington. Is he somehow trying to prevent Anna from probing into Sigma too far? Ben, in turn, has hired a private investigator, Hans Hoffman, who discovers that Jürgen Lenz's attested past as a medical doctor is entirely fictitious: he has no medical degree and never went to medical school. Ben now sees an old Nazi-hunter, Jakob Sonnenfeld, who tells Ben all about Sigma. Sonnenfeld knows of Max Hartman, and says that Max had worked for Sigma only as a means of buying freedom for himself and his two sisters. This puts a new complexion on the matter, and Ben begins to think that his father does not deserve the straightforward moral condemnation he had bestowed upon him.

Meanwhile, Anna is increasingly in trouble; she herself feels that she is being framed. She learns that the man she thought was Phil Ostrow was an impostor. Clearly, pressure is being put upon her from above. Ben now thinks that a man named Georges Chardin may know about Sigma; he appears to be living in Paris under the name Roger Chabot. Anna and Ben come to his apartment, but

Georges begins shooting at them. They manage to subdue him, and find that he is hideously deformed:

> They were staring into an almost featureless mass of scar tissue, wildly various in texture. In areas it appeared crenellated, almost scalloped; in other areas, the proud flesh was smooth and nearly shiny, as if lacquered or covered in plastic wrap. Naked capillaries made the oval that had once been his face an angry, beefy red, except where varicosities yielded coils of dark purple. The staring, filmy gray eyes looked startlingly out of place—two large marbles left on a slick blacktop by a careless child. (337–38)

He was meant to have died in a fire, but managed to survive. Chardin explains the true purpose of Sigma:

> "These leaders of capitalism accurately foresaw that the people of Europe, embittered and sickened by fascism, would, in reaction, turn to the left. The soil had been scorched by the Nazis, these industrialists realized, and without the massive infusion of resources at key moments, socialism would begin to take root, first in Europe, then throughout the world. They saw their mission as preserving, fortifying, the industrial state. Which meant, as well, muffling the voices of dissent. Do these anxieties seem overstated? Not so. These industrialists knew how the pendulum of history worked. And if a fascist regime was followed by a socialist regime, Europe might be truly lost, as they saw it." (341)

This is largely the same message that Peter had told Ben long before, but, because of Chardin's central role in the origin of Sigma and the dreadful injuries he has suffered (Sigma would not have made such efforts to silence him if he did not know the truth), his account is endowed with a convincing weight of authenticity and authority. He goes on to relate how, for the next several decades, Sigma members continually sabotaged leftist movements throughout Europe and the United States ("This cabal of industrialists and bankers had seen to it that the world was made safe for capitalism" [341]). And now, Chardin goes on to say, "Sigma has, of late, been undergoing one final transformation" (350). It is only a matter of time until . . . well, of course we still have almost 200 pages of this seemingly interminable novel to go, so Chardin cannot spill the beans just now: he is conveniently murdered by Griffiths, who has been lurking in an apartment across the street.

Griffiths, of course, takes potshots at Anna and Ben also, but naturally he misses. Fleeing out of Chardin's home, they see several other people who appear to be gunmen hired by Sigma. They escape by commandeering a velocipede and going along abandoned railroad tracks out of town. Anna now realises that Alan Bartlett had given her the assignment so that she could hunt down rebel members of Sigma and get them killed.

They now feel that Josef Strasser—who, along with Gerhard Lenz, had practiced some peculiar "experiments on children, on twins" (301), might be their last hope. He appears to be living in Buenos Aires. They go in disguise, Anna dressing up as a woman from India. In Buenos Aires, they are beaten up by a gang of thugs but are apparently rescued by the police—who turn out not to be the police. They form a bodyguard protecting Strasser. As they are recuperating in a hotel room, Ben thinks of Peter and gets all choked up; Anna too begins to weep. And so the inevitable (something the reader has been salivating for ever since the two paired up) happens:

> He could feel her heart thudding against his chest, her warmth. She raised her head off his shoulder and slowly, tentatively at first, placed her lips against his, her eyes closed tight. They kissed slowly, tenderly at first, then deeply and with abandon. His arms encircled her lithe body, his fingers exploring her as his mouth and tongue did the same. They had crossed a line each of them had invisibly and firmly drawn some time ago, a boundary, a high wall between natural impulses, containing and isolating the powerful electrical charges that now crackled back and forth between them. And somehow, when they made love, it didn't seem as awkward as he'd imagined it might be, when he'd allowed himself to imagine it.
>
> Finally, exhausted, they napped for half an hour or so, entwined in each other.
>
> When he awoke, he saw that she was gone. (404)

Take note, feminists: it is the woman who leaves after lovemaking! All one can say about this is that Ludlum mercifully eschews both the bathetic prose-poetry of Danielle Steel and her compatriots and the clinical emphasis on body parts of your routine pornographer. And, of course, he does not allow this bout of sex to interrupt the hectic flow of the narrative.

Ben and Anna manage to get Strasser's address from a private detective, Sergio Machado (who, shortly thereafter, is killed by a car bomb). They go to his house—and of course they are shot at. Actually, the shooters end up blowing away an elderly security guard who turns out to be none other than the redoubtable Trevor Griffiths. They had in fact been hired by Max Hartman to protect his son. Ben and Anna now go to the door. Strasser himself answers—but behind him is, apparently, a nurse. Anna has seen this scenario before. More gunfire ensues, and after all is said and done, both Ben's protectors (Israeli commandos—surprisingly incompetent, given their reputation) and the nurse are dead. But why should we be surprised that Griffiths himself is still alive?

> Images, shapeless and unfocused, devoid of significance or definition, outlines blurring into plumes of gray, disintegrating into nothingness like a jet's exhaust tracks in a windy sky. At first, there was only awareness, without even any defined object of awareness. He was so cold. So very cold. Save for the spreading warmth on his chest.
> And where there was warmth, he felt pain.
> That was good. Pain was good.
> Pain was the Architect's friend. Pain he could manage, could banish when he needed to. At the same time, it meant he was still alive. (425)

It is interesting that Ludlum resorts to prose-poetry not, in the way of our queens of romance, when describing the ultimate act of lovemaking, but the aftermath of bloodletting.

In any case, Strasser tells Ben and Anna that Gerhard Lenz was at work on some kind of molecular experiments. He says that Ben's father had never been in the SS—that was just a cover. He tells them that some big Sigma meeting is going on in Vienna, under the cover of an International Children's Health Forum, largely sponsored by the Lenz Foundation. Shortly after Ben and Anna leave, Griffiths crawls into Strasser's house and kills him.

Ben and Anna make their way to Vienna. Anna goes right to the Lenz Foundation to see Jürgen Lenz (who, we now learn, is not in fact the son of Gerhard). Ben finds that Lenz is funding research into progeria, or premature ageing. Can this be an extension of what Strasser and Lenz had worked on as Nazis? But Ben has more immediate concerns: Anna is now missing. Ben believes that the scientific activity is going on at a castle in the Alps near the town of Semmering—can Anna also be there?

Anna, for her part, was on the verge of revealing Lenz's real name, but was conveniently subdued and drugged. Ben now approaches the castle: he sees a group of children and teenagers in the lawn, apparently prisoners. Guards fire at him. Inside, Anna has been strapped to a bed, but she manages to pick the locks and free herself. Ben providentially discovers that there is a series of caves around the castle; perhaps one might even lead into the castle. Why should he doubt it? Led by an elderly cave-climber, Ben goes through the system of caves and gets into the castle. He finds himself in a storeroom where there are dozens of bottles containing fetuses. Overwhelming a guard, he puts on the guard's suit. He comes to an immense room where an array of famous elderly people are getting treatment of some kind. Then Lenz himself comes up behind Ben; the latter is captured.

Lenz, who, in the spirit of all such villains, now feels he has nothing to fear from Ben or Anna, spills the beans for their benefit and that of the reader. He explains that he is conducting experiments for the prolongation of life. But certain enzymes have to be taken from children. Ben now meets his old professor, John Barnes Goodwin, who looks a lot younger than one would have any reason to expect. Goodwin expatiates on the need for wise men to lead the world. Ben, under restraint, is being taken away, but just at that point Anna bursts in with a machine gun: she identifies Jürgen Lenz as (what no reader by this point has failed to guess) old Gerhard. They go to Lenz's office; he pulls out a gun and points it at Ben— but is interrupted by none other than Max Hartman. Max shoots Lenz, and Ben finishes the job by injecting an "opioid" (517) into him. Lenz dies. But now Ben and Anna realise that Lenz had managed to shoot Max; the latter dies also. But before dying, he had conveniently told his son that he could escape by means of Lenz's private helicopter. They get to the copter and take off in it—but find Alan Bartlett in the back, with a gun! Ben jostles the copter so that Bartlett loses his gun; they subdue him. But he isn't finished yet: he bites Ben in the neck. Ben and Anna finally push him out of the copter. The castle blows up: the dynamite used to block up the cave entrance was too large. But before that happened, those thirty-seven illustrious individuals had managed to escape (also the children in the yard), so the only victims were Gerhard Lenz's men.

We have at last reached the end—but of course, a novel like this cannot end without a suggestion that Sigma is still managing to live on, so that its nefarious attempts to suppress the valiant left and make the world safe for multinational corporations will continue.

In one sense, Ludlum has (if you will pardon my saying so) shot himself in the foot: this novel is so ludicrously complex that its chances of being translated into film or television are virtually nil. In fairness to Ludlum, it would be difficult to cut or truncate any significant segment of the work in a media adaptation without disfiguring the overall thrust of the novel. At the same time, even as a reading experience the novel consistently presents itself in visual terms: the interior monologues that Ludlum continually displays to reflect Ben Hartman's shifting emotions regarding his father are all so inane that they could be easily excised without any significant loss.

The amusing thing about *The Sigma Protocol,* and the chief factor—even beyond its preposterous plot or its telltale pulling of emotional punches at the end—that mitigates against its consideration as a serious literary work, is that Ludlum is so intent on a breakneck pace of action and incident that the reader is not given any time to reflect upon the political or moral significance of any of the subtexts running through it. Indeed, the reader experiences impatience whenever Ludlum does slow up the pace a bit and try to paint a scene a bit more tranquilly: several pages are devoted to the description of an elderly woman whose apartment Griffiths breaks into while planning to blow away Georges Chardin, but this passage is of no relevance to the overall plot and merely delays its progress.

Ludlum valiantly attempts to lend sociopolitical significance to his novel by his suggestion that Sigma has been secretly pulling the strings behind the scenes for half a century. After he hears the whole story from Chardin, Ben Hartman professes to undergo a cataclysmic change of heart:

> *My worldview was shattered that day, then and forever.*
>
> *Children, in history classes, are taught the names, the faces of political and military leaders. Here is Winston Churchill, here is Dwight Eisenhower, here is Franco and De Gaulle, Atlee and Macmillan. These men did matter. But they were, really, little more than spokesmen. They were, in an exalted sense, press secretaries, employees. And Sigma made sure of it. The men who truly had their hands on the levers of power were sitting around that*

*long mahogany table. They were the true marionette masters.*

*As the hours passed, and we drank coffee and nibbled on pastries, I realized what I was witness to: a meeting of the board of directors of a massive single corporation that controlled all other corporations.*

*A board of directors in charge of Western history itself!* (347)

Yes, I fear the italics are Ludlum's. The problem with all this is that it is all too obvious and hackneyed: if the "message" of *The Sigma Protocol* is that powerful economic forces (Sigma being merely a metaphor for them) are the true manipulators of the outward events of social and political history, then one would have to have spent one's entire life in a convent not to be aware of the fact. And the manner in which Ludlum expresses this cosmic revelation is too bombastic and self-important to qualify either as serious literature or as penetrating political insight.

Then there is the matter of the very high body-count in this novel. If the avowed purpose is merely to shock the reader, then—after the opening scene in the Zürich shopping mall—even this purpose fails through repetition and surfeit. The reader has not been allowed to have a sufficient emotional stake in any of the characters to care whether they live or die. Peter Hartman is no sooner plucked from (supposed) death and put on stage than he is blown away. Ludlum has attempted to invest him with some degree of emotional substance by having Ben ponder lugubriously over his fate, but it all amounts to very little. Ludlum also provokes mirth at his own expense by having Ben and Anna dodge death on so many occasions: if Sigma really were such a powerful organization, it is extremely unlikely that it could not have dispensed with these insignificant pests long before they became a threat.

Ludlum, even more egregiously than John Grisham, strives to whitewash those of his characters with whom he hopes the reader has identified. The early revelation—coming from Peter Hartman, and therefore presumably an unimpeachable source—that Max Hartman was a Nazi is successively overturned first by the claim (by Sonnenfeld) that he was acting as a Nazi only to save his family, and then by the discovery that he was not a Nazi at all. And Max's grotesquely implausible jack-in-the-box appearance at the end, so that he can blow Gerhard Lenz away, is no doubt envisioned by Ludlum as some kind of poetic justice, but is too ludicrously contrived for credence.

The tragedy is that, on the level of prose, Ludlum is a far from discreditable writer. Even though he at times descends to hackdom (as in the passage about Georges Chardin's deformities—the "proud flesh" and the "angry, beefy red"), his prose is on the whole crisp and even pungent. But, after decades of bestsellerdom, he has been suckered into giving the readers exactly what they want—a deliciously complex plot that nonetheless reads quickly, characters that are invariably stereotypes but are nonetheless lively and vibrant, and an adrenalin-filled narrative filled with chases, gunplay, close brushes with death, and more twists and turns than a New York street vendor's pretzel. But what does it all amount to in the end? I, for one, am hardly critical of the surprisingly liberal subtext—corporations are evil—of this novel, although I have no idea whether other Ludlum works are similarly left of centre in their political orientation. But no one comes to Ludlum for a lesson in postwar political and economic history: his sole purpose is to provide thrills, and in that humble function he succeeds to the best of his ability.

\* \* \* \* \* \* \*

Tom Clancy (b. 1947) is a full generation younger than Robert Ludlum, and his political and religious orientation is substantially different. He, too, served in the army (specifically, the Army Reserve Officer Training Corps), but from an early period he exhibited both political conservatism and fervent Roman Catholicism. Beginning his career as an insurance agent, he later became the owner of his own insurance company before writing *The Hunt for Red October* (1984), which became a spectacular bestseller. Relatively modest in fiction production, he has written only thirteen novels, but has produced fourteen works of nonfiction, mostly on military subjects. Four of his novels have been adapted to film. His recurring character, the CIA agent Jack Ryan, made his debut in *The Hunt for Red October.* But the demise of the Cold War and its seemingly transparent moral gulf between Americans and Soviets has caused particular problems for Clancy, as the recent novel *Red Rabbit* (2002)[5] shows.

*Red Rabbit* is a kind of historical spy novel, focused around the attempted assassination of Pope John Paul II by Mehmet Agça in 1981—a ploy that Clancy explicitly attributes to the KGB and its then leader, Yuri Andropov, by means of the Bulgarian secret service. I shall have more to say about the political and aesthetic implications of this conception later; here it can be stated that virtually all the leading figures (especially on the Soviet side) appear to be real, with the obvious exception of Jack Ryan and some of his British colleagues.

Ryan and his family have moved to London. In another thread that will eventually be linked up, another spy, Ed Foley, and his family move to Russia. At once we are treated to numerous unflattering portrayals of Soviet society and government. We are treated to an interior monologue by Andropov himself:

> *No,* Yuriy Vladimirovich told himself, *getting people to believe in Marxism wasn't all that hard.* First, they hammered it into their heads in grammar schools, and the Young Pioneers, and high schools, and the Komsomolets, the Young Communist League, and then the really smart ones became full Party members, keeping their Party cards "next to their hearts," in the cigarette pockets of their shirts. (18)

Hmmm . . . but isn't capitalism indoctrinated into American youth in just the same way, with the really smart ones becoming full members of the Republican party or the Chamber of Commerce or the Club for Growth? And what of the KGB? "Like the society it served, KGB applied a political template to reality" (28)—as if the American government doesn't! And again: "the problem with ideologues was that their theories did not always take reality into proper account, a fact to which they were mostly blind" (51). I can't think of a better description of the administration of George W. Bush. Various bleats of this sort fill this book, revealing an embarrassing inability on Clancy's part to acknowledge that the very same weaknesses he sees in the Soviet Union are fully as applicable to the United States.

Andropov, whose official title is the chairman of the Committee for State Security, wishes to transform the USSR, making it strong and feared again. But one of the thorns in his side is Pope John Paul II, who is lauded as follows:

> This had to be a man of deep faith, with the sort of core convictions that an earthquake couldn't bulge or crack. He'd been chosen by other such men to be the leader and spokesman for the world's largest church, which, by the way, also happened to be

Ryan's church [and, as it happens, Clancy's]. He'd be a man who didn't fear much of anything, a man for whom a bullet was his get-out-of-jail-free card, a key to God's own presence. And he'd be a man who felt God's presence in everything he did. He was not someone you could scare, not someone you could turn away from what he deemed the right thing. (44)

With bombast like this, we quickly see what kind of moral tale Clancy is about to spin. And so the plot moves on . . . slowly and blunderingly. Foley is station chief in Moscow; his wife, Mary Pat, is also an agent. I cannot help quoting one more political comment, put in Foley's head, that one can only hope Clancy now finds a bit awkward: "There was still torture here [in Russia], still interrogations that lasted into long hours. Due process of law was whatever the government at the time felt like it was" (81). I don't believe any comment is necessary on this.

The Pope, a Pole, has thrown down the gauntlet to the Soviet Union in a letter: "If the government of Warsaw persists in its unreasonable repression of the people, I will be compelled to resign the papacy and return to be with my people in their time of trouble" (81). This is, of course, when the Solidarity movement in Poland was gaining steam. Andropov is furious at this development:

> Warsaw *had* to camp down on those counterrevolutionary troublemakers in Danzig—strangely, Andropov always thought of that port city by the old German name—lest its government come completely unglued. Moscow had told them to sort things out in the most direct terms, and the Poles knew how to follow orders. The presence of Soviet Army tanks on their soil would help them understand what was necessary and what was not. If this Polish "Solidarity" rubbish went much further, the infection would begin to spread—west to Germany, south to Czechoslovakia . . . and east to the Soviet Union? They couldn't allow that. (87)

And so Andropov—after Clancy has made his atheist views crystal clear (*"No, there is no God"* [89])—wonders about simply getting rid of the pestiferous Pole ("And so, Karol had to die" [89]).

Andropov assigns Aleksay Rozhdestvenskiy to look into the easiest and simplest means to effect this result. At what point could an assassin get close enough to the Pope to shoot him? Aleksay (I can't be bothered to type the fellow's last name more than once) says that the best way to kill the Pope is to hire a Turk through the Bulgarian office. But while these discussions are going on, one Oleg Zaitzev, a minor functionary at the KGB who is relaying messages about the Pope, is plagued by the thought of killing the poor fellow: as he reflects in a dramatic one-sentence paragraph, "And they wanted to kill a priest" (171). Should he tell the CIA? Zaitzev, although presumably one of those millions of Soviets who has been neatly brainwashed to accept Marxism, displays anomalous independence of thought: he believes that "the course his country was taking" was "an evil one" (182)!

Andropov now talks about the mission with Ilya Bobovoy, head of the agency in Bulgaria. Andropov wants a second gunman to kill the first one, in order to silence him in case he is captured alive (he must have been a fan of Jack Ruby's). The killing of the Pope is discussed quite ruthlessly at a Politburo meeting:

> "It may be possible to eliminate the threat by eliminating the man who makes it," the Chairman replied, with an even, unemotional voice.
> "To kill him?" Ustinov asked.
> "Yes, Dmitriy."
> "What are the dangers of that?" the Foreign Minister asked at once. Diplomats always worried about such things. (228)

All eleven members of the Politburo agree to the plan, although some have reservations about it.

Meanwhile, Zaitzev has slipped a note to Ed Foley, whom he recognises as an American agent, in a Moscow subway train. Zaitzev then meets Mary Pat Foley, offering to turn over information if she can get him, his wife, and his child out of the USSR. He goes on to say that CIA communications in Moscow are seriously compromised—something Mary Pat finds more disturbing than anything else Zaitzev has said (*"Oh, shit*, Mary Pat thought. *They have a mole somewhere, and he might be in the White House Rose Garden for all we know. Oh, shit . . ."* [323]). The Foleys initially want to sneak the Zaitzevs through Hungary, but in an earlier passage we have learned that an American agent in Hungary has been captured picking up a dead-drop, so clearly that office is infiltrated also. So the plan shifts to getting the Zaitzevs out through the UK office—and this, at last, is where Jack Ryan comes in.

It is worth mentioning that Ryan is not having an especially good time in the merry isle. The poor fellow just doesn't get the lofty and recherché humor of "Fawlty Towers" ("It's what they call a comedy over here, Admiral. It's funny if you can understand it" [345]). Evidently we are to sympathise with Ryan for his denseness. His wife, an eye doctor, isn't faring much better. She is quite fed up with socialised medicine: in a gratuitous passage that has nothing to do with the overall plot, she is appalled that a woman requiring a routine eye procedure will have to wait nine to ten months for it, and later she is even more distressed when two surgeons walk out of an operation in progress to get lunch (and a pint) at a nearby pub. One would think that Clancy should be aware of the dangers of generalizing from a few bad examples—all one has to do is mention Abu Ghraib to settle the point. And as for the poor woman requiring the operation, I don't suppose she would be in much better shape in this country if she didn't have health insurance. But it's too easy to shoot Clancy down in this manner, so I'll move on.

Ryan, pondering the Zaitzev situation, wants to set up a scenario where dead bodies similar to those of Zaitzev, his wife, and his child are found by the Soviets, so that the latter think the Zaitzevs are dead, and so do not worry about his escaping and spilling what he knows. Very shortly, the situation works out exactly to their liking. A young British man dies in a fire: "it turned out he had no immediate family, and his ex-wife had no interest in him at all" (413). This body is sent to Patrick Nolan of the Metropolitan Police, who sends it to the British secret service. One down, two to go. An unmarried couple with a small child die in Boston—these people had no family to stir up a fuss either, and voilà! the duplicate corpses (with one left over for good measure, apparently) are found!

The plan is to set a fire in a room at the Astoria Hotel in Budapest, where the Zaitzevs would be staying. Having put the corpses into the room, Ryan, the Zaitzevs, and others attend a classical music concert. Somewhat peculiarly, the orchestra is playing Bach's "Toccata and Fugue in D minor." Is Clancy unaware that this is a work for organ solo? Presumably it is Leopold Stokowski's orchestral transcription, although Clancy makes no mention of it. All he can do is have Ryan suddenly find his inner aesthete: "This was as much Bach as Ryan had ever heard at one time [the piece lasts about fifteen minutes], and that old German composer had really had his shit wired, the former Marine thought" (496). Move over, Charles Rosen! Anyway, the room at the hotel is set on fire while Ryan and the Zaitzevs go to an airport in Yugoslavia, then fly to Manchester. Easy as pie!

Zaitzev is then interrogated, and he tells of the plot to kill the Pope—something that both the British and the American agents had heard dimly about, but the particulars of which they did not know. Ryan now goes to Rome to scout out the evident location of the shooting—St. Peter's Square, where the Pope mingles with the crowd one day every week, usually a Wednesday. At one point Ryan catches sight of a Russian agent named Strokov. He puts a gun to Strokov's back—but just then he hears gunshots elsewhere. Curiously enough, the American agents don't seem much concerned with the Pope himself, but are instead intent on capturing the perpetrators. Strokov later admits that the KGB had planned the whole affair, with Strokov himself assigned to kill Agça after the assassination. Later Strokov is found dead in his car . . . and so (a point of which Clancy seems entirely oblivious) it now appears that our "good guys" (the Americans and British) are largely indistinguishable from the "bad guys." This is the note on which the novel ends.

There are innumerable political, moral, philosophical, and aesthetic problems with *Red Rabbit,* and I can only hope that it is somehow unrepresentative of Clancy's work as a whole. Perhaps it is, only in the sense that it is based so clearly on an actual historical event. It is manifest that Clancy, who is both a conservative and a Roman Catholic, has chosen this event so that he can once more resurrect the evil, atheistic Soviets as the villains of the piece. No greater example of the desperation of hack spy novels at the fall of the Soviet Union can be found than this (but mercifully for them, Arab terrorism has now emerged as the new global evil, so one can no doubt expect a flurry of novels where valiant American spies battle with turbaned sheiks). What makes Clancy's choice of this incident particularly unfortunate is that *we all know how it turned out:* the Pope was indeed shot multiple times, but managed to survive, as did his assailant, Agça. This brute fact robs *Red Rabbit* of any conceivable suspense in regard to its outcome, and the reader is left helplessly witnessing what prove to be rather bumbling English and American attempts to foil the plot. If Clancy wanted to display the superiority of Anglo-American spies over their Russian counterparts, he has chosen exactly the wrong event to focus on.

It may be worth noting that Clancy's blithe attribution of direct KGB involvement in the assassination attempt is entirely fabricated. Numerous scholars since the fall of the Soviet Union have looked into the matter, and the end result is, at the very best, a verdict of "not proven." Garry O'Connor, author of a thoroughly researched biography of Pope John Paul II, writes: ". . . was Agça acting alone? Many vivid theories for and against this contention subsequently blossomed into circulation (according to one, the inebriated Brezhnev suggested to KGB chief Andropov that the Soviet world would be well rid of this turbulent priest)."[6] But O'Connor goes on to say:

> American security chiefs and agencies found nothing to pin the assassination attempt on Moscow, believing that neither Brezhnev nor KGB head Andropov would have ordered the death of John Paul—quite the reverse, as it would have compounded Russia's already serious difficulties with Poland and sparked off further unrest. As revealed in 1992 documents released by the post-Soviet government, a top-secret cable from Rome reported the wounding of the Pope "by an unknown assailant. The crime was perpetrated while the Pope was driving through a crowd of the faithful in an open automobile. . . . Early reports connect this attempt . . . with the complex political situation in the country [Poland]." But neither this cable nor anything else gave substance to the many allegations of a Communist plot that would follow. It seemed unlikely that, had Ağça been hired, he would have publicly proclaimed his intention beforehand. Yet as Robert Gates, director of the CIA, summed up in 1996, "The question of whether the Soviets were involved in or knew about the assassination attempt remains unanswered and one of the great remaining secrets of the cold war."[7]

This does not mean that Clancy is in error for attributing the plot to the KGB; he is certainly within his rights as an historical novelist to make this kind of conjecture, and to base an entire long-winded novel upon it. But it becomes transparently obvious that Clancy has chosen this scenario solely for the purpose of once more dredging up a cardboard villain whose perceived failings, both political and religious, can be held up to scorn in contrast to freedom-loving, God-fearing Americans. (The British, with their dangerous tendency toward socialism, are somewhere between these extremes, but their deficiencies serve, in Clancy's mind, as a warning as to where the United States should *not* go.)

As it is, it becomes so plain whose side Clancy is on that all the Soviet characters prove to be little better than caricatures. As Mrs. Foley reflects on one occasion, "Mary Pat called it the belly of the beast, and this one was one nasty fuckin' beast" (212). Clancy must surely be aware that our own CIA has been involved in its share of sordid doings—assassinations, overthrows of governments, and the like—in the past half-century, and that these activities are substantially worse than similar actions by the KGB precisely because the United States is supposed to be some kind of shining beacon of democracy and freedom. On only one occasion does Clancy address this point, and he does so with pathetic feebleness:

> The KGB had a very direct way of dealing with people it didn't like. CIA did not. They hadn't actually killed anyone since the fifties [thank God for small mercies], when President Eisenhower had used CIA—actually quite skillfully—as an alternative to employing uniformed troops in an overt fashion. But that skill hadn't been conveyed to the Kennedy Administration, which had screwed up nearly everything it touched. (346)

So it was all Kennedy's fault! So I imagine that the CIA's 1953 overthrow of the Iranian prime minister, Mohammed Mossadegh, to bolster the Shah of Iran—an incident that led directly to the revolution in 1979 and has substantially worsened the prospects for peace in the Middle East—was merely an attempt to avoid "employing uniformed troops in an overt fashion"!

Then there is the matter of Ryan's and other characters' ponderous discussions of God. Consider this priceless passage:

> "Father Tim at Georgetown liked to say that wars are begun by frightened men. They're afraid of the consequences of war, but they are more afraid of not fighting. Hell of a way to run a world," Ryan thought out loud, opening the door for his friend.
> "August 1914 as the model, I expect."
> "Right, but at least those guys all believed in God. The second go-round was a little different in that respect. The players in that one—the Bad Guys, anyway—didn't live under that particular constraint. Neither do the guys in Moscow. You know, there have to be some limits on our actions, or we can turn into monsters." (264–65)

It is difficult to chronicle all the intellectual failings in this passage. In the first place, Clancy doesn't seem to be aware that World War I wasn't, in the end, much less vicious than World War II (remember mustard gas? Gallipoli? the *Lusitania?*)—so that it is difficult to make a case that people who believe in God behave less heinously in war (or in any other context) than those who don't. And as for exercising "constraint," can Clancy have forgotten that it was the God-fearing United States that dropped the atomic bomb and killed 120,000 noncombatants?

Here's another passage that ranks high in buffoonery:

> People—even intelligent people—believed all manner of impossible things. It was sure as hell true in Moscow, where the rulers of this vast and powerful country believed in a political philosophy as out of tune with contemporary reality as the Divine Right of Kings. More to the point, they knew it was a false philosophy, and yet they commanded themselves to believe it as though it were Holy Scripture written in gold ink by God's own hand. So these people *could* be fooled. They worked pretty hard to fool themselves, after all. (337–38)

The only fool, I regret to say, is Clancy. Those telling parallels to religion are—although he is entirely unaware of it—the giveaway. It is exactly the contention of many that believers in God "believed all manner of impossible things," like the fact that a virgin can give birth, or that a body can be resurrected three days after its death, or that only the baptised will go to Heaven (Jesus said that: Mark 16:16), and so on and so forth. Clancy's point is that the fervency with which the Soviets believed in Communism (matched by the fervor with which most Americans believe in capitalism) renders it a kind of secular religion—but actual religions make just as many demands on people's incredulity as these ersatz faiths.

As for the Catholic Church, Clancy sings its praises in a passage so excruciatingly moronic that it deserves embalming in Lucite:

> The Catholic Church was not a perfect institution—nothing with mere people in it was or ever could be. But it was founded on faith in Almighty God, and its policies rarely, if ever, strayed from love and charity.

But those doctrines were seen as a threat by the Soviet Union. What better proof of who the Bad Guys were in the world? Ryan had sworn as a Marine to fight his country's enemies. But here and now he swore to himself to fight against God's own enemies. The KGB recognized no power higher than the Party it served. And, in proclaiming that, they defined themselves as the enemy of all mankind—for wasn't mankind made in God's own image? Not Lenin's. Not Stalin's. God's. (598)

With each passing sentence, one wants to plead with Clancy to shut up so as not to descend into still lower nadirs of buffoonery. The Catholic Church's policies "rarely, if ever, strayed from love and charity"? Well, aside from the six hundred years of the Inquisition, the murder of millions of "witches" and heretics, the forced conversions of Jews, Muslims, and other non-Catholics, the brutal religious wars of the early modern period, and sundry other peccadilloes. . . .

On a few occasions Clancy does attempt to deal with the social implications of capitalism, but he does so only to tie himself hopelessly into intellectual knots. At one point Ryan thinks to himself: "Generally speaking, talent went to where the money was, because smart people wanted large houses and nice vacations just like everyone else" (385–86). And yet, this epitome of worldly wisdom is directly contradicted by Ryan's later reflection: "Any opinionated asshole could make money, and his father-in-law [an investment banker] was one of them" (438)—and still later, "You do not need to be very smart in America to become rich" (522).

If it be objected that it is beyond the critic's function to argue with an author's political or philosophical views, I answer that Clancy so aggressively pushes them into the reader's face that some kind of response is mandatory; he would be the last person in the world to want the reader to read his work purely for the thrills and not for the "philosophy" underlying it. As it is, Clancy's work would not come out very well from a purely aesthetic examination, either. On the level of prose, it would be difficult to find a writer more given to clumsiness of diction. Even if we can ignore grammatical slips such as "alit" (92) for "alighted," "whomever it was" (210), or "a damned site [i.e., sight] more competent" (323), what can we do with a writer who states that "Hudson had a staff of three, including himself" (367)? In other words, the fellow had a staff of two.

Let it also be noted that, in spite of the relative thinness of the plot of *Red Rabbit,* the book is no less than 618 pages in length. How does Clancy fill up the pages? Well, largely it is by dwelling on the mundane actions of his (American and British) spies, evidently in an attempt to humanise them, as opposed to their robotlike Soviet counterparts. We are, for example, treated to six interminable pages telling in painful detail the procedures by which Ryan and his wife get up, have breakfast, and go to work in London (102–8). If this was Theodore Dreiser, there would be some sense in it; but Tom Clancy is no Theodore Dreiser. Clancy does much the same for Ed and Mary Pat Foley, also considerably slowing down the action as a result.

But the overriding problem with *Red Rabbit* is simply that Clancy has erred in his selection of a plot that, by its very nature, lacks suspense because every reader knows the outcome. Even whittling the book down to half its size would result only in the minimal benefit of concision; the absence of suspense would remain. Add to this the windy political and religious theorizing by a writer who is entirely out of his depth in these issues, and you have a work that is destined for the remainder shelves.

* * * * * * *

Clive Cussler (b. 1931), like Ludlum and Clancy, served in the military (the U.S. Air Force, 1950–54) and worked in advertising for a decade before writing his first novel, *The Mediterranean Caper* (1973). It took a little while for him to become a bestseller, but a majority of the nineteen novels featuring his recurring character, the pungently monosyllabic Dirk Pitt (two of them were co-written with his son, Dirk Cussler), have been pretty successful. He has also written six novels in the "Kurt Austin" series and three novels (all collaborative) in the "Oregon Files" series, whatever they may be. He has also written four nonfiction books, including *Clive Cussler and Dirk Pitt Revealed* (1998; with Craig Durgo), which I daresay is required reading for Clive Cussler scholars. His hero, Dirk Pitt, is a member of NUMA (National Underwater and Marine Agency). This entity is of course fictitious, but Cussler's financial success as a novelist has allowed him to create an organization of this very name, devoted to searching for sunken ships. Only two of his novels have been adapted for film, although there has been a documentary series on television, "Clive Cussler's 'The Sea Hunters.'" Whether the novel of his that I read, *Atlantis Found* (1999),[8] is representative of his work I shall leave to others to decide.

The omniscient narrator of *Atlantis Found* commences the story in the remote era of 7120 B.C., when a meteor crashes into the earth around what is now Hudson Bay, Canada. A worldwide cataclysm ensues; flourishing civilizations vanish without a trace. This event gives rise to the legend of Atlantis.

Moving considerably forward in time, the narrator now takes us to the year 1858, when a whaling ship, the *Paloverde,* is stuck in the Antarctic ice. Roxanna Mender, the wife of the whaler's captain, is caught in a blizzard while out for a walk. She catches sight of a derelict ship in the distance: it proves to be a British vessel from the 1770s. The rest of the crew, led to the site, explore it and find that it is the *Madras* (1779); the captain, Leigh Hunt, his wife, his infant child, and many crewmen are found dead and frozen on the vessel. Roxanna, for her part, finds a peculiar skull made of obsidian on board the ship. The relevance of these two flashbacks will become evident in the course of time.

We at last come to the present day—or, actually, the near-future, for the narrator now informs us that it is March 22, 2001. One Luis Marquez has bought an old gold mine, the Paradise Mine in Colorado, and made a fortune extracting gemstones from it. One day he finds a hidden room with a black skull in it. A renowned anthropologist, Thomas Ambrose, brings in a colleague, Patricia O'Connell, to examine the skull and the inscriptions in the room. Pat concludes that the writing is not ancient, but a code of some sort. As they are exploring, a cave-in occurs: Marquez thinks it was deliberately created by a blast of dynamite. There is a possibility that they will drown from the rising water flowing into the small room in which they find themselves. Pat verbalises the matter plangently. "'I wonder,' she whispered softly, 'what it's like to drown'" (49). Of course we know that she will not drown. A diver from a neighboring mine comes to rescue them. He is Dirk Pitt; or, as he announces in James Bond fashion, "My name is Dirk Pitt" (56). The explorers are not quite out of the woods yet, for they still need to get out of the cave system. As they make their way into a tunnel, they are confronted by three bikers. They inform the explorers that they are obliged to kill them because "You saw the skull and you saw the inscriptions" (68). Well, this will never do. Dirk sneaks behind them, knocking out one and killing two as they try to kill him:

> Pitt did not face the killers full-on, knees slightly bent, his gun gripped and extended in two hands directly in front of his nose, the way they taught in police academies or seen in action movies [naturally].

He preferred the classic stance, body turned sideways, eyes staring over one shoulder, gun stretched out in one hand. Not only did he present less of a target, but his aim was more precise. [He also looks more cool.] He knew that the gunslingers of the West who'd lived to a ripe old age had not necessarily been the fastest on the draw, but they were the straightest shooters, who'd taken their time to aim before pulling the trigger. (69–70)

If there is any better indication that we are in a modern, souped-up version of cowboys and Indians, I don't know what it is.

The explorers manage to get out at last. It is only at this time that we finally get a full-blown description of Our Hero, through the eyes of a sheriff named James Eagan, Jr.:

At first glance, he looked to Eagan to be forty-five, but he was probably a good five years younger than the tanned and craggy face suggested. The sheriff guessed him to be about six feet three inches, weight 185 pounds, give or take. His hair was black and wavy, with a few strands of gray at the temples. The eyebrows were dark and bushy and stretched over eyes that were a vivid green, a straight and narrow nose dropped from firm lips, with the corners turned up in a slight grin. What bothered Eagan wasn't so much the man's indifferent attitude—he'd known many felons who displayed apathy—but his bemused kind of detached interest. It was obvious that the man across the table was not the least bit impressed with Eagan's dominating tactics. (78–79)

This passage must set some kind of record for clichés. The most interesting thing about it (and even this is not very interesting) is that, in contrast to the lovely women in romance novels who always look much younger than they are, Dirk actually looks *older* than he is, with (no doubt "distinguished") grey at his temples. But the reason for this is his "tanned and craggy face," something evidently sought for by couch-potato men who yearn to be in Dirk's shoes. In a single paragraph we see how the suspense/spy novel exactly mirrors, for men, the wish-fulfillment fantasies of the romance novel for women.

The matter of the cave-in and subsequent fisticuffs is not quite resolved. Thomas Ambrose had actually been left behind, with the three bikers (two dead, one captured). But when Dirk and company return to the spot, both Ambrose and the bikers are gone. Dirk, in the nick of time (naturally), detects a booby-trap explosive on the site; they manage to detonate it without injury. Dirk concludes that Ambrose is allied with the killers.

Pat now tells of an archaeological dig in Chile where several explorers died. Could there be a connection to the Colorado incident? While dining at Luis Marquez's house, Dirk and Pat are nearly killed by an assassin—but a colleague of Dirk's, Albert Giordano, has arrived in the nick of time (naturally) to foil the plot. Giordano has captured the would-be assassin: it is Thomas Ambrose himself—or, rather, an impostor pretending to be Ambrose. This person speaks of a coming "Fourth Empire" before killing himself. It is at this point that Dirk, teeth no doubt clenched, thinks to himself: "He knew for certain that someone was going to pay, and pay big-time" (94). If this novel hadn't been published in 1999, I'd have said that Dirk was channeling Dick Cheney.

Pitt and Giordano now return to the mine. They find two divers in the now-flooded chamber, photographing the inscriptions. Subduing them, Pitt and his sidekick also take away the obsidian skull.

It is now March 27, 2001. The *Polar Storm,* commanded by Daniel Gillespie, nearly collides with a submarine off the coast of Antarctica. Gillespie, conveniently enough, ascertains that it is a U-2015—a *Nazi* submarine that has not been seen in more than fifty years. We are left to chew on this while returning to the actions of Pitt and Giordano, who have made their way (along with Pat O'Connell) to Washington, D.C. Pitt has opportunely contacted his godfather, a 400-pound gourmand named Sir Julien Perlmutter, who happens to know where another skull exactly like the one they found in Colorado can be located: it is in Fredericksburg, Virginia, in the possession of Christine Mender-Husted, the great-granddaughter of Roxanna Mender. When Pitt and Perlmutter show her the skull found in Colorado, Christine quite implausibly hands over her own specimen to them, along with documents pertaining to the *Madras* expedition.

Pitt and Giordano meet with Admiral James Sandecker, the (naturally) gruff head of NUMA. Pitt, looking over the documents provided by Christine, says that the *Madras* found its skull on an uninhabited island on the South Indian Ocean. Meanwhile, Pat has been working on the inscriptions in NUMA's high-powered computer centre. Max, a rather uppity computer who makes tart remarks to all and sundry, has ascertained that some of the symbols are a star chart. Max also determines that the chamber in Colorado was built in 7100 B.C. Of course, Pat and others express incredulity, but the reader, having already had a glimpse of the distant past, knows that the computer must be right.

Giordano and Rudi Gunn, the deputy director of NUMA, are now sent to the Indian island, called St. John. In a cave they find twenty ancient mummies. But as they are returning to their plane, it blows up—a time bomb had been planted on it, and they are (naturally) lucky not to have been killed in it. Shortly thereafter the two men see an unmarked helicopter land on the island. Six men in black coveralls emerge. Giordano and Gunn hide; Sandecker, in communication with them, states that rescuers will still take about two hours to come. So our valiant pair manage to kill *all six* of the intruders and destroy the helicopter, although Gunn is injured in the process.

Sandecker now orders Pitt to go to the *Polar Storm:* he thinks it may be near the wreck of the *Madras.* The crew presently find it; it is covered in ice. They find artifacts on board and take them back to the *Polar Storm.* Meanwhile, the Nazi submarine has surfaced. Pitt taunts the men on board by radio; they fire a machine gun at him but (naturally) miss. But the submarine is not done yet; it now fires shells at the ship, and several reach their targets:

> He [Dirk] pulled himself erect, not bothering to count the bruises and glass cuts. Acrid smoke filled his nostrils, and his ears rang, cutting off all other sounds. He staggered over to Gillespie and knelt beside him. The explosion had smashed his chest against the chart table, breaking three, maybe four, ribs. His eardrums were bleeding. Blood also seeped from one pant leg. The captain's eyes were open but glassy. "My ship," he moaned softly, "those scum are destroying my ship." (197)

It looks bad for the *Polar Storm*—but then, out of nowhere, a surface-to-surface missile destroys the submarine. It has come from the U.S. nuclear attack boat *Tucson*, providentially sent by Admiral Sandecker.

Pitt now dives down to the wreck of the submarine, but finds no documents of any relevance. Then something strange happens:

Suddenly, without warning, Pitt felt a hand on his shoulder. He froze, and his slowly beating heart abruptly accelerated and pounded like a jackhammer. The contact was not exactly a tight grip; it was more like the hand was resting between his arm and neck. Beyond shock lies fear, the paralyzing, uncontrollable terror that can carry over into madness. It is a state characterized by a complete lack of comprehension and perception. Most men go totally numb, almost as if anesthetized, and are no longer capable of rational thought.

Most men, that is, except Pitt.

Despite his initial astonishment, his mind was unnaturally clear. He was too pragmatic and skeptical to believe in ghosts and goblins, and it didn't seem possible for another diver to have appeared from nowhere. Fear and terror melted away like a falling quilt. The awareness of something unknown became an intellectual awareness. He stood like an ice carving. Then slowly, carefully, he transferred the dive light and briefcase to his left hand and removed the dive knife from its sheath with his right. Gripping the hilt in his thermal glove, he spun around and faced the menace.

The apparition before his eyes was a sight he would take with him to the grave. (218)

I have quoted this passage at such excruciating length to show just how bad Clive Cussler can be when he thinks he is being at his action-packed best. In his desperation to turn Pitt into some kind of superhero, he uncorks bombast piled upon cliché; and if he thinks that that simile of fear melting away from Pitt like a falling quilt reveals a talent for prose-poetry, he had better think again. The sight that Dirk will take with him to his grave is a beautiful (naturally) dead woman. Bringing her up to the surface, he and others examine her, but to little effect.

It is at this point that Sandecker informs Pitt regarding the so-called New Destiny Operation:

"This was a blueprint drawn up by top Nazis, in collaboration with the Perón government in Argentina, for the flow of immense wealth accumulated by the Nazis during the war. While other submarines were still maintaining combat patrols to sink Allied shipping, the U-2015 was traveling back and forth between Germany and Argentina on a mission of transferring hundreds of millions of dollars' worth of gold and silver bullion, platinum, diamonds, and art objects stolen from the great collections of Europe. High-level Nazi officials and their families were also transported along with the treasure cargo, all discharged in absolute secrecy at a remote port on the coast of Patagonia. . . .

"The story that circulated in unconfirmed reports suggests that Operation New Destiny was the brainchild of Martin Bormann. He may have possessed a fanatical adoration of Adolf Hitler, but he was smart enough to see the Third Reich crashing and burning in flames. [How else does one crash and burn?] Smuggling the Nazi hierarchy and a staggering amount of valuables to a nation friendly to Germany was his goal even before the Allied armies crossed the Rhine. His most ambitious plan was to smuggle Hitler to a secret redoubt in the Andes, but it fell through when Hitler insisted on dying in his bunker in Berlin." (222)

Well, at least we will presumably be spared the spectacle of Hitler still alive and well after all these years . . . or will we? In any event, the evils of Nazidom are such that no self-respecting spy writer can allow them to die at the end of the war. But what exactly does all this have to do with 9,000-year-old obsidian skulls and inscriptions? We will no doubt find out in time.

We are now introduced to Karl Wolf, a fabulously wealthy German businessman in Buenos Aires. He is one of sextuplets, the others being his five sisters. He runs Destiny Enterprises Limited. One of the sisters, Heidi, was on the U-2015 when it was sunk, and no doubt this is the corpse that Dirk fished up from the wreckage. Karl and his family are, of course, planning some huge event in only ten days' time.

Meanwhile, Giordano and Gunn have to be rescued. Pat, Pitt, and others come to the island. Pitt finds a series of maps that suggests that the makers of the maps "walked on Antarctica thousands of years before man" (243). For his (its?) part, Max the computer has partially deciphered the inscriptions. (Exactly how this is possible, if the language predates all living tongues, is never adequately explained.) They tell of a cataclysm in 7000 B.C.—a comet landing on the earth. A second comet is predicted to land—very soon, if the inscriptions are correct. The inscriptions tell of a civilization that spanned the globe and "developed a chain of coastal city-ports" (248), hence accounting for the obsidian skulls and inscriptions being found in such remote areas as this island and Colorado.

Pitt returns to Washington, where his lover, Congresswoman Loren Smith of Colorado, is waiting for him. She is (naturally) gorgeous:

> If the car wasn't enough to turn heads, the woman sitting behind the wheel was equally beautiful. The long cinnamon hair was protected from the light breeze outside the airport by a colorful scarf. She had the prominent cheekbones of a fashion model, enhanced by full lips and a short, straight nose and charismatic violet eyes. She was wearing an alpaca chunky autumn leaf brown turtleneck with taupe wool tweed pants under a taupe shearling coat that came down to her knees. (252)

I'll vote for her in a heartbeat! Cussler must have taken lessons from Danielle Steel in describing her outfit—can it be that Cussler has women readers after all? But what a gaffe he commits by describing her as only *just as* beautiful as (not more beautiful than) her souped-up car!

Loren is, conveniently, on the International Trade Relations Committee (is there in fact such a thing?—I suppose there are congressional committees for just about everything else, so why not this?), which allows her to provide Dirk with just the kind of help he needs, as we shall see presently. She in fact knows Karl Wolf ("a handsome and stylish man, a real charmer. Women don't forget men like that" [253]), but of course she doesn't really know what he's up to.

As Dirk is going to Sandecker's office late at night, he is assailed by an intruder, who flees and exits the building, driving off in a car. Pitt returns to Loren's car, pushes Loren out of the driver's seat (naturally), and gives chase. The first car stops at a townhouse in Georgetown. Pitt tackles the woman as she is trying to flee on a motorcycle: he is startled to discover her to be the identical twin of the dead woman from the submarine.

Sandecker now calls a meeting, at which one Dr. John Stevens reveals that the obsidian skulls appear to have an opening; inside is a globe with an engraved illustration of the world. He says that an ancient race, called the Amenes (the name is derived from the translated inscriptions), had "lift[ed] mankind from the Stone Age to the Bronze Age" (266). As if that wasn't enough, they have also predicted the arrival of the second cataclysmic comet—on May 20, 2001, less than two months away!

The FBI has identified the woman from the submarine as Heidi Wolf, and the woman captured by Pitt as Elsie Wolf, a cousin. Dr. Aaron Bell of the FBI thinks that the women have been genetically engineered. Pitt now interviews Elsie, even though his impression of her is not favorable: "The pure sense of evil about her seemed so concentrated he could reach out and touch it" (280). She tells him that the Wolf family, knowing about the predicted comet, has been planning for fifty years to survive it. But how, exactly?

Dirk and Loren now take a little time to have a nice meal at a swanky Washington restaurant. Both are dressed for the occasion:

> As he pulled the Ford up in front of Loren's town house in Alexandria, he was wearing gray slacks, a dark blue sport coat, and a saffron-colored turtleneck sweater. Loren spotted him and the car from her fourth-story balcony, waved, and came down. Chic and glamorous, she wore a charcoal lace-and-beadwork cardigan with palazzo pants pleated in the front under a black, knee-length imitation fur coat. She carried a briefcase whose charcoal leather matched her outfit. (284)

Well, if it is one of the traits of popular writers to reveal their erudition, then Cussler has certainly succeeded: I don't even know what palazzo pants are—nor, for that matter, where one can get a man's saffron-coloured turtleneck sweater. At all events, Loren has found information on the Destiny Corporation: it was founded in 1947 by "high Nazi officials who had escaped Germany before the surrender" (286). Wolf is building four colossal ships to preserve civilization (or at least his idea of civilization) after the fall of the comet.

Pitt and Giordano now go to the Chilean port where all these ships are being made. But they are startled to learn that Pat O'Connell and her teenage daughter are missing—as are Elsie Wolf and the body of Heidi. Pitt believes Pat is in the Chilean shipyard somewhere. He also thinks that "there is a far more sinister purpose behind their undertaking. A purpose with horrible consequences" (302). I daresay. Pitt and Giordano manage to penetrate the shipyard undetected. Meanwhile, back in Washington, Sandecker hears a story from an old German acquaintance of his: the burned bodies of Hitler and Eva Braun were carried out of their bunker and placed in the U-2015. But there is a still more remarkable detail: "'One of the canisters that was transported aboard my U-boat was kept frozen at all times.' He drew a deep breath [naturally]. 'It contained the sperm and tissue samples taken from Hitler the week before he killed himself'" (312). Er . . . one doesn't wish to be indelicate, but how exactly did Hitler perform the necessary procedure while being besieged in his bunker? Well, I suppose there must have a certain amount of down time. . . . The end result is that the genetic engineering that appears to have resulted in the Wolf sextuplets may have come from Hitler's DNA!

Pitt and Giordano, going up an elevator in the shipyard office, overcome some guards and force one of them to tell where Pat is being kept. She and her daughter are in one of the ships, the *Ulrich Wolf*. Pitt and Giordano manage to find out what room she is being held in, break into the room, seize Pat and her daughter, Megan, and leave—then change clothes with four ship workers. (Pat, for her part, had been put to work by Wolf to decipher the inscriptions from an Amenes' city in Antarctica discovered by the Nazis before the war.) Through a series of incredible maneuvers, they manage to escape the compound. They are not quite in the clear yet, however: they reach their plane and take off, but are pursued by helicopter gunships. But (naturally) they elude them and return to safety.

It is now April 10, 2001. In Buenos Aires there is a big celebration of Prince Charles's accession to the British throne (Queen Elizabeth, apparently believing that Charles has cooled his heels long enough, has charitably abdicated). Dirk and Pat boldly accost Karl Wolf and Elsie, exchanging various insults with them. Wolf says the end of the world has moved up a bit—only four days and ten hours from now. The U.S. ambassador to Argentina tells Pitt that Wolf is to visit his "mineral retraction facility in Antarctica the day after tomorrow" (370). This ties in with something that the old German admiral, Hozafel, has told Sandecker earlier: the Nazis had established an extensive base in Antarctica, upon the ruins of an ancient city.

Loren, Sandecker, Pitt, and others meet at the Buenos Aires airport. Loren has found that the Wolf family has sold all their assets in the last few days. But an astronomer, Dr. Timothy Friend, now states that there is no chance that the second comet will hit the earth. Then why are the Wolfs so sure that the cataclysm will come? The astute reader can theorise that this is because the Wolfs can manufacture one themselves. This conjecture suddenly becomes a reality when we learn that an "ice shift" from the poles could produce much the same result as a comet slamming into the earth. Could this be related to the Wolfs' nanotech facility in Antarctica? Is it the purpose of this facility, in fact, to detach the entire Ross Ice Shelf from the Antarctic continent? It would seem so: the Wolf operation has bored "a ten-foot diameter tunnel fourteen hundred feet through the ice in two months" (396).

Pitt and Giordano now fly to the U.S. base at Little America V, across the Ross Ice Shelf from Wolf's operation at Okuma Bay. They want to reach Wolf's facility in snowmobiles—but all are in use or out of commission! Is this a subtle criticism of American defensive readiness? Well, there's another possibility. The station chief, Frank Cash, suggests taking Admiral Byrd's old Snow Cruiser:

> "It was the inspiration of Thomas Poulter, a polar explorer, who designed and built a monstrous machine he hoped could carry five men and his pet dog to the South Pole and back. I guess you might call it the world's first really big recreational vehicle. The tires alone were over three feet wide and more than ten feet in diameter. From front to back, it measured fifty-six feet long by twenty feet wide and weighed thirty-seven tons fully loaded. Believe you me, she's some vehicle." (403–4)

I believe it. Conveniently, an old geezer nicknamed Dad has just resurrected and refitted her. (I shall not comment on the fact that this person, it later turns out, is named Clive Cussler.)

Pitt and Giordano undertake an arduous trip through the snow to Okuma Bay. (Apparently unbeknownst to them, a U.S. Marines Special Forces unit is also making its way there.) Pitt smashes the Snow Cruiser through a secret door made of ice—but, curiously, no alarm goes off. The Marines, for their part, have infiltrated the compound, but have been detected by Wolf's security force. A gunfight ensues, in which Cussler engages in the now predictable and moronic attempt at bantering humor during this tense moment:

> Giordano twisted around in his seat and stared back through the slanted rear window of the control cab. "I hope you paid your insurance premiums."

"Only liability and property damage. I never take
out collision."
"You should reconsider." (466–67)

Cussler should reconsider being a writer. Anyway, Pitt and
Giordano now come to an airplane hangar, housing planes that will
take the Wolfs to their ships in Chile. They destroy all the planes
with the Snow Cruiser. Now they strive to rescue the beleaguered
special forces unit. The Snow Cruiser destroys the control room,
breaking up the automatic countdown sequence: the world is saved!
But, depressingly for the reader (at least this one), there are still seventy pages to go. I suppose we need to make sure the Wolfs are
rounded up.

Sure enough, that's what Pitt sets out to do. He approaches
Wolf with a white flag, telling him that his computer has been dis-
abled and showing him that reinforcements have surrounded the remainder of the Wolf clan and associates. Incredibly, Pitt now asks
the special forces for temporary custody of Wolf and his two sisters;
he then takes them outside, where they will freeze to death.

The Amenes' site is now explored. Pat O'Connell, arriving by
plane, states that she and Giordano . . . are in love! I had wondered
what Pat's fate would be, since she is obviously no conceivable rival
to the fetching Loren. Pitt and Giordano are flown, along with the
Nazi relics captured from the Wolfs, to Washington. But they suspect a plot, as the plane is not landing at Andrews Air Force Base, as
it should. The plane lands instead at a private airstrip. At this point
Pitt and Giordano overwhelm the pilots and proceed to *drive* the
plane on the highway (its cables have been cut, so it cannot fly),
while two cars shoot at them. Giordano eventually disables these
pursuers. They are surrounded by police, but a timely call to the
White House results in their release.

And that, mercifully, is the end of *Atlantis Found.*

I do not believe I need say any more to convey the completely
preposterous conception and execution of this plot. Even for a sus-
pense/spy novel, a genre not known for its adherence to conventional norms of mundane realism, it is unbelievable from beginning
to end. The whole business about the ancient civilization of the
Amenes proves to be poorly fitted into the overall structure. In the
first place, it is inconceivable that the existence of a comet bearing
down on the earth would not have been known years in advance of
the event, and the revelation that there is in fact no such comet is
sprung upon us exactly at the time when the reader's suspicions are
shifting from a natural cataclysm to a manmade one. But Cussler

doesn't want to let this cat out of the bag until his narrative is well established, so he has to show—in his third-person omniscient voice—that there really was such a civilization whose remnants now span the globe. But even this part is incredible. Cussler informs us at one point that NUMA is a "far-reaching operation with two thousand employees that scientifically probed into every peak and valley under the seas" (263)—but in that case, why did it not come upon traces of the Amenes long before now?

As for Dirk Pitt, aside from his attention to *haute couture* (derived manifestly from James Bond), he is nothing more than your stock action-adventure hero, engaging in gunplay and fisticuffs at every opportunity and always conveniently escaping death, although not always escaping injury (which only allows him to display his gritty endurance of pain and violence for the sake of a higher cause). I don't get any sense of his character in this book: he is a stick figure just going through the motions that his author has laid out for him.

I trust I have cited enough of Cussler's prose to show its overwhelming inanity and triteness. It, like his plots and characterization, is hackneyed and stereotyped to the *n*th degree. We have read (or, more precisely, seen on television and film) all this too many times before. The eagerness with which Cussler wishes his book to be a kind of half-literate duplication of a film experience is shown by repeated analogies, as for example his description of one of the Wolfs' immense ships: "Even the most sophisticated Hollywood special effects could not come close to replicating the real thing" (315). But it is, in reality, Cussler's own work that cannot come close to duplicating the adrenalin rush that the standard action movie provides, because Cussler simply lacks the skills to create those kinds of effects, even assuming for the nonce that there is some literary value in doing so.

* * * * * * *

I have stated that the spy novel features geopolitical concerns that distinguish it from the conventional crime/suspense tale; but, if the above three novels are any gauge, the more popular exemplars of the form continue to return obsessively and repetitively to the same predictable villains (the Nazis and the Soviets—in Ludlum's novel we find international capitalists as minimally novel bad guys), and, moreover, either fail utterly to present any kind of compelling account as to why we should in fact prefer the "good guys" over the "bad guys" (as in the case of Tom Clancy) or (as in the case of Clive Cussler) are simply given an action-adventure scenario without even a modicum of sociopolitical theorizing. One would think that the complex international tensions engendered by the Cold War and its aftermath, with its spectre of nuclear holocaust and its intricate and shifting network of alliances, would provide writers with abundant fodder for searching investigations of the moral and political benefits and drawbacks of spying; but our popular novelists are content to engage in an endless succession of cops-and-robbers scenarios where moral and political lines are drawn with absurd clarity and the heroes always prevail over the villains. In the end, these popular novels prove to be indistinguishable from popular crime/suspense novels except insofar as entire spy agencies are concerned instead of random individuals from the ranks of either the criminal class or the police, and insofar as the plots present a façade of the broader stakes of the enterprise and thereby engage in a kind of fast-paced globe-trotting for the delectation of the stationary reader. The elementary (and, in reality, illusory) satisfaction of seeing unequivocally evil individuals or groups being subdued by valiant American or British agents appears to be all that readers of this kind of fiction desire— aside, of course, from the customary gunplay, fisticuffs, and other thrills endemic to the form.

# VI.

# MAVENS OF HORROR

## STEPHEN KING AND DEAN KOONTZ

The realm of horror fiction—supernatural, psychological, and various gradations between—is an even more complex literary and historical phenomenon than detective or mystery fiction. Although its antecedents can be traced as far back as the various monsters (Circe, the Cyclops, the Sirens) encountered by Odysseus in the *Odyssey*, it became a concrete literary mode only in the later eighteenth century, when Horace Walpole wrote *The Castle of Otranto* (1764). For the next fifty years, hundreds of Gothic novels were published, the great majority of them—in a rather uncanny parallel to the present day—entirely worthless and now deservedly forgotten. The few that distinguished themselves from the mass of rubbish—*The Mysteries of Udolpho* (1794) and other novels by Ann Radcliffe, *The Monk* (1796) by Matthew Gregory Lewis, *Melmoth the Wanderer* (1820) by Charles Robert Maturin, and (if indeed it is to be called a Gothic novel) *Frankenstein* (1818) by Mary Shelley—are themselves flawed masterworks, but nonetheless do have some enduring literary value.

The field was revolutionised by Edgar Allan Poe (1809–1849), who in the last two decades of his career so infused the horror tale with psychological acuity, intensity of style and narrative pacing, and a distinctive worldview that saw horror and corruption in every corner of human life and society, that subsequent practitioners were forced to follow his lead. Poe definitively established the short story as the preferred aesthetic medium for the horror tale. His most adept disciple or successor was the cynical Ambrose Bierce (1842–1914?), whose *Tales of Soldiers and Civilians* (1891) and *Can Such Things Be?* (1893) duplicated Poe's keenness of psychological insight, but utilised a cold, spare prose that occasionally produced even more chilling effects. In Britain, Poe's near-contemporary Joseph Sheridan Le Fanu (1814–1873) wrote both tales and novels, but the former are by far the more successful. The British Victorians took to horror—or, at any rate, to ghost stories—in substantial numbers, although the most accomplished work of this type was generated by that transplanted American, Henry James, in *The Turn of the Screw* (1898).

The later Victorian and Edwardian eras, especially in England, supplied such a fund of superlative horror literature that it has rightly been called a golden age. Such practitioners as the Welshman Arthur Machen (1863–1947), the Englishmen Algernon Blackwood (1869–1947) and M. R. James (1862–1936), and the Irishman Lord Dunsany (1878–1957), along with a host of other writers ranging from Henry James and Edith Wharton to F. Marion Crawford and Robert W. Chambers, raised the horror tale (generally in its supernatural mode) to such a level of literary artistry that their work has largely overshadowed the work of most of their successors. They achieved their distinction in various ways: exceptionally acute analysis of the psychology of fear; a prose style of exquisite modulation and suppleness; conceptions of a high degree of originality, drawing upon myth and legend but also evolving newer sources of terror in science and social turmoil. Their cumulative work showed how horror literature can be made the venue for keen analyses of the human psyche and its place in a cosmos of bewildering mystery.

In the 1920s, H. P. Lovecraft (1890–1937) engendered another revolution in the horror tale, broadening its scope to encompass the entire universe and thereby producing a fusion with the burgeoning field of science fiction. Some of Lovecraft's disciples, including Robert Bloch and Fritz Leiber, carried on the horror tale into the realms of fantasy, suspense, and science fiction. In 1939 August Derleth and Donald Wandrei, two of Lovecraft's closest friends, founded the publishing firm of Arkham House, initially for the purpose of preserving Lovecraft's works in book form; Arkham House went on to publish many of the leading writers of horror fiction in the succeeding decades, even though it was a prototypically small press that attracted less and less attention from the mainstream with the passing of years, so that it came to seem as if horror literature was a kind of caviar to the general, capable of being appreciated only by the sensitive few—or, in the eyes of hostile critics, by the psychologically aberrant.

Supernatural horror—the most dominant and representative phase of horror fiction—is a particularly difficult mode to pull off. It is sandwiched uneasily between the adjacent modes of fantasy (where the entire world or universe is the product of the author's imagination, as in the work of J. R. R. Tolkien or of his lesser-known but superior predecessor, Lord Dunsany), science fiction (where horror may be present, but is accounted for scientifically—or, more specifically, by extrapolated future developments of science), and crime/suspense (where fear of violence or death is generally subordinated to detection of the criminal or examination of his motives or psychology). The central difficulty is the very simple one of credence: how to make the reader engage in the "willing suspension of disbelief" that a supernatural event is actually happening? In the last century or so, such standard figures in horror literature as the ghost, the vampire, and the werewolf have become so stale and implausible that they can now only be used with the greatest of subtlety or as symbols for psychological states or social conditions (the vampire as social outsider, for example).

Some writers, abandoning the attempt to lend new life to these overused conceptions and unwilling to invent new ones of their own making, have shifted to the mode of non-supernatural or psychological horror, in which terror largely resides in the rather mundane fear of physical harm. Although there have been some signal triumphs in this mode—extending back, perhaps, to Robert Bloch's *Psycho* (1959), a prototypical specimen that remains influential—we have in recent years been faced with such a surfeit of such work that it is in danger of become self-parodic. Genre considerations come into play here as well: what makes a non-supernatural novel a genuine contribution to the literature of horror, as opposed to being a mere crime or suspense novel? If there is a sufficient emphasis on the psychological aberration of the criminal, then the work can perhaps be considered a tale of terror; but if the emphasis shifts toward pursuit of the criminal, then we have entered the realm of crime or suspense. From this perspective, the bestselling novels of Thomas Harris (*The Silence of the Lambs,* 1988) are very difficult to classify. Harris's early work, even if somewhat corrupted by the cheap tricks of popular writing, contains much merit from a literary perspective; his later works are less stellar.

Horror literature has long had to face prejudice and outright disdain from critics and readers, who regard such work as obscure, recherché, unpleasant, and even literarily spurious. Winfield Townley Scott made the curious remark that "I share Elliot Paul's refusal to regard weird tales, no matter who writes them, as great literature: there is 'enough horror in real life without dragging it in from outside,' as Paul once said."[1] Scott has unwittingly provided the aesthetic rationale for horror fiction, for it is precisely *because* there is "horror in real life" that it requires treatment in literature. The best horror fiction transmogrifies our fears of ghosts, vampires, werewolves, and more eccentric entities into a broader fear of our fragility and helplessness in an unknown and unknowable cosmos; while psychological horror, at its best, probes the human tendency toward crime, violence, and madness that can render the world a living hell.

But, sadly enough, horror fiction is often not practiced at so lofty an aesthetic level. Whether the level of mediocrity in this realm is any greater than that of any other is a difficult question to answer; at any rate, it is an unfortunate fact that, to many of the uninitiated, it is exactly these mediocre specimens, whether in literature or in film, that are taken as representative of the field as a whole. Horror and fantasy fiction first entered the realm of popular fiction in the pages of the *Argosy* (1882f.) and other proto-pulp magazines published by the Frank A. Munsey Co., which proved immensely popular for decades. The first magazine solely devoted to horror was the long-running pulp *Weird Tales* (1923–54), where Lovecraft and his disciples published much of their work. Their very appearance in this magazine has been held as a mark against them, but it was at this very juncture that the supernatural (even in the form of the innocuous Christmas ghost story) became generally banished from mainstream periodicals, so that these writers had no other markets to peddle their wares. Whether the existence of the pulp magazines engendered this banishment, or whether changes in literary fashion triggered the scorning of non-mimetic fiction from mainstream magazines, is a question that has not been satisfactorily answered.

It is, however, a sad fact that the overwhelming majority of work published in *Weird Tales* and other pulps of the 1920s, 1930s, and 1940s is subliterary rubbish. These magazines, selling from a dime to a quarter, by and large catered to relatively low levels of literary taste, although they were perused by a higher grade of readership, as well, and not necessarily as a purely guilty pleasure: for much of its run, items from *Weird Tales* appeared on the list of best short stories in Edward J. O'Brien's long-running series, *The Best Short Stories of the Year* (1915f.), as well as *The O. Henry Memorial Prize Stories* (1919f.), even if few were actually reprinted as the very best stories of the year. Nevertheless, the general contempt with which *Weird Tales* and its congeners was regarded was by no means unjustified.

The rise of the pulp magazines also coincided with the emergence of horror and the supernatural in the media of radio and film.

For the first several decades of the twentieth century, the examples of horror in these industries were really appallingly dreadful from an aesthetic perspective. For all the fondness with which we now regard Lon Chaney's *Frankenstein* (1931) or Bela Lugosi's *Dracula* (1931), they are very crude works as cinema. Lovecraft was quite right when he remarked harshly in 1933:

> It is not likely that *any* really finely wrought weird story—where so much depends on mood, and on nuances of description—could be changed to a drama without irreparable cheapening and the loss of all that gave it power. . . . What the public consider "weirdness" in drama is rather pitiful and absurd—according to one's perspective. As a thorough soporofic I recommend the average popularly "horrible" play or cinema or radio dialogue. They are all the same—flat, hackneyed, synthetic, essentially atmosphereless jumbles of conventional shrieks and mutterings and superficial, mechanical situations.[2]

Lovecraft, of course, was axiomatically regarding horror as at least potentially a branch of "high" culture, whereas the great majority of horror tales, radio shows, films, and (later) television shows were and are nothing more than claptrap designed to send shivers up the spines of the uncultured. Alfred Hitchcock—whose *Psycho* (1960; adapted from the 1959 novel by Robert Bloch) and *The Birds* (1963; adapted from a very bad novella by Daphne Du Maurier) are his most able ventures in, respectively, psychological and supernatural horror—is a rare exception; there are not many others.

Horror fiction became a best-selling genre only recently. Sparked by the spectacular success of Ira Levin's *Rosemary's Baby* (1967), Thomas Tryon's *The Other* (1971), and, especially, William Peter Blatty's *The Exorcist* (1971)—the latter two dominated the bestseller lists for 1971, and all three were turned into tremendously popular films, especially the first and the third—the 1970s and 1980s saw what has been called a horror "boom," as dozens of writers sought to capitalise on horror's sudden popularity by churning out novel after novel filled with vampires, serial killers, and other dreadful creatures. By the 1990s the "boom" was dying out of inanition, or perhaps by a surfeit of rubbish, and in many ways horror fiction has now returned to its roots as the province of a specialised readership.

The horror "boom," at least in its initial stages, is virtually synonymous with one writer: Stephen King (b. 1947). King, after graduating from the University of Maine, worked in such odd jobs as janitor and a labourer in an industrial laundry before teaching English for a few years at Hampden Academy. It was King who, having written a number of reasonably effective short stories in the late 1960s and early 1970s, suddenly burst into celebrity with his first novel, *Carrie* (1974). And yet, it is emblematic of the dominance of media in our culture that *Carrie* did not become a bestseller when initially published in hardcover, but only in paperback, after the tremendous popularity of Brian De Palma's film adaptation. It is a remarkable fact that nearly every one of King's forty-four novels (including the six he has written under the pseudonym "Richard Bachman," and two co-written with fellow bestselling horror writer Peter Straub), and even many of his short stories and novellas, have been adapted into film or television. More than any other author covered in this volume, Stephen King has become a brand name. His name on any book, no matter what the subject, is sufficient to ensure sales.

Indeed, in the last decade or more King has apparently become rather resentful of being labeled a mere "horror writer," and he has sought to escape from the shadow of this purportedly contemptible literary alcove into the more expansive realm of mainstream literature. In some senses he has achieved success (by which I now mean literary, not commercial, success) in this endeavor, and such works as *Gerald's Game* (1992), *Dolores Claiborne* (1993), and *Rose Madder* (1995) are either works of suspense or are altogether mainstream. In 2003 King, to the shock of some and the satisfaction of many of his devoted fans, who had heretofore loudly complained of the lack of seriousness with which he was presumably regarded by the literary community, received the National Book Award annual medal for "distinguished contribution to American letters."

And yet, it is my judgment—and I have read the great majority of King's works down to about 1995—that King's success (and I now refer to commercial, not literary, success) derives almost entirely from the fact that he is, to be blunt, not a very good writer.[3] His conceptions are stale and largely derived from the films, television shows, and comic books that he openly admits constituted his literary diet in youth (see his ruminations on the horror field, *Danse Macabre* [1981]); his prose is flat, plain, and mundane almost beyond belief and tolerance; his novels are shambles of extraneous verbiage, episodes that go nowhere, and characters who are stale, stereotypical, and hackneyed. It is exactly these qualities that both condemn him (rightly) in the eyes of many critics and engender his popularity among a readership that would find anything more literarily elevated beyond its scope and comprehension. His only virtue—if indeed it is a virtue—is his rather dreary prolificity: he has published one or more books in almost every year since 1974, and his production underwent only a momentary lapse after he was seriously injured by a car while walking along a road in his native Maine. It is exactly this rate of production that has kept him in the eyes of the public for so long.

There are, however, signs that his popularity is at last tailing off. During his early years, such other bestselling horror writers as Peter Straub and Clive Barker struggled to keep up with him and generally failed: neither was as prolific as King, and neither seemed to have the rapport with a wide and indiscriminate readership that King had. But, beginning in the 1990s, at the very time when King himself expressed a certain impatience with his being typecast as a horror writer and attempted to branch out into other realms, his popularity began to suffer a decline: his works did not remain on the bestseller lists quite as long as they used to, and some of them (*mirabile dictu*) were not immediately made into films or television, or adapted for media at all. What is more, other writers such as Anne Rice and Dean Koontz caught up with King in the horror realm and perhaps surpassed him. Nevertheless, King remains a force to be reckoned with in the rarefied world of bestsellers, so it is worth examining a relatively recent work to see exactly what makes it tick.

*Bag of Bones* (1998)[4] opens with the image of a woman, Johanna Arlen Noonan, running in a parking lot of a drugstore to investigate a car accident. She falls down dead—of a brain aneurysm, it is later determined. Her husband, the first-person narrator, Michael Noonan, is devastated. He is thirty-six years old; she was thirty-four and, it is learned, pregnant. Jo (as she is called) had not told anyone, even her husband, of this fact. Why not? Michael, it turns out, is a bestselling author—one can certainly not fault King for following the age-old literary advice of "writing what you know"—but, in an access of modesty, notes, "I was never a Clancy, Ludlum, or Grisham" (19), and goes on to say:

> I stood just outside the magic circle of the mega-bestsellers, but I never minded that. We owned two homes by the time I was thirty-one: the lovely old Edwardian in Derry and, in western Maine, a lakeside log home almost big enough to be called a lodge—that was Sara Laughs, so called by the locals for

nearly a century. And we owned both places free and clear at a time of life when many couples consider themselves lucky just to have fought their way to mortgage approval on a starter home. We were healthy, faithful, and with our fun-bones still fully attached. I wasn't Thomas Wolfe (not even Tom Wolfe or Tobias Wolff), but I was being paid to do what I loved, and there's no gig on earth better than that; it's like a license to steal. (19–20)

Admittedly, a passage likes this makes it a bit difficult to sympathise with Michael, even considering his dreadful loss of a spouse; indeed, the first several chapters of the novel are taken up with an anomalously detailed account of publishing practices—the exact time to launch a bestseller, the competition posed by such 800-pound gorillas as Danielle Steel and Mary Higgins Clark, and so on and so forth—that, it would seem, only professionals connected with the publishing field could find any conceivable interest in.

In any case, Michael manages to finish the book on which he is working, *All the Way from the Top,* a few weeks after Jo's death—but then makes the startling announcement: "And except for notes, grocery lists, and checks, that was the last writing I did for four years" (25). Once again, it doesn't seem as if anyone but Michael's putative fans would or should care one way or the other about this circumstance. No doubt for the prolific King, who recognises that one can't scare others without scaring oneself, this case of extended writer's block must be about the most frightening thing it is possible to contemplate.

Accordingly, we are treated to several more long and tiresome chapters about how Michael is unable to write, how his agent and publisher are pressuring him to churn out more books, and so on. It is not a good way to begin a book: it would be bad enough if King were writing an autobiography or memoir and telling of something actually happening to him, but in the case of this clearly fictitious character (however loosely based upon himself) who has done nothing to earn the reader's sympathy or consideration, it is beyond tedious. Early on we are given the theoretical justification for the book's title when Michael tells us that his writing teacher once told him something that Thomas Hardy is supposed to have said: that "the most brilliantly drawn character in a novel is but a bag of bones" (33). Michael, for his part, has recurring dreams of going to the cabin called Sara Laughs, situated on the shore of Dark Score Lake.

He spends six weeks in Key Largo, but his writing does not revive; so he decides to live in the cabin permanently.

Not long after arriving, Michael sees a little girl wandering alone on the road; thinking fast, he saves her before she suffers any injury. This girl is named Kyra, and Michael sees great significance in the fact, since he and Jo had wished to name their child Kia. She is the daughter of Mattie Devore, a young mother who lives in a trailer park. Her husband is dead. Michael wonders whether she is related by marriage to Max Devore, a wealthy computer pioneer:

> His company, Visions, had created scanning programs which could upload hard copy onto floppy disks almost instantaneously; it created graphic-imaging programs which had become the industry standard; it created Pixel Easel, which allowed laptop users to mouse-paint . . . to actually fingerpaint, if their gadget came equipped with what Jo had called "the clitoral cursor." Devore had invented none of this later stuff, but he'd understood that it *could* be invented and had hired people to do it. He held dozens of patents and co-held hundreds more. He was supposedly worth something like six hundred million dollars, depending on how technology stocks were doing on any given day. (110)

In comparison to Devore, Michael is, economically speaking, a pygmy. But Michael can't understand why, if Mattie is really related to Devore, she is living in near-poverty in a trailer.

Michael then gets a phone call from Max Devore himself. This call itself is suspicious, for how could Devore have obtained Michael's phone number, which is unlisted? In any case, Devore has heard of the incident involving Kyra and professes to be concerned: Kyra is in fact his granddaughter, and Mattie his daughter-in-law. But it is becoming evident that Devore is trying to elicit information that would be damaging to Mattie—perhaps to paint her as a neglectful mother—and Michael, who has already taken rather a shine to both Mattie and Kyra, gets angry and refuses to tell Devore anything, and in fact hangs up on him. It is not a smart move.

Very soon Michael learns from Bill Dean, the caretaker of Sara Laughs, that Devore wants custody of the child and will go to any lengths to get her. Dean tells of Devore's nearly insane determination, a quality manifested throughout his life:

"My own dad . . . said little Max Devore broke into Scant Larribee's tack-shed one winter because he wanted the Flexible Flyer Scant give his boy Scooter for Christmas. Back around 1932, this would have been. They found him near midnight, sliding down Sugar Maple Hill, holding his hands up to his chest when he went down. He'd bled all over his mittens and his snowsuit. There's other stories you'll hear about Maxie Devore as a kid—if you ask you'll hear fifty different ones—and some may even be true. That one about the sled *is* true, though." (139)

Around this time the first apparently supernatural incident occurs. Michael seems to be hearing voices in the cabin. One day he decides to set up a dictation-machine to record any sounds that may manifest themselves at night. On one occasion Michael finds that the machine has recorded something:

"*Oh, Mike,*" a voice whispered—mourned, almost—on the tape, and I found myself having to press the heel of one hand to my mouth to hold back a scream. It was what I had heard in Jo's office when the draft rushed past the sides of my face . . . only now the words were slowed down just enough for me to understand them. "*Oh, Mike,*" it said again. There was a faint click. The machine had shut down for some length of time. And then, once more, spoken in the living room as I had slept in the north wing: "*Oh, Mike.*"
Then it was gone. (134)

Well, now we're getting somewhere! Michael has heard that Jo had been to the town not long before and purchased two plastic owls. What could these have possibly been for? Michael goes down to the basement to look for them—and seems to hear something. He actually engages in a rather grotesque conversation with the ghost, or whatever it is, who holds up his or her end of the dialogue by banging once (for yes) or twice (for no) on the wall. All he learns from this spectral entity is that the owl figures are not down in the basement. Later he sees his refrigerator magnets—a seemingly random collocation of letters and numbers—spell out words; or, rather, one specific word: "hello" (158), the best that can apparently be done under the circumstances.

All this is a trifle absurd. It brings to mind the now corny "spiritualist" writing of the later nineteenth and early twentieth centuries, where these manifestations were apparently looked upon with awe and wonder; but with so many subsequent exposures of fraud and charlatanry, things like these seem either a charade or too inconsequential for credence. Surely a ghost can have something a little more interesting to say than "hello." The matter is compounded by the apparent casualness with which Michael regards these supernatural phenomena. Consider this passage, where again the refrigerator magnets are in play:

> When I returned to the kitchen to set the coffeemaker for seven A.M., I saw a new message in a new circle of magnets. It read:
>
> **blue rose liar ha ha**
>
> I looked at it for a second or two, wondering what had put it there, and why.
> Wondering if it was true.
> I stretched out a hand and scattered all the letters far and wide. Then I went to bed. (209)

Went to bed? Just like that? If this were a legitimate supernatural phenomenon, it would constitute such a cataclysmic overturning of our understanding of natural law that the last possible thing one could do is just go to bed. But, as I have suggested, we have now been so conditioned by the surfeit of supernaturalism in literature and the media that it now strikes us as merely something a little out of the ordinary.

King, in any event, commits what could well be the most serious aesthetic error in this novel by largely forgetting about these supernatural manifestations and focusing on the relationship between Mattie and Kyra Devore and the baleful Max Devore. For a custody hearing has now been set in motion by Max, and Michael is summoned to testify. He quickly gets in touch with John Storrow, a custody lawyer in New York, and hires him to defend Mattie—at his own expense. Mattie, meanwhile, supplies the history of her relations with her deceased husband, Lance, Max Devore's son. They had married in September 1994; Kyra had been born April 1995. Clearly Mattie was not the kind of daughter-in-law Max Devore had wished, and so Max refused to help them financially in any way. Lance had died when he fell off the roof of his trailer and broke his neck, dying instantly. Max, who had rather crassly purchased the goodwill of the townsfolk by various munificent bequests, is now seeking to win his granddaughter away from the scorned Mattie.

But Michael is most disturbed by one casual utterance on Mattie's part: she remembers having seen Jo in town some months previously, in the company of another man. Michael fears the worst: admitting that he has a low sperm-count, and remembering that Jo had been found in the drugstore parking lot with a bag of purchases that included a home pregnancy kit, he wonders whether Jo had in fact been impregnated by this stranger: is that why she had never told Michael about her condition? Is it these reflections that makes Michael have a long, bizarre sex dream involving Sara Tidwell, a long-dead black blues singer who had once lived in Sara Laughs, and for which he cabin was named?

Michael encourages Mattie to talk with John Storrow, and he begins to think that, with luck, things might progress very nicely with Mattie: "It sounded like we might have the expected fairy-tale ending, if we could keep our courage and hold our course" (226). Michael even begins writing again, reverting to an old IBM Selectric rather than a computer. Unfortunately, King chooses this juncture to spout pseudo-profundity about life, writing, and such:

> This is how we go on: one day at a time, one meal at a time, one pain at a time, one breath at a time. Dentists go on one root-canal at a time; boat-builders go on one hull at a time. If you write books, you go on one page at a time. We turn from all we know and all we fear. We study catalogues, watch football games, choose Sprint over AT&T. We count the birds in the sky and will not turn from the window when we hear the footsteps behind us as something comes up the hall; we say yes, I agree that clouds often look like other things—fish and unicorns and men on horseback—but they are really only clouds. Even when the lightning flashes inside them we say they are only clouds and turn our attention to the next meal, the next page. This is how we go on. (259)

The problem with a passage like this is not merely that it is almost intolerably banal—the entire intellectual or aesthetic content of it could be summed up in the first sentence, if not the very first phrase—but that it is uttered with a pomposity and seriousness as if

King were uttering some cosmic revelation to which only he is privy. King fancies that by scattering passages like this throughout his book, he might lend it a certain *gravitas* that a mere tale of supernatural horror would lack—that it would, in essence, fuse mainstream writing with supernatural writing. But the *gravitas* of supernaturalism comes from its expression and elucidation of our deepest fears and from its suggestion of wonders and terrors beyond our ken—not from windy probings of "deep" emotions by its characters. King is simply not up to the job of lending depth to his protagonists.

Michael now hears of a small African American boy who had died near his cabin in 1901. Could he be the son of Sara Tidwell, and is he the ghost that Michael heard in the basement? For the time being Michael cannot concern himself with this matter, for he has now learned that Jo had, in the last ten months before her death, been to Dark Score Lake on a number of occasions when she had told Michael that she had been going to meetings of various charities of which she was a member. Michael hopes that these visits were not for the purpose of seeing the mysterious man that Mattie Devore had seen her with; he latches on to Bill Dean's comment that Jo had become interested in local history and was planning to write about it.

Michael now has a dramatic confrontation with Max Devore himself, now in extreme old age and confined to a wheelchair, and his companion, Rogette Whitmore. Michael appears to be walking along a narrow pathway next to the lake called The Street, and it is here that Max and Rogette choose to confront him. A bitter argument over Mattie ensues, and it actually leads to fighting. Let it not be assumed that the presumably fit and healthy author has the advantage over a cripple and his female companion; for Max uses his wheelchair deftly to prevent Michael from passing, and Rogette reveals surprising power and ferocity. Michael actually tumbles into the lake, while Rogette pelts him with rocks. Just as he appears on the verge of drowning, something strange occurs: "Then I felt a hand seize me by the nape of the neck. The pain of having my hair yanked brought me back to reality in a flash—it was better than an epinephrine injection. I felt another hand clamp around my left leg; there was a brief but terrific sense of heat" (299). With this supernatural aid, Michael manages to struggle back to his cabin; but, in typical fashion, he merely thanks the spirit of Jo—who he believes had come to his aid—and . . . goes to bed. In all frankness, this scene with Devore and Rogette is probably the most compelling in the entire book: King's narrative is lively and vivid, and the crisp realism of his account contrasts strikingly with the unconvincing supernaturalism found elsewhere in the book.

Things are looking bad for Mattie: she has been fired from her job at the library. It is manifestly Devore's doing. All of a sudden, however, Devore's lawyer, Richard Osgood, brings Michael a letter from Devore: in it he announces that he will drop the custody fight if Michael agrees to "cease asking questions about him" (313). Astounded at this turn of events, Michael telephones Rogette and accepts the terms. The next morning he learns that Devore had killed himself the night before.

This certainly seems a providential solution of the problems facing Mattie, especially given that the romance between Mattie and Michael also appears to be progressing nicely. After dinner that evening, Michael kisses Mattie for the first time:

> She was very close, looking up at me, and I couldn't stop myself. I put the blame on summer, her perfume, and four years without a woman. In that order. I slipped my arms around he waist, and remember perfectly the texture of her dress beneath my hands; the slight pucker at the back where the zipper hid in its sleeve. I remember the sensation of the cloth moving against the bare skin beneath. Then I was kissing her, very gently but very thoroughly— anything worth doing is worth doing right—and she was kissing me back in exactly the same spirit, her mouth curious but not afraid. Her lips were warm and smooth and held some faint sweet taste. Peaches, I think. (339)

Very touching. Actually, this passage is a credible attempt at romance without sentimentality. So in spite of their nearly twenty-year age difference, wedding bells seem to be in the offing. Michael is, on another front, now relieved to learn that the mysterious man whom Mattie had seen Jo with was Jo's own brother Frank. Calling Frank, Michael learns that Jo was indeed writing something about the town:

> "All I know is that it started—whatever it was— with her doing research for an article. It was a lark, Jo playing Nancy Drew. I'm pretty sure that at first not telling you was just to keep it a surprise. She read books but mostly she talked to people—listened to

their stories of the old days and teased them into looking for old letters . . . diaries . . . she was good at that part of it, I think. Damned good." (350)

But what exactly was the subject of her investigations? That is something Michael still doesn't know.

Michael now has a long, involved dream about going back in time, in the company of Kyra, to the Fryeburg Fair; once again, Sara Tidwell is centrally involved. And in classic supernatural fashion, upon waking Michael is startled to find elements of the dream manifesting themselves in real life: his finger is sticky from the sap of a pine tree he had rubbed against in his dream. Even more remarkably, Kyra confesses that she has had the same dream. Meanwhile Michael learns that Mattie has been offered her job back: he is happy, but wonders whether this is just a ploy to keep her in town. John Storrow tells him, in fact, that Mattie stands to inherit $80 million from Devore's will—but she must stay in town for a year following his death, or until July 17, 1999. This doesn't seem like such a hardship, so Michael, Mattie, Storrow, and others hold a barbecue to celebrate their victory over Devore. All of a sudden, gunfire is heard—it is from a car driving by. George Kennedy, a private detective hired by Storrow, shoots at the car and blows it up. The shooter is one George Footman, a local thug hired by Devore. His shooting has been all too effective . . . for Mattie has been fatally injured and dies in Michael's arms.

I will be honest and say that Mattie's death surprised me, because King seems to have been leading his readers to expect the customary happy-ending union of Mattie and Michael. But King had lain the seeds for this turn of events by suggesting that the age difference between the two would preclude a satisfactory union, something that Michael himself articulates on almost the novel's final page:

> Have you set up a moral dilemma you don't know how to solve? Is the protagonist sexually attracted to a woman who is much too young for him, shall we say? Need a quick fix? Easiest thing in the world. "When the story starts going sour, bring on the man with the gun." Raymond Chandler said that, or something like it—close enough for government work, *kemo sabe*. (528)

Let us overlook the fatuous clichés in that last sentence. The only difficulty in this formulation is that King has not really established the "moral dilemma" in sufficient detail that the death of Mattie is seen to be aesthetically necessary. There are brief suggestions along the way, as Michael urges himself not to take advantage of the fact that he is footing Mattie's legal bills—he reminds himself that he must not pressure her for sex, or even for the expression of affection, since the inequality of their relationship would preclude its being genuine and unpressured. But beyond momentary remarks of this sort, there is very little on this subject.

Well, Michael must carry on. The first thing he does is to snatch Kyra up and take her back to Sara Laughs, since the townspeople are apparently coming after them. They make their way back there in the prototypical hail/rain/thunder storm. Once inside, he finds those missing plastic owls in Jo's studio, while all kinds of bizarre poltergeist phenomena are occurring all around them. Inside one of the owls he finds a number of old newspaper clippings; they tell a bizarre story. A great many of the townspeople had killed their own children over the years: can this be Sara Tidwell's revenge from beyond the grave for being raped and murdered by a gang of white boys—all of them ancestors of current inhabitants of the town—and for the death of her son, Kito, whom they had also killed? Michael now digs up a birch tree where Sara's spirit is embedded; Jo's spirit comes to aid him, battling with the spirit of Sara. There he finds the actual bag of bones of the title:

> Inside was what remained of them—two yellowed skulls, forehead to forehead as if in intimate conversation, a woman's faded red leather belt, a molder of clothes . . . and a heap of bones. Two ribcages, one large and one small. Two sets of legs, one long and one short. The early [*sic;* does King mean "earthly"?] remains of Sara and Kito Tidwell, buried here by the lake for almost a hundred years.
>
> The larger of the two skulls turned. It glared at me with its empty eyesockets. Its teeth chattered as if it would bite me, and the bones below it began a tenebrous, jittery stirring. Some broke apart immediately; all were soft and pitted. The red belt stirred restlessly and the rusty buckle rose like the head of a snake. (497)

This is reasonably effective: King conjoins physical disgust (the presence of decomposing bones) with supernatural menace. It is clearly the climax of the novel. Michael now pours lye over the bones, causing them to melt away.

But Michael is by no means out of the woods. When he returns to the cabin, he finds that Kyra has gone. He knows at once that Rogette has taken her. Giving chase, he sees Kyra on the dock over the water, struggling to get away from Rogette. Suddenly the ghost of Mattie appears, startling Rogette and causing her to drown in the lake. Michael walks away with Kyra, knowing the horror is finally over.

In an epilogue we find that Michael is attempting to adopt Kyra. This is being done purely out of altruism and love: she is not in fact wealthy and does not stand to inherit Devore's millions, for Rogette had lied about the details of the will.

*Bag of Bones* is itself a kind of shambling bag of bones, with too many elements in it that do not fit well together. It can be seen from this summary that the whole business about the custody battle over Kyra between Devore and Mattie/Michael is simply a time-wasting and space-consuming red herring: it serves no integral purpose in the novel, whose central supernatural premise is the ghostly revenge of Sara Tidwell. This latter feature is presented so sketchily and fragmentarily throughout the novel—chiefly in the form of those preternatural dreams to which Michael is subject—that its final revelation toward the end carries little impact: the reader has not been sufficiently prepared for this turn of events because King, like a too-clever detective writer, has dropped too few hints along the way that might lead convincingly to this dénouement. In effect, King has deliberately padded this 529-page book with all manner of extraneous scenes, characters, and incidents in order to keep the Sara Tidwell element under wraps until its purportedly surprising exposure at the end—but the element is so well hidden that it fails to carry any effective punch.

King, clearly, is keen on the custody issue, for in an author's note he makes a point of stating that "To some extent, this novel deals with the legal aspects of child custody in the State of Maine," going on to note that he had asked for help from an attorney to guide him in the intricacies of the matter. But no matter how convincingly or accurately it is presented, there can be no denying that it simply has no, or little, place in a novel whose true focus is and should be elsewhere. King also, no doubt, wishes to lend weight to his novel by founding it upon a racist incident where ignorant whites (including the young Max Devore) raped and killed a talented and vibrant black musician, but again this facet is not emphasised with the force required to make it aesthetically or morally significant.

One of the worst features of this incoherent novel is that King has failed to tie up a number of loose ends at the end, as if he had simply forgotten about them. Who or what was the entity that was causing the thumping down in the basement of Sara Laughs, and who was the creature doing the refrigerator-magnet writing? So far as I can tell, King has failed to tell us, or even to think that he needs to tell us. Was it the spirit of Sara Tidwell, or perhaps of her small child? Or someone else altogether? I suppose King is no longer obliged to explain the very existence of these spirits or ghosts. They have appeared in so many previous novels and tales, on television, and in film, that their presence is simply accepted as something mildly unusual instead of what it really is—a sign of a radical deficiency or error in our understanding of how the universe operates.

As it is, the most obvious feature of this novel, as of all King's writings, is his down-to-earth, blue-collar, almost plebeian prose style. He has no doubt heard many criticisms of what has come to be called his brand-name realism, and sure enough on the very first page he makes a point of citing such commercial entities as Rite Aid, Radio Shack, Fast Foto, and Blockbuster Video. This is a childishly easy means of creating verisimilitude and eliciting reader recognition, and King is consciously working in a supernatural tradition—begun in the 1940s and 1950s with such writers as Ray Bradbury and Richard Matheson—that eschewed the exotically Gothic settings of Bram Stoker, H. P. Lovecraft, and others for the mundane realities that the great majority of us face on a daily basis. And King's workingman's prose style similarly enhances the effect of a regular guy telling us a tale around a fireside:

> I left the house, checked to make sure the door was locked, and walked back up the driveway, swinging the flashlight beam from side to side like a pendulum—like the tail of old Felix the Krazy Kat in the kitchen. It occurred to me, as I struck north along the lane, that I would have to make up some sort of story for Bill Dean. It wouldn't do to say, "Well, Bill, I got down there and heard a kid bawling in my locked house, and it scared me so bad I turned into the gingerbread man and ran back to Derry. I'll send you the flashlight I took; put it back on the shelf next to the paperbacks, would you?" That wasn't any good because the story would get around and people would

say, "Not surprised. Wrote too many books, probably. Work like that has got to soften a man's head.
Now he's scared of his own shadow. Occupational
hazard." (88)

The use of "low" language in supernatural fiction can occasionally be effective: such stories as F. Marion Crawford's "The Upper
Berth" (1886) and Rudyard Kipling's "The Mark of the Beast"
(1890) are narrated by bluff, no-nonsense, non-literary types who
establish their fundamental down-to-earthness in the plainness of
their speech, leading the reader to suspect that such a person is not
likely to be taken in by impostures and, more significantly, not
likely to be frightened by anything except the genuinely supernatural. But King's prose is at times so mundane that it confounds its
own purpose: when the supernatural does manifest itself, King frequently lacks the vocabulary to express it effectively and convincingly. He is entirely incapable of writing a passage like this, taken
from the climax of Lovecraft's "The Call of Cthulhu," as that baleful entity pursues a hapless ship in the Pacific:

> The Thing cannot be described—there is no lan-
> guage for such abysms of shrieking and immemorial
> lunacy, such eldritch contradictions of all matter,
> force, and cosmic order. A mountain walked or
> stumbled . . . The Thing of the idols, the green, sticky
> spawn of the stars, had awaked to claim his own. The
> stars were right again, and what an age-old cult had
> failed to do by design, a band of innocent sailors had
> done by accident. After vigintillions of years great
> Cthulhu was loose again, and ravening for delight.
> . . . Slowly, amidst the distorted horrors of that
> indescribable scene, [the ship] began to churn the le-
> thal waters; whilst on the masonry of that charnel
> shore that was not of earth the titan Thing from the
> stars slaved and gibbered like Polypheme cursing the
> fleeing ship of Odysseus. Then, bolder than the sto-
> ried Cyclops, great Cthulhu slid greasily into the wa-
> ter and began to pursue with vast wave-raising
> strokes of cosmic potency.[5]

This passage, while seemingly overwritten, is in fact appropriate to its function in the story, for Lovecraft has taken care to manage the pacing of the story in such a way that this cataclysmic dé-

nouement is fitting and appropriate. His elevated language, with its powerful allusions to myth and folklore, evokes the mingled awe and terror that Lovecraft is aiming for here. But King's prose is so deliberately flat and mundane that it is incapable of rising to this level—or if he attempted it, he would only bring ridicule upon himself for pomposity and bathos.

\* \* \* \* \* \* \*

Like King, Dean Koontz (b. 1945) was a high school English teacher for several years, and he actually began writing novels earlier than King. His first, *Star Quest* (1968), was a science fiction novel, as many of his early works were; and the majority of these were published in paperback, under as many as nine pseudonyms. Koontz has been an appallingly prolific writer, having published eighty novels in less than forty years, along with several books of nonfiction, including the helpful volume *How to Write Best-Selling Fiction* (1981). Although, in recent years, he appears to have attracted a following as large as, and perhaps even a bit greater than, King, whose own popularity appears to have flagged somewhat of late, Koontz has had a much poorer record of achieving that summit of bestsellerdom, the film adaptation: only five of his novels have been turned into movies.

In *The Taking* (2004)[6] we are introduced to Molly Sloan, a novelist (what leads so many horror novelists to have writers as protagonists?), and her husband, Neil. Molly, plagued with insomnia, is startled by the sight she sees outside the porch of her southern California home: "The porch swarmed with wolves. Slinking out of the storm, up the steps, onto the pegged-pine floor, they gathered under the shelter of the roof, as though this were not a house but an ark that would soon be set safely afloat by the rising waters of a cataclysmic flood" (9). This is the end of the first chapter; on the very next page we find that these are not in fact wolves but coyotes. Already the prospects that Koontz is a respectable novelist, willing to eschew a cheap end-of-chapter shiver, look pretty dim. In any case, the coyotes are acting peculiarly, almost as if they are beseeching Molly. She actually opens the door and goes out among them. After milling around her for a time, they flee. It is still raining, and Molly detects that the rain has a peculiar odor: "Within that mélange of subtle but exotic scents had been a vaguely familiar odor, smoky and ammoniac, that Molly had not been quite able to identify. Although she had flushed the smell from her hands, it now returned to her in memory, and this time she was able to name it: semen" (19). Well, this is a pretty kettle of fish!

Neil, for his part, is usually a sound sleeper, but now he cries out in his sleep. Molly, for some reason, thinks there may be an intruder in the house, but Neil lets her know that he is merely having a nightmare. It is, however, a dream of a peculiar sort:

> Tipping his head back, studying the bedroom ceiling with evident anxiety, the initial roughness in his voice smoothing into a solemn silken tone of mesmerizing intensity, he said, "Huge. In the dream. Massive. A mountain, rock blacker than iron, coming down in a slow fall. You run and you run . . . but you can't get out from under. Its shadow grows ahead of you faster . . .faster than you can hope to move." (24)

By this time, other bizarre things are happening. Molly had already tried to call 911 but heard only "an audial tapestry of eerie, oscillating electronic tones" (20) over the phone. The hands of clocks are spinning madly forward, music boxes spring to life, a mirror fails to reflect the contents of the room in which it is placed. At 2:44 A.M., all the weird phenomena abruptly cease. But we don't seem to be out of danger just yet. A television news broadcast reports anomalous weather developing over the Pacific Coast. Unusual amounts of rain seem to be falling all over the world, even in the parched Middle East. The source of these bizarre conditions seems to be waterspouts in the South Pacific, but later these waterspouts are sighted elsewhere. A worldwide cataclysm seems to be taking place. True to form, Koontz concludes chapter nine with Molly's melodramatic utterance: "Let's get out of here. Now. Quickly" (63).

This, however, proves to be easier said than done. Molly and Neil go to the house of their neighbor, the widower Harry Corrigan, and find him dead—he has killed himself with a shotgun. But his house is a shambles, leading Molly to wonder if there had been an intruder; but if so, why didn't he attempt to use the shotgun on the intruder? Molly wonders: "He retreated to the bathroom and blew his brains out to avoid coming face-to-face with whoever tore down the bedroom door" (68). But very quickly Molly and Neil find bullet holes here and there, but no blood, leading them to wonder why these deadly shots had had no effect on the putative intruder.

Things quickly become still weirder. A strange presence is heard, reciting verses from . . . T. S. Eliot. (There are epigraphs from Eliot scattered throughout the book.) It proves to be the dead but reanimated corpse of Harry Corrigan! Neil, ever resourceful, blows the creature away, explaining his action with unwitting irony, "'Cause this isn't the movies" (75). Well, maybe not, but it's pretty close: so far there has been nothing even remotely believable in this farrago of oddities, and it is in fact exactly like a bad B-movie. Neil now makes the suggestion that Harry's body might have been animated by some kind of parasite. Molly, in turn, asks the rather obvious question: Why was he reciting lines from T. S. Eliot? Neil doesn't have much of an answer to that, except to note that Eliot is one of *Molly's* favorite writers.

But this seems to be the least of their worries. The entire world is coming apart at the seams, as a desperate radio broadcaster notes: "Listen to this, America, listen close and hard to this, and *know your enemy*. This is not global warming, sunspots, cosmic radiation, this is not some inexplicable spasm in the planet's climate. This is *the war of the worlds*" (83–84). This point seems to be confirmed by a report from the International Space Station, which states that an "unknown craft" (84) has docked there. Creatures are passing through the metal hatches and killing all the astronauts. Then one of them speaks in an alien language: *"Yimaman see noygel, see refacull, see nod a bah, see naytoss, retee fo sellos"* (87).

Molly at this point draws an odd conclusion: "Although she knew nothing of their meaning, she sensed arrogance in those words: arrogance sharp with a sense of triumph, bitterness, blackest hatred, and rage beyond the capacity of the darkest of human hearts, rage beyond all understanding" (88). How exactly it is possible to derive all this from an incomprehensible utterance is difficult to understand; but it becomes quite clear that Koontz is setting up these horrible alien entities as creatures of pure evil—so that hating and killing them, for the sake of preserving our noble and valiant human race, can be rendered morally justifiable. It is too much effort for Koontz to create a morally ambiguous enemy; in his black-and-white world, there are only good guys and bad guys.

Molly and Neil are struggling through the omnipresent rain in their SUV (what else?). Koontz, fatally addicted to teasing the reader, now has Molly think she sees a baby in an abandoned car—but it proves only to be a doll (90). But an even weirder sight now assails her: she sees a figure walking along the road, and it turns out to be her father, Michael Render, a "murderer" (95) who was supposedly in jail. Can he have escaped, or has the whole criminal justice system collapsed?

Molly and Neil make their way to a mountain community called Black Lake, where there is a lot of tough talk about how the U.S.

army can conquer whatever danger the world is facing: "We got the Marines, Army Rangers, Delta Force, we got the Navy Seals" (104). The last may certainly be helpful in all this rain. As the people of this community gather in a tavern, some dogs approach Molly with curious interest and sniff her. The occupants tell of the bizarre manifestations they have witnessed, similar to what Molly and Neil have seen. The people seem to be naturally dividing themselves, in accordance to the different courses of action they wish to pursue: one group merely wishes to drink themselves to oblivion, thinking there is no hope for humanity; a second group embraces dogmatic pacifism; a third are fence-sitters who say they need more information before taking any action; and the fourth are the fighters. It is pretty obvious whose side Koontz is on:

> The fourth group, only slightly less numerous than the fence-sitters, were those who preferred to stand up and fight, regardless of the odds against them. Among them were as many women as men, folks of all ages and persuasions. Angry, energized, they had brought most of the guns and were eager to strike back.
>
> They pulled up two more chairs and welcomed Molly and Neil, inferring from the shotgun and the pistol that they might be like-minded. This spirited group had put half a dozen tables together to form a U, the better to jointly speculate on all the possible what-ifs, as well as to discuss strategy and tactics for each contingency. (115)

Bravo! There is just one awkward point: Against whom are they to fight? Surely it would seem that the fence-sitters are, objectively speaking, in a rather more rational position: Koontz himself grudgingly admits that the fourth group "knew next to nothing about their enemy" (115). Neil now suggests that they hole up at the local bank—can this be a subtle nod to the virtues of capitalism? Well, maybe not; as Vince Hoyt, a football coach, explains a trifle bombastically:

> "I never coached a single game where I ever thought a loss was inevitable, not even in the final quarter when the other team had us by four touchdowns, and I have no intention of trading that attitude for a loser mentality now. Damn if I will. But there is

one other good thing about the bank. The vault. Armored walls, thick steel door. It'll make a hell of a final bolt-hole if it comes to that. If they want to tear the door off and come in after us, we'll make a shooting gallery of them, and take a slew of the bastards with us." (118)

I'm aware of the ubiquity of sports in contemporary culture, but the comparison of this situation to a football game strikes me as more than a little grotesque.

The focus momentarily shifts to one Derek Sawtelle, leader of the first group. He is a "long-tenured professor of literature at the state university in San Bernardino" (119). Koontz makes little secret of his contempt for this person: "Lacking an athletic physique, too kind to punch people out in barroom brawls or to cheer the bloody spectacle of a bullfight, or to dangle a wife from a high-rise window by her ankles, Derek could model himself after his heroes only by immersion in literature and gin. He had spent his life swimming in both" (120). One wonders, if this were the case, how Sawtelle has managed to preserve his lofty position for so long. But let it pass. Sawtelle, who has read a lot of science fiction, thinks the aliens are merely refashioning the earth to suit their needs. Human beings are mere insignificant obstacles. Molly refuses to believe this, but Sawtelle then takes her into the men's room, where some odd-looking fungi are growing, "fat and round and clustered in such a way that they resembled the coils of a gathered serpent" (126). Could the aliens be drawing up water from the oceans and lacing it with seeds from their own world, so that it comes down in the rain to supply nourishment for them? Molly, of course, finds the fungi not only repulsive but positively evil:

> Nevertheless, judging only by the evidence of her eyes, she felt that this thing was profoundly malignant. On an intuitive level, she *knew* that it harbored malice, that in some strange way it dreamed of violence, as a trap-door spider might dream of sucking the juices from the beetle that sooner or later would fall into its lair, though this thing dreamed of cruelty with a glee that no spider could ever experience, with a ferocity that transcended nature. On a level even deeper than intuition, in that realm of belief that is of the heart rather than of the mind, and might be called faith, she had no doubt whatsoever

> that this life form, whether fungous or not, whether
> plant or animal or something between, was not just
> poisonous but *evil.* (132)

I must confess that this is one of the most preposterous passages I have ever read, and it is compounded by the added nonsense of Molly's thought, "it seemed to have no rightful place in a universe created by the God of light" (132). Granting that it may be a bit difficult to feel sympathy for fungi, nevertheless the notion that Molly could have understood the "profoundly malignant" nature of this entity, that it "harbored malice" and so forth, is too ludicrous for credence. It is a sad fact that, throughout the universe, the only creatures of whom we have any knowledge who seem "profoundly malignant" and "harbor malice" are human beings. To get around this awkward fact, Koontz is obliged to invest his own alien entities with such levels of vileness—going well beyond mere physical loathsomeness and entering the realm of moral viciousness—that readers, unless they be self-professed misanthropes, are obliged to indulge in this orgy of hatred against the perceived enemies of humanity.

One cannot help contrast this staggeringly naïve and crude moral dichotomy with the extraordinary subtlety of Lovecraft's portrayal of alien entities in "The Colour out of Space" (1927). The creature or creatures that are apparently imbedded in a meteorite that lands on a farmer's property in Massachusetts are so different in every regard from humanity that their morals or psychology cannot be determined; even though their presence corrupts all plant and animal life so that it turns a sickly grey and crumbles to dust, their motives in so doing remain inscrutable—and are the more terrifying for that. Possibly they are not even conscious entities, in any sense in which we understand the term. But this kind of intellectual, psychological, and moral restraint is beyond Koontz's powers; he must have his cardboard villains.

Anyway, things look pretty bleak for our brave remnants of humanity in the tavern. (It need hardly be stated that everyone, from Koontz on down to the least adept of his many readers, knows that humanity will in fact prevail in the end.) Molly goes to the ladies' room—and sees Michael Render standing nearby. We are now given the short and sordid annals of his life:

> Twenty years earlier, when he destroyed his last
> hope of winning legal custody of Molly, Michael
> Render resorted to the instrument of persuasion that
> he now claimed to find unsatisfactory: the gun. He

had come to her elementary school to take her from her classroom. Having asked to see his daughter on some pretense that the principal had found unconvincing, Render realized that he'd aroused suspicion, whereupon he pulled a pistol and shot the principal dead. . . .

With the principal dead, Render had gone in search of Molly's third-grade classroom, killing one member of the faculty en route and wounding two others. He found her room and grievously wounded her teacher, Mrs. Pasternak, and would have abducted Molly if the police had not then arrived. (140)

Well, we can't possibly waste any sympathy on him. He has, in any case, broken out of his prison. But all he does is taunt Molly for a while and then go out a window.

There is now some further discussion among the four groups of human beings. Koontz labels the first group as "fugitives from reality" (151), but then, in reference to the fighters, notes: "With hope, all things were possible" (151). If that isn't a flight from reality, I don't know what is.

More weird phenomena. A doll begins to cry, talk, and move of its own accord. It claws out its own eyes and tongue with its hands, but manages to get in one last utterance before doing so: "all your babies will die" (157). Ah, yes! the babies. One must always be concerned about the babies. Mirrors in the tavern show people with all kinds of horrible injuries that their bodies do not in fact have. The lights go out; the doll disappears. Molly is not alone in wondering about the purpose behind this apparent psychological torture: "If they can replace our entire environment with theirs, scour away human civilization in days or weeks, eradicate it more efficiently than a seven-continent nuclear war, they wouldn't bother to screw with our minds like this" (168). A dog comes up to Molly, looks at her intently, and then brings her a rose. She interprets this, by a course of reasoning that I fail to follow (it must be her vaunted intuition), to mean that the dog will lead them to other small children in the community who need help. How could I have overlooked that! Always the children!

The rain now suddenly stops. As the group of fighters leaves the tavern, the headless body of a mailman pleads with them to help. It is not entirely clear what they can do for the poor fellow. They enter a house, which seems to have become alive: the walls are full of fluttering noises. They find two small children inside. Suddenly the door closes behind them—is this a trap? They can't seem to get the door open, but a dog does the trick. As they leave the house, they finally encounter the actual aliens whose existence they have suspected all along: a UFO comes down from the sky and floats just above them. Then it simply moves away.

Our valiant crew make their way to the Catholic church (naturally). Molly is horrified to find a severed hand in a marble reservoir of holy water. Three children and two men are in the church. Koontz makes the odd remark that Molly "respected the privacy of their worship and their penance" (212). I can't say that I'm an authority on the Catholic church, but what exactly these people have done to require a *penance* escapes me. The two men actually apologise to Molly for leading her and her group into a possible trap—for there is something baleful in the basement of the church. There are in fact dead bodies—exhumed from coffins, apparently—scattered all over the church. These figures now arise and slowly take positions at all the doors of the church. The recently deceased priest, Father Dan Sullivan, takes his place at the altar. He has a hideous tentacular entity growing out of him. A huge spider-like creature bursts through the floor from below and eats one of the men. As the rest of the (living) human beings are fleeing, the entity nabs a second man with its stinger. But at least the three children are saved! Of course, those corpses standing like sentries at all the doors have to be blown away with shotguns, but I suppose that couldn't be helped.

The church burns to the ground. The rescued children (who were not related to the two men they were with in the church) say that their parents just floated up through the ceiling of their house into the sky. As Molly is digesting this piece of information, she sees a reptilian hand reaching down from the trees: "Four knuckles per finger, endowed with black claws as pointed as rose thorns, the scarlet hand released the limb and vanished into foliage as the nimble creature proceeded ahead of them" (241). Molly now makes further reflections on the nature of the entities:

> She couldn't explain to herself how an extraterrestrial species, a thousand years more advanced than humanity, with the wisdom to beat the limitations of the speed of light and cross galaxies in a clock tick, could be so barbarous, so pitiless. A civilization sufficiently sophisticated to construct ships larger than mountains and machines capable of transforming entire worlds in mere hours ought also to be a civiliza-

tion exquisitely sensitive to suffering and injustice. (245)

I fear that this course of reasoning is not very sound: certainly the astounding scientific or technological achievements of the human race have not engendered any corresponding moral or psychological advance. Molly, however, now wonders whether these entities could constitute a "*hive,* in which every individual lacked a conscience, lacked even the concept of pity, reveled in cruelty, and had no personal identity different from those of all the other billions of its kind. Then each might direct its evil urges outward from the hive, bend its intellect to the creation of dark technologies, in the interest of furthering the evil of all" (246). Once again Koontz reveals his deficiencies as a moral philosopher: if these entities lack a conscience, then they could not possibly be guilty of *evil* (except from the human perspective which sees any actions hostile to humanity as evil), and would simply be amoral.

At any rate, Molly and her band decide to go back to the tavern. She finds it empty, but some weapons are still there—and, more disturbingly, some torn clothes. The guns have not been fired. She descends the stairs into the basement (how many times have we seen this in horror films?), and hears a voice *behind* her—it is a waitress, Angie Boteen, naked, holding a broken beer bottle in her hand. She seems to be in a kind of trance. Angie asks Molly to cut her, making Molly wonder whether the creatures enter through the blood. Angie goes on to say that there is a creature in the basement "with faces in its hands" (262). Then, incredibly, Angie sinks through the seemingly solid concrete floor.

Molly now finds a little girl, Cassie, for whom she had been searching. Cassie explains the curious business of the faces in the hands: "They can take your face and keep it in their hands, and show it to you, and other faces, and crush them in their fists, and make them scream" (271). Molly wonders whether human children are being deliberately spared by the entities. Worse, could Neil and Molly and other adults have been used to "harvest" children? Can even dogs be trusted?

Molly now enters a house, leaving Neil to guard the six children they are now with. A large man attacks her. She manages to escape by biting his face. The man wants to sacrifice the children (naturally) and manages to wrestle away the gun that Molly had been carrying. He holds it to her neck, but when he is momentarily distracted she cuts him with a pair of scissors, gets the gun back, and blasts him away. Bravo! She now sees the fungi, scattered over nearly every surface, peel back and reveal the faces of the dead: "These were not real faces, but watching them in a paralytic state of awe, of dread, Molly suspected—and quickly came to believe—that each represented a human consciousness, the mind and memory of someone who had actually lived. They had been stripped out of their physical bodies at death and somehow captured in these hideous structures" (303).

Nevertheless, Molly is reassured on one point: something that her attacker had said leads her to believe that "the kids are untouchable" (305). Well, that's a relief. Molly and Neil make their way back to the bank; she sees only four people there, but that's not the worst of it: "They had no faces" (310). Molly goes into the bank vault and finds five children inside . . . with Michael Render. After a brief and tense discussion, she shoots him several times—but "no blood spilled from him" (315), because he is already dead. The figure of her father now changes shape into a monster:

> What stood before her was not her father, but a simulacrum of exquisitely convincing detail. Now it changed, and became what it really was: a mottled black-and-gray *thing* with a face that seemed to have once imploded and been badly reconstructed. Eyes as large as lemons, protuberant, crimson with elliptical black pupils. From shoulders ridged with spiky plates of bone, leathery wings hung unfolded along its sides. (316)

Somehow, Molly "knew that it was filled with hate and fury an frustration" (318). How she knows that is a mystery.

Now the immense mother ship of the aliens appears. The rain starts again, but stops the next morning. The sun comes out for the first time in thirty-six hours. All the fungi that had covered the ground and trees are gone. Can the horror be over so suddenly, as in *The War of the Worlds*?

It certainly appears so. Let us ignore the fact that this resolution is staggeringly anticlimactic: even in the absence of some titanic battle with the disgusting aliens, the reader is surely owed something a bit more exciting and interesting than the mere cessation of weird phenomena. So the critical question becomes: How does Koontz explain all the odd things that have happened in his book? The supernatural incidents have been of such a bewilderingly diverse sort that it would seem difficult to encompass them in any kind of convincing account. What is Koontz's solution?

Well, in effect, there is no solution. First of all, he asserts that all the adults who survived the alien Armageddon "had been *chosen* not just to save the children but for the talents he or she could bring to this larger purpose" (329). The religious undercurrent of this utterance is elaborated upon—after a fashion—in the few chapters that remain, for it appears that the aliens were really conducting a kind of purging because humanity had become so corrupted by violence, lack of faith, and other evils that the only solution was to get rid of them all. As Molly thinks to herself in self-important italics:

> *An extraterrestrial species, hundreds or thousands of years more advanced than we are, would possess technology that would appear to us to be not the result of applied science but entirely supernatural, pure magic. . . .*
> New thought: *A supernatural event of world-shaking proportions, occurring in a faithless time when only science is believed to have the power to work miracles, might appear to be the work of an extraterrestrial species hundreds or even thousands of years more advanced than we are.* (336)

Molly now recalls that bit of gibberish that one of the aliens had spoken: *"Yimaman see noygel, see refacull, see nod a bah, see naytoss, retee fo sellos."* She figures out that this is a reverse phonetic rendering of the phrase: *"My name is legion, is Lucifer, is Abbadon, is Satan, eater of souls"* (337). So it appears that those human beings who had been "taken" (by drifting up through ceilings and such) are headed for you know where. But there are, of course, two places they could possibly end up: "Of the countless millions who had been taken, floated through ceilings, drawn through floors: Some had screamed in the transit but some laughed. Different destinations" (337).

All this, I fear, is an explanation that is no explanation. The problems with it are myriad. In the first place, this explicitly religious (and specifically Christian) accounting for all the bizarre phenomena in the novel will simply fall flat on those who happen not to accept Christian dogma. It will seem like cheating, like trickery. We have not struggled through this windy and maladroit narrative just to be told that the solution could have been found in our family Bible. Secondly, Koontz has dodged the really hard work of *making the supernatural phenomena plausible:* by merely saying that it was all the product of some nebulous force (whether it be God or the devil or angels or whatever), he has freed himself of the difficulty of making any individual supernatural event (Harry Corrigan spouting T. S. Eliot, the existence of the spider-like creature in the church basement, and so on) credible and believable. Even the supernatural must have some kind of logic to it, otherwise it will seem random and unmotivated, as it does here. In particular, the chief supernatural phenomena of the omnipresent rain (which Koontz lamely likens to a kind of Noachic flood) and the proliferation of the hideous fungi (which Koontz neglects to explain at all, either their existence or their sudden disappearance) are left utterly unaccounted for.

But the worst part of Koontz's "solution" is that it unwittingly endorses a kind of Social Darwinism that he would presumably be the first to hold in abhorrence. If the people who are left on earth were "chosen" because of their various "talents," it means that the ones who were "taken" had no particular talents to offer to the newly cleansed planet—they are simply "unfit" to live, and must be whisked off to other realms, whether it be above or below. I am certain that the pious author would be horrified at this conclusion, but his own "explanation" leads inevitably to it.

*The Taking*, in effect, is a mess. Its religious resolution solves nothing, and the whole novel seems like a trick that has been played on the reader. The supernatural incidents come to seem like jack-in-the-box surprises to make the reader jump every few pages, and they cannot be incorporated into a unity. Koontz would have been better off if he had recalled H. P. Lovecraft's advice on writing weird fiction:

> In writing a weird story I always try very carefully to achieve the right mood and atmosphere, and place the emphasis where it belongs. One cannot, except in immature pulp charlatan-fiction, present an account of impossible, improbable, or inconceivable phenomena as a commonplace narrative of objective acts and conventional emotions. Inconceivable events and conditions have a special handicap to overcome, and this can be accomplished only through the maintenance of a careful realism in every phase of the story *except* that touching on the one given marvel. This marvel must be treated very impressively and deliberately—with a careful emotional "build-up"—else it will seem flat and unconvincing.[7]

By this criterion, Koontz's *The Taking*, with its preposterous plethora of supernatural events, is exactly the sort of "immature pulp charlatan-fiction" that rightly earned Lovecraft's disdain.

\* \* \* \* \* \* \*

As I have mentioned, the "horror boom" of the 1970s and 1980s has by now dissipated. King and Koontz regularly reach the bestseller lists, but Clive Barker has apparently taken to writing children's books, and Anne Rice has proceeded from her entertaining (and not entirely contemptible) vampire novels to metaphysical tracts full of pompous philosophizing. Meanwhile, horror films continue to proliferate, but in spite of their extensive special-effects budget continue to be not much better than their crude B-movie predecessors of decades ago. This literary genre, at least of late, has been particularly susceptible to influence from film, as many popular writers strive to imitate the startling (but often irrational and unmotivated) effects meant to make readers (or viewers) jump out of their seats; but their work seems doomed to oblivion. Some genuinely talented writers do work in the horror tradition—one need only mention such sadly little-known writers as Ramsey Campbell, Thomas Ligotti, or Caitlín R. Kiernan—but their work does not reach a mass audience; perhaps mercifully so, for it may be that that keeps them from prostituting their talents as so many others have.

# VII.

# BLOOD, THUNDER, AND RELIGION

## DAN BROWN AND IRVING WALLACE

Dan Brown's *The Da Vinci Code* (2003)[1] is certainly a remarkable publishing phenomenon. It remained on the *New York Times* hardcover bestseller lists for a remarkable 166 weeks, scattered from the time of its initial publication to the summer of 2006. This record of endurance shatters that of Richard Bach's ineffable *Jonathan Livingston Seagull* (1970), which was the best-selling novel of 1972 and 1973 but remained on the *New York Times* bestseller list for only a period of 102 weeks (combined hardcover and paperback).[2] But unlike that harmless piece of fluff, whose popularity seems to epitomise the vacuous 1970s, *The Da Vinci Code* claims to have considerably greater intellectual substance, specifically in some spectacular claims about the nature of religion and the functioning of the Christian—and in particular the Catholic—church. Its portrayal of the Catholic sect called Opus Dei called down furious denunciations upon Brown's head for anti-Catholic prejudice; these denunciations were redoubled when a big-budget film version, directed by Ron Howard and starring Tom Hanks, appeared in 2006. In addition, Brown has had to fight off several claims of plagiarism, as other authors have contended that he has taken the central idea of his novel from their works. He was accused of such borrowing from Lewis Perdue's novel *Daughter of God* (2000), but in a subsequent copyright infringement suit the court ruled in favor of Brown. Other claims have also been rejected.

Brown himself is a pretty unlikely figure to inspire this kind of controversy. A former English teacher at Phillips Exeter Academy, he had previously written only three other novels: *Digital Fortress* (1998), *Angels and Demons* (2000), and *Deception Point* (2001).

Although all these books were reissued upon the success of *The Da Vinci Code,* none has captured the public imagination, and only recently (2009) has *Angels and Demons* been turned into a blockbuster film—presented, anomalously, as a sequel to *The Da Vinci Code.*

*The Da Vinci Code* opens dramatically with the murder of Jacques Saunière, curator of the Louvre. But before he dies, he manages to pass on a secret in some manner that is not immediately explained. The murderer is identified as one Silas, an albino.

The focus of the novel is on Robert Langdon, an authority on religious paintings. Langdon, who "viewed the world as a web of profoundly intertwined histories and events" (15)—I would be interested to know what historian doesn't—was to have met Saunière (who himself had written "books on the secret codes hidden in the paintings of Poussin and Teniers" [15]) after a lecture that the latter had delivered just prior to his death. Langdon is working on a book on "the iconography of goddess worship" (23), which is Saunière's area of expertise. When he comes to the Louvre in expectation of meeting Langdon, he is naturally shocked to find that Saunière has been murdered.

Brown devotes some entertaining early pages to Silas, who wears a *cilice* ("a leather strap, studded with sharp metal barbs that cut into the flesh as a perpetual reminder of Christ's suffering" [14]). This fellow's mantra is *Pain is good*—a slogan Silas had taken from his teacher, Father Josemaría Escrivá (14). After killing Saunière, he proceeds to flagellate himself:

> Silas turned his attention now to a heavy knotted rope coiled neatly on the floor beside him. *The Discipline.* The knots were caked with dried blood. Eager for the purifying effects of his own agony, Silas said a quick prayer. Then, gripping one end of the rope, he closed his eyes and swing it hard over his shoulder, feeling the knots slap against his back. He whipped it over his shoulder again, slashing at his flesh. Again and again, he lashed.
> *Castigo corpus meum.*
> Finally, he felt the blood begin to flow. (14)

It is a small mercy that Brown doesn't trouble to translate that Latin phrase ("I punish my body").

We soon learn that Silas is a member of Opus Dei. This Catholic organization has just opened a brand new headquarters and conference centre in New York. Escrivá's book, *The Way* (1934), had caused the order to expand throughout the world: "Opus Dei was a global force" (29). And yet, as Bishop Manuel Aringarosa, president-general of Opus Dei reflects, the order has a bad reputation:

> "Many call Opus Dei a brainwashing cult," reporters often challenged. "Others call you an ultra-conservative Christian secret society. Which are you?"
>
> "Opus Dei is neither," the bishop would patiently reply. "We are a Catholic Church. We are a congregation of Catholics who have chosen as our priority to follow Catholic doctrine as rigorously as we can in our own daily lives." (29)

But this rational response does not satisfy everyone, especially in light of some random instances where some Opus Dei members ("a few misguided souls" [29]) have engaged in questionable behavior:

> Two months ago, an Opus Dei group at a midwestern university had been caught drugging new recruits with mescaline in an effort to induce a euphoric state that neophytes would perceive as a religious experience. Another university student had used his barbed *cilice* belt more often than the recommended two hours a day and had given himself a near lethal infection. In Boston not long ago, a disillusioned young investment banker had signed over his entire life savings to Opus Dei before attempting suicide.
>
> *Misguided sheep,* Aringarosa thought, his heart going out to them.
>
> Of course the ultimate embarrassment had been the widely publicized trial of FBI spy Robert Hanssen, who, in addition to being a prominent member of Opus Dei, had turned out to be a sexual deviant, his trial uncovering evidence that he had rigged hidden video cameras in his own bedroom so his friends could watch him havin sex with his wife. "Hardly the pastime of a devout Catholic," the judge had noted. (29–30)

But now Opus Dei, and perhaps the entire Catholic church, is threatened by a danger much more serious than the derelictions of a small number of its members—a danger that Aringarosa coyly neglects to elaborate to the reader. It would appear to have something to do with Saunière's murder. For we now learn the appalling fact that the curator was found naked, spread-eagled, and with a pentacle on his body drawn in his own blood. This pentacle, Langdon helpfully points out to the reader, is not (as Hollywood would have it) the symbol of the devil, but of Venus. In his left hand Saunière is holding a black-light pen, "originally designed by museums, restorers, and forgery police to place invisible marks on items" (39). It appears that the curator has written a cryptic message on the floor with this pen. It is as follows (43):

13-3-2-21-1-1-8-5
O, Draconian devil!
Oh, lame saint!

Virtually the entire novel is spent on the decoding of this message.

All this is happening in the Louvre, with Langdon and a Paris police prefect, Bezu Fache, examining the body. At this point Sophie Neveu, from the cryptography department of the Paris police, interrupts Fache's interrogation of Langdon with the startling announcement that she has "deciphered the numeric code" (51) and that Langdon is to contact the U.S. Embassy immediately. When he calls the number that Neveu gives him, he hears a message—*from Neveu:* "Mr. Langdon. . . . Do *not* react to this message. Just listen calmly. You are in danger right now. Follow my directions very closely" (53).

In fact, Neveu goes on to say, Fache suspects Langdon of committing the murder. She points out that Saunière had written a fourth line of text: "P.S. Find Robert Langdon" (67). Neveu realises that this message was meant for *her:* "P.S." does not mean *post scriptum,* but refers to her childhood nickname, "Princess Sophie"—for she is Saunière's granddaughter.

We now get a little background on the murderer, Silas. He comes from a broken home, where his father, "enraged by the arrival of an albino son" (55), beat and ultimately killed his mother. The boy, in turn, killed his father, then fled to Marseilles, where he "was forced to live alone in the basement of a dilapidated factory, eating stolen fruit and raw fish from the dock" (55). Other dreadful things happen, and Silas (not his name at the time) finds himself in a prison in Andorra, where Manuel Aringarosa himself—then only a "missionary from Madrid" (57)—comes to him and takes him under his wing, becoming his teacher and mentor. Prior to murdering

Saunière, Silas had extracted from the curator the crucial piece of information that he had sought—the fact that a keystone sought by Opus Dei was in the Saint-Sulpice church in Paris. Why Opus Dei would want this object is not explained at the time. In any event, Aringarosa asks the abbé of the church to let Silas into it that evening—at one in the morning. The abbé passes on this unusual request to Sister Sandrine, who reluctantly agrees. She, however, does not have warm thoughts about Opus Dei:

> Opus Dei had always made her uneasy. Beyond the prelature's adherence to the arcane ritual of corporal mortification, their views on women were medieval at best. She had been shocked to learn that female numeraries were forced to clean the men's residence halls for no pay while the men were at mass; women slept on hardwood floors, while the men had straw mats; and women were forced to endure additional requirements of corporal mortification . . . all as added penance for original sin. It seemed Eve's bite from the apple of knowledge was a debt women were doomed to pay for eternity. (41)

Brown knows that his contemporary, middle-class audience will look askance at this kind of unreasoning prejudice, so to this extent he might be accused of anti-Catholic bias; but, to be blunt about it, Catholics—and perhaps Christians as a whole—have brought this hostility upon their own heads by adherence to the Bible, which is unequivocally an anti-feminist tract. And certain other religions one could name are no better in this regard.

In any event, Silas goes to the church and looks for that elusive keystone. He seems on the verge of finding it. And Bishop Aringarosa now thinks that, "if all went as planned tonight in Paris, [he] would soon be in possession of something that would make him the most powerful man in Christendom" (107). A mighty tall order! What could it be? We are, inevitably, not told—yet.

Meanwhile things are heating up for Langdon and Neveu. Langdon, in a sudden flash of insight, suddenly understands the meaning of the last two lines of the code. They are an anagram, standing for: "Leonardo da Vinci! / The Mona Lisa!" (98). This happens while the two are fleeing for their lives, for they have decided that any further interrogation by the police will prove dangerous. As Langdon is about to leave the Louvre, he realises that the letters P.S. in that fourth line may also refer to the *Prieuré de Sion*

(Priory of Sion), "one of the oldest surviving secret societies on earth" (113), with such luminaries as Botticelli, Sir Isaac Newton, Victor Hugo, and . . . Leonardo da Vinci as members. Indeed, "Da Vinci presided over the Priory between 1510 and 1519 as the brotherhood's Grand Master" (113). Neveu, for her part, remembers as a little girl finding a golden key with the letters P.S. on them among her grandfather's effects. They discover that Saunière has written another message on the glass covering the painting of the Mona Lisa: "So dark the con of man" (124). This would seem like another anagram, but it is not decoded immediately by our two intrepid investigators. Indeed, at this point Langdon is captured by a museum security guard—but Neveu comes to his rescue and frees him by threatening to destroy another da Vinci painting. As they are fleeing the building, Neveu announces that she has solved the new anagram: it is "Madonna of the Rocks," another painting by da Vinci, behind which is the golden key she remembered from her childhood.

Silas, for his part, finds that he has been tricked by Saunière and the Priory of Sion: the thing—whatever it is—that he is looking for is not in Saint-Sulpice Church. He takes out his anger on the nearest available victim: "A sudden explosion of rage erupted behind the monk's eyes. He lunged, lashing out with the candle stand like a club. As Sister Sandrine fell, her last feeling was an overwhelming sense of foreboding" (136). That's putting it mildly. If we had any sympathy at all for Silas because of his ravaged childhood and upbringing, it disappears with this entirely unprovoked murder of an innocent woman—and a nun at that.

Langdon and Neveu continue to flee the police, using various dodges to escape detection. Langdon now notices that the golden key looks peculiar—it has black-light writing on it: "24 rue Haxo" (156). Can this be some sort of headquarters of the Priory of Sion, of which Saunière was clearly a leading member? Neveu asks for the history of the Priory, and Langdon obliges in a rather longwinded manner (157f.). The upshot of the whole business is that the Priory appears to be guarding the Holy Grail. At any one time, only four members of the Priory know the whereabouts of the Grail. It was thought to be in England, but is in fact in France. Langdon and Neveu now realise that the key they are holding opens a Swiss bank deposit box. Can the solution be so easy as this? Is the Grail in the box? (Hardly: we are only on page 172.) They go to the Paris branch of the Depository Bank of Zürich, enter the bank vault, and get the deposit box. It contains a wooden box that appears to have something *liquid* inside it. But while this is happening, a guard has recognised the two fugitives and called Interpol. Police quickly surround the bank—but the obliging bank manager, wishing to protect the privacy of his apparent clients, contrives to get them out in a delivery truck. Another close shave!

Langdon and Neveu open the wooden box and find inside a cylindrical object called a *cryptex*—an object invented by Leonardo "to protect information written on the contained scroll or *codex*" (199). Neveu explains:

> "We require a password," Sophie said, pointing out the lettered dials. "A cryptex works much like a bicycle's combination lock. If you align the dials in the proper position, the lock slides open. This cryptex has five lettered dials. When you rotate them to their proper sequence, the tumblers inside align, and the entire cylinder slides apart." (200)

It is, however, not advisable, in the absence of knowledge of the proper sequence, simply to break the cryptex: Leonardo "designed the cryptex so that if you try to force it open in any way, the information self-destructs" (200). The cylinder's compartment is surrounded by vinegar, and any attempt to break the object will end up destroying the papyrus document within.

It is at this point that Langdon and Neveu figure out that Saunière was himself the Grand Master of the Priory of Sion, and that they are holding the keystone to the location of the Holy Grail. The bank manager, André Vernet, tells them that the other three members of the Priory are also dead. Vernet, thinking that Langdon and Neveu are the murderers of all four of these members, now demands the wooden box at gunpoint—but of course our valiant heroes manage to elude him.

Langdon now wishes to consult with Sir Leigh Teabing, a Grail expert who (conveniently) lives in an historic castle near Versailles. They make their way there and are suitably impressed with the accommodations:

> The butler guided them through a lush marble foyer into an exquisitely adorned drawing room, softly lit by tassel-draped Victorian lamps. The air inside smelled antediluvian, regal somehow, with traces of pipe tobacco, tea leaves, cooking sherry, and the earthen aroma of stone architecture. Against the far wall, flanked between two glistening suits of chain mail armor, was a rough-hewn fireplace large

enough to roast an ox. Walking to the hearth, the butler knelt and touched a match to a pre-laid arrangement of oak logs and kindling. A fire quickly crackled to life. (226)

Teabing tells them the *true* story of the Grail. It all has to do with the history of the Bible, and of how the Bible as we know it came to be. As Teabing states pompously: "Almost everything our fathers taught about Christ is *false"* (235). He tells the story of how the church deliberately suppressed certain writings about Jesus and not merely declared them non-canonical, but sought to destroy all copies of these texts, now declared to be heretical. Teabing explains: "'It was all about power . . . Christ as Messiah was critical to the functioning of Church and state. Many scholars claim that the early Church literally *stole* Jesus from His original followers, hijacking His human message, shrouding it in an impenetrable cloak of divinity, and using it to expand their own power'" (233). He goes on to say that "The Holy Grail is not a thing. It is, in fact . . . a *person"* (236). (Those ellipses are Brown's, and this is how the chapter ends.)

Teabing has come to this conclusion by an analysis of da Vinci's *The Last Supper.* The "person" in question is a woman: the painting depicts a woman to Jesus' immediate right. This is none other than Mary Magdalene; she was Jesus' wife. Jesus in fact wanted Mary to carry on the church after his death—a circumstance that allows Teabing to conclude: "Jesus was the original feminist" (248). We are pointedly meant to recall how anti-feminist Opus Dei has revealed itself to be. Let it pass that at least some of the leading writers and thinkers of ancient Greece and Rome were, by all accounts, rather more feminist than Jesus (in the Roman Empire, widows could inherit their deceased husbands' property, something that did not happen in the West until well into the nineteenth century). In any case, Jesus had a child by Mary. Moreover, both Jesus and Mary were of royal blood: this is the real meaning of *Sangreal,* which does not mean *San Greal* (Holy Grail), but *Sang Real* (royal blood). When Jesus was crucified, the pregnant Mary fled to France and gave birth to a child, Sarah. Jesus' line has descended through this child all the way down to the present day. Can it be that Neveu, who was called "Princess Sophie" as a child, is related to Jesus? Brown leaves us with a cliffhanger at the end of this chapter, but in the next he brings us down to earth by stating that, no, Neveu is not related to Jesus.

Meanwhile, Teabing has learned, through his servant, that Langdon and Neveu are fugitives from the police. They convince him, however, that they had nothing to do with Saunière's death; and they further inform him that the other three members of the Priory of Sion with knowledge of the Grail have also been murdered. The question is: Why now? What is the point of killing these individuals at this particular moment in history? It turns out that the Priory was on the verge of publicizing the truth about Jesus. Langdon now springs the great surprise upon Teabing: the "keystone" is in a wooden box that Langdon is hiding under the couch. He also manages to open a secret compartment in the box that reveals four lines of text in characters he does not recognise.

While all this is happening, Bezu Fache—who, it comes as no surprise, is allied with Opus Dei (272)—and other members of the police have surrounded the house. The truck by which Langdon and Neveu fled has a homing device, so the police know exactly where they have gone. The murderer Silas also knows—he has been informed of Langdon's whereabouts by someone known only as the Teacher. Is this Fache? In any case, just as Langdon is reading those four lines of inscrutable text, he is knocked out by Silas. Silas demands, at gunpoint, the keystone from Neveu and Teabing, but by a clever contrivance they manage to subdue him. At this point the police burst in, but in some fashion or other our valiant trio—Langdon, Neveu, and Teabing—manage to escape in a Range Rover. They go to Bourget Airfield and leave for England in a private plane.

They now discover that the four lines of text are written in Leonardo's patented mirror writing (this is actually reproduced on page 298). By reading this writing (written in English) in a mirror, they ascertain that the five-letter code they are looking for is *sofia* (Greek for wisdom). Using this code, they open the cryptex—only to find *another* cryptex inside! All this is happening while they are in the air, but as they are about to land in Kent they realise that the British police are already there. Teabing, being a nobleman, manages to sneak Langdon, Neveu, and Silas (whom they have bound and gagged and taken with them) into his limousine before the police can arrive to question them. A piece of paper accompanying the second cryptex reveals yet another versified conundrum of some kind, which appears to have something to do with a knight buried in Temple Church—the "church built in London by the Priory's military arm—the Knights Templars themselves!" (338).

But things go awry from an unexpected direction. It transpires that Teabing's servant, Rémy Legaludec, is an ally of Opus Dei. They are everywhere, by gum! As the others explore the church,

Rémy frees Silas and gives him a gun. At gunpoint (always at gunpoint), the two miscreants take the second cryptex; they also take Teabing as a hostage. For their part, all Langdon and Neveu can do is to go to the library of King's College for help in deciphering the verses about the knight. (The librarian delivers what is probably a fitting commentary on the entire novel: "What is this? Some kind of Harvard scavenger hunt?" [379].) They manage to figure out that the knight referred to is Sir Isaac Newton.

Meanwhile, Rémy drops Silas off at the London headquarters of Opus Dei. There, Rémy meets the ineffable Teacher—who poisons him and takes the cryptex. Meanwhile, the police have been notified that Silas is at Opus Dei headquarters. When spotted, he flees, and in a scuffle contrives to shoot Bishop Aringarosa. At this point we do not know whether this injury is fatal. Langdon and Neveu head, of course, to Westminster Abbey, where Newton is buried. They look at the tomb of Newton and finally come face to face with the Teacher—it is Sir Leigh Teabing himself.

Teabing now spills the beans: Saunière and the other members of the Priory of Sion had betrayed the Grail. The Priory had planned to reveal the truth at the turn of the millennium, but the curator had been intimidated by the church into keeping a lid on the secret: his family (meaning his wife, his son and his wife, and his son's son—Sophie's brother) had been killed, an incident that understandably has haunted Neveu all her life. Now Teabing is going to publicise the truth once and for all.

This development is of some interest. Up to this point, the reader's sympathies have presumably been carefully guided to elicit hostility to Opus Dei, and perhaps to the Catholic church as a whole, for its role in suppressing the truth about Jesus; but Teabing's revelation that it was he and his associates who killed the four members of the Priory of Sion, not to mention the hapless Rémy, has the effect of making the Grail supporters seem as despicable as the church itself. This perception is augmented by a revelation by Bishop Aringarosa (who, yes, is still alive) that, five months earlier, he had been summoned to the Vatican to be told that the Catholic church would be severing its ties to Opus Dei—it had become "a liability and an embarrassment" (416). Teabing had learned of this development and had offered Aringarosa the Grail as a means of securing power and prestige. So clearly Teabing is not interested in abstract truth, but merely in wielding power.

Back in the present, Teabing (yes, at gunpoint) demands that Langdon team up with him to find the Grail. Langdon threatens to destroy the cryptex so that the secret of the Grail will remain hidden;

Teabing doesn't think Langdon can bring himself to do this, but Langdon does in fact throw the cryptex in the air. Teabing tries to catch it, but it falls to the ground and breaks. Does this mean that the secret is lost forever?

Well, no. Langdon had managed to open the cryptex earlier and taken out a map that indicates the whereabouts of the Grail (which, presumably, provides definitive proof of the true history of Jesus, Mary, and the rest). Bezu Fache and the police come into the abbey and arrest Teabing. Langdon and Neveu now follow the final clue—the map in the second cryptex. It leads them to Rosslyn Chapel in Scotland. There they meet Sophie's grandmother and brother: they had not in fact died in the car accident that had killed Sophie's parents; Saunière and his wife had come up this scheme to protect themselves—*for they are in fact descendants of Jesus Christ.* The grandmother scoffs at the idea that the church pressured Saunière not to reveal the truth about the Grail: "Heavens no. . . . There is nothing in the Priory doctrine that identifies a date at which the Grail should be unveiled. In fact the Priory has always maintained that the Grail should *never* be unveiled" (444). But where *is* this bloody Grail? It turns out that it is not in Rosslyn Chapel at all but... under the Louvre. So we end where we began—how symmetrical!

It is by no means clear to me why *The Da Vinci Code* has elicited all the interest that it has: it is, in reality, nothing more than a scavenger hunt, or perhaps more accurately a jigsaw puzzle. And the peculiarly cerebral nature of the puzzle, involving anagrams, mirror-writing, clues in Latin and Greek, and the like, makes one wonder how it could have attracted the millions of readers that it is. No doubt it has something to do with Brown's presumably provocative treatment of religion, in particular his (far from original) speculations on the "truth" of Jesus' life. And yet, those who maintain that Brown has a bias against religion, or the Catholic church, or even against Opus Dei—and who have, in a rich irony, written any number of books attacking or explicating *The Da Vinci Code,* a few of which have themselves appeared on nonfiction bestseller lists for a brief interval—seem to be straining at gnats. There is very little evidence of any kind of explicit religious animus in Brown's book. If there are any who think that Brown is an iconoclast on the level of Nietzsche, Thomas Paine, H. L. Mencken, or Bertrand Russell, then they cannot possibly be familiar with any of these thinkers. The most searching treatment of the nature of religion in *The Da Vinci Code* occurs relatively late in the book, in a brief discussion between Langdon and Neveu:

Langdon smiled. "Sophie, *every* faith in the world is based on fabrication. That is the definition of *faith*—acceptance of that which we imagine to be true, that which we cannot prove. Every religion describes God through metaphor, allegory, and exaggeration, from the early Egyptians through modern Sunday school. Metaphors are a way to help our minds process the unprocessible. The problems arise when we begin to believe literally in our own metaphors." (341–42)

I can't see anything here that would raise the temperature of anyone but a fundamentalist—either Christian or Islamic. It is a small point that Langdon deems as "fabrication" something that could conceivably be true, but for which there is no evidence. The conversation continues, with Langdon remarking:

". . . The Bible represents a fundamental guidepost for millions of people on the planet, in much the same way the Koran, Torah, and Pali Canon offer guidance to people of other religions. If you and I could dig up documentation that contradicted the holy stories of Islamic belief, Judaic belief, Buddhist belief, pagan belief, should we do that? Should we wave a flag and tell the Buddhists that we have proof the Buddha did not come from a lotos blossom? Or that Jesus was not born of a *literal* virgin birth? Those who truly understand their faiths understand the stories are metaphorical."

Sophie looked skeptical. "My friends who are devout Christians definitely believe that Christ *literally* walked on water, *literally* turned water into wine, and was born of a *literal* virgin birth."

"My point exactly," Langdon said. "Religious allegory has become a part of the fabric of reality. And living in that reality helps millions of people cope and be better people." (342)

There are a number of evasions here that an atheist or true iconoclast could pounce upon. In the first place, it is not at all the same thing to say that a literal belief in miracles is identical to "religious allegory" becoming "a part of the fabric of reality." In the second place, there is no reason to think that religious belief necessarily leads to being "better people": any number of sociological studies have found very little difference in behavior between the religious and the non-religious; or, at any rate, no greater inclination toward antisocial behavior among the non-religious than among the religious. The position that Langdon (and perhaps Brown, if—as is by no means certain—Langdon is expressing the author's view at this point) is staking out is the mainstream, non-fundamentalist credo that, for all that some features of a scripture (whichever scripture you happen to believe in) may be myth and metaphor, there remains a core residuum of value—even if it is only moral value—in religion that can lead both to psychological comfort for the individual and benefits for the society as a whole. It does not appear that an acceptance of Brown's theory of Jesus' life would have any fundamental effect upon Jesus' moral teachings, or even—if one wishes to press the point—upon his presumed divinity, which does not rest upon his not having married or procreated.

The one passage where Brown could be accused of bias occurs much earlier, when Langdon is pondering the clue, "So dark the con of man," left by Saunière. He thinks to himself: "Nobody could deny the enormous good the modern Church did in today's troubled world, and yet the Church had a deceitful and violent history. Their brutal crusade to 'reeducate' the pagan and feminine-worshipping religions spanned three centuries, employing methods as inspired as they were horrific" (124–25). Brown goes on to spell out the familiar history of the witchcraft persecutions in the Middle Ages, which he attributes (not entirely accurately) to the church's prejudice against women; and he concludes: "During the three hundred years of witch hunts, the Church burned at the stake an astounding five *million* women" (125).

There are numerous problems with this formulation, and from both sides of the religious spectrum. Firstly, the persecution of witches extended over a far greater period than merely three hundred years: the first known trial for witchcraft in the Christian era occurred in 373 C.E., and the last person executed for witchcraft in Europe appears to have been a woman in Germany in 1775. It is true that the great majority of witchcraft persecutions occurred between the fifteenth and the seventeenth centuries, and it is presumably these three centuries that Brown is referring to. But many people aside from women—including old men, children, and even infants— were victims. Secondly, Brown's figure of five million women killed is wildly exaggerated, and appears to have been based in part upon British scholar Pennethorne Hughes's conjecture that as many as nine million people died during the witch-hunts of the Middle

Ages and Renaissance; but this figure has been uniformly discredited by later scholarship, which has established that probably several hundred thousand people were executed between the twelfth and the eighteenth centuries.[3]

Brown's discussion here is merely meant to augment the overall thrust of the book that the Christian church suppressed the "goddess" to advance an exclusively male agenda:

> The days of the goddess were over. The pendulum had swung. Mother Earth had become a *man's* world, and the gods of destruction and war were taking their toll. The male ego had spent two millennia running unchecked by its female counterpart. The Priory of Sion believed that it was this obliteration of the sacred feminine in modern life that had caused what the Hopi Native Americans called *koyanisquatsi*—'life out of balance'—an unstable situation marked by testosterone-fueled wars, a plethora of misogynistic societies, and a growing disrespect for Mother Earth. (125–26)

There are problems with this formulation also—the Catholic church, at any rate, venerates the Virgin Mary to such a degree that she can be considered a deity scarcely less significant than Jesus himself—but what is evident is that this diatribe against the church really has little value in itself, but is merely designed to advance the plot.

Brown might perhaps have left himself less open to attack by the forces of religion had he not asserted, somewhat pompously and arrogantly, that his book is based on "facts." A heading called "Fact" prefaces the book, in which he very briefly notes that the Priory of Sion was a real organization with Da Vinci and others as members, and that the "Vatican prelature known as Opus Dei is a deeply devout Catholic sect that has been the topic of recent controversy due to reports of brainwashing, coercion, and a dangerous practice known as 'corporal mortification'" ([1]). Even this seems relatively mild, and assertions by various opponents of Brown in op-ed pieces and elsewhere that Brown had portrayed Opus Dei as a "secret society" are directly contradicted by the text. What is more, Brown's antagonists have not noticed that, in the course of the book, both the Catholic church and Opus Dei itself emerge untainted by any touch of scandal, "coercion," or violence. The true villains prove to be Teabing and others who wish to publicise the "truth" about Jesus in order to discredit and even destroy the church. Brown notes that the church was not involved in any campaign to suppress the Priory of Sion's revelation about Jesus' marriage, and states explicitly that Teabing "had exploited both the Vatican and Opus Dei, two groups that turned out to be completely innocent" (428). And if one were to think that the unsavory characters Silas and Aringarosa are, in Brown's mind, somehow representative of the organizations they represent, Brown again declares: "His [Teabing's] dirty work had been carried out unknowingly by a fanatical monk and a desperate bishop" (428).

Examining *The Da Vinci Code* from a purely aesthetic perspective, there turns out to be surprisingly little to say. Brown engages in the obvious suspense tactic of telling his story alternately from one side (Langdon and Neveu) and the other (Silas and Aringarosa, and later Teabing): accordingly, the reader in one sense stays one step ahead of both, knowing facts and events to which neither side is privy, but not knowing the *full* story until the end. This rapid switching back and forth has something to do with the abundance of short chapters—105 chapters, plus a prologue and an epilogue, in 454 pages. Some chapters are exactly one page long. But in reality this is one more instance of the short-attention-span syndrome we have seen in so many recent popular novels, which not only echo the quick change of scene found in contemporary movies but which all but proclaim themselves as fleshed-out screenplays hoping desperately to find a producer and director to translate them to the pinnacle of the popular writer's wish-fulfillment fantasy, the big screen.

I have already observed that suspense and adventure novels, in spite of their surface patina of realism, are in reality works where genuine realism almost never comes into play—if by realism we mean a depiction of how events actually happen in the world and how people actually react to those events. Almost everything in *The Da Vinci Code* is preposterous and unbelievable—it is not remotely possible that anything like the given scenario could possibly happen. In particular, the elaborate succession of "codes" and cryptograms and such is so ludicrous—and so obviously designed merely to tease the reader into continuing to turn the pages—that any sense of reality is obliterated from the start. In particular, the idea that a dying man (Saunière) could have taken the trouble to write out an elaborate puzzle in his death-throes immediately brands *The Da Vinci Code* as a work of fantasy. We (I will consider myself, for the nonce, among the millions of eager page-turners of Brown's novel, even though I frankly could not turn the pages fast enough to reach the end of this piece of pseudo-literary cotton candy) are willing to suspend disbelief entirely purely for the sake of learning the outcome.

I shall have more to say about *The Da Vinci Code* after examining a much earlier novel that strikingly anticipates many of its themes: Irving Wallace's *The Word.*

\* \* \* \* \* \* \*

Irving Wallace (1916–1990) proves to be a surprisingly interesting literary—or almost-literary—figure. He became a freelance magazine writer at the tender age of fifteen, continuing in that work into the 1950s. He served four years in the U.S. Army Air Force (1942–46) and worked as a screenwriter (1949–58). This latter experience no doubt gave him a good sense of what the public wants, and he gradually turned to writing. His first book was a nonfiction work, *The Fabulous Originals* (1955), and his first bestseller was a novel, *The Chapman Report* (1960), about the sexual lives of a group of wives in an exclusive community. Wallace sensed that novels featuring a lively mix of sex, race, religion, and other hot topics would prove sure-fire sellers, and he accordingly produced a succession of blockbusters, including *The Prize* (1962); *The Man* (1964), about the first African-American president; *The Plot* (1967); *The Seven Minutes* (1969), an entertainingly salacious novel about a controversial book that reveals a woman's sensations during the seven minutes of sexual fulfillment; and *The Word* (1974).[4] Four or five of his books have been filmed, and *The Word* was turned into an eight-hour miniseries on CBS. Several novels of the 1980s similarly treat religion in a purportedly controversial way, but I have not read them.

*The Word* is, fundamentally, the story of Steven Randall, the head of a relatively small public relations firm in New York. At the very outset, his scepticism is emphasised, as he remembers the religious training he received in youth: "How familiar it was to him. The Tomb is empty. The Lord has arisen. He has appeared. The Resurrection. In memory, it had been the most meaningful and secure time of his life. Yet, he had spent years ridding himself of this crippling voodooism" (3). That last phrase—written before the rise of the Moral Majority and the entire modern fundamentalist movement—would have been quickly deleted by Dan Brown's copyeditor today, even if Brown had had the *cojones* to write it, even as a character description. And yet, Steven's father, the Reverend Nathan Randall—who happens to be in a coma—is (understandably in light of his profession) very religious: "His father would say—God is everything—and he would look to God and give his love to God" (5). We receive at the outset a poignant description of Steven's grief at his father's condition:

> He could still feel, inside himself, the lump of agitation that he had carried along the entire day, but now he could better analyze it, and what was curious was that the smallest part of this unhappiness came from grief over his father. He tried to rationalise his unfilial reaction, and decided that grief was the most intense of the emotions and therefore the shortest-lived. The very intensity of grief made it so self-destructive that one's survival instinct rose up to draw a sheet over grief and hide it from mind and heart. He had drawn the sheet, and he was no longer thinking of his father. He was thinking now of him-self—realizing how heretical his sister Clare would find this, if she could know—and he was thinking of all his own recent dyings. (7)

This is really quite creditable—perhaps not in the Dostoevski league, but something Updike or Roth need not be ashamed of. The "dyings" that Steven is concerned about are the troubling circum-stances of his own personal life—specifically, his separation from his wife, Barbara, who has custody of their thirteen-year-old daugh-ter, Judy, and the tedium of his work, impelling him to seek a way out of it. In fact, Steven's company is being bought out by Cosmos Enterprises. This sounds promising, but there is a catch. Steven is friendly with one Jim McLoughlin, who heads the Raker Institute, a concern devoted to unearthing ethical behavior by big business. Ogden Towery III, the owner of Cosmos, understandably despises McLoughlin, who he sees as a meddlesome muckraker.

Steven's life is turned upside down, although he has no imme-diate realization of it, when he is approached by George L. Wheeler, a religious book publisher, about a "brand new Bible" (2). This doesn't sound, on the surface, terribly promising: if all Wheeler has is a new translation of the Bible, how will that be any news?—and why does he need a public relations firm to trumpet it to the world? Meanwhile, there are other troubles in Steven's personal life. He is shocked to learn that his daughter, Judy, was thrown out of private school for taking drugs—and not for merely the lesser or relatively harmless ones, as Barbara explains: "I'm talking about speed. I'm talking about bennies, bombitas, dexies, crystals, jolly beans, meth.

I'm talking about amphetamines, Steve, the kind you pop in your mouth and the kind you inject" (25). On top of this, Barbara announces that she wants to marry Dr. Arthur Burke, the psychiatrist who is treating Judy. Steve indignantly refuses to grant Barbara a divorce, and she calmly retorts that he is not likely to prevail in court, given what could be dug up about him: "Your behavior in the past and the present. Your irregular life. Your drinking. Your affairs. The young girl you're keeping in New York" (31). Clearly, Steven is not a model husband or father, or even a model human being.

Steven is at least relieved to hear that his father is slowly recovering. A friend of his, Tom Carey, a minister, has a lengthy discussion with Steven about the state of the Christian church. Tom believes that the church is out of touch with people and the way they live today: "The church is simply not keeping pace, is not reaching and holding enough human beings" (45). He goes on to say: "If the church can't reform, there's only one thing that can save it. A miracle" (46). Tom wonders whether a figure like the Reverend Maertin de Vroome, a "Protestant revolutionary in Amsterdam" (45), can help: de Vroome feels that all the "superstitions about miracles and the Ascension, the events after the Resurrection, destroy the effectiveness of the New Testament and limit the church in its activity. The only thing important in the gospels, de Vroome insists, is the basic wisdom of Christ" (45). This means emphasizing "a program of humanistic action and social involvement" (45).

Meanwhile, Wheeler is being increasingly insistent that Steven take up the publicity work for his new Bible. Steven, for his part, wonders whether accepting the job might help in his father's recovery: "How pleased his father would be to learn that his son was going to become involved in the Good Book and good works" (54). Towery is also urging him to accept the Wheeler offer. Wheeler provides more details about his new Bible:

> Five publishers—Wheeler in the United States, and the leading Bible publishers in Great Britain, France, Germany, Italy—were combining their resources to bring out a brand-new International Bible—no, not the complete Bible, but a New Testament, actually. This New Testament would be freshly translated and contain exclusive information never before published, on some unrevealed archeological discovery. It would be the definitive New Testament, the most perfect one in the history of Christianity.... (58)

Even so, Steven doesn't think this sounds very exciting. He wonders why Wheeler is going to so much effort and expense to publish the book, and so he declines the offer. Wheeler then tells him the truth: six years ago, Professor Augusto Monti found some papyri in Ostia (the port that served Rome) that turned out to be the original source of the Synoptic Gospels: the Gospel of James (brother of Jesus). This gospel tells the entire life of Jesus (the Synoptic Gospels—Matthew, Mark, and Luke—have large gaps in their coverage of Jesus' life, especially in his later youth and early adulthood). More spectacularly, it states that Jesus did not die on the cross in 30 A.D., but lived on for another nineteen years. Jesus continued to preach, actually coming to Rome itself, and died in 49 A.D.—the date of the actual Resurrection. The Gospel of James provides an eyewitness account of that event. Steven (now called Steve throughout the rest of the book) ponders the implications of this new find:

> Randall had closed his eyes. Behind them spun a bright pinwheel carrying images of both his recent past and his present. He visualized the human images on that pinwheel responding to this most sensational find in nineteen hundred years. He saw them electrified and aglow with renewed faith in the meaning of life. . . . The Gospel of James would revive the Saviour's message of love and peace and would comfort and heal His human family. (67)

A Dr. Evans, of the National Council of Churches, states to Steve as he sails on a ship to London with Wheeler and others: "With the advent of the new Bible, universal skepticism will cease" (77). There is, of course, a problem with this view. Even if the Gospel of James includes an eyewitness account of the death, resurrection, and ascension of Jesus, what reason is there for shedding all scepticism over this event? Have not other eyewitnesses been deluded, or dreaming, or hallucinating, or simply lying? And there remains the awkward fact (never mentioned in *The Word*) that Jesus states, in all three Synoptic Gospels (and hence presumably in the newly discovered gospel), that his second coming will occur within the lifetime of those who hear him—a prophecy that obviously has not come true. How could Jesus, if he was divine, be so catastrophically wrong on so central a feature of his eschatology?

But perhaps it is expecting too much of a popular writer to wrestle with these issues. Indeed, at this point in the novel I had already gained the sensation that Wallace's ultimate scheme was to reveal the new gospel as a fake, perhaps through the efforts of Jim McLoughlin, who is mentioned at this very moment as "off somewhere on his highly confidential mission" (72). Let us see how well my prophecy—er, guess—is fulfilled.

Wheeler, in any case, is highly hostile to "dissident clergy" like Maertin de Vroome, who "is spreading his tentacles everywhere, subverting and undermining Protestantism throughout the Western world" (92). It is expressly stated that de Vroome is a disciple of the "heretic" (92) theologian Rudolf Bultmann, an actual figure who promoted the notion of "demythologizing" the Bible—stripping away its layers of miracle and myth to reach the core of moral and social teaching found in the New Testament. (This tendency, of course, is as old as the Bible itself, and was anticipated by such earlier figures as David Friedrich Strauss, Ernest Renan, and other proponents of the "higher criticism" of nineteenth-century biblical scholarship.)

Steve has boarded the boat in the company of Darlene Nicholson, his current squeeze. Indeed, one morning he awakens "to find that what was stifling his breath was Darlene's soft breast, her exposed left breast pressed against his lips" (68). I quote this passage only because it is the first of many indications that Irving Wallace himself has a serious breast fixation. But for a popular (male) writer, that is harmless enough. However, one of the members of Wheeler's party, a seemingly straitlaced Bible expert named Naomi Dunn, appears interested in Steve, as this exchange, in which Steve offers to share a drink with her, attests:

> Randall rose to his feet. "Be my guest. Where shall we go? Would you prefer the Riviera Lounge?"
> She shook her head. "Too big, too crowded, too much string music." Her normally rigid features softened. "The Atlantique is more intimate." She removed her horn-rimmed glasses. "Wouldn't you like something more intimate?" (94)

One might think this would lead directly to some cheesy sex romp, but it is not quite that straightforward. Naomi informs Steve that she used to be a nun; she left the order not because of a lack of devotion, but "It was simply that I wasn't cut out for the stern routine and discipline of the convent" (98). After several drinks, they go back to her room—ostensibly so that she can give him some papers to read. But things take a hot turn quickly: she asks him to undress her, and he discovers that she is wearing nothing under her dress. But now she announces: "I don't fuck. I don't like it. But I do everything else, anything you want to do" (102). Holy crap! as Ray Barrone's father might say. So we get a pretty clinical description of what, in the business, is called 69:

> She came up on her knees quickly, turned her knobby back and narrow buttocks toward him, straddled his chest, and then stretched out on top of him. Her hands cupped his testicles, and her tongue flicked around the tip of his penis, and then her mouth closed over it.
> As she hung above him, he could see the protruding lips of her vulva. His fingers clutched at her buttocks, brought her down closer and closer to him. (102)

And so on. Quite frankly, this really doesn't do it for me. I suppose Wallace was writing at a time when he could really not call a spade a spade, but the use of such terms as "testicles," "penis," "vulva," and even "buttocks" instead of . . . well, their coarser synonyms seems a trifle like an elementary course in medical school. But perhaps Wallace intends this entire scene to be clinical and unstimulating: after it is over, Naomi merely states: "Thank you. . . . The only favor I ask is that you forget his ever happened. I'll see you at dinner" (103). For his part, Steve reflects a bit tritely, "There are no saints, only sinners" (104)—and then proceeds to quote Immanuel Kant! I wonder if Dan Brown or any of our other bestselling writers have even heard of the German metaphysician.

The ship arrives in London. Wheeler had been expecting to meet Florian Knight, a renowned biblical scholar, but learns that he has taken ill and will not be able to join them in Amsterdam, where Resurrection Two (as the unveiling of the new Bible is termed) is planned. There seems to be something suspicious about this incident, but at the moment we do not know exactly what. Even though Knight had been working on the new Bible, he had only learned the previous day of its true nature. Steve looks up Valerie Hughes, Knight's fiancée, and gets Knight's address from her. He sees Knight, who says he is in fact not ill; but he speaks disapprovingly of Dr. Bernard Jeffries, another biblical scholar on Wheeler's team: "Dr. Bernard Jeffries is a beastly, bloody liar, who has used me for the last time. I'm damn tired of being put out among the dustbins, cleaning up behind him, while he goes on higher and higher" (123–24). Knight is furious at being kept in the dark about the Bible project. Meanwhile, Valerie tells Steve privately that Knight is embittered because he has just finished a new biography of Jesus that is now unpublishable because of the new find. Nevertheless, Valerie thinks that she can persuade Knight to rejoin the project.

Steve is now alarmed to read a headline in a newspaper that de Vroome has suspected the existence of a new translation of the New Testament and denounced it: "We do not need one more New Testament to make religion relevant in this changing world. . . . We need radical reforms within religion and the church itself, changes in the clergy as well as interpretations of the Scriptures, to make religion meaningful once more" (130). Steve is less concerned about de Vroome's opinion of the new Bible (which he has clearly not seen) than with the mere fact that word about it has somehow leaked out, in spite of the nearly fanatical lengths to which Wheeler and his cohorts have gone to keep the find under wraps. Steve wonders whether Florian Knight is teaming up with de Vroome and has leaked the news to him.

Coming to Amsterdam with Wheeler's team, Steve is taken aback to be confronted outside his hotel room by Cedric Plummer, the reporter who had written the article about de Vroome. How did Plummer know Steve would be there? Steve exchanges angry words with him, quite literally telling him to drop dead.

Wheeler's headquarters are at the Hotel Krasnapolsky (the Kras for short). Steve begins to confer with his appointed staff about publicity plans. None of them have seen actual page proofs of the new Bible. Steve would like to see a copy himself, although he is well aware of the risks: "I'll promise them we'll be careful. I know the risks involved. In fact, I had a dangerous run-in this morning" (160). Naomi believes that Steve ought to have a confidential secretary, and she recommends one Lori Cook, who is "fanatically devoted to the project—and to religion" (163). She does, however, have an infirmity—a crippled leg. Is there something suspicious about the readiness with which Naomi is offering Lori for this position? We'll see. In any event, Steve manages to get galley proofs of the Bible. He is then driven back in a limousine to the Amstel Hotel, where he is staying; but he decides to walk the last six blocks, with the limo following him. It is not a wise decision. He is attacked by several men in a car and almost loses his briefcase containing the Bible before the men flee with the approach of the police. This is, I believe, one of the relatively few moments of actual violence or fisticuffs in the entire novel; and, of course, being in a sane country, there is no gunplay. Steve emerges relatively unhurt, with the Bible still in his possession; but it is dawning upon him how much this entire project is fraught with danger.

Indeed, Steve's entire belief structure is slowly undergoing change, and it is passages like this that raise *The Word* reasonably close to the level of actual literature:

> What he felt inside was a sense of peace. It was also a sense of security. It was, above all, a sense of purpose, although to what end he was not certain, and somehow that did not matter. . . .
>
> What pervaded his being, he was aware, could not yet be called by the name of faith—that is, unquestioning faith in an unseen and divine master or master planner who provided humans with motivation and purpose and was the explanation for the inexplicable. What had overcome him, and could not be more easily understood by him, was the beginning of a belief, a belief that his being on earth had a meaning, not only for himself but also for those whom his life brushed against or touched. In short, he was not here by accident or chance, and therefore he was not expendable, a waste, a cipher dancing in a void until the ultimate darkness. (175–76)

This may not win Wallace a ranking with Bertrand Russell, but it shows his ability to depict the gradual development, even transformation, of his central character. It is worth remembering this passage when we reach the end.

Steve now reads portions of the Gospel of James. It reveals that the Romans had executed Jesus for sedition; they had not been egged on by the Jews, as the Synoptic Gospels stated. Wallace quotes actual biblical scholars casting doubt on the story of Pontius Pilate's reluctance to execute Jesus, maintaining that this is part and parcel of a not-so-subtle anti-Semitic bias in the New Testament from which Wallace manifestly wishes to dissociate himself. Steve goes on to reflect that Jesus' sayings "had uncanny relevance to the world today" (188). He notes that James reports no miracles, at least until the very end of his story: Jesus happens to survive his initial crucifixion, goes to Rome, then to Puteoli (a port city near Rome), where he is captured by the Romans and burned at the stake. Later he is resurrected and ascends to Heaven. All this is told by Wallace with at least the patina of learned scholarship, and with liberal quotations from the Gospel of James, complete with annotations by scholars explaining the discrepancies between its account and that of the Synoptic Gospels. The whole exercise is a praiseworthy venture into biblical scholarship that not many popular writers could have pulled off.

A further indication of Steve's personal transformation is that he now calls his wife, Barbara, and says that he will not contest the divorce. This is not merely for the sake of his daughter, as Steve explains: "I'm not doing it for Judy's sake. I'm doing it for your sake, Barbara. You deserve some happiness" (199). Good boy! Steve's girlfriend Darlene, who has overheard the conversation, now thinks that she and Steve can get hitched—but Steve throws cold water on that idea: "Darlene, marriage was never part of our arrangement. Think back. Did I ever promise to marry you? From the start, I made it clear to you, if you simply wanted to move in and live with me, that was fine, that was great. We'd live together. Have some fun, I never spoke of anything more" (201). Darlene, furious, leaves immediately and goes back to New York.

Freed of this increasingly unwelcome burden, Steve resumes work. He is puzzled at the fact that the file on Professor Augusto Monti, the discoverer of the gospel, is so skimpy. He feels it important to interview him, as this person's first-hand account of the momentous discovery could be an important component in the overall publicity for the project. But Monti is curiously reluctant to speak to Steve or anyone else. Steve decides to go to Milan to meet Monti—but he only sees his daughter, Angela—who, *naturellement,* is lovely:

> She was, he guessed, five feet six inches in height. She wore a broad-brimmed Italian straw hat, outsized lavender-tinted sunglasses, a low-cut sheer yellow silk blouse that revealed two wisps of bra which did little to contain the overflow of her provocative breasts. A wide leather belt hugged her slim supple waist, and a rust-colored summer skirt enhanced the curves of her voluptuous hips. (210)

Note those "provocative breasts"! I also could have done without the "voluptuous hips." In any event, Angela Monti tells Steve all about her father's discovery. They seem quite taken with each other, and Steve hires her to work on Resurrection Two.

Steve now goes to Paris to interview Henri Aubert, a scientist who dated the manuscript using carbon-14 dating techniques. While not absolutely exact, Aubert reports that his tests confirm that "the papyri could come from the period when the brother of Jesus was alive to write the true story of the Messiah. The Ostia Antica discoveries were absolutely authentic ones" (227). Aubert makes a point of noting that he was once a militant sceptic:

> "When I became a full-fledged scientist, I departed from my faith completely. I decided religion was *merde*. I became a cold bastard. You know how it is when one finds something new, a new attitude. One is inclined to go overboard. Once I had settled upon my unfaith, my scientific approach, I would only give my respect and belief to that which came out of a laboratory, in effect, to that which one could see, feel, hear, or logically accept. This condition persisted after I left my schools. I worked and lived for the now, the present, this time on earth. I was not interested in the future and the hereafter. My sole religion was Fact—and God was not Fact, the Son of God was not Fact, and neither hell nor heaven was Fact." (230–31)

All this is a trifle crude, but it at least shows why Aubert became a believer after his own vaunted science confirmed (at least in his mind) the authenticity of the new gospel. His wife, incidentally, is extremely orthodox—and what is more, her father "is one of the leaders of the Sociedad Sacerdotal de la Santa Cruz et Opus Dei. It is known in public as Opus Dei" (232)!

But Steve himself is still not convinced. He feels the need to dig deeper. He now goes to Mainz to see Karl Hennig, the printer of the new Bible. But he is stunned to see the loathsome reporter Cedric Plummer coming out of the building housing Hennig's printing facility. What could this possibly mean? In any event, we are treated to a learned dissertation about the history of typesetting that would make James Michener proud. But all is not well at the Hennig plant. There seems to be some resentment of Hennig among the younger workers. Hennig, for his part, was forced to compensate for the decline of Bible sales in Germany (he echoes his fellow German Nietzsche in declaring, "God is dead" [250], at least in the sense that religion was on the decline in Germany and elsewhere in Europe) by publishing all manner of popular works, including pornography. It seems that his workers are dissatisfied at Hennig's shift back to publishing what they feel is an unprofitable religious publication, and they are threatening to strike; but Hennig makes major concessions and offers a generous contract, and the strike is averted. Hennig then drives Steve to Frankfurt, so that he can catch a plane back to Amsterdam. Hennig takes Steve to his hotel, the Frankfurter Hof—where again Cedric Plummer is spotted. Steve recalls that Hennig told him that he has an appointment at five o'clock at the Hotel Intercontinental—can it be to see Plummer?

But other matters quickly engulf Steve's attention. First on the agenda is Angela. After a romantic dinner in Amsterdam, they go back to Steve's hotel room for some transcendent sex. The passage is far too long to quote, but Wallace emphasises that this is far more than just a roll in the hay. Take cognizance of this response by Steve after it is over:

> He had never, in so many nights in a life of so many grownup years, offered or taken, given or received, an orgasm born and released entirely of love, never once, until this night on this bed with this young woman in Amsterdam. He wanted to weep. For wasted years? For final joy? For the millions of others on earth who would live and die without knowing this ultimate oneness? (259)

Speak for yourself, bub! But we are clearly meant to see that Angela is, as far as Steve is concerned, the one and only. Far more than the soft-breasted Darlene or the staid but secretly lustful Naomi, Angela is clearly a soul mate whose relationship should extend far beyond the completion of the Resurrection project.

But curious things are afoot—literally. Lori Cook, Steve's crippled secretary, has a vision and can suddenly walk. Steve remains sceptical, but to Wheeler it is nothing short of a miracle:

> "We're in, Steve. . . . I can tell. I can feel it inside. Those theologians know it's a miracle, the first divine miracle that can be credited to our International New Testament. Even if Protestants don't look upon miracles as the Catholics do, they can't ignore evidence like this. They've got to be impressed by the powers of our New Bible. . . . Once we get the go-ahead, I want you ready to run with this, Steve. After the announcement is out, you can pull the cork

on Lori's story. Can you think of a better endorse-
ment on earth than this?" (268)

There is, as Steve manifestly perceives, something a bit sordid—an unseemly combination of reverence and self-aggrandise-
ment—about this whole incident. But worse things are about to happen. Steve now discovers that a confidential memo that he had sent
out about the place and time of the announcement of the new Bible
(to take place on July 12) has fallen into the hands of Maertin de
Vroome, who plans to anticipate the announcement by two days.
Wheeler, alarmed, states that his own announcement must now be
moved up to July 8.

Shortly thereafter, Cedric Plummer accosts Steve and says that
de Vroome wishes to see him. Steve agrees, and the two go to
Vroome's church. The reverend comes into the room holding two
Siamese kittens! (Isn't there a James Bond film in which the villain
spends his entire time stroking an Angora cat on his lap?) De
Vroome outlines his religious views at length (292f.). He feels that
Wheeler and his band are just out for money and power, seeking to
frighten people back into blind faith. He tells Steve that Wheeler
was close to bankruptcy before Cosmos Enterprises offered to buy
him out. Lori Cook, he states, was always able to walk normally; she
is merely a neurotic who "saw that she could gain more attention
and indulgence by playing Bernadette, so now she is playing this
new role" (300). Karl Hennig, the printer, was a Nazi book burner in
youth. Henri Aubert cannot have children—he has had a vasectomy;
his wife, now pregnant, has been impregnated by Charles Fontaine,
the French publisher of the new Bible. Professor Monti had attempted to cheat the peasants who owned the land where the discovery was made; caught in the act, he is now living in disgrace in
Rome.

It is an overwhelming indictment, and Steve is profoundly
shaken. De Vroome urges Steve to come to his side to debunk the
new discovery. Steve refuses and delivers his own indictment:

> "I think you are no less selfish or ambitious than
> those I now work for. But you, Dominee, I believe
> you are more fanatical. You may see it as a necessity,
> and for a good end, but I could not work for a man so
> righteous, so unbending, so certain he alone knows
> truth. I could not become a turncoat, and help you de-
> stroy the very thing I have finally come to believe
> in—the Word—yes, the Word which we are going to

give to the world. It is a message you know nothing about, and if I have my way, you will not know anything about until it safely belongs to the world." (304)

Steve reflects that, even though de Vroome (assuming he is even speaking the truth) has revealed various personal failings in the people on the Resurrection project, has so far produced no credible evidence that the actual gospel is a fabrication.

Nevertheless, Steve feels he has to pursue the intriguing threads of suspicion that de Vroome has outlined. He first discovers, to his shock and amazement, that Angela is the one leaking information to de Vroome. Confronting her about this and about her father, she denies the story about her father, saying it was invented by colleagues envious of his discovery; and as for the leak, she manages to persuade him that the real leaker is Florian Knight. Steve confronts Knight, who admits his guilt in the matter but pleads for leniency: he says he had actually managed to secure a proof of the Bible the day before and was going to turn it over to de Vroome, but in reading it he was overwhelmed with love of Jesus, and in fact had a vision of Jesus, and then found that his poor hearing is now restored. Another miracle! Knight goes on to reveal that Hans Bogardus, the librarian of Resurrection Two, was his liaison with de Vroome. Steve dutifully hunts Bogardus down, but the latter is defiant: he has information that will "reveal it [the new Bible] as a fake" (332). Well, well! Now we are on to something. . . . (Bogardus, incidentally, goes on to say that Cedric Plummer is his gay lover!—something we are evidently to look upon with disfavor, if not actual distaste.) Bogardus tells Steve: "Look at Papyrus Number 9, fourth line from the top" (334). Steve does so. The line appears to reveal a small and rather arcane historical error (too complicated to explain here) on the part of James in relation to Jesus' capture in 49 A.D., but it certainly seems as if this is not the kind of error that an eyewitness could possibly have made. Does this one small flaw deflate the genuineness of the entire document?

Steve relates all this to Wheeler, but the latter is preoccupied with other matters: de Vroome is trying to blackmail Hennig (by threatening to reveal his Nazi past) into supplying him with an advance copy of the Bible. Wheeler tells Steve not to fire Bogardus just yet. Steve then goes to Aubert in Paris, who admits to having the vasectomy, and also makes the key admission that even though the *papyrus* on which the Gospel of James was written dates to the time of Jesus, the *writing* may not. Aubert goes on to say that the writing could be authenticated by consulting the leading Aramaic scholar in the world—Abbot Minos Petropoulos, who lives in the monastery of Simopetra on Mt. Athos in Greece. Steve is puzzled as to why this authority is not working on Resurrection Two. Telephoning Angela on the matter, he is informed that she and her father had in fact gone to see Petropoulos at the monastery and that the latter had authenticated the papyrus, but he was too sick to work on the project. But Aubert immediately declares that this whole story is impossible: no women are allowed on Mt. Athos. Steve continues to be shaken at this additional evidence that his beloved Angela is either a liar or some kind of double agent.

Evidently attempting to win some kind of award for frequent flying, Steve makes his way to Mt. Athos to see the learned scholar. He reaches the monastery after three arduous days, much of it on foot. Petropoulos tells Steve that he had heard from Bernard Jeffries about the discovery and had corresponded with Monti, but never met him. So Angela was indeed lying! Petropolous looks at a copy of the dubious papyrus that Steve had brought, and he concludes that the translators have probably made some kind of error—that the error may not in fact reside with James himself. Steve is encouraged, but wants Petropolous to look at the original papyrus. The scholar agrees.

Steve returns to Amsterdam, where he attempts to see the original papyrus. He and Wheeler go to the vault where the papyri are stored—and are stunned to learn from the curator that Papyrus 9 has been stolen! Steve is, understandably, "sick . . . from distrust" (369). Something about the whole Resurrection project is beginning to smell very bad. Wheeler then tells him that the missing papyrus has been found—it had fallen into the back of the drawer. This seems a bit convenient, but Steve is somewhat relieved. He lets Petropolous look at the papyrus, and the scholar confirms his belief that there has been a small translation error in the line in question but that the papyrus as a whole appears to be genuine. Steve, however, is still troubled: could the genuine papyrus have been switched with a fake? Small things take on immense implications. Why, for example, was an infrared photograph of the papyrus so much poorer in resolution than the original? Steve looks at the photograph—it looks different from the one he had initially shown Petropoulos. He goes to see the photographer, Oscar Edlund—but is alarmed to find that his darkroom has been damaged by a fire the previous evening, destroying the negative of the questionable papyrus. Steve nonetheless confronts Edlund and shows him the photograph of Papyrus 9; Edlund, who has studied the papyri with extraordinary care and attention, thinks the photograph does indeed look a little peculiar.

Steve now wants to see Petropoulos again, but Wheeler intervenes and refuses, angrily telling Steve to stop wasting time trying to verify the papyrus—not the assignment he was hired for—and get back to work with the publicity campaign. Steve then confronts Angela about her manifest lying about the Mt. Athos trip. She, in turn, makes an impassioned plea to Steve, saying that she had lied to prevent him from losing his faith and descending into cynicism:

> "Your irrational, defensive, self-protective cynicism. Maybe it is self-protective for you, Steve, and keeps you from hurt. But it is also anti-life, and it stands between you and life, prevents you from accepting or giving deep love, true love. A person without faith cannot love. I heard you on the phone from Paris. I perceived you were again doubting the authenticity of my father's find. I saw you losing the little trust you had gained. You were becoming again the Steve Randall who could not be close to his parents, his wife, his child, to anyone." (392)

There is considerably more of this, and it is all rather eloquent.

Steve, for his part, states that his doubts about the papyrus will be resolved if he can see Professor Monti in Rome. So he and Angela go to Rome—but Steve is astounded to learn that Monti is in an insane asylum. Angela, who has known this all along, says that he is usually catatonic, but has occasional periods of lucidity. During one of these moments Steve shows him the papyrus; Monti makes the simple but cataclysmic claim: "I wrote this" (401). Monti thinks he is James, the brother of Jesus.

As Steve returns to his hotel, he meets de Vroome, who makes the bold announcement that the papyri are forgeries. How can he know? "Because I have just seen the forger himself and I have learned all the details of the hoax" (412). De Vroome states that Cedric Plummer received a letter from a French expatriate in Rome, Robert Lebrun, who says that he forged the documents. Lebrun approached Monti with a fragment of parchment and encouraged him to go dig at a particular site in Ostia Antica, where Lebrun had buried his forgery. But after the discovery was made, Lebrun began to demand more and more money from Monti, otherwise he would expose the forgery. Is this what caused Monti's mental collapse? Lebrun was then about to turn over evidence of the forgery to Plummer for $20,000—but when he saw de Vroome with Plummer, he thought that Plummer was on the side of religion and that he wanted to obtain the evidence only to destroy it. Lebrun fled from the appointed interview and is now in hiding.

Steve now makes his own efforts to hunt down Lebrun. He looks through Monti's papers and finds an appointment book for May 8 of the previous year. It reads: "Appuntamento con R. L. da Doney. Importante" (434) ["Appointment with R. L. at Doney's. Important"]. Steve suspects that Doney's, a café, is a regular haunt of Lebrun's, and so he waits there. Sure enough, Lebrun shows up. Lebrun is, however, suspicious of Steve and refuses to turn over the evidence to him. Then Steve tells Lebrun of Jim McLoughlin and the Raker Institute. This manages to convince Lebrun that Steve is on his side. He tells Steve at great length about how he produced the forgery: he worked on it while imprisoned at Devil's Island for many years. He had become embittered against religion because, although he was befriended by the prison's curé, Père Paquin, and although he served in an army unit made up of prisoners from Devil's Island who fought valiantly against the Germans in World War I, after the war he was merely imprisoned again instead of being pardoned, as he had been promised; and Père Paquin had done nothing. So Lebrun spent years studying Aramaic and then in preparing the forgery (he had in fact been a forger, which had led to his imprisonment). After Lebrun's lengthy account, Steve admits laconically to himself: "Faith had fled" (464).

Steve telephones Wheeler and tells him the whole story, but of course Wheeler refuses to believe it; he calls Lebrun a "twentieth-century Judas" (468). But Wheeler makes a telling slip at one point, calling Lebrun an ex-convict: Steve had not mentioned that detail, and so he knows that Wheeler was previously acquainted with Lebrun. The next day, Lebrun doesn't show up for a meeting with Steve to present proofs of the forgery. Worried, Steve manages to find out where Lebrun lives. He is dead—the victim of a hit-and-run accident. By now it is becoming clear that the extent of the "hoax" is immense, perhaps more than a single man can combat. Steve goes to the morgue to see Lebrun's corpse; he pays for Lebrun's funeral expenses and so gets possession of the few belongings on Lebrun's person. One of these items is a railroad ticket to Ostia Antica. Following a hunch, he goes to the site and finds a missing piece from Papyrus 3 on which Lebrun had written in invisible ink. He hears voices outside the area where he has been digging: it is the mother of the boy who had led him to the site, along with a policeman. Steve manages to flee and escape them.

Steve now plans to go to Paris to have Aubert confirm the papyrus fragment—but he also calls de Vroome to tell him that he will now work with him. At Orly Airport in Paris, he is stopped by customs officials: they take the bit of papyrus. Steve tries to fight with them but is easily subdued. This could only be the work of de Vroome, who was the only one who knew of his coming and of his possession of the papyrus. Why has de Vroome double-crossed him? At a hearing, de Vroome testifies, to Steve's amazement, that the papyrus fragment is authentic and not a forgery. Steve thinks Wheeler has somehow bought de Vroome off. In fact, Wheeler has offered de Vroome the general secretaryship of the World Council of Churches, a position of authority that the power-hungry cleric can ill resist. Wheeler now asks Steve to recant his testimony; if he does so, Wheeler may be able to get the magistrate to release him. Angela comes to Paris to persuade Steve to follow this course of action; but he refuses, and in a dramatic scene in court Steve makes the following utterance:

> "What I learned in Rome, what I saw with my own eyes, has convinced me that the papyrus fragment I was led to and which I brought into France, as well as the entire collection of papyri and the parchment that serve as the basis for the International New Testament, is a modern fabrication, a sham and a fraud, produced by a master forger's hand. I believe the products of Professor Monti's find are worthless, and the Jesus offered by James the Just and Petronius is a graven image and a spurious Christ. Despite earlier testimony to the contrary, I still maintain the evidence I had on my person upon entering France was a forgery—worthless, I repeat—and therefore I committed no crime. I trust the court, taking into consideration my own firsthand knowledge and investigations, motivated by no personal gain, will find me innocent. Moreover, I pray the court will return to me the missing portion of Papyrus Number 3, which is in some sense a legacy left to me by Robert Lebrun, so that I may have its contents assessed and examined by more objective experts elsewhere in the world. I have nothing further to add." (540)

Steve is, as expected, found guilty—but is then released.

The new Bible is announced with great fanfare. It creates a religious revolution. Steve sees members of his own family transformed and wonders whether the end has justified the means. Then his father dies. Steve decides to resume his exposé of the Bible—he had written an account of his involvement with it, and now he plans to team up with Jim McLoughlin to champion the truth. He even thinks he can get back together with Angela:

> "Hello, Angela," he called to her. "I love you, you know."
> She came running, plowing through the snow, toward him. "Darling," she called back, "my darling!" And then she came into his arms at last, and he knew, he knew that he would never let her go. (568)

And that is, at long last, the end of *The Word.*

It can be seen from this summary that *The Word* is a kind of mirror-image of *The Da Vinci Code:* whereas, in the latter, the forces of religious orthodoxy appear to be attempting to suppress a (genuine) ancient document that reveals cataclysmic truths about Jesus, in *The Word* the forces of religious orthodoxy are determined to disseminate a (false) ancient document that reveals cataclysmic truths about Jesus. But aside from this, and the fact that the nature of the puzzles in each case are unusually intellectual (unusual, that is, for popular fiction), there is very little resemblance between the two works, either on the level of plot or in overall aesthetic significance. The fact is that *The Word* is a surprisingly creditable novel, for all its flamboyance, its occasional descents into explicit sex, and the final, rather corny suggestion that Steve will somehow reunite with his true love, Angela. These blemishes do not tarnish a novel that otherwise accomplishes one of the principal goals of legitimate novels—the portrayal of a fundamental development of character in one or more protagonists. Steve Randall emerges as a vital and vibrant figure in *The Word,* and his gradual metamorphosis from a rather cheap cynicism regarding religion to belief in religion's power to transform lives to, finally, a clear (but not cynical) realization that the falsities and hypocrisies that can corrupt religion and the religious must be eradicated, is handled ably. Wallace has the restraint to end his novel just as Steve is about to begin his crusade to reveal the falsity of the new revelation that Wheeler and his cohorts are pushing; and there is no guarantee of his success. But Wallace does suggest that Steve has gained a new and burning purpose in life that may impel him to put aside his tendency toward meaningless sex with the Darlenes of the world, and will also endow him with a sense of direction for which, at the novel's opening, he had openly been searching.

There is no such transformation among the characters in *The Da Vinci Code*. After all the breathless permutations of the plot, Langdon and Neveu seem pretty much the same as they were before; each new twist only jolts them with momentary surprise, as it does the reader, but effects no fundamental alteration in their worldviews. Wallace's plot, although substantially more convoluted than Brown's, is also expounded in a superior fashion: his plotting is tight but without the frenetic pace of *The Da Vinci Code,* and he is content to let the inherent power of the core idea sink gradually into the reader.

Indeed, from a religious perspective, *The Word* is far more subversive than *The Da Vinci Code*. Wallace is not reluctant to portray the forces of religion as either so fanatical (Wheeler) or so cynical (de Vroome) that they simply do not care that the revelation they are propounding to the world is a falsehood. If this novel had been published in 2003—at a time when both Protestant fundamentalism and Catholicism have become considerably more aggressive in sniffing out and condemning what they perceive to be the banes of heresy and atheism—it could well have set off an even greater firestorm of controversy than *The Da Vinci Code*. Wallace is fully cognizant of the power of religion to transform lives; indeed, he expresses the point with poignancy toward the end, as Steve sits in church watching his family members absorb the new Word:

> He sat on the ash wood seat between his mother, Sarah, her smooth, pudgy face blissful as she hung on every utterance from the pulpit, and his father, Nathan, the elderly gentleman's features partially restored to a semblance of his onetime vigor, the light blue eyes dancing after the cadence of his protégé's from the pulpit. Only the cane propped beside him and the thick slowness of his speech reflected the remnants of the stroke he had survived. Beside his father, Randall could see Clare, his sister, and next to her, Swedish jaw thrust forward, Ed Period Johnson. Shifting slightly on the bench, Randall inspected those who were sitting beyond his mother, first Judy, her long corn-silk hair covering much of her angel face, his alert, clear-eyed daughter, and then Uncle Herman, fatter but less vacuous tan in earlier times.

They were all intent, entirely devoted to the Reverend Tom Carey's sermon, hearing what was still fresh to them, the sign, the wonder of Christ risen. (551)

And Steve's own transformation throughout the entire novel is summed up with the compact sentence that follows: "But Randall, he had heard it, he had heard it, lived with it, bought it, questioned it, doubted it, fought it, been defeated by it" (551).

I repeat that *The Word* probably does not qualify as genuine literature; but it comes surprisingly close to it, and far closer than *The Da Vinci Code*. It is a depressing thought that popular literature has, over the course of two or three decades, sunk even lower toward the nadir of trashiness, but such seems to be the case. But what the authors of both books are attempting to capitalise upon is the volatile mix of religion, sex (although there is mercifully relatively little of that in *The Da Vinci Code*, aside from the inherent sexual tension generated by the now commonplace pairing of a male and a female investigator plunged into all manner of scrapes and near-death experiences), and violence that they rightly see as a sure-fire recipe for controversy, and hence for sales.

# VIII.

## GLAMOUR, FASHION, AND SEX

### JACQUELINE SUSANN, JACKIE COLLINS, AND JUDITH KRANTZ

"Sex sells" is one of the oldest adages in advertising, and it is no doubt a venerable adage in literature—popular or high—as well. But, as far as Anglo-American literature was concerned, it took an enormously long time for explicit sex to make its way into print. To be sure, any romance novel, from Samuel Richardson onward, contained an undercurrent of sexual activity, even such "aberrant" activities as fornication, masturbation, and even rape; but the diction used to hint at these matters was entirely decorous, triggering only the imaginations of particularly salacious readers. Actual print pornography was no doubt circulated covertly, and Grove Press has made a pile of money reprinting vintage items of Victorian pornography, such as the magazine *The Pearl* (1879–80) and such "novels" as *The Autobiography of a Flea* (1888) and *My Secret Life* (c. 1890). But this material was on a level even below that of the burgeoning popular literature of the period.

Popular and pulp magazines of the early twentieth century helped to usher in the overt sexuality that now forms a ubiquitous presence in all entertainment media. Such magazines as *Snappy Stories* (1912f.) and *Saucy Stories* (1916f.)—the latter founded by H. L. Mencken and George Jean Nathan, then editors of the highbrow fiction magazine, the *Smart Set,* for the sole purpose of making money off of the booboisie—led to even more specialised journals such as *Spicy Detective Stories.* Some of the material in these magazines could be pretty racy, albeit without the use of four-letter words or clinical descriptions of genitalia. Consider this passage from Howard Wandrei's story "Too Good-Looking" (*Spicy Detective Stories,* December 1937):

> Arrestingly attractive though she was, Marcia exhibited no hint of bodily consciousness in her bearing. The gray silk piqué of her dress held the delicious swell of her bosom with nearly the economy of a brassiere, and the choice contours of her figure were magnificent, caused more than one lingering glance to follow her. She walked with an unconsciously provoking hip-sway, and her long legs were unexampled perfection. A hundred and eighteen pounds of potent, physical allure; a sultan's ransom on the hoof.[1]

But even this kind of coy suggestiveness was slow to make its way into books, even of the cruder sort. One of the difficulties was censorship. As early as 1873 Anthony Comstock had formed the New York Society for the Suppression of Vice, and he and his colleagues—who quickly formed similar organizations in many other states—forced the passage of the Comstock Law of 1873, barring the distribution of purportedly obscene materials through the mail. The result was that thousands of books, magazines, and other publications were suppressed over the next half-century. Publishers had very little recourse: either they had to defend their products in expensive litigation in the courts, or they had to withdraw their materials without a fight, losing much revenue in the process. The result (acknowledged even by such an iconoclast as Mencken, who despised Comstock and chafed under the strictures imposed by his actions) was a self-censorship in which book and magazine publishers simply declined to issue sexually daring material at the outset, to save bother. But Comstock and his lieutenants eventually overplayed their hand, especially when they attempted to ban manifestly serious literature—everything from Theodore Dreiser's *The "Genius"* (1915) to such venerable French classics as Gautier's *Mademoiselle de Maupin* and Flaubert's *Madame Bovary.* Losing some spectacular cases, they eventually became an object of ridicule. (They did manage to ban James Joyce's *Ulysses* from the US market from its initial serialization in a magazine [1918f.] until 1933.)

Accordingly, the trend toward greater sexual explicitness in all levels of literature forged inexorably ahead. Matters were aided by the increasing raciness of the films of the period, prior to the Hays Code of 1934: anyone who has seen Claudette Colbert prancing around with almost nothing on in *Cleopatra* (1934) will know that very little was left to the imagination in some of these movies. The postwar period saw an expansion on several fronts. Gore Vidal created a sensation—and a bestseller—with *The City and the Pillar* (1948), one of the first openly gay novels, containing a beautiful (and tasteful) description of a sexual encounter between two teenage boys. Ten years later another bestseller emerged: Vladimir Nabokov's *Lolita* (1958), the third-leading seller of that year, remaining on the *New York Times* bestseller list for 54 weeks. Of course, nothing in the book—nor in the delightfully wicked film version of 1962—had anything explicit, for the true "perversity" of the novel is not that Humbert Humbert wants to seduce Lolita but that the twelve-year-old sexpot, who has already lost her virginity, succeeds in seducing *him;* in any case, anything remotely explicit would have quickly led to the novel's suppression. (The film, of course, resorts to the cowardly compromise of making Lolita a sixteen-year-old and is therefore a bit less scandalous.)

By this time pornography itself was being mainstreamed. *Playboy* began publication in 1953, attracting a more sophisticated audience—by means of its exhaustive interviews of celebrities of all sorts, its meritorious fiction, and other features—than cruder magazines like *Rogue* (1955f.) or *Cavalier* (1952f.) ever could. There has been a gradual expansion in the display of female body parts in *Playboy,* a tactic carried still further by Bob Guccione's *Penthouse* (1969f.) and Larry Flynt's *Hustler* (1974f.), whose vulgarity puts it pretty much beyond the pale. Given that the Fifties saw the birth of *Playboy,* rock 'n' roll, and other elements that radically sexualised American society, those naïve conservatives who look back upon that decade as a kind of golden age of "Leave It to Beaver" moral uprightness must be accused of being seriously delusional.

But for all that, the Sixties were the true birth of the sexual revolution. It is difficult to chart the countless ways in which sex permeated the culture, from the androgyny of the mop-headed Beatles and their imitators to the sultriness of Elizabeth Taylor to the increasing sexualization of television commercials. At the same time, a parallel tendency in which "glamour" (always with the supercilious *u*) was infused in the entire entertainment industry, particularly Broadway and films, was encouraging bored housewives and tired businessmen to become voyeurs of actors, actresses, models, and other purveyors of panache. Fashion magazines such as *Cosmopolitan, Vogue,* and countless imitators enticed women of all shapes and sizes to become sex objects under the guise of beautifying themselves, and also carried celebrity profiles of the seemingly unattainable Hollywood stars and starlets whose larger-than-life images on the big screen made them akin to demigods.

Popular literature was not slow to pick up the trend, and one of those who most successfully rode the wave of sex and glamour was Jacqueline Susann (1921–1974). Susann had begun life as a model and actress, appearing in Broadway shows from as early as 1937 to as late as 1970. After writing a nonfiction work, *Every Night, Josephine!* (1963), about her raising a pet poodle, she attained spectacular success with *Valley of the Dolls* (1966),[2] which, as we have seen, was far and away the best-selling novel of that year, ultimately selling close to 10,000,000 copies in hardcover and paperback.

*Valley of the Dolls* is the loosely interlocking story of three young women, Anne Welles, Neely O'Hara, and Jennifer North. The narration is deliberately fragmented, jumping from one woman to the next, and a synopsis is likely to suffer from the same difficulty. But we proceed.

Anne is a woman from Lawrenceville, Massachusetts, who has come to New York to escape the stiflingly conventional atmosphere of her hometown:

> She would *never* go back to Lawrenceville! She hadn't just left Lawrenceville—she had escaped. Escaped from marriage to some solid Lawrenceville boy, from the solid, orderly life of Lawrenceville. The same orderly life her mother had lived. And her mother's mother. In the same orderly kind of a house. A house that a good New England family had lived in generation after generation, its inhabitants smothered with orderly, unused emotions, emotions stifled beneath the creaky iron armor called "manners." (5)

But let us not be deceived by this Theodore-Dreiser-for-the-poor description: Anne is not a wild young thing looking to plunge into sex, drugs, and rock-'n'-roll. For one thing, it is the year 1945, just after the end of the war, and certain rules of propriety and decorum exist even in New York. Secondly, Anne explicitly admits to herself that she is looking for love, even though her cynical mother, speaking perhaps more truly than she knows, retorts, "You'll only find that kind of love in cheap movies and novels" (7).

In any case, Anne is hired by Henry Bellamy, a Jewish theatrical attorney who warms to her like a benevolent uncle. His small office is abuzz because a young Anglo-American lawyer, Lyon Burke, is about to return to the firm from the war. Anne is assigned to find him an apartment. An insurance salesman named Allen Cooper, who has taken a shine to Anne, offers to let Lyon have his apartment—Allen has another place. Allen turns out to be a fabulously wealthy son of a real estate tycoon (although Anne was ignorant of the fact, being very naïve and not reading the society columns), and he now wants to marry Anne. But when he kisses her, he doesn't get the reaction he expects: "She stood there limply—then abruptly broke the embrace. God, it had happened again! At his kiss, a surge of revulsion had swept through her" (25). That "again" refers to the fact that, years before in Lawrenceville, Anne had actually ended up "kissing most of the boys in town" (!) but found the experience repulsive: "Mother, I don't think we have one decent kisser in all of Lawrenceville" (6). But now that a sophisticated New Yorker has kissed her and elicited the same response, Anne fears the worst: "She knew the truth now. She was frigid. That awful word the girls at school used to whisper about. Some girls were born that way—they never reached a climax or felt any real passion. And she was one of them. God, she couldn't even enjoy a kiss!" (26).

Meanwhile, Anne is getting better acquainted with Lyon Burke, listening to his deep thoughts about serving in the war:

> "I suppose if you're in it, nothing matters but getting out alive," she said quietly.
> "You don't chance thinking even that far ahead," he answered. "You think from day to day. If you allow yourself to think of the future—any personal future—you lose your nerve. And suddenly you recall all the senseless time-wasting things you've done . . . the wasted minutes you'll never recover. And you realize that time is the most precious thing. Because time is life. It's the only thing you can never get back. You can lose a girl and perhaps win her back— or find another. But a second—this second—when it goes, it's irretrievably gone." His voice was soft, remembering, and she noticed the fine lines around the corner of his eyes. (33)

Well, I can certainly sympathise about the idea of "senseless time-wasting"—although perhaps not in a manner that would flatter Jacqueline Susann. While imaginary violins continue to play in the background, Lyon tells Anne a sob story about a fellow soldier, poor farmer boy from Pennsylvania, who yearned to get back to his fields but was blown up by a land mine. The implication is obvious: Anne is falling for Lyon. The question is: Is Lyon falling for Anne?

But there is the matter of Allen Cooper to contend with. He and his father (oddly named Gino) are pressuring Anne to commit to marrying Allen. Presently an article appears in the newspaper announcing that Anne and Allen are engaged. Anne is besieged by reporters at her office. Henry, incredulous that Anne doesn't want to marry Allen and be on easy street for the rest of her life, actually warns her against Lyon, whom he likes personally but who he says is a bit of a playboy ("He's a guy, free and single. And any girl who appeals to him is the right girl—for the moment. And there are a hell of a lot of moments and a hell of a lot of right girls around this town" [48]). Henry wants to fire her, but he grudgingly relents and lets her stay on, so long as she (publicly, at least) remains engaged to Allen—no doubt she can use her feminine wiles (assuming she has any) to stall him for a while.

One of Henry's clients is an ageing actress named Helen Lawson, and we are treated to words of wisdom regarding the status of decrepit celebrities: "Age settled with more grace on ordinary people, but for celebrities—women stars in particular—age became a hatchet that vandalized a work of art" (68). Well, that must be comforting to all the non-celebrity women out there. At any rate, Helen is starring in a new Broadway musical, *Hit the Sky,* hoping that it can catapult her back into the spotlight. Helen seems a pretty tough cookie, but in an unguarded moment she tells Anne, "All I ever wanted was love" (74), and proceeds to recount the sad tale of her numerous failed marriages. But Neely, a vaudeville performer who is Anne's roommate, gives her the real dope about Helen's past:

> "Anne, I sit and gab with the girls all day. Everyone knows Helen sang in a speakeasy that was owned by Tony Lagetta. She was mad for him. But he was Italian and Catholic and had a wife and seven kids. He'd lay her, sure—but that's all. When she made it in her first show, Henry Bellamy stepped in and made her drop Tony. She was getting too famous, and if the wife sued it could hurt Helen's image. She had a long affair with Henry, but she still slept with Tony on the sneak. Everyone knew but Henry. He just kept managing her and making her a star and a millionaire. Then Tony found someone else, and Helen got so mad she married the first guy who came along—the artist. By this time there were

no more speakeasies and Tony ran some fancy joint—a French-Italian restaurant—and Helen used to bring this artist she married in and neck with him to get Tony jealous. I guess it worked, because one day the artist comes home and he finds Helen and Tony having this little reunion. . . . He left her and he was never the same. He got married again—but he was a drunk." (81)

My, how sordid! While Anne tries to take in this dreary tale, Helen labels her a dodo for still being a virgin at the age of twenty ("You make it sound like a disease," Anne replies sullenly [88]). This would have been music to Allen Cooper's ears, for he too is pressuring Anne to have sex; they have a serious conversation on the matter:

> "Anne, I think you're afraid of sex."
> This time she looked at him. "I suppose you're going to tell me that I'm unawakened . . . that you will change all that."
> "Exactly."
> She sipped the champagne to avoid his eyes.
> "I suppose you've been told this before," he said.
> "No. I've heard it in some very bad movies."
> "Dialogue is often trite because it's real. And it's easier to sneer at the truth."
> "The truth?"
> "That you're afraid of life—and living." (96)

This is a pretty ingenious argument for bad writing, but Anne remains unconvinced ("Do you think it's natural to reach twenty and still be a virgin?" "Virginity isn't an affliction" [96]).

*Hit the Sky* is set to open in New Haven. Neely has a bit part in the show, and to Anne's shock she announces she has had sex with her boyfriend Mel:

> "It hurt a lot and I didn't come. But Mel made me come the other way."
> "What are you talking about?"
> "He went down on me."
> *"Neely!"*

"Now Anne, stop acting so prissy. Just because you're not hot for Allen doesn't mean I'm a tramp. I happen to be in love with Mel."

"And that makes it right."

"You're darn right it does! We both want each other. Nowadays people don't get married just to do it. Mel respects me and loves me just as much today as he did yesterday. Even more, because how he *really* loves me. And I love him. Besides, we can't get married yet. He helps support his folks. But if the show's a hit and I can count on my hundred a week, then we'll get married." (100–101)

Now we're getting somewhere! This is pretty explicit stuff for 1966, at least between the covers of a book that purports to be "serious" and not (what it actually is) a sleazy sex romp. And yet, one suspects that Susann is projecting the sentiments of 1966 upon an age that was very different; indeed, her portrayal of the postwar years is notably unconvincing, and as the novel lumbers through twenty years of American history one gains not the slightest sense of shifting moral or sexual values as society passes from the age of Truman and McCarthy to that of Kennedy and the Beatles.

Anne still has her eyes on Lyon. The show turns out to be a great success in New Haven, and the two are engaging in a romantic walk in the cold Connecticut air. Then:

> Without a word, he spun her around and led her back to the hotel. They didn't speak until they entered his room. It was a duplicate of the colorless old-fashioned room that had been assigned to her. Lyon took her coat. For a moment he stared at her tenderly, then he held out his arms. She rushed to him, to his lips, cold from the night air but firm and demanding as they met her own. Her arms slid around him. She was surprised at the urgency with which she returned his kiss, as if she had always been waiting to kiss like this. She clung to him, her mind spinning deeper and deeper into the wonder of that kiss. (111)

Can it be that Anne is not frigid after all? Well, she and the reader have to wait a bit, for she and Lyon engage in more tiresome yakking about whether they really love each other or not; in fact, at one point he asks her (nobly, in his mind) to leave, just to make sure she doesn't do anything she regrets—but she says that she wants to stay, so the clothes-shedding resumes:

> She felt herself responding to his embrace with an ardor she had never dreamed she possessed, her mouth demanding more and more. She couldn't kiss him deeply enough. His hands caressed her body, gently, then intimately. Yet her emotional excitement dominated all physical sensation. To have him in her arms . . . to be close, to feel free to kiss his eyelids, his brow, his lips . . . to know that he wanted her, that he cared. . . .
>
> And then it was happening. Oh God, this was the moment! She wanted to please him, but the pain caught her unaware and she cried out. He pulled away immediately and released her. (114)

So Lyon has discovered she is a virgin! It appears that he has never had a virgin before. He stops temporarily, but she is so mortified at his surcease that he resumes. Evidently he climaxes, but she doesn't. All she can conclude is: "All at once she knew—this was the ultimate in fulfillment, to please a man you loved. At that moment she felt she was the most important and powerful woman in the world. She was flooded with a new sense of pride in her sex" (115).

At this point Anne realises that she can no longer keep Allen on tenterhooks. She tells him definitively that she cannot marry him, and he responds bitterly. Helen Lawson, for her part, is also angry with Anne over her breakup with Allen, for she had been making sheep's eyes at his father, Gino, and now that plan is jeopardised. To Anne's horror, Helen tells her that she herself had had relations with Lyon:

> "All you got left is maybe a few more bangs from Lyon Burke before he gets bored with you. And he gets bored easily. I know—I had my innings with him six years ago." She smiled at Anne's incredulous stare. "That's right, me and Lyon. I was doing a new show and he had just joined Henry Bellamy. He was playing it smart—gave me the big romance treatment. He liked being seen with me. But at least I wasn't a jerk like you. I took it for what it was worth—enjoyed him in the kip and when it petered

out that was it. And believe me, I had more to offer him than you, a two-bit secretary." (136–37)

Anne is shattered by this news, but somehow she and Lyon manage to reconcile, especially when he tells her that he loves her. It doesn't hurt that, on a subsequent lovemaking session, he brings her to climax, causing her to exult: "I function, Lyon—I'm a woman!" (141). So it seems as if things are heading toward a satisfactory conclusion. Lyon even asks Anne to move in with him . . . but he explicitly denies that he wants to marry her. Or rather, he states that he is in no position to marry, as he is endowed with certain old-fashioned ideas ("I do think a husband should support his wife" [143]). He thinks that he may be able to support her if he fulfils his dream of becoming a novelist, so, to Anne's disappointment, they eventually agree that they *might* get married after he finishes the novel he has begun working on.

The narrative now shifts to Jennifer North, a beautiful actress who had befriended Anne during the rough times she had had in New Haven. Jennifer also wants love, but sex is OK with her also ("That's what a great body was for, to get things you wanted" [150], she thinks to herself as she strokes the luxurious fur coat she received from an admirer after a toss in the hay). She has just annulled her marriage with an Italian prince because she discovered that he had no money. Now she is carrying on with one Tony Polar, a famous crooner of the day, but she has other admirers as well. Not all these admirers are of the male persuasion, for we learn that, while at a school in Switzerland, Jennifer had had an encounter with a young woman named Maria:

> That night Maria undressed and stood before Jennifer proudly. She had a lovely body, but Jennifer felt a secret delight in the knowledge that her own was superior. She dropped her clothes to the floor shyly. She heard Maria's startled gasp as she exposed her breasts.
>
> "You are more lovely than I dreamed," Maria said softly. Her hands stroked Jennifer's breasts lightly and endearingly. She leaned over and rested her cheek against them. "You see, I love your beauty and respect it. A man would be tearing into it now." She ran her fingers gently over Jennifer's body. To her amazement, Jennifer began to feel a sensation of excitement. . .her body began to vibrate. . . . (158–59)

Hot stuff! There is a bit more of this, but very soon we leave Jennifer in the lurch and move on to our third star, Neely.

Neely has not been idle. She had filled in for another actress on *Hit the Sky* and performed a couple of numbers, creating a sensation ("One critic had actually called her the freshest new talent to come along in many a season" [162]). She quickly gets some voice lessons, leaves Henry Bellamy for another agency, and gets a Hollywood contract. She is pressing her fiancé, Mel of the skilful tongue, to move to California—but he is worried that in doing so he will just be her appendage.

Jennifer now returns to our attention. She is concerned that Tony Polar won't ask her to marry him; so distraught is she over the matter that she has trouble sleeping. A woman named Irma, who has replaced Neely in the musical, gives Jennifer some little red pills colloquially called "dolls" (175)—they are Seconal. Jennifer is a bit apprehensive at first:

> Should she try one? It was a frightening idea, that a little red capsule as tiny as this could put you to sleep. She walked to the small pantry and poured a glass of water. She held the pill for a second, feeling her heart pound. This was dope—but that was ridiculous! Irma took one every night, and she was fine. Irma had been nervous going into the show and she was still nervous seven months later. . . .
>
> Well, one pill couldn't hurt. She swallowed it, replaced the bottle in her bag and rushed to bed. (175)

It works like a charm. Her doctor, however, refuses to give her any ("He turned her down cold" [176]), so she goes to a disreputable M.D. who gives her a prescription. More calm and self-assured, Jennifer now teases Tony, flagrantly exhibiting her body to him and demanding that he marry her that night if he wants to gain possession of her charms. While this is going on, a telegram is delivered to her room—it is for Anne (Jennifer had moved into Anne's apartment after Neely had left), and tells the awful news that Anne's mother is dead. In a bizarre seriocomic moment Jennifer relates the news to Anne by phone while being pawed by Tony:

> "Hello, Anne? A telegram just came for you. Sure, one second." She ripped it open. Tony gently

> but firmly pushed her on the bed. She held the tele-
> gram and the phone and silently tried to push him off.
> She clamped her hand over the phone. "No, Tony!
> Not now. No!" He was on top of her. She looked at
> the wire. Tony's mouth found her breasts. Oh God. . .
> "Anne . . . yes, I'm here . . . Anne. . .Good Lord, your
> mother is dead!" She felt Tony enter her, roughly,
> pounding into her. She clenched her teeth and kept
> her voice even. "Yes, Anne. That's all it says. I'm
> terribly sorry." She hung up. Tony had fallen across
> her, panting in satisfied exhaustion. (179)

It is difficult to know whether Susann has intended this episode to be a species of grotesque buffoonery or not; I suspect the latter. But Jennifer's ploy doesn't work: after being satisfied, Tony casually refuses her demand to go to Maryland to get married, and just walks out. Jennifer continues to play hard-to-get (or should that be harder-to-get, since she didn't exactly resist his advances in the telegram incident) and takes more red pills in the process. Finally she persuades Tony to marry her. Jennifer is thrilled, thinking everything is now satisfactory, but Tony is apprehensive: he is terrified of what his sister, Miriam (who is much older than Tony and raised him as a child) will say. Miriam, for her part, fears the worst:

> Miriam slammed the receiver down. But he was
> right. Jennifer had been too slick. She sighed. She
> had been so careful, and now it would all probably go
> up in smoke. So far the public and everybody had
> been fooled. They accepted Tony's childish replies as
> part of his charm. Some even thought it a clever pose.
> Only Miriam knew the truth, and she had hidden it
> from everyone—even Tony. With a woman he func-
> tioned as a man, physically. His talent as a performer
> was a gift. He did everything right when he sang,
> automatically. But mentally and emotionally, Tony
> was ten years old. (186)

That can't be good.

Meanwhile, Anne is faring none too well herself. Lyon has finished his novel, but is now in the process of rewriting it. They don't seem any closer to getting married than before. Anne has had to spend a lot of time in Lawrenceville handling her mother's estate. Lyon comes to visit—and ends up loving the quaint little town and

Anne's house in particular. He actually wants to live there. This is Anne's worst nightmare, for she hates the house and the town, and New York had given her her first taste of freedom and expansiveness:

> "Lyon, don't you understand? Just as you have certain principles—you couldn't let me support you in New York—well, I have my blind spots too. Not many—in fact, just one. Lawrenceville! I hate it! I love New York. Before I came to New York I lived here, in this mausoleum. I was nothing. I was dead. When I came to New York it was like a veil lifting. For the first time I felt I was alive, breathing." (197)

So she refuses to live with Lyon in Lawrenceville. He abruptly returns to New York and, for all practical purposes, vanishes. Sometime later Anne gets a letter from him, announcing that he has gone back to England to write. The letter concludes:

> *I loved you, Anne. But you are too wonderful to accept such a small part of a small person who tried to scatter himself in so many directions. So I shall concentrate on writing—at least in that way I can hurt no one but myself.*
> *Thank you for the most wonderful year of my life.* (201)

Get out the handkerchiefs, friends!

Jennifer and Tony have moved to California, but she finds life there somewhat less than enchanting. She meets Neely, who has become a big star. Her manager has given Neely some green pills to lose weight, but they make her jittery, so Jennifer helpfully recommends the red ones ("They're beautiful little red dolls that take all your cares away and give you nine blissful hours of sleep a night" [207]). Neely, for her part, is fed up with Mel: he is a "drag" and only "gets in the way" (207). Jennifer herself is none too confident of her situation with Tony. She wonders if Tony is tiring of her, and so she determines to have a baby to cement their relationship. Presently she announces to Neely that she is two months pregnant. Neely quickly gives some advice: "Well, there's a guy in Pasadena. He's supposed to be very good. . . . First he tries shots, then if they don't work. . . . The abortion is easy. He even gives anesthesia" (210). (Remember that this is supposed to be the year 1947.) This is of course not the advice that Jennifer wants. But when Miriam learns of Jennifer's condition, she is furious (in reality, she is terrified that this will only make matters worse for Tony and herself, given Tony's infantilism). She blurts out (what is in fact the truth) that Tony has been having an affair with Betsy, a singer on his radio show. Jennifer, crushed, flees to New York and files for divorce. Miriam follows her to New York, finally spilling the beans about Tony's condition. In fact, it is much worse than what it seems:

> "The kind of condition he has is passed on. The doctors don't really know what causes it, but there's a good chance that Tony will be completely insane by the time he's fifty. And his child will be born with the same condition. If it's lucky it might have the mentality of a twelve-year-old, but it could have even less. . . . The baby inside you probably won't inherit Tony's voice—but it will inherit his sickness." (219–20)

It is not entirely clear whether Miriam is really telling the truth or making this up just to persuade Jennifer to get rid of her baby; her apparent sincerity, along with medical papers she produces, suggest the former. At all events, her spiel has the desired result: Jennifer has an abortion.

Anne, trying to get over her breakup with Lyon, meets a man named Kevin Gillmore, the owner of Gillian Cosmetics. He wants Anne to be his exclusive model for his products, which would include television spots. Anne ultimately agrees. And what of Neely? Well, by this time she is also taking yellow pills (Nembutals), and indeed is popping them like candy: "She stretched luxuriously in the large bed and sipped some Scotch. Eleven-thirty and she was still wide awake. Maybe she should take another doll. She had already taken two . . . maybe another red one. She had to be on the set at six. She wandered into the bathroom and popped a red pill into her mouth. 'Come on, you little doll, do the job'" (232). She has now married a fellow actor named Ted Casablanca (!!) and has given birth to twins. But Ted is fooling around with both men and women. One day Neely finds Ted with a sweet young thing (female) in their swimming pool. This is the last straw. She wants a divorce, but the head of the studio says this would be bad for her "girl-next-door" image. Things change, however, when she wins an Academy Award. Now she can dictate terms to her studio, and the first thing she does is to demand that she get a divorce from Ted and that Ted be dropped by the studio.

Neely becomes increasingly temperamental and hard to work with. Her two most recent films lose money, and she is having no fun being a star. She reflects on her past, starting out as a vaudeville performer:

> ". . . I hate people who say it was all so wonderful when they were starving. It stunk. One-night stands, cold trains, dim-witted audiences . . . but there *was* something that kept you going and made you feel good—hope. It was all so lousy that you knew it had to get better, and you dreamed of the big time or security and thought it would be so wonderful if you could just latch onto a piece of it. And that hope kept you going so it didn't seem bad. But when you sit here and think, Geez, here it is . . . this is it . . . and it stinks. Then what?" (244)

At this point I was a bit disconcerted by the fact that Susann was actually reaching some minimal level of profundity. Indeed, the whole narrative of Neely is, in this novel, Susann's one claim to literary merit.

More years pass; it is the year 1956. And the unthinkable happens: the head of the studio takes Neely off a picture and puts in a younger star. Is Neely already washed up? She rushes home and appeals to her little friends: "She went into the house and grabbed a bottle of Scotch off the bar. Then she went to her bedroom, pulled the blinds to shut out the daylight, shut off her phone and swallowed five red pills. Five red ones hardly did anything now. Last night she had only slept three hours with five red ones *and* two yellows. She undressed and slipped into bed" (254). She wakes up to find herself in a hospital. The head of the studio now reinstates her in the film, but this is only a device on his part, for he has planned to have a physician say that she is not well enough to work. Neely, however, outsmarts him, telling the Hollywood news sheets that it was the studio that had started her taking the pills in the first place. But the head of the studio has one more trick up his sleeve. He has the director of the film, Sam Jackson, make Neely do repeated takes of a given scene, and then make the unprecedented demand that she come back after dinner to finish the work. She refuses, and this allows the studio to replace her with a younger star.

Anne, by this time, has gotten involved with Kevin Gillmore. She is thirty-one and Kevin is fifty-seven, having been previously married for twenty-five years to a woman who died. He is of course pressing Anne to marry him, but she doesn't feel the kind of love for him that she felt for Lyon. Given their difference in age, it is not surprising that their lovemaking is unadventurous:

> She recalled their first union. She had been unable to do more than submit. She allowed him to take her, to satisfy himself—nothing more. And he never asked for more. Sometimes she forced herself to respond in a tepid way, and Kevin seemed to accept this for passion. Soon she realised that with all his worldliness, he was totally unsophisticated about the act of love. Obviously he had been quite pure when he married his wife, and she must have been equally chaste and unimaginative. They probably had never progressed beyond a few limp kisses and the mechanical act of intercourse. After his wife's death there must have been girls, and some of them must have gone all out—but he probably related this kind of sex to girls of loose morals. Anne was a lady, as his wife had been. And so he accepted her frigidity as the normal attribute of a lady, and being a gentleman, he expected nothing more. (263)

A far cry from the time, years before, when Anne was shocked to hear of Neely being serviced by Mel! If this is Susann's way of showing the development of her character, well, so be it. Neely in fact comes to visit Anne and Kevin, and appears to make a bit of a recovery as far as her health is concerned. Kevin wants her to do an hour-long show of her songs on television. Remember that this is the era of live television, where a blunder would be visible for all to see. Neely initially resists the idea, but then she creates a sensation by some impromptu singing at a nightclub. Kevin continues to press her about the TV gig, but to no avail. Neely how has a run-in with the deathless Helen Hawson, who has just performed in a flop on Broadway. They bump into each other in a ladies' room—and Neely pulls off Helen's wig and attempts to flush it down the toilet!

Neely now finally agrees to the television show, largely to prove to Helen Lawson that she is not washed up. She thinks it will be easy, but the rehearsals prove difficult. She becomes terrified of going on live television—at one point she takes a lot of pills and falls unconscious. The show has to be abruptly cancelled, and she receives a one-year suspension from all work.

Let's get back to the long-lost Jennifer. The last we heard from her, she had been persuaded by one Claude Chardot, a French film producer, to star in a series of arty sex films in Paris. She achieves tremendous celebrity in this role. Now Claude gets an enormous offer from Hollywood to have Jennifer work in American films. Jennifer is now "*the* sex goddess of Europe" (284). But she has put on a little weight, and has to lose ten pounds—so she undergoes sleep treatment in Switzerland, where she will be asleep for eight days. She also has a facelift.

Anne comes to visit her while she is recuperating at Idlewild. There is random talk of love:

> "Still looking for the stars-in-your-eyes kind of love?" Jennifer asked. "You know, Anne, I guess a woman can either love or *be* loved, but it's almost impossible to have both."
>
> "Why?"
>
> "I don't know, but it just doesn't seem to work out that way. You should know. Allen loved you, even wanted to marry you. And Kevin loves you. Yet you could walk away from either of them and feel nothing. *You* loved Lyon . . . and he was able to walk away from you." (287)

Anne is startled to learn that Kevin has had a heart attack. (We are now in the year 1960.) He begs Anne to marry him if he recovers; she reluctantly agrees. Neely, for her part, is attempting to make a comeback, but the effort fails: a big new picture in which she was to have starred is abruptly scrapped, at a loss of half a million dollars (evidently a lot of money, even for Hollywood, at the time). Neely now moves in with Anne. Later she is arrested for disturbing the peace. She goes to London, then to Spain, and then just disappears.

Jennifer is now engaged to Winston Adams, a senator who is "about fifty—attractive, brilliant and immensely popular" (297). She wants children, even though she has by this time had a total of seven abortions. On Anne's advice, Jennifer gets a checkup—and discovers that she has polyps in her uterus. This is declared to be nothing serious, but then a lump in her breast is discovered—the breast must be removed. Jennifer wants to flee the hospital, but Anne persuades her to stay. Then Winston comes, somewhat indelicately calling her breasts his "babies" (305). She sneaks out of the hospital at 3 A.M., goes to a hotel, takes some sleeping pills, and dies. She had written Winston a note: "I had to leave—to save your babies" (307). How touching!

After Jennifer's funeral, Neely shows up out of nowhere. Still trying for a comeback, she this time *tapes* a show for television—and creates another sensation ("Neely was back on top" [308]). But later Neely is crushed to discover that her voice is gone. The doctors think it may just be nerves, but Neely is inconsolable. She actually delivers a soliloquy to God:

> "Hey, God, are you really up there?" she said. "Are you a big white-haired man with a beard? Do you understand me? Tell me, what went wrong? I never asked for too much. Geez, all I wanted was an apartment and a guy to love me. I tried—why did you fuck it up all the time? Why in hell did you give me a voice if you didn't want me to be great? Why did you take it away?" (312)

There is more of this, but that should suffice. Neely now takes all the pills and liquor she can find, and also slits her wrists for good measure. But then, terrified of the prospect of dying, she calls the operator for help. She manages to survive somehow.

Anne recommends that Neely take the sleep cure, and they find a place in upstate New York for her. But a doctor, after looking at Neely's medical records, thinks this is not the answer: she really needs a year-long treatment to cure her sleeping-pill addiction. Kevin and Anne reluctantly agree to this, knowing that Neely won't like it. In the clinic Neely deliberately stages a tantrum, hoping that she might get some pills that way. Instead, she is confined to a bathtub. Finally she is given some drink to make her sleep. She undergoes many other travails at the clinic. This whole episode is really rather grim and effective, and once again underscores the fact that, of all the characters in this book, Neely is the one that commands some modicum of respect as a vital, real-life figure and not just a stereotype.

Anne is now shaken up by the sudden arrival of Lyon Burke—who is "more overpoweringly attractive than ever" (344). He is there for six weeks on a writing assignment. Anne still feels powerful emotions for him—but feels guilty about betraying Kevin:

For a long time she sat very still. Lyon was back. Nothing had changed. But it had—she was no longer twenty, and the years had brought changes. There was Kevin, who had given her love, trust—and her career. Kevin needs me, she thought, and in walks Lyon, just for a visit, and I act like an idiot, ready to kick over the traces and forget all the years without a word. Tomorrow I'll call him and say I'm busy. Or maybe I won't even call. Let him wait, like I waited so long.

But she knew she would see him. (346)

Sure enough, they have dinner, even though Kevin, who knows all about her previous involvement with Lyon, has pleaded with her not to see him. After dinner the inevitable happens . . . they have sex. It's just like before—in every sense of the term. Lyon loves her, but he wants to remain in London: "I'm just cut out to be a loner," he announces (349). When Anne comes back to her apartment, Kevin is there. A grim confrontation ensues. Anne vows not to see Lyon again. Some weeks later she sees Lyon at a restaurant with another woman—"Anne felt physically ill" (352). Kevin, who is there with her, taunts her about it, daring her to call him later and ask to come over. She does so—and Lyon somewhat hesitatingly agrees to see her. At this point Kevin storms out; clearly their relationship is over. While she is with Lyon, Kevin calls and pleads for forgiveness—but she refuses and stays with Lyon, even though he is still offering her no future.

Anne wonders about going with him to London—but Harry Bellamy, ever the avuncular protector, says that she must try to keep Lyon in New York. Henry offers to lend Lyon the money to buy his firm; Lyon grudgingly agrees. Lyon and Anne now agree to marry. Meanwhile, another member of the firm, George Bellows, is working with Neely, who has gotten fat (she is now up to 160 pounds) but has recovered her voice. George thinks there is a possibility of making Neely a star on the concert circuit. By now Anne is pregnant. Neely's concerts are a great success. But Neely doesn't want to go to a performance in Hollywood by herself; she wants Lyon there for support. Lyon doesn't want to leave Anne in her condition—but then he learns that it was Anne herself who had surreptitiously supplied the money for Lyon to purchase the firm. He is furious at this slander on his manhood, and decides to go with Neely to Hollywood.

Anne's child—named Jennifer Burke—is born on New Year's Day 1963. Lyon softens a bit when the baby is born, but Anne still senses an "intangible difference" (382). Lyon, indeed, is spending a lot of time away from home. Then Anne hears rumors that he is having an affair with Neely. Henry Bellamy confirms the rumors. He says that the only way to get Lyon back is to wait it out—no doubt Neely will show her bad side and end up alienating Lyon. Now it is Anne who, in this period of stress, says she wants a doll. Henry gives her a bottle of 65 Seconals. She takes one and continues taking the pills as Lyon and Neely prolong their affair. Then the baby gets a high fever; in fact, she has pneumonia. Slowly she recovers, and Anne and Lyon seem somewhat reconciled. But then Lyon continues to spend more and more time with Neely. Gradually he tires of her insistent demands. One day Neely is reported to be near death from an overdose of pills. Lyon comes to her; she demands that he remain with her; he refuses. He drops her from his company, and she signs with a rival.

On New Year's Day 1965 Anne reluctantly throws a party for a variety of celebrities. At one point she overhears Lyon talking with Margie Parks, a young Broadway star. It becomes obvious that they are fooling around. Resignedly, Anne takes another doll.

And that, my friends, is the end of *Valley of the Dolls*.

Perhaps it was imprudent of me to have provided such a detailed synopsis of this novel, but it would appear to be the only way to convey its utterly meandering plot and immense length (it is nearly 250,000 words). What strikes us as we reflect upon the plot threads involving the three central figures (Anne, Neely, and Jennifer) is that they really have very little to do with one another. Each of them could have served as the focus of a single, shorter novel of much greater unity of construction. What is also strange is that, although Susann clearly wishes us to see Anne is the principal heroine of the novel—she is the exclusive focus at the beginning and very largely the focus at the end—she proves to be a relatively colourless character, and her blandness continually forces her to yield the spotlight to Neely, the one dynamic figure in the book. It is *her* travails—her gutsy rise from cheap vaudeville acts to the pinnacle of Broadway and Hollywood, then her inexorable decline from addiction to pills, her repeated attempts to regain her standing, beset by failure and humiliation, and finally her horrific stay at the detox clinic—that inexorably draw the reader's attention.

So what, if any, is the "message" of *Valley of the Dolls?* It is painfully obvious that Susann has attempted, in her clumsy, pathetically earnest way, to write a "serious" novel about love, sex, show business, and addiction—but I trust that my synopsis adequately reveals that she is just not up to the job. With the exception of Neely, all her characters are stereotypes, and their "growth" or development is of the most superficial sort. If Anne's sexual awakening from a prudish virgin to the mistress of a powerful executive is meant to reflect the liberalization of sexual mores from the 1940s to the 1960s, it is effected in a manner that entirely ignores the complex network of political, social, and economic forces that brought about the change in the first place. I have mentioned that there is not the remotest trace in this novel of any historical contextualization: for all we know, we could be in some never-never-land of the imagination instead of the New York or Hollywood of the postwar era.

The story of Jennifer is the most disappointing of the three plot threads. For long periods of time she is simply absent from the narrative, and her transformation from a pretty young Broadway bit player to European sex star is simply stated bluntly rather than described in detail. As a result, her succumbing to cancer produces no effect upon the reader, for there has been no genuine attempt at eliciting the reader's emotional attachment to her. She is merely an obvious metaphor: the cancer that affects the exact part of her anatomy that the world most prizes—and, in the end, she most prizes herself—could perhaps be thought to reflect upon the objectivization of women and society's view of them as purely sexual creatures, but the whole episode is handled too crudely to be effective.

As for Anne—she has awakened sexually, but the "love" that she sought still eludes her, in spite of her finally obtaining the man she thought she loved, Lyon. He proves to be exactly the philanderer that Henry Bellamy told her at the outset he was, and she can only reconcile herself to this realization by the fact that she is comfortably situated and has a ready supply of those "dolls" that can provide the mental oblivion she craves.

The amusing thing about *Valley of the Dolls* is that, in the absence of any genuinely serious purpose behind the novel in spite of its author's desperate attempts at lending it weight and substance, it turns out to be nothing but a glimpse into the lives of the rich and glamorous—full of sex, pills, disappointment, betrayal, and hardship. It turns readers into voyeurs greedily lapping up the varied sexual escapades (including lesbianism) and pill-popping of its protagonists, thereby simultaneously allowing them to envy their sexual freedom and their ready access to drugs and stardom and to rest comfortably in their own mediocrity by showing them that these celebrities really aren't happy, and perhaps never will be. This is a valuable lesson that all the tabloids and celebrity gossip rags have learned: it's one thing to have heaps of money, to be in front of the cameras at every turn, and to hop from one bed to another with insouciance; but stolid middle-class burghers must be reassured that these demigods and demigoddesses really don't have it as good as you or I in our fifth-floor walkups.

As it is, it was the prurience of *Valley of the Dolls,* and not its feeble ventures into pseudo-profundity, that propelled it to bestseller status. In spite of its raciness, it is somewhat less explicit than Gore Vidal's incalculably superior satire, *Myra Breckinridge* (1968)— whose most notorious scene, an anal rape of a hapless male acting student by the transsexual Myra (using a dildo), still has the power to shock and appall. The film version of *Valley of the Dolls*—with Barbara Perkins as Anne Welles, Patty Duke as Neely O'Hara, and the late lamented Sharon Tate as Jennifer North—appeared to universal derision but immense success in 1967. What followed thereafter could almost have come out of a Jacqueline Susann novel. She herself went on to write another bestseller, *The Love Machine* (1969), about a powerful yet vulnerable television executive and his many love affairs with willing women. This was itself turned into a sleazy film in 1971, but a year earlier, in the summer of 1970, *Beyond the Valley of the Dolls* appeared. This film had nothing to do with anything Susann ever wrote; it was meant solely to capitalise on the raunchy success of the book and film of *Valley of the Dolls.* Its director was the breast connoisseur Russ Meyer; its screenplay was written (will he ever live it down?) by . . . Roger Ebert. Susann, appalled at what the film would to do her lofty literary reputation, attempted to secure a court injunction to prevent the release of the film, but failed.

*Beyond the Valley of the Dolls* and the notorious film of *Myra Breckinridge* appeared almost simultaneously and inspired various amusing disquisitions on the decline of Western civilization. One of them was by Charles Champlin, entertainment editor of the *Los Angeles Times.* He wrote in part:

> "Myra" is both dirtier and more aberrant than "B.V.D."—something I would have said was impossible. It is more aberrant not only in its famed transsexual content, but in its whole shaping view of existence. . . .
>
> "Myra" has been put together with more style, skill and even wit than "B.V.D." But the effect of this is only to amplify a reasonable viewer's contempt for the operative cynicism involved.

It leaves an inference that American civilization had perhaps reached a slightly higher level—before it fell apart—than "B.V.D." would have led us to believe.

What the existence and the nature of this movie say about the present and the future of this society is in fact appalling to contemplate.[3]

And so on.

It was, after all, during this period that saw the emergence of such films as *Carnal Knowledge* (1972)—rated X when it appeared, although now it would barely get an R rating—and the largely forgotten *Bob and Carol and Ted and Alice* (1969), which also inspired a flurry of commentary about the prevalence of group sex, wife swapping, and other such signs of decadence. And let's not forget such musicals as *Hair* (1967) and *Oh, Calcutta!* (1969), the latter quite shamelessly designed to rake in the bucks by relentless displays of nudity and even a (presumably simulated) live sex scene onstage. And yet, it was such weighty writers as Philip Roth (*Portnoy's Complaint* [1969], all about masturbation) and John Updike (*Couples,* 1968), who, along with Vidal, definitively ushered in the sexual revolution as far as the higher strata of American literature were concerned.[4] The Supreme Court lent its aid to the matter by liberalizing censorship laws so as to make it increasingly difficult to suppress sexual content in literature or film—logically so, since no one was being forced to see a sex film or read a bawdy book. And of course we can't overlook Alex Comfort's *The Joy of Sex* (1972), which, as a *New York Times* bestseller for a total of 437 weeks, may be the best-selling book of all time, or at least of the twentieth century.

By this point, other genres of popular literature got into the act, and sex began to show up in the mystery, suspense, spy, and even horror novel. William Peter Blatty's *The Exorcist* (1971) contains a scene in which the teenage Regan MacNeil abuses herself with a crucifix while shouting to herself, "You bitch! Let Jesus *fuck* you, *fuck* you!"[5] This passage retains the power to shock even those who (like myself) do not feel any sense of the religious blasphemy of the act. Television executive Sidney Sheldon, who as producer of "I Dream of Jeannie" was not allowed to show Barbara Eden's navel on screen, gained his revenge by a series of blockbuster mystery/adventure bestsellers liberally dosed with sex, chiefly dealing with a succession of woman who are raped or brutalised but ultimately gain vengeance upon their abusers. The novels are of course complete trash.

And so we come down to the present day. The irony is that the pervasiveness of sex in the media—including, now, the Internet—makes (pseudo-)literary erotica pretty tame. There is no way that the print medium—or, in general, the medium of words, however conveyed—can possibly match the immediacy of effect, as far as sexual arousal is concerned, of photography, films, or television. But that hasn't deterred writers like the British novelist Jackie Collins (b. 1941), sister of actress Joan Collins, whose twenty-four novels, beginning with *The World Is Full of Married Men* (1968), exploit the sex/fashion/glamour schtick with relentless determination. Collins didn't become a bestseller until *Chances* (1981), but since then she has had six novels adapted for film or television. One of more recent ventures is *Thrill!* (1998).[6]

*Thrill!*—the exclamation mark is a dead giveaway—is largely the story of Lara Ivory, a movie star who is described as a "devastatingly pretty girl" (13). Right at the outset, however, we learn that "The sad truth was that for a star such as Lara, no relationship was easy" (14); in fact, she found it hard "to cope with the loneliness of being by herself" (15). Although Lara is, on the whole, portrayed sympathetically—at least as compared to other figures in the book—she has by no means had an easy time of it, and even now, at the height of her fame, is faced with all manner of troubles.

She was married for four years to Richard Barry, a well-known director. Richard is now married to one Nikki, and they all seem to be friends. Lara has just finished shooting *French Summer* in the Riviera, after which she proceeds to the Hamptons to shoot a film called *The Dreamer.* Nice work if you can get it! In that film a young actor named Juan Lorenzo has a small part. Remember that name! He will be with us presently.

Lara, ever the sensitive actress, wants to take on a low-budget film being produced by Nikki about a woman who takes revenge on a group of men who gang-raped her. The film, sensibly called *Revenge,* seems a worthy, if tough and gritty, project, quite out of character with the kind of frothy romance films that have made Lara a living legend. In her ham-fisted way, Collins suggests that something deeper is at work:

> Of course, it wasn't a star vehicle, but if the script was good, she was definitely interested. She had all the success she could ever possibly want—why not take on something risky? Something that

would stretch her as an actress? Something that could maybe help her avenge her past?

Lara Ivory—beautiful movie star. If people knew the real truth. . . .

If they only knew. . . . (53)

Did I mention that this bit of deathless prose comes at the end of a chapter? That phrase "real truth" is a bit of a puzzle—I would be interested to know what a "false truth" could be. And I'm not going to touch that "stretch her as an actress" with a . . .

Nikki, for her part, isn't faring too well herself. Chief among her problems is her daughter, Summer, not quite sixteen, who speaks to us in a perfectly unconscious parody of the rebellious teen:

"Bummer!" Summer exclaimed. "Richard's not home and there's no food."

"Tell me what you'd like, and I'll send the maid to the market."

"Forget it, Mom. I'm gonna hit the beach. I plan on getting a way cool tan."

*So much for mother-daughter bonding,* Nikki thought ruefully. (59)

So much for believable characters, think I.

After some more coy hints about Lara's past ("Nikki knew Lara didn't like talking about her childhood; it obviously hadn't been very happy" [85]), we suddenly get the full story in a painfully long passage of self-important italics: Lara's father had killed her mother and brother in a fit of jealousy, then shot himself in front of her eyes (89–91). This had all happened when Lara was six. She seems to have made a remarkable psychological recovery, but her one problem appears to be her inability to maintain a steady relationship with a man. Richard was certainly no prize, for all his power as a director. In spite of his relatively recent marriage to Nikki, he is having sex with his assistant, named (you guessed it) Kimberly ("He reached for Kimberly and her musky scent. She melted into his arms as if she belonged there" [107]). What's worse for Nikki (although she doesn't know it yet), her former husband, a psychiatrist named Sheldon Weston, has been having sex with his own daughter, Summer, since she was ten. A pretty kettle of fish!

Lara, on the set of *The Dreamer,* appears to be falling for Joey Lorenzo, in spite of her stated determination not to get emotionally involved with anyone in the acting profession. Joey, indeed, is craftily playing hard-to-get: "Lara had given him an opening, and he hadn't taken it. The only sure way to score with a woman who could have any guy she wanted was to play hard to get. Right now she was sitting at home thinking that she couldn't have him, and that's exactly how he *wanted* her to feel" (153). This seems to suggest that all Joey wants to do is to have sex with Lara, and perhaps that is indeed all he wants at the outset. In a romantic encounter on the beach, they actually do have sex—but no penetration is involved; Joey only strokes her to climax:

> Next he raised her hands above her head, while he bent his mouth to her left breast and drew in the nipple as if he were suckling milk.
> "Ohhh. . . ." Before she could help herself, she came with a series of shuddering convulsions that shook her body from top to toe. And he hadn't even touched her where she craved to be touched. (195)

This scene is perhaps meant to be contrasted with an earlier passage in which the hapless Summer, finding herself in a limo with Mick Stefan, a rather crude but (apparently) hugely talented director hired by Nikki for her film, gives him head. Note the distinction between the selfish Mick, interested only in his own pleasure with a randy but powerless teenager, and the sensitive Joey, pleasuring one of the world's greatest movie stars without a thought of his own gratification!

Things take a sinister turn, however, when one Alison Sewell is introduced. She is an unattractive photographer who had become fascinated with Lara and stalked her; she was sent to prison for her pains. Now she is on the verge of being released, and her feelings for Lara are not pleasant ("Lara Ivory was going to pay" [200]). The reader is forced to file that away for the time being, for Alison is still behind bars.

At a dinner party at Nikki's house, Lara, Joey, Mick, and Aiden Sean (the co-star for Nikki's film) are gathered. Summer makes a grand entrance. Mick is freaked out, because he had not in fact known Summer's identity—or, rather, her parentage—while she serviced him in the limo. He later confronts her in private:

> Mick grabbed Summer's attention on the way in to dinner.
> "Whyn't [sic] you tell me who your mother was?" he demanded, mouth twitching.

"You didn't ask," she retorted flippantly.

"And how come you didn't call me?"

"'Cause I knew you'd be mad when you found out my mom was Nikki Barry."

He looked perplexed. This little Lolita was confusing him. (234)

It apparently doesn't take much. In any event, Lara now pressures Nikki to give Joey a part in the film. Nikki agrees reluctantly.

A bit later, Aiden blurts out to Nikki the story of Mick and Summer in the limo. (Summer had come on to Aiden also.) As if that wasn't enough of a shock, Nikki now learns of Richard's philandering, and she demands that he leave the house. Still later, Summer and her friend Tina have a bit of lesbian sex while a sleazy actor, Norman Barton, watches. Nikki, fed up with her daughter's behavior, packs her off to her father in Chicago.

It is only at this time that we learn more about the sad early life of Lara Ivory. She grew up with a cruel aunt (naturally), Lucy, who treated her like Cinderella. She escaped by latching on to one Morgan Creedo, a two-bit country singer who was "glamour personified" (318) to the naïve Lara. She shacks up with him, but life is no peaches and cream with him either ("Morgan Creedo proved himself a sonofabitch. He made Lara Ann into his love slave" [321]). But then Morgan dies in a car accident, and Lara is left alone again. What is the rest of her story? We have to wait a few more chapters....

The redoubtable Alison Sewell is now out of prison. Someone has tipped her off to the grim gang-rape scene in Nikki's film. Alison surreptitiously photographs it while it is being shot, and the pictures are quickly published in a "particularly down-and-dirty tabloid" (359) named *Truth and Fact.* A huge scandal erupts. Richard, meanwhile, has taken a violent dislike to Joey and wants to pry him away from Lara. He unearths Madelaine Francis, an agent in her late forties who had represented Joey years before and also been his lover. She spills the beans about how Joey had actually stolen money from her and then dumped her when he no longer needed her. It is by this time obvious that Richard was the one who tipped Alison off. Madelaine tells Lara about Joey's sordid past, and Lara is shattered. (But of course we all know that Joey is really a good person down deep, and that he and Lara will eventually ride off into the sunset as a happy couple.)

Lara, deeply upset, has moved out to a cabin on the beach. Alison has been following her; is she actually planning to kill Lara?

Meanwhile, we learn more about Joey's own life. The money he had taken from Madelaine was actually designed to pay off his mother's gambling debts. But there was an altercation with his mother's boyfriend, in which his mother killed the boyfriend with his own gun; Joey took the rap for his mother, spending six years in jail. See what a wonderful boy Joey really is? Back in present time, Joey learns where Lara is staying and goes there to plead his case—only to find Alison in the process of strangling Lara. He fights with her, and she conveniently falls over a cliff.

Other loose ends are now being wrapped up. Summer has fled from her father's tyranny and returned to Los Angeles. Sheldon comes there and, with Nikki, they hunt her down to the apartment of Norman Barton, where Tina spills the dreadful truth about Sheldon's abuse of his daughter. Nikki is outraged, of course, but thinks that this may be a way of getting closer to her daughter.

By this time, we have learned the sordid truth about Richard Barry. Years before he had been a small-time actor and male prostitute who had actually been involved in murder and other unsavory activities. It is he, we learn, who is the author of various short and pungent italicised chapters (not to be confused with the italicised sections about Lara's past) that pepper the book. In any case, he is now making his way to Lara's cabin when he is conveniently killed in a mudslide. This opens the way for Lara and Joey to be united in holy matrimony.

The remarkable thing about *Thrill!* is that every single character—even, to a large degree, the sympathetically portrayed Lara Ivory—is motivated chiefly or exclusively by sexual passion. Virtually no other emotion is put forth as determining the behavior of any character, unless it be equally shallow portrayals of revenge (Alison Sewell) or envy (Richard Barry). Consider this passage:

> Lara picked up her glass of nonalcoholic fruit punch. "Actors don't interest me," she said firmly, thinking—in spite of herself—that this one [Joey] did.
>
> "Haven't you ever heard the words 'location fuck'?" Nikki said mischievously. "It's a perk of the business. One great fling with a fantastic-looking guy, and at the end of the movie you both go your separate ways. Everyone does it."
>
> "Is that what you used to do before you met Richard?"

Nikki nodded enthusiastically. "You bet your sweet ass."

Roxy danced by, clad in a tiger-print jumpsuit. She was clinging tightly to her trucker, rubbing up against him as they rocked and rolled their way past.

*Hmm . . .* Lara thought, trying to get her mind off Joey, *Yoko's right—he* is *a fat one.*

Roxy was followed closely by Yoko with *her* boyfriend, a well-muscled hunk who looked as if he belonged on the cover of *Playgirl.*

Right behind them came Trinee, accompanied by her fiancé, a solid tree trunk of a man who favored a kind of crazed Mike Tyson look and towered over the diminutive Trinee.

Lara waved, happy to see everyone having a good time, forcing her thoughts away from Joey once and for all.

"Oh boy," Nikki said, sitting back and observing the passing couples. "There'll be plenty of fucking on the beach tonight!" (112–13)

At this point it hardly need be reiterated that all the characters in *Thrill!* are shallow stereotypes, ranging from Lara herself (who overcomes childhood trauma to become a megabucks movie star) to Joey (seemingly a low-down troublemaker but with a heart of gold) to Summer (rebellious teenager) to Nikki (would-be feminist who has trouble with men) to Richard (powerful film director with sordid past) to Alison (ugly hanger-on of the stars filled with hatred and resentment) and on and on down the line.

And yet, in spite of Collins's obsession with sex (which she then transfers to all her characters), it becomes evident that she is, in effect, writing a kind of souped-up romance novel, for the core of the plot features exactly the "love-conquers-all" scenario found in Danielle Steel and her congeners, even if it is laced with all manner of sexual scenarios that they would not dare to include in their pages—at least not in Collins's salacious language. No doubt she and others of the sex/fashion/glamour school realise that average housewives will not tolerate a novel that is *only* about sex—this is too close to the pornography that they have been conditioned to regard as beyond the pale—so that some effort must be made to surround the sex with a patina of true love to make the sex a bit more morally palatable.

* * * * * * *

Judith Krantz (b. 1927) is quite a bit older than Jackie Collins and virtually of the same generation as Jacqueline Susann, to whom she has been compared; but she took to writing novels about a decade later than Collins. She gained experience for her sex/fashion/glamour novels by working as a fashion publicist in Paris in 1948–49 and then by being a contributing writer to such magazines as *McCall's* (1956–59), *Ladies' Home Journal* (1959–71), and *Cosmopolitan* (1971–79). She struck it rich with her first novel, *Scruples* (1978), and has since written ten more. Three of them have been adapted as television miniseries; none has reached the big screen. The one that I sampled was *Spring Collection* (1996).[7]

The events of *Spring Collection* are largely seen through the eyes of Frankie Severino, who is "second-in-command" (2) at Loring Model Management in New York City. The owner of the agency is one Justine Loring. Frankie is waiting for the results of a somewhat unusual contest sponsored by Jacques Necker, a Swiss billionaire, who wants three models to introduce the first spring collection of Marco Lombardi, a young fashion designer whom Necker is banking on to become the next Calvin Klein or Tommy Hilfiger. One of these three models will receive the sum of $12 million for four years of work. The fashion world is stunned, as Frankie is as well, when all three models are chosen from her agency. It is only at this point that Justine admits that Necker is her father, with whom she has been estranged for many years. So was this contest merely a ruse for Necker to reestablish relations with his daughter?

Justine is to accompany the models to Paris, a full two weeks before the opening of the show. She is convinced that Necker is merely trying to gain power over her. But, as we begin seeing events from Necker's perspective, we come to understand that he is merely trying to make it up to his daughter for abandoning her mother many years before:

> He had to tell Justine that he was more deeply ashamed of how he had treated her mother than he was of anything in his life. He had to tell her that for the past thirty-four years he'd blamed himself endlessly for having deserted Helena Loring. They'd both been barely nineteen, both students in New York, when she had discovered that she was pregnant. He'd fled in a blind panic, returning to Switzerland, leaving Helena alone, unprotected. Nothing

could ever excuse his foul cowardice. His punishment had been bitter, yet far less than he deserved. It
was not an accident, he thought in his darkest moments, that his [current] wife, poor Nicole, had been
unable to conceive, but a judgment on him, visited on
a woman to whom he had been resolutely faithful until her death several years ago. (16)

Nowhere does Krantz explain how this apparently impoverished
nineteen-year-old student became a billionaire a few decades later.

Justine, knowing none of this, seeks to foil what she believes to
be Necker's nefarious plan by feigning illness and sending Frankie
to Paris in her place. Frankie, for her part, has been married to and
divorced from an Irish sportswriter, Slim Kelly. On the plane ride to
Paris she admits to herself that she was (and apparently still is) in
love with Mike Aaron, a college classmate who is on the plane with
her. Frankie is full of sage wisdom on the fashion industry and,
more broadly, on what might be called the philosophy of female
beauty. Here's a specimen:

> I have a theory that when every girl child is born,
> a multitude of fairies gather around her crib, the fair-
> ies in charge of distributing perfect skin and great
> legs, the fairies who hand out symmetrical noses and
> full lips, the fairy of wide eyes, the fairies of chinli-
> nes, of cheekbones, of beautiful hands and long
> waists. Every once in a great while, one time in tens
> of millions, every last one of the fairies—with the
> frequent exception of the tooth fairy—will decide to
> bestow her particular gift on just one baby and of
> those few babies, some will grow up healthy in the
> Western world, and of these little females, some will
> become models. It's not abnormal that this happens,
> it's just the random way nature, and fairies, work.
> (26)

I don't think any commentary is necessary on this.

As the narrative continues to shift irritatingly from Frankie's
first-person voice to omniscient third person, we are now introduced
to Marco Lombardi, a thirty-five-year-old roué who has developed
what appears to be a purely physical relationship with a wealthy
Texas heiress, Peaches Wilcox, age forty-seven. With the pressure
of the opening building, he visits Peaches, wanting merely "a brief,

brutal relief from nervous tension, the kind of animal release only a whore could give you, and he never used whores" (48)—but he does use Peaches. She is, however, at this particular moment having a swanky cocktail party with some fellow Texans, and she does not respond immediately to Lombardi's importunate demands for physical release. So he does what every red-blooded, non-gay man in his position would do: he drags her into the bedroom and rapes her:

> As he ground it [his penis] into her he found himself so intoxicated by the novelty of her dryness and her resistance that he no longer heard her begging him to stop. The universe was reduced to the monstrous orgasm he felt building from the base of his spine. A man threatening him with a gun couldn't have stopped him now as he used Peaches mercilessly, quickly losing himself in a series of spasms that made him cry out as wordlessly as an animal. (51)

Charming fellow! Peaches, though furious, merely dusts herself off and returns to her party.

Back in New York, Justine has bought a townhouse that needs a bit of work. Reluctantly, she hires a contractor ("Why did she *know* that he was going to rip her off? Why did *everybody* know that about contractors?" [61]) to do some repairs. One Aiden Henderson comes over. In spite of her longtime hostility to men ("it seemed to Justine, as she observed the messy love entanglements of her models, that men were *not* to be counted on . . . that the expression 'a good man' was an oxymoron" [58]), she accepts his invitation to dinner with alacrity! By now it is already obvious where this is leading. Only a bit later do we learn that Justine herself, some years before, had been Marco Lombardi's love-slave ("it had taken her years to recover from the deliberate cruelty of Marco Lombardi's successful attempt to destroy her innocence and betray her confidence. Perhaps she'd never truly recovered. In any case, her first experience with love had been tainted forever" [90]). Her relations with Aiden become increasingly implausible. He makes some error regarding a furnace, and Justine has to evacuate her townhouse for the weekend. Conveniently, he offers to put her up in his own loft—and she accepts! To be sure, she has regrets:

> She could be settling into a warm luxurious hotel by now, Justine thought, she could be surrounded by

a secure, impersonal network of room service and phone operators and assistant managers, she would have ordered flowers up from the lobby florist, bought all the new magazines and be snugly prepared to ride out whatever the elements brought to the city, but no, she'd allowed a whim, a vagrant impulse, to overtake her judgment and now she was captive of a man she had met only twenty-four hours earlier, much too up close and personal with a virtual stranger who had already proved himself a prime fuckup. (96)

As if this episode, seen through Justine's eyes, is not ridiculous enough, Krantz suddenly switches the narrative voice again and lets us see into Aiden's mind, so that we can see that he's a good guy after all and not some kind of serial rapist:

Had he been dreaming or had Justine been leading him on back there in the basement? Was he some kind of exotically low new experience for her? A weekend with a contractor or how I got to wallow in the depths of depravity with a man who works with his hands? Well, he had a surprise for her. He'd only asked her to stay because he had a businessman's responsibility to provide her with shelter and she'd insisted that hotels depressed her. (98–99)

Well, that's a relief! Justine, indeed, is amazed at Aiden's apartment, which he has transformed into a kind of huge log cabin, with wood paneling all around. They are regaled by Aiden's cat, Rufus—and actually give it milk! (Either Aiden or Krantz must be inexperienced in the care of cats, for domesticated cats cannot drink cow's milk without regurgitating.) But the cat occupies a key function: he leads them to Aiden's bedroom, with the predictable result. Mercifully, Krantz spares us any physiological details of their lovemaking: no doubt the whole scene is intended to contrast pointedly with the savagery of Marco Lombardi.

Let's get back to Paris, where the real action is. Necker is of course crestfallen that Justine has not come to Paris. He knows full well that her claim of illness is a lie. But he is stumped as to how to get her over the water. He does the next best thing, befriending one of the models—a black woman named Jordan Dancer (!), taking her to Versailles, asking her about Justine and also about herself, at which point she spills the beans about her tough life as a "woman of color":

> "Being black is more than constricting enough. My roommate at college was a terrific girl named Sharon Cohen. We used to talk for hours about being Jewish and being black. She said that just once she'd like to see what it was like to be introduced as Jordan Dancer, to see how people would relate to her if they didn't know, the minute they heard her name, that she was Jewish. I told Sharon I'd like to live inside her skin for a week and find out what it was like not to be put into a definite category the split second I walked into a room, long *before* I was introduced! That was one argument Sharon didn't win!" (159)

This, apparently, is what passes for profundity in a Judith Krantz novel.

Then there is another model, Tinker Osborn. She too gets a chance to tell her life story, as she has struck up a friendship with a would-be artist named Tom Strauss. She relates what the world of children's beauty pageants is like:

> "The child's pageant walk is the absolute opposite of a runway walk. I walked like an automaton, a windup toy, a good, good, *good* little girl with the best possible posture, a little princess reviewing the troops. [??] I stood up absolutely stiff and straight, head held high, chin up, eyes straight ahead, and I learned not to swing anything, not even my hair—the judges hate the slightest hint of overt sexuality— Lolita would never make it to the Little Miss Most Adorable Nashville contest." (130)

There is quite a bit more of this, but this should suffice. Tom, in fact, thinks that what Tinker has told him amounts to a "Gothic horror story about herself [told] without varnish, without self-pity, in an analytical way, not hiding her fears and wounds but not giving in to them, certainly not asking for advice or help" (130–31). In any case, Tom takes Tinker back to his apartment, and Tinker insists that he paint her (presumably nude); but Tom doesn't do portraits—he paints only abstracts. And so he puts her to bed—literally. She is exhausted and merely falls asleep. Touchingly, he does a pencil sketch of her while she sleeps. But Krantz isn't going to disappoint her readers so cruelly: when Tinker wakes up, the two of them profess their love for each other, and the inevitable happens: "Holding his breath, Tom touched his fingertip to the faint rose of one nipple and felt it rise immediately. Mad, utterly mad, he thought to himself as he threw off his clothes. She would make him mad and she would make him whole and she would be everything in the world to him" (142). I imagine this is what passes for prose-poetry in a Judith Krantz novel.

Our final model, April Nyquist, spills her guts to Maude Callendar, a hard-nosed fashion reporter accompanying the girls. April seems to be a kind of ice-princess from the frozen north of Minnesota: she admits in a candid moment to Maude not only that she has not had a sex life, but that she has never found men very appealing. She is beginning to think that she doesn't want sex at all. Well, this will never do in a Krantz book; and the moment we learn that Maude is a lesbian who is clearly attracted to April (151–52), we know what will follow. But Krantz will, of course, make us wait. Frankie, meanwhile, has been trying in vain to keep her girls on a short leash, for she knows that any kind of romantic or sexual involvements can only lead to trouble. She speaks in no charitable terms of Tinker's new friend: "The stage-door Johnnies who lie in wait for models are beyond slime" (165). Quite frankly, this is probably the single best sentence in the book.

Back to Justine in New York. To put it crudely, she has been fucking Aiden's brains out:

> She knew what she looked like. Lips puffed and swollen, cheeks and chin covered with whisker burn, eyes languid and almost unfocused, with circles under them from lack of sleep, tangled hair that had only been towel dried, since Aiden didn't have a blow-dryer. She looked utterly fucked-out, completely, thoroughly fucked, up, down and sideways. It felt one hell of a lot better than it looked. They'd never tried to make the Knicks game, they'd never changed the sheets, much less made the bed, they'd barely stopped to eat and she'd resented the showers they eventually staggered into together because soap dissipated the way Aiden smelled. (175)

And yet, while all this is happening, Justine still has time to dwell with poignant angst on the cruelties of the fashion world:

What normal woman, in the name of God, would pay good money every month to have it rubbed in her face how far short she fell of a ridiculous, impossible, manufactured ideal that was constantly *changing?* What kind of collective insanity allowed the magazine editors to get away with the manipulative crap they wrote to sell cosmetics and clothes? And it wasn't just an American phenomenon, there were some *thirty* fashion magazines published by the supposedly sensible French. (178–79)

Evidently a case in point is now to be presented to us. Marco Lombardi is consumed with doubt about the success of his forthcoming show. He has fired his usual fitting model, Janine, "a plain, supremely professional woman of thirty-five" (191), and insists, against all precedent, of using Tinker. It would appear that she inspires him:

As Marco finished Tinker's scalp and felt its warmth he had released a fragrance that was natural to her, a fragrance that acted on his imagination as a powerful stimulus. Suddenly ideas, unbidden, were leaping in his mind, fresh, thrilling ideas, so vivid and complete that he knew absolutely that there was no need to stop and note them in his sketchbook because he would never forget them. And Tinker was the source of these ideas. (197–98)

Well, it appears she inspires him in more ways than one, for we learn that he has fantasies of having sex with her ("As slowly as she dared she would force herself to bend her head toward his cock, still not fully hard, and take him awkwardly into her dry, quivering mouth" [201]—and so on and so forth). Her problem is that she is not very good at the runway walk, and so he insists on teaching her the tango as a way of improving. At the end of one session he tries to make his fantasy a reality by having her suck his cock; she not only refuses but does the sensible thing and grabs his balls and gives them a good squeeze ("'Aah!' he screeched, gasping in pain" [206]).

Frankie is not missing out on the fun, either. She has palled up with Mike Aaron, and, in the most unbelievable of the many unbelievable moments in this novel, he suddenly admits that he has been carrying a flame for her all this time! Get a load of this:

> "It's the *personhood* of you that I love, the hu-
> man *beingness* . . . the way your nutty little mind
> works, what passes for your sense of humor, your
> strong sense of values even when you're wrong, your
> wacky attitude . . . you know who you are and you
> *are* who you are. I love the way you make me feel
> that I'm a completed person. I love the way I want to
> take care of you. When I'm with you I feel that I've
> come home—home in the way everyone imagine
> home should be." (219)

This is the phoniest monologue I've ever heard outside of an e-Harmony commercial. But no matter; the inevitable happens:

> With intermissions and catnaps, of course, all af-
> ternoon and well into the evening, together in a big
> bed overlooking the Seine, with street noise that
> made a rapturous bumble [???] outside the double-
> glazed windows of our room. We didn't talk a lot.
> [Thank heaven for small mercies.] We were making
> our first trip together through a landscape too in-
> tensely interesting to be interrupted by words. I can't
> tell you the details, because I'm modest about things
> like that, but . . . never mind. Let's just say that when
> Mike and I made love I realized that I'd never truly
> been with a man before. (220)

The stamina that Krantz's characters exhibit for this kind of sexual gymnastics is quite remarkable.

But there's trouble back in New York. Firstly, Necker has sent Justine a fabulously expensive antique desk costing, apparently, millions of dollars. Justine, still not understanding Necker's motives, is deeply resentful, thinking once again that he is trying to buy her forgiveness. Secondly, there is the matter of Dart Benedict, an unsavory manager of another modeling agency. He is offering to buy Justine's business, allowing her to stay in a management role. But she peremptorily refuses, knowing that Dart has a habit of sleeping with his models. Later she regrets being so blunt, for now she has made an enemy of him. We shall see shortly where this leads.

April Nyquist is disheartened that Lombardi is clearly favoring Tinker, who therefore seems in line to win the grand prize of the contest (the $12 million contract). Maude Callendar comforts her, and then proposes a tumble in the hay as a means of releasing her pent-up sexual energy. A very long lesbian sex scene follows (241–47), about as explicit as one could possibly want ("Her fingers, deep inside April, were clutched and unclutched by the powerful spasms that lasted a long time until they eventually came farther apart and finally stopped entirely" [246]).

Jordan, for her part, goes with Necker to an antique shop, where she overhears a courier reporting the delivery of the expensive desk to Justine. Jordan, unaware of Necker's relationship to Justine, thinks that Necker is actually in love with her; but presently Necker confesses the truth to Jordan. She takes pity on him, recommending that he confront Justine in New York.

And what of Peaches Wilcox? She has decided to throw a lavish cocktail party for the Loring models. Each model makes a dramatic entrance, as also do Frankie and Maude. April now makes no secret that she is a lesbian. Dart Benedict is there: he is brazenly trying to steal the models away from Loring. Marco and Tom Strauss nearly come to blows over Tinker, but Necker intervenes. Frankie, bewildered by all these complications, calls Justine and demands that she come to Paris and take matters into her own hands. Incredibly, Justine asks Aiden for his advice, as if he knows anything about the matter; but in the course of their heated discussion, he proposes to her! At this point she decides to come to Paris.

We are now at the dress rehearsal of the show, and Frankie delivers a kind of paean to supermodels:

> As a group they were plunged into a dense atmosphere of dedicated self-absorption that was deeply knowing and totally privileged, in equal proportions. They were wrapped in the knowledge of their meritocracy, which consisted of the dead-simple fact that at this particular moment in time they were the chosen of the chosen, the anointed. Rules that bound other women had been suspended for them. Their faces, in spite of their youth, carried the weight of so much fantasy that walking into a room filled with top models was ten times more impressive than finding yourself backstage in the presenters' makeup room on Oscar Night. (312)

I'll have to take Krantz's word for that last remark, since I'm not ever likely to be at either event. Anyway, the show is now about to begin. Tinker is acting strangely: she doesn't like the music that will accompany her walk; in fact, she wants to tango! She has been so conditioned to that dance that she doesn't think she can perform without it. Marco takes her aside and gives her a drink called Goddess. He says she must not tell anyone about this drink. Under its influence, he finally manages to make her the "abject slave" (330) he has long sought: "'Kneel between my legs,' he ordered" (330).

Tinker now goes on to the platform. At first she seems splendid, but then she stumbles and begins to swear loudly. Necker jumps up to the runway and leads her off. At this point Justine meets him— and with remarkable alacrity they reconcile! *Très vite, n'est-ce pas?* Necker decides that he will name April and Jordan co-winners of the prize. And in spite of Tinker's embarrassing lapse, the show is a tremendous success.

The next day, Necker confronts Marco about what he did to Tinker. He says that he has sold Marco's contract to . . . Peaches Wilcox! So Marco will now be a slave in his turn! Jordan now confesses that she is in love with Necker, in spite of their difference in age, race, and such. He tries to talk her out of it, but she in turn urges him to think the matter over. Tinker says that she will stay in Paris to find herself; she will give up modeling. April has dumped Maude for a "dark-haired French beauty, a startlingly sultry little piece named Kitten" (354). Necker announces that he is in fact marrying Jordan, and Justine is delighted. Frankie sums up the whole book by declaring that "the last two weeks had been like an extended, real-life episode of the 'Love Boat'" (351).

It would seem that, at this juncture, I should be a bit fatigued of saying what a deeply silly book this is. It is not merely the insouciance with which people leap into bed with one another that renders *Spring Collection* so preposterous; it is that they perform so many actions entirely contrary to their own professed beliefs and characters. Justine is the most unbelievable of all, first falling in love at a moment's notice with Aiden Henderson after harboring a decades-long suspicion of men as a result of her broken home, and then reconciling with her estranged father after only a few minutes' talk with him at a fashion show. Frankie, whose tough, racy narration is one of the few elements of genuine entertainment in the book, is scarcely less incredible, somehow managing to win over her boyhood crush after a few days. Each of the models is nothing but a farrago of clichés and stereotypes, and Dart Benedict is the standard cardboard villain brought in to lend a bit of tension to the proceedings. He seems to disappear after the cocktail party, with no harm being done. Marco Lombardi is the lecherous fashion designer who gets his comeuppance at the hands of the woman he brutalised. And so it goes.

I am obliged to believe that there are readers out there—mostly women, but perhaps some men?—who are actually interested in the details of the fashion world that Krantz displays so bountifully. But her efforts to find deep meaning in the whole enterprise fall ludicrously short. She just doesn't have the talent to lend depth to the characters or scenarios she is exhibiting. She is not quite so humorlessly earnest as Jacqueline Susann, and indeed one gets the impression after a time that her casual forays at profundity and deep emotion are merely a makeshift cover for her predictably frequent bouts of heterosexual and lesbian sex (I don't imagine that gay male sex ever soils her pages). She evidently feels the need to make at least a token gesture toward seriousness so that her work is not branded frankly as pornography. But genuine, unabashed pornography seems to me a lot more honest than the slimy mix of pseudo-profundity and sexcapades that we find in *Spring Collection.*

\* \* \* \* \* \* \*

I don't imagine that much analysis need be made of the increasing sexualization of contemporary entertainment—books, television, film, and the Internet. Even on higher aesthetic levels the motivation seems very largely to be titillation, and there is scarcely any "literary" novel in recent years that does not include some kind of sexual episode, usually described with a fair degree of explicitness. I am not prepared to lament the prevalence of sex in popular entertainment: on one level it could be said that, however crassly it is exhibited, it at least reveals an awareness of the significance of sex as a motivating factor in human life, although on another level its particularly prurient examples (ranging from such things as the incessant and increasingly explicit sexual situations on such television shows as "The O.C." or "Grey's Anatomy" to the entirely needless nudity in recent James Bond films) suggest that the repressed upbringing to which many Americans are still subject creates an unhealthy and salacious fascination with sex that purveyors of entertainment are all too eager to satisfy. There is no compelling reason to heed conservatives' call for censuring—or even censoring—this material: no one is being forced to partake of it, and it is in fact far easier to avoid it than many of our self-styled hand-wringing moralists seem to imagine. One excellent place to start is to eschew the novels of Jackie Collins, Judith Krantz, and their ilk.

# CONCLUSION

I trust I have established, without fear of contradiction, that the great majority of bestsellers (for surely the twenty-odd books discussed here are representative of a substantial range of bestsellers published in recent decades) are, from a purely aesthetic standpoint, inferior—that they embody severe flaws in the basic craft of writing, ranging from lifeless prose to stereotyped characters to implausible action to contrived plot twists to artificially neat resolutions to calculated efforts at meaning and profundity to crass exploitation of controverted subjects, and so on and so forth. Two overriding questions, which I posed in the introduction, now need to be addressed:

1. Why do so many people read these books?
2. What, if anything, can or should be done about it?

It should be evident that the overwhelming majority of readers of popular fiction are not seeking an abstract aesthetic experience but are merely aiming for a relatively emotion-free means of transiently engaging their attention, oftentimes at odd moments—while riding the subway or the bus, while on vacation, while waiting in line at the DMV. Even if a book proves to be "gripping" or "engrossing"—as a result either of fast-paced action or of supernatural terror or of love or sex between characters with whom the reader has momentarily identified—the ultimate effect is usually highly ephemeral. I myself, if I had not taken detailed notes on the books I read, would have promptly forgotten them a few days, perhaps a few hours, after finishing them. (I suppose it is conceivable that those who read only one or two books a year might keep them in memory a bit longer, since the experience of reading anything—at least, anything as arduous as an entire book—must be for them a distinctive experience. I have not conducted any interviews with such readers.) In this sense—to answer another of the questions I posed at the outset—the experience of reading a bestseller would seem precisely analogous to that of doing a crossword puzzle or watching a football game. They are meant to amuse, but after they are finished they are forgotten and the serious work of life resumes.

The act of reading a "serious" book is so different as to be of an entirely different order of experience. Its purpose is simultaneously aesthetic and intellectual—aesthetic in evoking an appreciation of the author's skill at the manipulation of words, at the creation of vital and vivid characters, and at the invention of scenarios that are fresh, genuine, and resonant of actual emotional conflicts in which human beings find themselves; and intellectual in forcing the reader to confront profound questions relating to life and society for which the author poses no simple or contrived solutions. Optimally, such a work is never forgotten, and can be read over and over again to bring out new levels of meaning. Most significantly, such a work permanently affects the reader's vision of the world and perhaps even affects the reader's behavior in large or small ways.

Is it simply the case that most readers wish an experience of the first sort—transient amusement—rather than the second? Is it that they have no desire to engage in a profound and genuine emotional experience that might shake them from their certitudes and presuppositions? Do they ask of their popular fiction—as they apparently ask of their films, television, and music—that it merely tickle them for a few hours before it is put aside? It would seem that the answer is yes. But this raises the further question: Why is this the case?

In the introduction I quoted Gore Vidal's comment, made almost in passing in his discussion of the decline of the audience for the serious novel, regarding "appalling education." To be sure, neither secondary nor even college education appears to prepare most readers for absorbing genuine as opposed to ersatz literature. Matters are not helped by the hopelessly jargon-laden, obfuscatory, and impenetrable brand of literary criticism practiced by a substantial majority of academicians—work that is intended only for a small band of other academicians and not even the general literate public, let alone the public at large. There was a time not so long ago when sound handbooks of literary appreciation—perhaps the best of which, still valuable today, was Cleanth Brooks and Robert Penn Warren's *Understanding Fiction* (1943), reprinted as late as 1979—were designed, at least theoretically, for the general public, and provided valuable guidance to basic principles of literary appreciation. But it would appear that the majority of literary critics, academic or otherwise, now regard this kind of work as beneath their dignity or interest.

My general feeling, however—based upon nothing more than a somewhat sporadic study of the phenomena associated with best-sellerdom—is that advances in education will have only a minimal effect in producing greater numbers of culturally sophisticated readers. As I have mentioned, even those with college degrees—even degrees in the humanities—do not, as a rule, read serious literature and eschew popular froth. It is widely acknowledged that few individuals read the "classics" after they leave college, and it is widely known that publishers will not take the economic risk of issuing "classics" if they are not assured of substantial college sales. If, then, even this class of people cannot be counted on to keep above the level of popular rubbish, there is little hope for the rest. The bottom line, in my impression, is that the great majority of purportedly literate people—and those who actually read books constitute, overall, only about a quarter of the total adult population[1]—are, as far as aesthetic appreciation is concerned, not merely *uneducated* but *ineducable*. As H. L. Mencken stated in a somewhat different context (in reference to the level of intelligence needed to make democracy viable):

> I doubt that the art of thinking can be taught at all—at any rate, by school-teachers. It is not acquired, but congenital. Some persons are born with it. Their ideas flow in straight channels; they are capable of lucid reasoning; when they say anything it is instantly understandable, when they write anything it is clear and persuasive. They constitute, I should say, about one-eighth of one per cent of the human race. The rest of God's children are just as incapable of logical thought as they are incapable of jumping over the moon. Trying to teach them to think is as vain an enterprise as trying to teach a streptococcus the principles of Americanism.[2]

I'm not sure I take quite as dim a view of the situation as this, but I suspect it is more true than otherwise.

There is another aspect of bestsellerdom that needs to be addressed—a social aspect. This aspect is perhaps not quite as strong as it used to be, since films and television, so much easier to absorb than whole books, have become the chief subject of common parlance around the office cooler or coffeemaker, but it is present nonetheless. There is a kind of social pressure exerted upon individuals to keep up with the latest popular books as a means of facilitating social intercourse—whether it be an immense and controversial blockbuster such as *The Da Vinci Code* or the latest novel by Danielle Steel or James Patterson or any other writer with a wide following. I myself remember, as a teenager, feeling some kind of compulsion to read bestsellers—ranging from the steamy novels of Irving Wallace to Alvin Toffler's *Future Shock* to, yes, *Jonathan Livingston Seagull*—in order to be culturally current. It hardly makes a difference that these books generally fade in a short period of time, to be overtaken by the next wave of ephemera. It takes considerable fortitude to resist what William H. P. Faunce, president of Brown University about a century ago, rightly labeled the tendency to be "too desperately contemporary."[3]

The devoted consumer of popular fiction (assuming there are any such who have actually troubled to read this book), exasperated by being so roundly abused as a yahoo, will naturally reply: What the hell is wrong with reading trash? If it provides transient amusement, what of it? What's wrong with being transiently amused? If popular fiction can be likened to eating a bag of popcorn, what's wrong with eating popcorn every now and then?

My answer to this is that the great majority of readers of popular fiction appear to read nothing but popular fiction, and that of the lowest quality. In other words, they eat nothing but popcorn, and bad popcorn at that. A steady diet of this kind of writing is not merely time-wasting, in the most literal sense of the term; it corrupts one's taste so that genuine literature seems boring (it doesn't move as fast as the latest page-turner by James Patterson or Clive Cussler), uncomfortably ambiguous (it doesn't provide neat solutions to artificial problems; it doesn't present a coherent scenario of good guys vs. bad guys), and, overall, "difficult" (prose that is idiosyncratic and therefore slow going; the thrashing of weighty issues that can leave the reader depressed, confused, or unsatisfied; the occasional absence of readily identifiable or sympathetic characters). The systematic reader of popular fiction will conclude that such books are actually "bad" because they do not embody the meretricious qualities found in the standard bestseller.

But the situation is even worse than this. The failure to read good literature creates a sense that one's actual, real life is boring—because it itself does not conform to the artificially heightened action sequences of trashy fiction. Whereas good literature can invest even the commonest events of life with an intellectual, moral, and even aesthetic meaning that renders them vital and significant, bad literature creates the expectation that life can only be interesting if it is a succession of car chases or torrid love affairs or involvements in high finance or world intrigue. This is the true reason why "escapist" literature is harmful: it does not (as its proponents allege) provide a welcome relief from the tedium of daily life; it renders daily life tedious because it fails to demonstrate how that life, while seemingly plain and uneventful, is in fact full of meaning and significance.

The second question I have posed here—what, if anything, can or should be done about the dominance of generally low-quality bestsellers among those who read books at all?—is one that cannot be answered in a sanguine manner. The bestselling authors themselves have no interest—and usually no ability—to write any better than they do. Publishers who have staked a substantial proportion of their profits on these blockbuster sellers are not likely to shift gears and promote serious literature that has little chance of selling widely. And, as I suggested above, it is probably a hopeless cause to try to steer readers toward better fare. But this last point does offer some small glimmers of hope.

The fact is that there is a fairly wide array of "popular" or genre literature that is several cuts above the level of most bestsellers. If one wishes to read a detective or mystery or suspense story, the work of writers as various as Dashiell Hammett, Raymond Chandler, James M. Cain, P. D. James, Ruth Rendell, Ross Macdonald, and several others one could name stand out as substantially meritorious. If horror fiction is to your taste, you are much better off reading the work of Edgar Allan Poe, Ambrose Bierce, H. P. Lovecraft, Shirley Jackson, and such contemporary writers as Ramsey Campbell, Thomas Ligotti, and Caitlín R. Kiernan instead of the latest release by Stephen King or Dean Koontz. The work of John le Carré, Eric Ambler, and others raises the spy novel to the level of literature. Even the romance novel has its gradations of quality, and Sandra Brown ranks considerably higher on the aesthetic scale than Danielle Steel. What is often forgotten or ignored is that these writers—some of whom reach as high as the second rank of greatness in general literature—are genuinely "entertaining" in ways at least approximating those of the cruder popular writers. Their work is artfully crafted so that the reader's interest is consistently maintained from beginning to end; they feature characters that are vibrant and realistic but also readily identifiable; and their prose can hardly be said to be "difficult" in the sense that such dense writers as John Fowles and Thomas Pynchon are usually classified as "difficult." Better efforts might therefore be made to sort the wheat from the chaff when it comes to genre fiction, or even to mainstream fiction. Such leading twentieth-century novelists as Evelyn Waugh, George

Orwell, Aldous Huxley, F. Scott Fitzgerald, Sinclair Lewis, and Toni Morrison are far from inaccessible to even the casual reader.[4]

But, as I have remarked, things are not likely to change anytime soon—and if they change, they may well change for the worse. The overwhelming dominance of the media—especially films and television—will probably cause bestselling books to mimic these media even more than they now do, with the result that prose will become even more simple-minded, emphasis on "action" even more dominant, and the need to achieve any kind of adrenalin rush—whether by the expression of extreme emotions on the part of characters (in the manner of the always shouting Kiefer Sutherland of *24*) or the display of ever more spectacular or bizarre incidents, even if they do not arise naturally from the scenario or cannot be reconciled to the development of the plot—becomes ever more urgent. If, as I have noted, the aesthetic difference between Irving Wallace's *The Word* and Dan Brown's *The Da Vinci Code* is at all representative, popular fiction has in fact declined over the past thirty years. How much lower it can go it is beyond my powers of prophecy to conjecture, and also beyond my interest. Now that I have done the public service of writing this book, I'll go back to reading the good stuff.

# NOTES

## Introduction

1. Gore Vidal, "The Top Ten Best Sellers According to the Sunday *New York Times* as of January 7, 1973," in *Matters of Fact and of Fiction* (New York: Random House, 1977), p. 3. The article appeared in the *New York Review of Books* for May 17 and May 31, 1973.
2. The titles are Mary Higgins Clark's *Moonlight Becomes You*, Sue Grafton's *"O" Is for Outlaw*, Patricia Cornwell's *Black Notice*, Stephen King's *Bag of Bones*, and Judith Krantz's *Spring Collection*. The first three were reviewed in the *Book Review*'s "Crime" column.
3. The titles are John Grisham's *The Chamber*, Tom Clancy's *Red Rabbit*, Stephen King's *Bag of Bones*, and Dan Brown's *The Da Vinci Code*.
4. See Alice Payne Hackett and James Henry Burke, *80 Years of Best Sellers 1895–1975* (New York: R. R. Bowker, 1977), pp. 65f.
5. Gerard Manley Hopkins, Letter to R. W. Dixon (15 August 1883); *The Correspondence of Gerard Manley Hopkins and Richard Watson Dixon*, ed. Claude Colleer Abbott (London: Oxford University Press, 1935), p. 114.
6. Cf. Kenneth Levine, *The Social Context of Literacy* (London: Routledge & Kegan Paul, 1986), p. 84, who, in reference to eighteenth-century England, notes the proliferation of "new and modified genres of popular literature including, most notably, local newspapers, weekly reviews, chapbooks, ballads and religious tracts."
7. Levine, p. 77.
8. Levine, p. 90.
9. Nina Burgis, "Introduction" to *David Copperfield* (Oxford: Clarendon Press, 1981), pp. xxxi, l.
10. David F. Mitch, *The Rise of Popular Literacy in Victorian England* (Philadelphia: University of Pennsylvania Press, 1992), p. 75.
11. John E. Maher, *Labor and the Economy* (Boston: Alleyn & Bacon, 1965), p. 280.
12. Maher, p. 317.
13. See Peter Haining, *The Penny Dreadful* (London: Gollancz, 1976).
14. Edmund Pearson, *Dime Novels* (Boston: Little, Brown, 1929), pp. 4f.

15. Carl F. Kaestle et al., *Literacy in the United States* (New Haven: Yale University Press, 1991), p. 172.
16. See Michael Denning, *Mechanic Accents: Dime Novels and Working-Class Culture in America* (London: Verso, 1987), p. 29.
17. On this issue see Sam Moskowitz, *Under the Moons of Mars: A History and Anthology of "The Scientific Romance" in the Munsey Magazines, 1912–1920* (New York: Holt, Rinehart & Winston, 1970).
18. See Dana Gioia, chairman of the National Endowment for the Arts: "A few of my favorite boyhood writers have now, I am sorry to say, entered the fringe of the academic canon. In my heart, however, they remain forever beyond the reach of pedagogic good taste—H. P. Lovecraft, H. G. Wells, Ray Bradbury, Olaf Stapledon, Arthur C. Clarke, and Isaac Asimov . . ." "The Lonely Impulse of Delight," *Stanford Magazine* (July–August 2006). Some of these authors have done far more than "enter the fringe" of the canon and are likely to endure far longer than Gioia himself, only a middling poet, will.
19. H. P. Lovecraft, Letter to C. L. Moore (c. 7 February 1937), *Selected Letters 1934–1937,* ed. August Derleth and James Turner (Sauk City, WI: Arkham House, 1976), pp. 397–98.
20. Gore Vidal, "A Note on the Novel" (1956), *Rocking the Boat* (Boston: Little, Brown, 1962), p. 149.
21. On this general subject see Thomas Whiteside, *The Blockbuster Complex: Conglomerates, Show Business, and Book Publishing* (Middletown, CT: Wesleyan University Press, 1981).
22. See Kaestle et al., p. 296.
23. *New York Times* (1 January 2006): C8.
24. Luc Sante, "Rising Crime" (a review of Patrick Anderson's *The Triumph of the Thriller*), *New York Times Book Review* (18 February 2007): 12.
25. Most of the biographical data that I have culled on these authors comes from the online edition of *Contemporary Authors* (Thomson Gale).

## 1. *Queens of Romance*

1. Danielle Steel, *Bittersweet* (New York: Delacorte Press, 1999). All references to this work are derived from this edition and appear parenthetically in the text.
2. Danielle Steel, *The Ring* (New York: Delacorte Press, 1980). All references to this work are derived from this edition and appear parenthetically in the text.
3. Barbara Taylor Bradford, *A Sudden Change of Heart* (New York: Doubleday, 1999). All references to this work are derived from this edition and appear parenthetically in the text.
4. See S. T. Joshi, *The Angry Right: Why Conservatives Keep Getting It Wrong* (Amherst, NY: Prometheus Books, 2006), p. 161.

5. Nora Roberts, *Midnight Bayou* (New York: G. P. Putnam's Sons, 2001). All references to this work are derived from this edition and appear parenthetically in the text.

6. See, e.g., Janice Radway, *Reading the Romance* (Chapel Hill: University of North Carolina Press, 1984); Carol Thurston, *The Romance Revolution* (Urbana: University of Illinois Press, 1987).

## 2. *An Aesthetic Pretender*

1. H. L. Mencken, "The Sawdust Trail," *Smart Set* 46, no. 4 (August 1915): 154; rpt. in *H. L. Mencken on American Literature,* ed. S. T. Joshi (Athens: Ohio University Press, 2002), pp. 189-90.

2. "It's a Bird! It's a Dream! It's Supergull!" *Time* 100, no. 20 (13 November 1972): 58.

3. Ibid., p. 59.

4. John Grisham, *The Chamber* (New York: Doubleday, 1994). All references to this work are derived from this edition and appear parenthetically in the text.

5. John Grisham, *The King of Torts* (New York: Doubleday, 2003). All references to this work are derived from this edition and appear parenthetically in the text.

## 3. *Mistresses of Mystery*

1. One of the earliest, and still among the best for its sensitivity and enthusiasm, is Howard Haycraft's *Murder for Pleasure: The Life and Times of the Detective Story* (New York: D. Appleton & Co., 1941). See also Julian Symons, *Mortal Consequences* (New York: Harper & Row, 1972), revised as *Bloody Murder: From the Detective Story to the Crime Novel* (Harmondsworth: Penguin, 1985), and Colin Watson, *Snobbery with Violence: Crime Stories and Their Audiences* (London: Methuen, 1971). Tony Hilfer's *The Crime Novel* (Austin: University of Texas Press, 1990) is a more theoretical study. More pertinent, from the standpoint of popular fiction, is John G. Cawelti's *Adventure, Mystery, and Romance: Formula Stories as Art and Popular Culture* (Chicago: University of Chicago Press, 1976). Less insightful is Patrick Anderson's *The Triumph of the Thriller* (New York: Random House, 2007).

2. S. T. Joshi, *John Dickson Carr: A Critical Study* (Bowling Green, OH: Bowling Green State University Popular Press, 1990), p. 139.

3. Mary Higgins Clark, *Moonlight Becomes You* (New York: Simon & Schuster, 1996). All references to this work are derived from this edition and appear parenthetically in the text.

4. Sue Grafton, *"O" Is for Outlaw* (New York: Henry Holt, 1999). All references to this work are derived from this edition and appear parenthetically in the text.

5. Patricia Cornwell, *Black Notice* (New York: G. P. Putnam's Sons, 1999). All references to this work are derived from this edition and appear parenthetically in the text.

## 4. *Pulse-Pounding Suspense*

1. James Patterson, *The Lake House* (Boston: Little, Brown, 2003). All references to this work are derived from this edition and appear parenthetically in the text.
2. James Patterson and Howard Roughan, *Honeymoon* (New York: Little, Brown, 2005). All references to this work are derived from this edition and appear parenthetically in the text.
3. James Patterson, *The Big Bad Wolf* (Boston: Little, Brown 2003). All references to this work are derived from this edition and appear parenthetically in the text.
4. Stephen King, *Bag of Bones* (New York: Scribner, 1998), p. 183.
5. Nelson DeMille, *Plum Island* (New York: Warner Books, 1997). All references to this work are derived from this edition and appear parenthetically in the text.

## 5. *Cops, Robbers, and Spies*

1. Julian Symons, *Bloody Murder: From the Detective Story to the Crime Novel* (1972; rev. ed. Harmondsworth: Penguin, 1985), p. 216.
2. Ian Fleming, *Thunderball* (1961; rpt. New York: Signet, n.d.), p. 41. All references to this work are derived from this edition and appear parenthetically in the text.
3. Ian Fleming, *On Her Majesty's Secret Service* (1963; rpt. New York: Signet, 1964), p. 137.
4. Robert Ludlum, *The Sigma Protocol* (New York: St. Martin's Press, 2001). All references to this work are derived from this edition and appear parenthetically in the text.
5. Tom Clancy, *Red Rabbit* (New York: G. P. Putnam's Sons, 2002). All references to this work are derived from this edition and appear parenthetically in the text.
6. Garry O'Connor, *Universal Father: A Life of Pope John Paul II* (New York: Bloomsbury Publishing, 2005), p. 244.
7. Ibid., pp. 248–49.
8. Clive Cussler, *Atlantis Found* (New York: Penguin Putnam, 1999). All references to this work are derived from this edition and appear parenthetically in the text.

## 6. *Mavens of Horror*

1. Winfield Townley Scott, "His Own Most Fantastic Creation: Howard Phillips Lovecraft," in *Lovecraft Remembered,* ed. Peter Cannon (Sauk City, WI: Arkham House, 1998), p. 9.
2. H. P. Lovecraft, Letter to Farnsworth Wright (editor of *Weird Tales*), 16 February 1933; in *Selected Letters 1932–1934,* ed. August Derleth and James Turner (Sauk City, WI: Arkham House, 1976), p. 154.
3. See my chapter, "Stephen King: The King's New Clothes," in *The Modern Weird Tale* (Jefferson, NC: McFarland, 2001).
4. Stephen King, *Bag of Bones* (New York: Scribner, 1998). All references to this work are derived from this edition and appear parenthetically in the text.
5. H. P. Lovecraft, "The Call of Cthulhu" (1926), in *The Dunwich Horror and Others,* ed. S. T. Joshi (Sauk City, WI: Arkham House, 1984), pp. 153–53.
6. Dean Koontz, *The Taking* (New York: Bantam Books, 2004). All references to this work are derived from this edition and appear parenthetically in the text.
7. H. P. Lovecraft, "Notes on Writing Weird Fiction" (1933), in *Collected Essays, Volume 2: Literary Criticism,* ed. S. T. Joshi (New York: Hippocampus Press, 2004), p. 177.

## 7. *Blood, Thunder, and Religion*

1. Dan Brown, *The Da Vinci Code* (New York: Doubleday, 2003). All references to this work are derived from this edition and appear parenthetically in the text.
2. See Keith L. Justice, *Bestseller Index: All Books, by Author, on the Lists of* Publishers Weekly *and* The New York Times *through 1990* (Jefferson, NC: McFarland & Co., 1998).
3. See Jeffrey B. Russell, *A History of Witchcraft* (London: Thames & Hudson, 1980), p. 11.
4. Irving Wallace, *The Word* (New York: Simon & Schuster, 1972). All references to this work are derived from this edition and appear parenthetically in the text.

## 8. *Glamour, Fashion, and Sex*

1. Howard Wandrei, "Too Good-Looking," in *The Last Pin* (Minneapolis, MN: Fedogan & Bremer, 1996), p. 231.
2. Jacqueline Susann, *Valley of the Dolls* (New York: Bernard Geis Associates/Random House, 1966). All references to this work are derived from this edition and appear parenthetically in the text.

3. Charles Champlin, "'Myra Breckinridge' Plays on Decadence," *Los Angeles Times* (25 June 1970): Sec. 4, p. 16.
4. See James Atlas, "The Laureates of Lewd," *GQ* 63, No. 4 (April 1993): 202–7, 242.
5. William Peter Blatty, *The Exorcist* (New York: Harper & Row, 1971), p. 190.
6. Jackie Collins, *Thrill!* (New York: Simon & Schuster, 1998). All references to this work are derived from this edition and appear parenthetically in the text.
7. Judith Krantz, *Spring Collection* (New York: Crown, 1996). All references to this work are derived from this edition and appear parenthetically in the text.

## *Conclusion*

1. See Helen Damon-Moore and Carl F. Kaestle, "Surveying American Readers," in Carl F. Kaestle et al., *Literacy in the United States* (New Haven: Yale University Press, 1991), p. 196.
2. H. L. Mencken, "The Fringes of Lovely Letters," *Prejudices: Fifth Series* (New York: Alfred A. Knopf, 1926), p. 202.
3. Quoted by H. P. Lovecraft, "The Case for Classicism" (1919), *Collected Essays* (New York: Hippocampus Press, 2004), 2.37.
4. This point has recently been made eloquently by Michael Dirda in *Classics for Pleasure* (Orlando, FL: Harcourt, 2007).

# INDEX

# ABOUT THE AUTHOR

S. T. JOSHI is a widely published critic and editor. He is the author of such critical studies as *The Weird Tale* (1990), *H. P. Lovecraft: The Decline of the West* (1990), and *The Modern Weird Tale* (2001). For Penguin Classics, he has prepared three annotated editions of Lovecraft's tales, as well as editions of the works of Lord Dunsany, Algernon Blackwood, and M. R. James, and the anthology *American Supernatural Tales* (2007). His exhaustive biography, *H. P. Lovecraft: A Life* (1996), won the British Fantasy Award and the Bram Stoker Award from the Horror Writers Association. He is coeditor of Ambrose Bierce's *Collected Short Fiction* (2006; 3 vols.), and has edited several editions of the work of H. L. Mencken. He is coeditor of *Supernatural Literature of the World: An Encyclopedia* (2005; 3 vols.) and the editor of *Documents of American Prejudice* (1999), *Atheism: A Reader* (2000), *In Her Place: A Documentary History of Prejudice against Women* (2006), *Icons of Horror and the Supernatural* (2006; 2 vols.), *The Agnostic Reader* (2007), and other volumes. Among his writings on politics and religion are *God's Defenders: What They Believe and Why They Are Wrong* (2003) and *The Angry Right* (2006). He has compiled bibliographies of H. P. Lovecraft (1981; rev. 2009), Ambrose Bierce (1999), Gore Vidal (2007), H. L. Mencken (2009), and other authors. He lives with his wife, Leslie, and five cats in Seattle, Washington.

www.ingramcontent.com/pod-product-compliance
Lightning Source LLC
Chambersburg PA
CBHW021216090426
42740CB00006B/247